Sarah you are always there just in time. Just in time when I start to give up the business. Just in time when I get in my own head and say it's impossible. Just in time when I start listening to others and stop trusting the Lord with my business. I always come back to boot camp to reenergize myself. God puts you in my space always just in time....

Jennifer Harrison

Your story, all of your books, everything you put out keeps me going with motivation and hope that I can make this business something I can be proud of. I'm in a verbal/mental/emotional abusive marriage and he is anti-Young Living. It is discouraging in every way, but you give me hope that I can do this. With God and a starter kit, I can build from the bottom up. I can rise from the ashes!

Cailin Eckard

Your transparency and realness made me realize that I can do this!! Do the work and the results will follow!!

Jennifer Hiltz

Your words have given me hope, dreams, inspirations, hope for freedom, strength, and courage, But most of all, you have shown me the love of God and what obedience ~~~~ *my family but also to the ones I come*

Karrie Toth Spears

TO:

FROM:

DATE:

Unstuck

HOW TO TALK TO
HUMANS
& GET THEM TO RESPOND
TO YOU

Sarah Harnisch
Young Living Diamond

Book 2 of 3 in the Gameplan Trilogy

DEDICATION

This book is dedicated to the thousands of leaders across the globe who work tirelessly every day and feel their efforts are in vain. It's for every leader who's given their oils away without a kit sale. It's for every leader who sat in an empty classroom. It's for every leader that has invested in someone only to see them end up on another team. It's for the tens of thousands of hours poured out and the feelings of treading water. This is a love letter from me to you. I know those broken places; and I have felt those hurts. You are not alone! I believe you have it in you to go all the way, if you do the actions that will lead to growth. Just like the chess piece on the cover of this book, you are anointed  *as royalty and set apart. May the sentences on these pages give you new fight, new words, and new ways to connect. You cannot do what you were called and created to do when you're beaten down. It's time to rise up, dream, move your feet, and get Unstuck.*

With deep love,

Sarah

Hang out with me on
Instagram: @sarahharnisch
Facebook: Oil Ability with Sarah

2nd Timothy 1:9

"He has saved us and called us to a holy life—not because of anything we have done but because of His own purpose and grace. This grace was given us in Christ Jesus before the beginning of time."

CONTENTS

Dedication • VII

Introduction • XIII

A FRESH START ON A STUCK BUSINESS

1. Why Young Living is the Best Job in The World • • • • • • • • • 3
2. No One Is Listening • 9
3. The State of Stuck •17
4. Mojo Method 1: Utilize Your Forgotten Warm Market • • • • • 23
5. Mojo Method 2: Purple Bags • • • • • • • • • • • • • • • 27
6. Mojo Method 3: Vendor Events • • • • • • • • • • • • • • 31
7. Mojo Method 4: Friends of Friends • • • • • • • • • • • • • 35
8. If All Your Mojo Methos Fail You • • • • • • • • • • • • • 43

CLEAR THE WAY: DITCHING MENTAL ROADBLOCKS

9. You Are Not Forgotten • • • • • • • • • • • • • • • • • 49
10. Why Don't People Respond to You? • • • • • • • • • • • 53
11. Tongue, Head, Feet • • • • • • • • • • • • • • • • • • • 59
12. The Art of Listening • • • • • • • • • • • • • • • • • • • 65
13. How to Collect Contact Information • • • • • • • • • • • • 73
14. You Are Telling Me to Do Things I Have Already Tried • • • • • 79
15. Fear • 85

FUELING CONNECTION

16. The Key to Growth • • • • • • • • • • • • • • • • • • • 95
17. How to Get People to Respond 101 • • • • • • • • • • • • 99
18. Perfect Persistence: 7 to 15 Conversations • • • • • • • • • 103
19. Diamond Rising Decks: Follow Up at It's Best • • • • • • • • 111

15 CLASSES TO MOVE YOU FORWARD

20. Methods of Teaching • 121

21. Class 1: The In-Person Class • • • • • • • • • • • • • • • 133

22. Class 2: Purple Bags • • • • • • • • • • • • • • • • • • • 157

23. Class 3: Textable Classes • • • • • • • • • • • • • • • • 167

24. Class 4: DVD Teaching: Playing the Role of the Host • • • • • 173

25. Class 5: Oils on the Body: The Personal Loan, Informal Sharing 179

26. Class 6: Online Classes: Vimeo, Zoom, YouTube • • • • • • • 187

27. Class 7: Social Media Classes: Facebook & Instagram, Featuring Diamond Christie Rose • • • • • • • • • • • • • • • • • • • 199

28. Class 8: Lunch & Learn, Sip & Sniff, Simple Swap, Ditch & Switch • 211

29. Class 9: Speed Oiling • • • • • • • • • • • • • • • • • • 217

30. Class 10: Make and Takes That Work • • • • • • • • • • • 221

31. Class 11: Speaking at Events • • • • • • • • • • • • • • • 227

32. Class 12: Teacher Training Classes • • • • • • • • • • • • 231

33. Class 13: Classes for Business Owners • • • • • • • • • • 237

34. Class 14: Blogging and Vlogging • • • • • • • • • • • • • 243

35. Class 15: Vendor Events • • • • • • • • • • • • • • • • • 249

A BIT MORE: TALKING TO HUMANS 102

36. Things That Don't Work • • • • • • • • • • • • • • • • • • 261

37. Leading Sentences That Start Conversations • • • • • • • • 269

38. Expanding Your Circle: How to Tap into Friends of Friends • • • 277

39. How to Craft Your Personal Story • • • • • • • • • • • • • 287

40. Essential Rewards 101: ER Without the Sales Pitch • • • • • 293

41. Closing A Class in A Way That Leads to Kit Sales • • • • • • 311

LIGHTEN YOUR LOAD: AVOID COMMON MLM MISTAKES

42. The Grass Is Greener on The Other Side Syndrome • • • • • 319

43. A Spirit of Contentment • • • • • • • • • • • • • • • • • 325

44. The Curse of Expectations • • • • • • • • • • • • • • • • 333

KEEP THE MOMENTUM!

45. Rinse and Repeat: The Story of Kathy: 12,000 to 19,000 OGV in 12 Weeks • 341

46. Closing Out with Hope • 349

APPENDICES:

Appendix A: Simple 101 Script (oils) • • • • • • • • • • • • • • • • 357

Appendix B: 102 Script: Toxin Free Life (Thieves) • • • • • • • • 369

Appendix C: 103 Intro to NingXia Script • • • • • • • • • • • • • 381

Appendix D: 104 Script: Savvy Minerals • • • • • • • • • • • • • 393

Appendix E: Closing Scripts • • • • • • • • • • • • • • • • • • • 403

Appendix F: Teacher Training • • • • • • • • • • • • • • • • • • • 409

Appendix G: Essential Rewards in Clear Language • • • • • • • • 415

Appendix H: How to Use the Gameplan System • • • • • • • • • 417

Appendix I: Gameplan Resources • • • • • • • • • • • • • • • • 421

Appendix J: Young Living Ease • • • • • • • • • • • • • • • • • • 423

Appendix K: FAQ • 427

Appendix L: Who Gets Paid? • • • • • • • • • • • • • • • • • • • 445

Appendix M: Poaching • 447

Appendix N: Advanced Strategy + Basic Compensation Plan Training • 449

Appendix O: Gameplan 3 Topics: Research Outlined • • • • • • • • 453

If you have felt shame, confusion, or just plain hopelessness about reaching people with Young Living, THIS is the book for you. With the candid voice of a wise mentor and the practical advice of someone who has been through every mountain and valley in this business, Sarah will clearly guide you around what's tripping you up, and show you what your next step is. This book filled me with hope and excitement for me and my team, and gave me fresh tools and perspective for reaching our goals. You can't stay stuck after reading this book!

Trina Holden

INTRODUCTION

THE MOST PAINFUL PART OF MY STORY, FOR THOSE THAT NEED A WAY OUT

*written with permission from my first-born son

October 2012

I woke up to the sound of two children screaming in pain outside my bedroom door. My oldest son, Gabe, is autistic. Until he was 7 years old, he did not speak. He is the first born of five kids and I spend most of my day protecting him from the other children, and protecting the other children from him. On this day, Noah, the littlest, was having a bit of fun and tossed a Lego at Gabe as he was walking by. Gabe took it personally and started shoving dog treats down Noah's throat until he was choking and his lips were turning blue. Though almost never intentional, Gabe does not always have an "off" switch to recognize when people are getting hurt. He is a good son who can't find the right words to describe how he feels. Everything physical with Gabe has an emotional root that has to be found.

Still half asleep, I used my body as a shield. I jumped in the middle of the boy's fight to try to calm Gabe down, explaining to him that Noah was playing. Gabe regrouped and decided he wanted the tablet our fourth born son Ben was using. When he did not hand it over mid-math-lesson, Gabe slapped Ben's face so hard that he left a red handprint with five fingers across Ben's 8-year-old face. I sat on the floor trying to calm Noah down. I now had two children squealing in my living room. Before I could get up to go to Ben, Gabe had already left the room. I put ice on Ben's face and heard another cry coming from the garage moments later.

When I was sure the other two were ok, I ran into the garage and saw through the glass window in the door that my 10 year old daughter, Grace, was laying on the sidewalk in a small puddle of blood in the pouring rain, with two skinned knees. She had gotten into the van thinking she could run an errand with me. When Gabe came into the garage and saw her there, he got upset. He thought he was going on the errand instead. He grabbed her by the hair, threw her outside the door, and locked her outside in the rain, making faces at her through the glass.

All of this happened in the span of ten minutes.

When you are the mom of an autistic child, some days are easier and some days are harder. This was a hard day, when every thought and every moment needed to be centered toward my son. It was a day when very little laundry got done, dishes sat untouched; and we ate baked potatoes for dinner, because I needed something with little prep. I get through each day and collapse into bed knowing I could be a better mom, knowing I could have handled situations better, wishing for a normal life that didn't involve constant character correction. I am broken. I am tired. I need a break. I need someone to step in and save me. I need someone to give me time off and fix my frustration. I need someone to teach me deeper patience and give me rest.

After 4 or 5 hours of sleep, I hear my alarm go off at 3 a.m., and it's time to go into work. : I have anchored news for nearly 20 years. I LOVE it. It's an outlet for me. It allows me to be creative, hunt for facts, and research without feeling like I'm walking away from my family. In the span of six hours, I will read 39 newspapers, write over 60 stories by hand, and cut up hundreds of soundbites. I will watch the lead stories on seven networks then tell those stories myself. When I get through with one newscast, I have 22 minutes until the next one. Each story must be accurate, balanced, and hold the listener's attention, yet be told with power in as few words as possible.

Doing that 40-60 hours a week is mentally draining; and when I get off my shift between 10 and noon each day, I walk into my home depleted. The kids are ready for the day, well rested, and already at one another. The whole cycle then begins all over again: protect Gabe from the kids; protect the kids from Gabe; try to get in a seven-hour homeschool day with an 8th grader, 6th grader, 5th grader, 3rd grader, and 1st grader. Play mom taxi and shuttle to activities. Cook good food. Collapse. Repeat.

I felt stuck.

I love my kids. I love my job. I love my husband, but love isn't enough to make my body go anymore. Our bills are unpaid. I've gone 15 years without a family vacation or even an overnight date night with my husband. We live check to check. Despite all the work that I do every day, I have 20 dollars a week to live on after our mortgage, food, utilities, van payment, and student loans are paid. There is no fat in our budget. There is nothing to trim! We have no internet, no cable t.v.; and it seems like so much work for so little yield.

Worst of all... there's not a way out! I have another 10 to 15 years of this kind of life. A subsistence life. A life I'm not ungrateful for; but one that takes me to the pit of nothing every single day. One that drains the deepest part of who I am emotionally and physically. How do I carry on like this, feeling so depleted?

March 2013

For the first time in my life, I considered giving up. It actually completely dumbfounded me that the thought crossed my mind. I was the joy girl! I was the one that made everyone smile. I was the one that did hard things with no complaint. I was the one that brought the room up. I was Sarah smile. No one had any idea how worn I was. I just went through the motions. I was a mom on auto pilot.

I was driving home from anchoring news one morning. It was blustery and cold in upstate New York. I had not seen the sun in 12 weeks. The sky today was overcast, as usual. I live on a near-mountain. It's actually on the foothills of the Adirondack Mountains but our "hill" is only a few hundred feet shy of being classified as a mountain. There are parts of it with steep drop-offs. We live on the edge of a state park where I love to run, with 200-foot-tall pine trees that make the air smell amazing. It's my get-away place.

On this day, I was extra depleted. I'd only had an hour of sleep before my shift. The day before was unbelievably hard with Gabe. We tried him on a series of doctor-ordered medications that resulted in many intense side effects. Last night, he was throwing apples at the walls inside my house, making apple sauce; and running through each room turning the faucets on systematically, over and over and over again. We had an entire wall in our home ruined from splattered apples. No one got hurt. My kids made it to bed without any injuries.

My morning anchoring was rough. I was ten minutes late and got reprimanded and written up. I had an argument with my boss about news content and why I chose a certain story. I didn't time any of my stories out right and got a second reprimand. My writing was off. I didn't feel like I did a good enough job to be there that day. Five million people turned on the radio trusting what I was putting out; and that particular day, I felt mediocre at my job; mediocre at being mom; mediocre at just about everything. I felt like I was not enough. I felt like I was never enough. I had not been enough in a very long time.

Have you ever had a moment, driving on a road, where you wonder in your head what would happen if you veered to the side and went right off the cliffside? Your family would hurt for a season; but life would go on. The pain for you would stop. Someone would take on your responsibilities, and the rhythm of your family would eventually resume. That was my day. I had those terrible, awful thoughts that I was worthless; that my life had no value; that I was stopping fights only to see new ones the next day; that so many others would do a better job at this "mom" thing than I would; that I was too tired to cook correctly; that I was too "done" to take care of my kids correctly. I was engaged in a full-on pity party.

I paused and looked around the hill, my hands on the steering wheel, alone. I knew in that moment that I was about to make a massive decision. I continued those dark thoughts. I never thought about anyone else in my home, just my own frustration of the daily juggle, never keeping up, always doing everything halfway, running from emergency to emergency. I was tired of giving. I was tired of surviving. I was so deeply tired that a few days of naps would no longer save me. This kind of tired required a new kind of rescue, one I did not know how to do.

Right at that moment a song came on the radio. I am so grateful that it played because I might have made the wrong decision. I may have driven past the road to my house where my kids were waiting for their momma, unassuming, and into the state park. I might have driven right to the overlook, with its 1600-foot drop off and never hit the brakes. Because that song played, I stopped.

I pulled over to the right side of the road and just sat in silence, me and the music. The song was "Worn", by Tenth Avenue North. Even the sounds of the notes were on repeat, the same eight notes playing over and over again, just like me. The words went like this:

I'm tired

I'm worn

My heart is heavy

From the work it takes to keep on breathing

I've made mistakes

I've let my hope fail

My soul feels crushed

By the weight of this world

And I know that you can give me rest

So I cry out with all that I have left

Let me see redemption win

Let me know the struggle ends

That you can mend a heart that's frail and torn

I want to know a song can rise

From the ashes of a broken life

And all that's dead inside can be reborn

'Cause I'm worn

I was worn. I was in a place of no release. As I sat there, I had no words, only tears. Somehow those tears must have translated into a prayer that was heard by the Lord, because a series of miracles happened next.

The first miracle was a sunbeam. It started as a little pinpoint on the top of my leg.

I noticed it immediately.

If I could live anywhere, I'd asked the Lord for a Victorian mansion on a beach, preferably in Hawaii or Florida. He gave me a ranch house next to a trout pond in upstate New York. Gloomy, cold 8-months-a-year, New York. So you see, a sunbeam is HUGE in New York, especially in March.

That little beam started as a dot on the top of my leg; but then it started spreading across the van. It moved across my leg and grew larger. It filled my entire seat. Then it filled the seat next to me. The van began to get warm. It was like I could feel the presence of the Lord right there with me, in that space. He was saying, "you're not alone."

The little beam of sunshine spread further. I looked out the window and it filled the whole field to my right. It filled the field to my left. It left me so stunned that I stepped out of my van on that deserted road wondering what was going on. I looked up into the sky. There was not a cloud in sight... not a single one. God cleared the sky to have a conversation with me about weariness. He cleared the sky and brought me some sunshine to show me that I meant something to Him; and that life, of any size, had value and meaning. He cleared the sky to tell me I was precious, and that though this was a season of serving, it was worth fighting for.

I stood there for ten minutes on that silent road. I stood with the warmth on my face. I stood there with no breeze. I stood there in the cloudless sky. I did not have the strength to speak. There were only tears. God knew that I was sorry for my thoughts... my thoughts of giving up... of quitting. He heard me, and he answered. He parted the sky and answered my heart.

After a few minutes of just standing there, I got back in my van and cried out. "Why Lord?? Why am I always weary?? I understand that I put too much on my plate. I know that I say yes too often. I know that I have made a million mistakes... but why is this so HARD? When does it get easier? When do I get rest? When I make a concerted effort to slow down, it's always sabotaged by the next emergency. This is a marathon with no finish line. I'm not running; I'm crawling. I need release. Please... can I quit my job?"

That's when miracle two happened. You might think I'm completely crazy by writing this, so I'll shoot straight with you. I rethink this whole story and I think I'm crazy for remembering it. You may not believe in a God of any kind. There are many times in my life I've had the same doubts. But as sure as the sun is in the sky, I heard the voice of God. He gave me an audible "No."

I started sobbing. If I could not leave my job, then the struggle would continue. I could not cut my kids, which meant no break. There was nothing else to cut. My life was divided in two: work and children. One had to go for me to stand up.

If I knew then what I know now, I would have realized that His answer actually was, "It's coming." In that moment, all I could handle was yes or no; and that's exactly what God gave me. So I asked Him, "why?? Why can't I have some water on my parched throat? Why is there no end? Why is it trauma every day? Why don't I get a resting place?" Then I heard His voice in my head say simply, "When you are weary, you rest in me. When you are strong, you do it all yourself. Until you can learn to lean on me when you're strong, you're not ready for an easier plate. Learn to be still."

Then it hit me. I was so tired because I was swimming upstream. I was doing it all on my own. I didn't need anyone. I pushed until I could push no more, then wondered why no progress was made.

Maybe I am speaking to you, and maybe I'm not. If you've ever had that quiet space of depletion, that deep place inside you where the race is too much; let's meet at that place. It may be your overwhelming job; the care of your parents; finances that are unbelievably stressful and unfixable in your lifetime; children; an abusive relationship; a spouse that leaves you broken; a church that has hurt you; friends that have hurt you in places that can't be fixed in this lifetime.

Here's the thing: all those burdens are too hard for us; but none of them are too hard for God. He's the designer of the universe; the One that spoke and an earth formed. Our troubles are so small compared to what He can take on.

Then miracle three occurred: I got it. I was where I was because I refused to lean on the Lord. I did it all alone. I'm not going to tell you I've got it all figured out, because I think it takes a lifetime to grasp and ten thousand more mistakes. I can tell you one thing. I turned my key in the ignition and veered to the right on my road instead of going straight into the state park. That moment when the skies parted and I heard that audible "no", I had a realization that I could stay where I was and do it on my own or I could surrender and get on my knees and try a new way. This was everything I needed that day. It was a water oasis in a desert of lost.

When I pulled into my driveway, the fourth miracle happened. It didn't need to. God had already gotten my attention. He'd already made his point that my weariness was my stubbornness. It was my contentment in a sea of me. I didn't have His vision. I didn't have His drive. However, I am so thankful I had His mercy and grace; or I'm not sure I'd be a Young Living Diamond right now. I'm not sure I'd even be here right now.

When I got out of my van, the sun was gone. The sky was a sea of clouds. Not a single beam peeked through. Why is that a miracle? Because God showed me one more time, like an exclamation at the end of a powerful sentence, that He controls the skies and the seas and He can order my day. He can bring peace where there is chaos, if only I lean into Him. The first part of your journey is to look into the clouds. Look into the dark places and leave them at the cross. Pause and surrender. Pray for hope. Pray for vision. Sometimes we're so tired we can't even see the possibilities. That's where I was. Be bold and pray for a way out; but don't, for a moment, believe it will be your doing that gets you there. There's a great big God that loves you deeply that plays a huge role in the end of the story; but only if we stand down and stop swimming against the strong current; and only if we turn our palms up and release. That's when the real miracle starts.

If you're in a place of struggle, weariness, or total exhaustion, a place with no way out, then this book is for you. I found my way from the cave. I passed the road to the cliff and kept going. I am on the other side. This is my surrender story. It's how I got out. The center of the story is always my Lord and Savior! He's the one who opened the sky. He's the one that will never forget you, never leave you and never forsake you, no matter how many days pass by without the sun on your face.

If you're ready for the how, keep reading. If you're so broken and lost you can't learn right now, then go back and read this story again, and cry. It's good to cry and release. It's a form of moving from where you are. If you have some oils with you, inhale Sara, Inner Child, Three Wise Men, or Release. They are good for broken places.

I can tell you in a sentence that we find Young Living, run to Diamond, and make major changes that impact the course of our lives in positive ways. However, I'll save the rest of the Cinderella story for the end of the book. For now, let's start walking from where you are, even if it's just a period of processing in your brain on how you want to do this thing before you take action. Hope starts in many ways. If you have forgotten to dream, let's start there.

PART ONE

A Fresh Start on a Stuck Business

It was April of 2018 when I showed up at the Gameplan LIVE event in Columbia, SC., so hungry and needing this to work. I also came from radio, but after a failed marriage and being a single parent I had nothing. My options were running out. We connected at the table that night and Sarah started handing me all these signed copies of Gameplan and Gameplan workbooks. I ask her "who do I give these to?" She said "your leaders." I told her I didn't have any—and then she spoke words into me that I will never forget. She told me that that was about to change and that I could do this. She said God was not done with me. I believed her. Within a matter of a couple of months I went from having no leaders to having 5 legs and 57% ER. Sarah, you have changed my life and I will never be able to thank you enough.

Ellen McGraw

CHAPTER 1

WHY YOUNG LIVING IS THE BEST JOB IN THE WORLD

I've written quite a bit on this topic already; and you can check it all out in more expanded forms in the Gameplan Mini: Build A Life Beyond Survival Mode, or the full Gameplan book (book 1 in this series). For the sake of the purpose of this book, however, I think in some form it needs to be reiterated again, because you may have tried this "network marketing" thing so many times you're truly starting to wonder if it actually works. This is your answer that the Young Living system of running a business has not just blessed thousands, but tens of thousands of families globally. It is proven. Here's what you need to ask: why are you here? Why are you considering Young Living? What brought you to this book in the first place? Most importantly though... why have you never given up?

The answer can be summed up in one sentence: This is the best job in the world. I truly believe that with my whole heart. I believe it while still continuing to fill in as a news anchor, because news is in my blood; and I'll be 90 before I stop, unless they throw me out. I will do what I have done for decades because I LOVE the craft. But news is not the best job for me. It drains me physically and pulls me from my family.

And I believe that for you, too. Your job doesn't mean it's the best job for you, even if it's a job you adore.

I think the best way to explain why Young Living is worth fighting for is to paint a before and after picture of my life pre-Young Living and post-Young Living Diamondship. I'm not promising you riches; I'm simply sharing my journey. I will say that I believe anyone can build this business if they put their mind to it, regardless of their personality or friend circle size. We'll dig into that DEEP later in this book. It all comes down to the art of loving humans. It's a simple skill, that once mastered, opens a doorway blazing wide for your cold market (those you don't know). We'll train hard on that one skill for this entire book. That skill, repeatedly, without giving up, and by being consistent, can build a Diamondship.

I lived in the projects for a dozen years before Young Living. I lived in two projects housing developments, actually in two different towns. I'm talking cockroaches, food pantries, WIC assistance, cinderblock walls, AND going-to-bed-without-power-in-our-jackets-on-in-minus-30-degree-weather projects! I am 41; and 39 years of my life on this earth have been in poverty, by American standards.

So when I tell you that Diamonds make 26,000 dollars a month according to the Income Disclosure Guide, that's freedom to me. Money doesn't solve everything; but it makes the road much easier. Money didn't drive me to start Young Living, oils did. I knew I wanted every oil in my house when I saw them work. I knew I could not afford them. So out of the sheer love of building my oils supply to protect my children and home with non-toxic products, I taught classes. I shared by sitting in front of people and pouring my passion all over them. That one action, 288 times, landed me at Diamond.

The first blessing was financial, for sure, even if it was inadvertent; but there were other things that came with it that completely caught me by surprise. You see, I had no idea what network marketing was. I'd never done it before. I had anchored 60,000 newscasts and read my children to sleep; but this whole "business" thing was quite foreign.

The second blessing was several rank ups. It started with one or two close friends that I watched hit Star, then Senior Star, Executive, and Silver. One of them is now running for Diamond this year; and the other, Platinum. Those one or two friends became 800 friends in the span of a couple years. We have a couple hundred people hit new ranks every month. I know what those ranks did for my family; so that means every single month, I watch my friends get blessed just as I have been blessed. It's pretty neat to do a job where your friends get the same perks, the same freedom, and the same paycheck. That's rare. In a newsroom, my coworkers don't get to experience that. I don't anchor a newscast and see their paycheck go up. I don't watch them anchor a newscast and see my paycheck go up. But when I teach a class, the people above me are paid on that volume. And when my leaders below me teach, I'm blessed with new ranks and new OGV and a higher check. We do better when we help each other. Leaving a story for the anchor after me didn't increase my pay. If they left something for me, it didn't increase their pay. But that's exactly how it works in network marketing. If you help the team by training them in business and in aromatherapy, your check is blessed as they pass the training and knowledge along. In network marketing, you do better when you help your friends rank up. When you raise Silvers, you get the biggest paycheck. In the act of raising leaders, you're spreading freedom all over your team, and you get a front row seat to watch it for a lifetime. That's a perk I've never had at any other job in my life. What if... walk with me for a moment, it's not just you; but your best friend, your mom, your sister, and two high school friends all went Diamond at this? You'd get to experience this lifestyle with the people you love the most, knowing they are cared for. That's a pretty big job bonus.

The third thing that changed for me was the sheer number of friendships I had. When I started, I could count on one hand the number of women I texted monthly, or spent time with. Now, I have friends in all 50 states, because we have labored in the trenches together. We've built a legacy together. We understand what no-show classes feel like. We understand disappointment with a leader. We understand getting shut down on a kit by a family member. We've walked the emotional side of this business together, and celebrated victories side by side. The people that are in my life now I wouldn't change for the world. I can't believe I spent the first 40 years of my life without them. I've been forever changed for the better by watching their fight. They have made me a better leader... and a better mom.

For 22 years, I woke up at 3am to start my shift by 4am. Anchoring is a frantic, high-stress job. I type 120 words a minute for 6 to 8 hours straight, five days a week. Now, my alarm goes off at about 8am. I get a quick run in. I have some devotion time. My kids come upstairs around 9am. We have smoothies, worship, and jump into school; and I am not tired. I can be there for my teen's midnight pouring-of-the-heart sessions. I am a present mom. If I need time off, that Diamond check is still there every single month. As I type this, I'm on a flight to Seattle en route to a Young Living cruise to Alaska. I'll be on that boat for seven days with 4500 oilers, sitting in hot tubs, going kayaking with my kids past Alaskan glaciers, doing some dog sledding, eating some really good food, and sitting up late into the night giggling with a half dozen of my own leaders that won the trip as well. When I come home, my check won't be down by a whole week of pay. It's not because I took one of my two weeks of yearly vacation. It's because I built residual income that's there whether I punch that timecard or not. THAT is worth fighting for.

Last year, I got a 600 percent pay raise. My largest pay raise in my life was 3 percent. That's about 100 dollars a month at my white-collar job. That's the reason I went to college for 8 years. That's the job I took a 70-thousand-dollar student loan to get. For this job, I never went to college. I never took out a single student loan. And I get paid more than a rocket scientist. That is GOOD payoff. For this job, I got a raise because I taught more classes. I connected with more humans. I shared my love of chemical free living; and I told people why they needed to protect their homes. Not only do I get a clean house in this deal; but I get to protect my family, friends, and hundreds of people I've never met; and make sure there aren't cancer-causing chemicals in their cabinets, too.

I think the best part of Young Living is willable income. With every other job I've had, I worked for years to build a 401k that may take care of my kids in the event of my death for maybe six months. At my last job, it took me a decade to save 17,000 in a 401k matching program. We live on 3,000 dollars a month. That's six and half months of income my mom would have to take care of my kids. However, she has them for life! That's not security! Even a life insurance policy would barely cut the bill caring for five kids. My mom would have to take on multiple jobs. W ith Young Living, let the company know who you want to get your check in the event you're gone. That information stays on file. One person you designate spends the 100pv to get your check, and they receive your paycheck and distribute it as directed, like a trustee. That means a Diamond check of 35,000 divided among my five kids would be 7,000 a month, every month, forever! Poverty over! That's the face of freedom.

Have I convinced you yet? This has changed my entire life. I could go on to tell you that we are now debt free, including our home. We're retired and using our clocks as we choose; and many, many other things. suffice it to say there is peace in our home. There is release. It took a lot of fight to get there; this fight leads somewhere. This is an investment you WANT to make.

Now you're ready for Unstuck.

Let's dive in.

This is what
#diamondrising
looks like

YOUNG LIVING *Ranks* AVERAGE MONTHLY INCOME

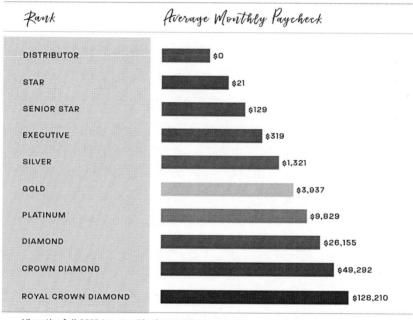

Rank	*Average Monthly Paycheck*
DISTRIBUTOR	$0
STAR	$21
SENIOR STAR	$129
EXECUTIVE	$319
SILVER	$1,321
GOLD	$3,937
PLATINUM	$9,829
DIAMOND	$26,155
CROWN DIAMOND	$49,292
ROYAL CROWN DIAMOND	$128,210

View the full 2018 Income Disclosure statement at:
https://static.youngliving.com/en-US/PDFS/IDSOnlineVersion_PDF_US.pdf

*Can you handle the no's if you know
they are not a personal rejection?*

Sarah, I bought your book at convention. My sister took it from me that day read it and has been on fire! She sold 3 kits at the Salt Lake City Airport on her way home from convention and one of them has turned into a business builder, and is coming to a Leadership retreat I'm doing in two weeks. My sister has already given my book to one of her downline members, so I guess I will wait for the true launch. I just wanted to share the impact your book has had already!

Lisa LaMunyon

CHAPTER 2

No One Is Listening

You see it.

You know where a Young Living business goes. The average Diamond makes over 26,000 dollars a month, according to the 2018 Young Living Income Disclosure Guide.

You want it. You want freedom. You are weary, and you need a leg up.

But wanting it isn't enough to get you there. It takes rolling up your sleeves and sharing essential oils constantly. The more you get the script in front of faces, the faster you get to freedom. It's simple math: the more classes you teach, and the more people that get on Essential Rewards, the faster you rank. Network marketing works. Network marketing works. You know what to do. However, despite your best efforts, no one is listening.

You can't seem to cross that bridge. You have wisdom that needs to be passed on! However, getting your friends to a class is the hardest part.

Let me start with a sprinkle of hope. Then I will share a powerful story from my team. Then we'll dive into why no one is coming to your classes. We'll tackle some mindset training. And I will give you more than a dozen different ways to teach, with scripts and words to invite people, and step-by-step powerhouse training (that works) on how to build relationships and get results.

Let's look at the facts. There were more than 20 new Diamonds in the month of November 2017. That's 20 new people running businesses doing a quarter-of-a-million-dollars a month in volume. Throughout the year of 2016, there were 57 new Diamonds. In 2017, there were 148 (three times more). In 2016, there were 2,251 new Silvers, Golds, and Platinums. In 2017, there were 4,821. That's a 214 percent increase in ONE year. How are they doing it??

You see the success stories... they are everywhere!! How can they pull it off while you sit there at the same rank, month after month, year after year??? Why can't you be one of those numbers?

Let me start with a short story of inspiration, and then I'm going to guide you through your frustration, because I know in my deepest heart of hearts that you have what it takes to be a Royal Crown Diamond with Young Living. I believe in you! One of the hardest steps to this business is getting you to believe in yourself.

Meet Rachael. She is my sister. She is a Young Living Gold. She has had 103 no-show classes. You read that right... 103!! I just got some stats from her and she said she's only had about 25 classes where anyone showed up. Most of them were only one or two people at a time.

Despite tremendous adversity, she's sitting on a monthly OGV (organizational group volume, which includes her purchases and the purchases of everyone under her) of 70,000. She is two-thirds of the way to Platinum rank.

How can that be???

Tenacity.

Tenacity and mindset. If you want this, there is one thing that you have to keep at the forefront of your mind. These are the most important words in this book: **the biggest obstacle on your way to Diamond is yourself**. We have the same amazing oils. We have the same 24 hours in a day. We have the same tools. The ones that get to Diamond are the ones that see that the goal is possible. Then, it's just a matter of walking out the steps necessary to get it. If you can get past your own view of yourself, you have a Diamondship in the bag.

About two years ago, I took my sister with me to the Gold retreat with Young Living. When you hold Gold rank for three straight months, Young Living pays to take you to the first Young Living farm at Saint Mary's. You will see founder Gary Young's first tractor and see how his first distillery yielded just a few drops of Lavender after a year. It's incredible.

Before that trip, my sister did not see that Diamond was possible for her. I shared inspiring stories, she had watched me climb up the ranks; and yet there was not even a small part of that that translated to a rank up for her. I'd highly recommend that when you win these retreats, you take an up-and-coming leader. Take someone you see potential in, rather than your spouse. Your spouse will get it (if they do not already) when they see your check. You do not need to win them over. You DO need leaders; so invest in your leaders.

There was something about the social proof of that trip. As Rachael sat at tables with Diamonds, Platinums, and shiny new Golds, it generated an entire mindset shift. She came home and was *unstoppable*. And despite class after class of no-shows, she never gave up. There is a saying that three in four people you speak to will say no. If you can emotionally detach yourself from the sale of the starter kit, "no" loses its sting. I think for Rachael it was more like 19 in every 20 that said no. That is a big burn! She kept going despite the rejection. Her advances were small, and her pace was slow.

That's not how you build this thing!

It's not a fiery explosion to Royal Crown Diamond. For most, it's built brick by brick, class by class, mortar by mortar, piece by piece, conversation by conversation. Those that are actively not giving up and committing to teach at least once a week usually make Diamond within four years (if you look at the average time to rank among the Young Living Diamonds). That time stamp is for those that find their mistakes, look at what they are doing wrong, and step into places that scare them. Those that correct their errors, they are the ones that rise. This book will help you find those mistakes. It's not that network marketing doesn't work, or that it's not "for you". I truly believe *anyone* can do this if they see it. It could just be that the tactics you are using may not be best for you to grow. If you find your weaknesses (most of the time it's mindset), and you alter your course and return to the things that brought you kit sales in the first place, you will build freedom.

For Rachael, one snowy winter evening, after dozens of classes, a single leader signed up in DuBois, Pennsylvania in a church basement. They caught the vision and started moving. Then another leader came along on a different leg months later. For her, 19 in 20 people continued to say no; but then finally there was another yes. Even though she was picking up the last of the grains on the ground of the field; the little that she gathered blew up into a solid Goldship. Why? She saw the goal; and she never, ever gave up. Can you handle the no's if you know they are not a personal rejection?

Rachael WILL hit Royal Crown Diamond. It may take her longer than most; but I know she'll hit it because of one thing, and one thing alone: **she sees it.** Because she sees it, she stays the course. She knows the route. She anticipates rejection, yet she is steady, consistent, and faithful. When she finds another leader, she never gives up on them, even if their pace and vision move slower than hers. Those little grains on the ground are growing into something amazing: **freedom.**

Step one to filling classes is mindset. If there's a small part of you that thinks you truly don't have what it takes, I want to walk you through an exercise. It only takes a few minutes; but if you don't know your "why" each day, you won't wake up to fight for it. Make a list of the desires of your heart. Those are the small things that you have seen in your head for a long time: a family vacation, a little speedboat to take your kids out on, a hammock for the backyard, being debt free, giving generously to missions, helping a family that you have watched struggle for a very long time, putting grassfed beef and pastured eggs on the table for your babies, the release from a stressful job for you or your spouse, an hour a day to take care of your body or get more rest, a weekly date night, or time for deep friendships. Those dreams were meant to be chased! Those desires were put there by a great big God who loves to love on His kids. When you pursue them, you are pursuing His goals for you. Inadvertently, you will touch thousands of lives.

Do you know one of the biggest problems I see with Young Living distributors? Your dreams are too small. Gary Young was successful because his dreams were HUGE. I have so many leaders come to me and tell me that a Silvership is enough for their family. It's enough to get free oil. It's enough to be debt free. Do you know what my response is?

How dare you!

How dare you think only of your own family? That is such a small circle! Don't you want to impact the widows, the sick, and the poor? Don't you want to change lives? Don't you want to be the hope-bringer? Don't you want a front row seat to watch miracles and freedom EVERY SINGLE DAY? Do you want to see the course of entire families' lives changed forever? Do you want to witness generational wealth? Don't you see what is ahead of you when you pursue dreams bigger than what can impact just your family alone? The larger your organization grows, the more lives have been changed. You are a course-corrector for thousands of people, if only you will see past the four walls of your home.

The high end of the income disclosure guide shows that a Royal Crown Diamond makes over 258,000 thousand dollars a month. What would that do to your life? You'd be debt free in one month. Then what? What dreams will you chase? Would you carry yourself differently if that amount was deposited into your bank account on the 20th this month? Then again in the next month, and the next, forever and ever, until you are gone? Then that same check blesses your kids, grandkids, and great-grand kids as generations of families fall in love with oils, and a lifestyle that is clean for their bodies? Network marketing is like baking a cake, selling it, and getting paid on that one cake for the rest of your life. Then your kids get paid on it . Then it will be your grandkids, and then your great grandkids; because Young Living is a legacy. Your hustle for two to four years blesses your GRANDKIDS and GREAT-GRANDKIDS. Isn't it worth it?? It's willable income that is there long after you are gone. (To read more about willable income, pick up a copy of the full 300-page *Gameplan* book at oilabilityteam.com.)

If you want to impact not dozens of families, but tens of thousands of families, you have to start thinking like a Royal Crown Diamond right now. The only difference between you and the Royal Crown Diamonds is that you're a few steps behind them. They've just had more classes. Walk with that attitude and mindset, and you will get there. You will change the future for so many people on your team.

Why? Because you believe it's possible.

When you believe it's possible, your leaders believe it's possible. Your distributors believe it's possible. People you have never met are inspired by your infectious passion. It's not hard for you to get people to classes. It's because you have the three things that can get them there: passion for the products, belief that they work, and compassion to meet people exactly where they are without judgement.

What I want you to do today is to write down those dreams. Let your mind walk them as if they have already happened. Write down the most sacred places in your heart, the things you have seen for years but haven't been able to get to, or the places where you've given up hope.

It's time to dream again.

It is the visionaries that take the world to great places. It's the Thomas Edisons, Eli Whitneys, and the Gary Youngs. It's time to follow their path and MOVE.

What does passion look like? It looks like oiling every single day, trying new things, playing, experimenting, and learning to research. It's spending 300pv on your order to try out products you've never owned, just to have the experience and the knowledge that you can pass on. It's the infectious love of a Clean Living lifestyle... one without yuck in your drawers and cabinets; and one that causes your neighbors, friends, and even people you don't know (like the guy sitting on the airplane next to me right now) to turn their head and wonder what it is that you have that's so different, so special. If you don't have passion, and your oils are sitting on a shelf collecting dust, it's going to be very hard for you build a team. They will copy what they see. If your oils are dusty, theirs will be too. If your lifestyle doesn't promote oiling, they won't have anything to follow. If you're teaching classes with pop in your hand, and your home is filled with poisons in your cabinets, they will be confused. You demonstrate the lifestyle by accepting the Simple Swap, going room to room and purging toxic ingredients out your home, and oiling with purpose and intent every single day. If a day goes by and you don't have oils on your body or in your diffuser, you have lost a day of training yourself. You have lost another story. Try new things. Then each day, you will learn just a little bit more that you can pass on with passion. *You don't need to know it all. But if you aren't out there gathering your own stories, it'll be awfully hard to tell the stories when you meet new people.* It'll be hard to get them excited because you have not experienced the lifestyle. Step one is to oil. Write your own story. Generate experiences. *Play* with the products. Then when your paths cross with a non-oiler, you will be an inspiration at best, and get their attention at the least. Attention is the entire focus of this book. If you have their attention, you can grow something completely amazing with Young Living. It all starts in your own home first. You cannot inspire others to live a lifestyle you yourself are not living.

Start with the commitment to play. That will generate excitement and stories, which leads to passion; and with passion, people will listen. They will follow hope.

You don't need to know it all. But if you aren't out there gathering your own stories, it'll be awfully hard to tell stories when you meet new people.

For over three seasons I've been overwhelmed and quiet, trying to listen to my "calling" trying to define my goals, explore "who" I am so that I can be strong enough to move forward with sharing the oils and growing a vial business for me and my family. Wasting time, wasting energy, I continued for weeks running in place getting nowhere. I received Sarah's new book "Ignite" as a gift from my upline. An hour into reading it (I'm a slow reader and distracted Mom), I got to page 21 and my world changed with just a sentence or two. Sarah's work, her words, and her ministry released me from my personal paralysis!

Aimee W. Hart

CHAPTER 3

THE STATE OF STUCK

I get hundreds of messages every single day telling me that people's warm market (those they know) has dried up. They do not know another person on this earth. Everyone has already been asked about essential oils. The market is saturated. Sharing is useless. No one will come to class.

First of all, you're speaking death over your business. Stop that! Proverbs 18:21 says: "Death and life are in the power of the tongue."

Listen to your speech for the next 24 hours. What are you speaking over your business? Are you cursing your business with your own tongue?? If you are speaking failure, you need to stop it! I am a Diamond today; but a breath ago, I was a Star. I know that place where you are, looking up the Young Living mountain, wondering if the journey is even possible or realistic. You are about to witness financial miracles! You have so much ahead of you that's worth fighting for! If you don't see it, though, you won't fight. I am here to tell you, on behalf of all of the Diamonds, _it **IS**_ _realistic for you_. We have all been there; and for many of us, it feels like it's only been a few moments. I remember the panic looking at each rank up requirement; and the disbelief and doubt floating around in my head,

...ain a certain OGV or be a leader that was worth following. ...wn you if you let it; and if it owns you, you're getting robbed of ...hat will change generations. You do not build a network market- ...siness in a day. You build it relationship by relationship. Expecting overnight riches is unrealistic. Expecting to build a legacy income piece by piece, with hard work, is practical and probable, if you do not give up. The biggest mistake I see is those that quit too soon. Failure starts in your head.

Here is what I want you to do to get your thoughts in the right place. Make a list of everything you believe about your business right now that's simply not true. "I can't find any leaders." "No one will come to my classes." "I will never hit Diamond. It's taking SO long." "No matter what I do, I CAN'T get that leg over a certain volume." "No one wants the lifestyle. I talk to them about Essential Rewards, but they just don't join. Every month I start my business back at zero all over again."

Now, I want you to write down the reciprocal of that. "I will find powerful, dynamic leaders with integrity that can stand on their own two feet." "My classes will change thousands of lives." "I will hit Diamond at the perfect time for my family. God makes no mistakes with the pace of my life!" "That leg is going to cross, because I can do ALL things through Christ who strengthens me". Not: "all things "but" speak in front of people", or "all things "but" grow a leg", or "all things "but" raise leaders". "All things" means "**ALL** things." It means you CAN do things that scare you, because we serve the God of the impossible.

He's the God that has a track record of taking small people to do really big things. You think He can't help you grow your business? He breathed a universe into existence! Stop doubting and start moving. Your doubt is disassembling His work. It is unraveling the amazing plans He has for you, if you'll only step out of a place of fear. Tell yourself, "my passion for Clean Living will inspire those I love to walk the same step on Essential Rewards". Every home I walk into will have Thieves soap in the bathroom, diffusers in the bedrooms, and a full oils rack on the wall. I CAN do this, because I believe in the products, and so do they."

Once you have written all your opposites down, take 60 seconds and repeat them to yourself every single day. There is a point where you will start to believe it. Get into the practice of not allowing fear into your head. It has no place there. Fear crowds out hope. Fear destroys productivity and keeps you in a place of captivity. If you want to be free, fear has to go.

I am about to debunk a few HUGE network marketing myths, (the biggest out there), and tie them right into Young Living with facts and logic. They're those lies we love to believe because we are looking for an excuse to stay in our comfort zone. The myths are: the market is saturated. "Everyone I know is already doing oils, or has said no." "All my friends have signed with someone else." "I am too late." I don't know anyone." The reality is that if you step outside your door, and you see humans, you can do this business. Let's knock these things out and get your mind in a place where you are ready for growth. Let's look at facts instead of living in the land of doubt.

Young Living has six million active distributors GLOBALLY. There are 300-million people in the United States. **If a room were filled with 300 people, only six would have a Starter Kit, and 294 would not.** That's if every distributor in Young Living lived in the United States, which is not true. That tells me that saturation is a myth. The actual problem is that you keep asking the same circle of friends. Get outside your circle and outside your comfort zone. That's where the Lord can really start to use you.

296 out of 300 are pretty good odds! We also know that the average person knows 2000 people by the time they are 20 years old (according to network marketing guru, Dani Johnson). You might be thinking to yourself that there is NO way you know that many people. However, if you started tracking it, you'd be shocked at how many people you DO know; and if you truly think you don't know anyone else, then you just have to master the art of talking to people you don't know. There are nine billion people on this earth. That's a lot of possibilities! I'll talk you through the art of relationship building in this book, too. We'll go through it step by step, following in the path of the people before you that have sold Starter Kit after Starter Kit and built the relationships that lead to Essential Rewards. If you stick with the basics and do them over and over again, they work. You are about to get unstuck.

My strategy when I first start to build is to sign my family and friends immediately. Then I tap into the friend circles of every member of my team. That's how I built to Silver so swiftly—not by knocking out every single person I know, but by befriending the friends of others. When that dries up momentarily, (it's never really dry—it's just your mindset), I will start with my semi-warm market—people I've known a while but we're acquaintances or have not talked in a while. Once I am fully confident in my "30 second script" to get them interested, I will break it out on my cold market, or people I've never met in my life. You can do that list completely backwards and still get results, but most people are more comfortable when they first start signing their mom and their best friend over the gas station attendant. You just have to get good at listening to the needs of humans—whether they are humans you know, or humans you don't know. All humans have needs. Be their solution and you'll have a Starter Kit sale.

In my little town of Corning, New York, there are 12-thousand people. There are 10 thousand on my team. You may think I've saturated this area, but only about 600 people from my town are on this team. And they are not just from Corning—they are from about 30 surrounding towns, too. Even in the shadow of a Diamond, there is a lot of room to spread your wings and fly.

Let's talk about you for just a second. I am writing this book for so many different people. Perhaps you have just started the business, and you look at the task of even becoming a Silver, and doing 10,000 in sales every month. It seems impossible. How can you grow an organization like that? That was the same feeling I had when I saw the rank qualification chart for the first time. If you have not seen that chart, log into your Virtual Office at youngliving.com and click on "Rank Qualification". That's the button where you watch YOU. The chart looks like this:

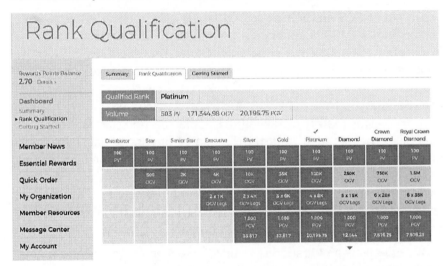

We'll go into it in more depth later on; but I want you to focus on one line right now. That second line shows all the OGV (organizational group volume) you need by rank. A Star needs 500 OGV every month. It resets back to zero when the clock strikes midnight on the first. A Senior Star needs 2000 in OGV every month. An Executive needs 4000, a Silver 10,000, a Gold 35,000, a Platinum 100,000, and a Diamond 250,000 every single month. Crown Diamonds need 750,000 in volume each month; and Royal Crown Diamonds 1.5 million.

That is completely overwhelming! Here's the thing though, it's not about you. It's the power of duplication, which happens through great leadership. **You were born to lead.** You are not the one generating all that volume. It's the passion and love you have passed on to every single person on your team. It's every single Essential Rewards order, and every leader teaching classes beneath you because of the fire you started in them. It's not overwhelming when you divide the numbers among the scores of people who have the same love that you have. They get that love when you ignite passion.

You may have taken off when you first started your business, but you have plateaued. For many, it's only for a few months, or maybe it's been many, many years. You had fantastic volume, and then bit by bit, it dropped off, you lost rank, and you lost hope. Maybe you lost 70 or 80 percent of your volume and are truly starting to believe that network marketing does not work; or you might fall into the third category of the water-treader. You hit a rank, and you have been treading water for a very long time... never advancing, never receding, always the same, but never the Diamondship your heart longs for. Perhaps you've never gotten off the ground. You can't master the art of the first kit, or the fifth kit. Getting started seems impossible. You need the right words to say, and even if you found them, getting people to respond just isn't working.

Here's the thing: the underlying issue is always the same: "mojo". You need mojo to be confident. A confident distributor is a distributor that people will follow and trust. Getting just one Premium Starter Kit sale will fire up your mojo, I swear. You will become bolder than you have in a long time. Instead of looking at the insurmountable task of growing your volume by 4000 OGV, or even 500 OGV for a Star, focus on this one single thing: **one kit**. One kit is all it takes for fire. Part of the problem is a goal that's too large. That is different than dreaming big dreams. Dream those dreams! Dream for Royal Crown Diamond or more. However, strategize and plot just one brick at a time. Goals and dreams are quite different. I knew that once I caught the vision of the business, I would go all the way to the top, no matter how many ranks Gary Young came up with. Since I started, I have never looked at all of the work that I had to do in one sitting. It's always been one kit at a time, one relationship at a time, one class at a time, one leader at a time, one brick at a time. That's how you get the snowball rolling up the hill, so it can eventually take off on its own, blowing up your OGV.

Your doubt is disassembling His work.

I have been devouring my beta copy of Unstuck. Girl...your whole heart was poured into every single word. It is INCREDIBLE. It is your best book so far!!!! Since I've been reading it, I dropped the fear I was still carrying and decided to power through it. Every person I've spoken to this week has been interested and receptive to learning more. I think it's because I found my confidence in the fact that EVERYONE needs oils and they are feeling that energy. WOW! Thank you so much for writing Unstuck

Jodie Wright

WAY TO GO! I really love your scripts and personal testimonies and experiences. It's all so very helpful! I am hoping to get back in the game and hit Silver by the end of the year!

Heather Findlay

CHAPTER 4

MOJO METHOD 1: UTILIZE YOUR FORGOTTEN WARM MARKET

How do you get your mojo back? I like to put myself in a place where I am virtually guaranteed to get that one kit, so I can get my boldness and my fire back (or maybe develop mojo if you've never had a kit sale!) You will be unstoppable with mojo. Mojo sets the tone for your belief system. When you believe, it's a straight track to Diamond. All you have to do is walk. It's already done. If there is one thing missing from your trek through all the ranks, it's the true, doubtless understanding that you have what it takes to run a multi-million-dollar business. Say that out loud until you believe it; because you just doubted! That's not ok!!! I caught you right in the middle of questioning yourself!! Speak it with me: "I have what it takes to run a multi-million-dollar business."

The month I went Diamond, some good friends of mine, Jim Bob Haggerton and his beautiful wife Cindy, said I was going to make it, "with grace and ease." That's a prayer I love to speak over my leaders. Not only will you meet your goal, I want you to repeat to yourself that it's going to happen in a low-stress way, "with grace and ease." We did hit it with both grace and ease, by the way, blowing 25,000 OGV past what we needed, in the shortest month of the year. Not to mention, we had a day and a half before the end of the month. Our legs and our OGV both crossed for the first time within hours of one another! On my website, oilabilityteam.com, there is a button for this book under the "share" tab. Look for downloadable graphics for each month of the year that say "I WILL NAIL THIS RANK WITH GRACE AND EASE!" Go print it off and put it where you'll see it every day. You HAVE this. Walk in it.

Back to mojo: here's the thing, your confidence is low. That's most of the problem. Simply put yourself in a place for easy kit sales. My favorite thing to do when my mojo is low is to make a list of every person I know. That's your warm market list. It's every name on your Facebook friends list, every name on Instagram, the people you're connected with on Linked In, Twitter, and Snapchat, your Christmas card list, wedding card invites from a decade ago, your address book, all your saved contacts in your cell phone, the people in the cubicles next to you at work, etc.... Then I carry that list with me for 30 solid days and continually add to it. I add the people in my small group at church, the parents of the kids on my daughter's basketball team, the friends where I volunteer, the teller at the bank, the lady at the post office, the gas station clerk I see every day, etc. You'll be blown away at how many people you actually "know". Then start building relationships one by one, getting oils on their bodies, and see where it leads. Just start crossing names off the list one at a time. If everyone is still continually telling you no, try to have three or four conversations where you are building your relationship before you ever even make mention of oils. It's ok, those conversations are an investment. If you need to see what a warm market list looks like, there are demos of the list in the Gameplanner and in the Gameplan workbook.

---

*Mojo sets the tone for
your belief system.*

There are 4 ways I get my mojo back. Utilizing my warm market is only one of them. I find that when I use that list for some time, then walk away from it, then return to it again, names I'd mentally crossed off the list are back on with new conversations and blocks I'd placed around people aren't still there. Revisit the list several times a year and add names and rekindle contacts.

These mojo methods are tried and true tricks that I use every single time my head gets in the gutter. The other three methods are purple bags, vendor events, and friends of friends. Let's look into each of those next. You can start utilizing some of these tips even as you're working through *Unstuck* and the *Unstuck* workbook—because they work! Don't look at the huge puzzle with all its pieces on the table. Look at the next thing only: signing one person. You can do it. You can get your mojo back."

If you hand out samples or purple bags and expect nothing back, that's poor stewardship of the business the Lord is trusting you with.

I love talking about Young Living, but I'm my own worst enemy. I find myself in the middle of fear, paralysis and with not enough confidence to step out freely and start the conversation. I can't wait to read your book. I'm hoping it will help me to get out of my own way!

Paula DeFur Hunter

Thank you!!!!! Your scripts and quotes have given me the confidence I needed to get myself "Unstuck". I am struggling to maintain Executive, but I already have my mind on Silver! Thank you for all that you do and share.

Nena Sledge

CHAPTER 5

Mojo Method 2: Purple Bags

The second way I get my mojo back is by being prepared. 80 percent of your business is simply carrying the right tools on you for when the time arises and people ask you about oils. If you have no tools, it's harder for them to order, and you'll have to have more conversations and direction to make it happen. To be prepared, I use the **famous purple bag**. There's an entire write up with hyperlinks for free on how to assemble the bags on my website at, oilabilityteam.com/follow-up-bags. What's included?

- a 101 or Toxin Free life cd (so they can listen as soon as they drive away. It's as if they attended a full class)

- a photo of the starter kit (discoverlsp.com, then "fliers")

- instructions on how to order and a cover sheet (free printables at: https://oilabilityteam.com/follow-up-bags/)

- your contact information

- Fearless and the Fearless calendar (free printable at: https://oilabilityteam.com/fearless-tools/)

- *Your Gameplan: Build A Life Beyond Survival Mode* (prospecting tool)

If you put that little bag into someone's hand, make sure you collect their contact information before they walk away! Allow them a few days to listen to the cd and read *Fearless* then contact them to follow up. It yields great results! I average 6-8 kit sales a month just by carrying these little bags on me and doing great follow up. I find my way around the mountain of sharing by always being prepared, because every second I have is precious; and the seconds need to matter. If I have "classes" on cd, and photos of the kit on my body, I see results when conversations arise.

How do I use purple bags? I make up about 100 purple bags at the beginning of each month and carry five or so in my purse and in the glove compartment of my family van. I'll give you more detail when we get into the part of this book where I break down all the various ways of sharing oils.

Let me address collecting contact information for a moment, because that can be quite scary. How do you ask for it from someone you have just met? Isn't that... stalkerish? Not really. You have invested in them by giving them knowledge. I generally don't ask for the cell phone number and address of a new acquaintance; but I have no problem asking, "would you mind if I Facebook friend you, so I can check in and see how you are doing?" Very rarely will they say no. It's a safe place. They can always unfriend me after I walk away, and no personal information was exchanged. Then I invest in them and build the relationship. As soon as I am in my car, I shoot them a quick message saying, *"This is Sarah, your creepy oils lady! Thank you for letting me pour into you today. I really believe that cd is the answer to what you have been looking for. Take a listen to it on your way home, and I'll check in on (Wednesday) to see if you're ok! I am sorry you had such a stressful day today! You made a difference for me just with your kindness!"* If you always ask for something back, you'll yield much higher results with purple bags. If you hand them out and expect nothing, you are giving away your paycheck (It's the same thing with samples of oil, by the way.) That is poor stewardship of the business the Lord is trusting you with.

By tracking your warm market and working through that list name by name, and carrying purple bags, for chance encounters, you can kickstart your OGV growth to hit the next rank. I am always surprised at who is NOT on my team yet when I go track my warm market list. Some are good friends. I'd cry if they fell in love with oils elsewhere! When I say "chance encounters" with purple bags, what I really mean is that there truly is a technique to it. It's not chance at all. You already have a heart, passion, and deep love for essential oils. Develop that love even more by being watchful of the needs around you. It may be someone coughing nearby that would really benefit from a Thieves cough drop, or a man standing in line with you that's in noticeable pain and could use a dollop of Cool Azul Pain Cream. It may be someone looking for hand sanitizer (you know which one to give them), or a roll or two of Stress Away. It could be someone on the beach that could use Young Living Mineral Sunscreen, or a friend at a campfire that would be blessed by Young Living Insect Repellant. It could be a momma who has not tried the Seedlings line. I have handed all these things out in lines of stores or in casual conversations wherever I am. Nearly all of those encounters have yielded results with a purple bag and contact information. It's about meeting them where they are, without judgement. The secret is paying attention to what is going on around you, and meeting needs.

Let's say you're not there yet. That step of offering something to a total stranger is foreign, and frankly it's terrifying. You need another step in the process to warm up your mojo and build your confidence. Let's take a few steps back. What if I gave you a market that's completely cold (not a single face that you know)... but they're coming to YOU looking for product? That's even simpler than classes, because these folks are actually walking into a marketplace with the intent of making a purchase. In your home, they may come solely for education, and be caught off guard by the offer of a Premium Starter kit at the close of the class. Not with this method. With the right training, even the shyest distributor can have significant success.

It's time to talk about Mojo Method #3: vendor events.

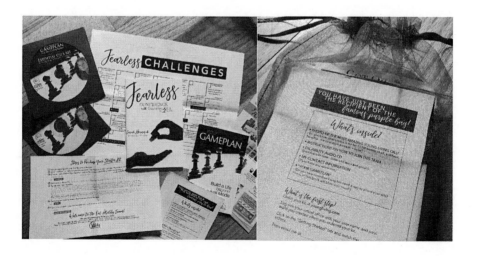

Sarah , I over think things over and over! You really have helped me to have a more "go for it " attitude without fear! My heart goes out to you for allll you do for all of us!! I cannot wait for Unstuck! I want my leadership to be as fearless as yours!!!

Candi Frost

You are truly amazing at opening people's eyes to why they are stuck!

Stacie Lubben

As I was helping a new lead just now learn about who and what Young Living is all about, my mind kept coming back to your voice and words, Sarah. Being genuinely interested in the needs of people is what it is all about for me. I get SO excited to share with others!

Michelle Ballard Heater

CHAPTER 6

MOJO METHOD 3: VENDOR EVENTS

What am I speaking about? Vendor events. A customer walks right into your "store" looking to make a purchase. If you are prepared, it's even simpler than classes, and requires no friend circles. It's a great place to start if it's been a dry spell or if you have plateaued. I will go into great depth on how to pull off a vendor event later in this book when I prep you on different types of classes. I'll give you all the dangers, pitfalls, and scripts to make it work. It's the longest write up ever penned on how to pull off a professional vendor event and knock it out of the ballpark with kit sales. Our team averages 4-6 kits per event by using this system, depending on foot traffic. With the right tools and training, this method is infallible. One of my sweet leaders, Theresa Yeager, built from 8000 OGV to 35,000 OGV in 18 months solely with a weekly Saturday vendor event. She's now a Gold en route to Platinum. It's as simple as a 30-second script, flip kits, and a computer to sign them. I'll outline it all step by step in the second half of this book.

This is a very viable method of building that can snap you out of a slow zone and get you back to sharing confidently. This may not be the primary way that you build the technique that you use; and that's completely ok. If you're using it just to get your head in the right place, that's a really good reason to start here.

Here is a quick bulletpoint list to get you started until you get to the full chapter on Vendor events:

- Book an event now as you prepare
- Design the setup of your table, but keep it simple. The center-piece should be the starter kit. Don't showcase every product Young Living makes. Add a giveaway basket and purple bags, and a place for them to sign up and you're off and running
- Make sure you have Diamond Deck contact me cards on hand—order them now. They are a game changer for the amount of information you can collect in 30 seconds from a passerby
- Start memorizing your 30-second script to get their attention (that's in the Appendix of this book)
- Order a few flip kits under the One Time Order button to have on hand
- Also order a few pocket desk reference guides to give to those that get kits
- Have purple bags made up for those that get kits

Other than that, skip to the Vendor Event chapter and read up on all the things that will make you event fantastic! The larger the foot traffic, the more people you can expect.

This is a phenomenal way to build, despite two large obstacles. You have to do the foot work to get the vendor events booked, sometimes months in advance—and pay fees to have a table. The follow up is also trickier with a person you only saw for a few moments. But I have tips to get you through both of those things in the Vendor Events chapter in this book.

If you're in a rut, this is a great way to pull yourself out. There are Diamonds that built mostly with vendor events quite successfully. Funnel people to what you want, which is a starter kit sale and Essential Rewards, then give them concise training information and action steps and follow up with them. That's the secret to success with this way of building.

Thank you Sarah for all that you have done! Your books, your inspirational write ups... they mean a lot to me, especially Gameplan. Unstuck will give me clearer input to move to next level. As for my leaders, I do hope they know how important it is for them to get out from comfort zones and do things that scare them. I cannot WAIT for Unstuck.

Arin Ya'acob

CHAPTER 7

Mojo Method 4:
Friends of Friends

Sign Your Circle

The first thing I do when I'm starting to build is sign my circle. It's my starting place.

I sign my mom, my best friend, the people I know who would support me no matter what I do. I avoid the naysayers. I keep my head in the land of positive. My mom may never do the business, but I sign her anyway because I want her to be carried along and get the benefit of the check. That's worked really well for us. She's almost a Platinum (they have checks of $9,829 a month, according to the 2018 Income Disclosure Guide.

The next thing I do is make a list of friends that I know that know people. They may never do the business, and they may never even order monthly; but I teach for them and their friends. One fired up friend will fill classes for you! Start signing their circles. Maybe you have 15 people with 3 or 4 people under them. That's significant! The average Silver has around 100 people on their team. If you think about it, say you have 15 friends on two legs with four people signed under them. That would be sixty people on your team. You'd already be two-thirds of the way to Silver.

I think one of the most important things you can do when you sign someone is to sign their circle as quickly as you can, right after they get their kit. That's when they have their initial fire for oils. I believe it's just as important to tap into their friend circles quickly as it is to explain Essential Rewards and get them into lifestyle swapping and buying from themselves. On the Distributor cards on the Diamond Rising Deck (there's a whole chapter on those later in this book, and they will revolutionize how you do follow up), it asks to teach to your new members friends. I mention it in the very first 101 class they attend—that we want to train their friends and family for them, so they understand the power of Thieves and the oils that God created.

I like to set their first class up before their kit even arrives, if they are willing. I use that class as an opportunity to go through the Starter Kit and show them how to use their reference guide and place their 100pv+ order monthly on Essential Rewards. I tell them if we sign three people at that class, their kit was free- -and it's not a hardship on their budget. If we get those three on Essential Rewards, they have made tremendous headway to placing an ER order every single month and never paying for it. Their family's NingXia and oils each month would be free, even if they never have an inkling to do the business. If they are willing to spend 100pv, I'm willing to teach and tap into their circles of friends and family. That's how you build OGV swiftly: not just relying on the people you know, but the people that others know.

I also keep my eye out for people who need the business. I've lost count of how many Walmart employees, restaurant staff members, etc... that I've signed. Have an eye for the needs around you and share in that space. If they don't express an interest, kick the dust from your feet and move to the next person. There is a big, wide planet outside your door, and many, many people that need the hope you have to give. Walk.

When I first started in Young Living, I taught a class and had 12 women show up. Six of them got kits.

My organization looked like this:

Month 1, July 2014:

Members: 7

Name	Level	Member ID	PV	OGV
	<=		>	>
⭐ HARNISCH	0		308.00	1,023.00
HILL	1		215.00	215.00
SULLIVAN-KNAPP	1		100.00	100.00
SAVAGE	1		100.00	100.00
CLEVELAND	1		100.00	100.00
RUMSEY	1		100.00	100.00
SOUTH	1		100.00	100.00

Month 2, August 2014:

Members: 27

Name	Level	Member ID	PV	OGV
	<=		>	>
⭐ HARNISCH	0		304.00	2,366.75
ARINGTON	1		439.00	439.00
SULLIVAN-KNAPP	1		100.50	222.50
STANLEY	1		215.75	215.75
KRACHT	1		215.00	215.00
STEWART	1		127.75	127.75
RUMSEY	1		122.75	122.75
YEAGER	1		120.00	120.00
SOLTYSIK	1		100.00	100.00

Month 3, September 2014:

Members: 63

Name	Level	Member ID	PV	OGV
	<=		>	>
☆ HARNISCH	0		481.50	6,221.50
☆ STANLEY,	1		1,553.75	2,348.00
☆ SULLIVAN-KNAPP,	1		255.00	1,151.25
☆ SPENCER	1		100.00	1,021.00
RHODES	1		306.00	406.00
SOROKES,	1		239.00	239.00
KRACHT	1		115.00	115.00
KRASINSKI,	1		100.00	100.00
PINE	1		100.00	100.00
YEAGER	1		92.00	92.00

Month 4, October 2014:

Members: 118

Name	Level	Member ID	PV	OGV
	<=		>	>
⑤ HARNISCH	0		351.25	14,739.50
☆ SULLIVAN-KNAPP	1		1,105.00	4,828.00
☆ STANLEY,	1		2,650.50	4,582.00
☆ SPENCER,	1		101.00	736.00
☆ RHODES,	1		326.75	726.75
WALKER	1		366.75	366.75
RUMSEY	1		219.00	319.00
KRACHT	1		103.00	303.00
COLE,	1		271.25	271.25

How on earth did I go from 1000 OGV four weeks into my business to 14,000 OGV 12 weeks into my business, and 118 members? Is it because I am a rockstar? No, not at all. In fact, I built this just a short time after I'd moved 750 miles across the country—so you know it wasn't done by people I knew. I didn't have any friends. I knew a couple of people from work, and that catapulted me because I relied on their friend circles to grow my team. When they were on fire with their new kit, I sat down with their mom and three friends to help them get the kit for free as well, and off we went. I taught a class a week consistently. It had nothing to do with the people I knew. It had everything to do with the people my few acquaintances knew. Their friends of friends are what built me to Silver in twelve weeks.

Don't be afraid to pop the question on how to get repaid for their kit right at the onset of enrollment. You'll be amazed how many people say yes.

I use words like this:

"I know you're going to fall in love with Thieves! It's going to feel really good when you walk in your mom's house and see Thieves on the counter instead of her dish soap with blue or green dye. Would you like me to teach this same class—with all the science—for her as well? If three people get a kit under you, you'll get $50 dollars per kit, which effectively pays you back for nearly every dime you're spending right now. Even if you never build a business with this, you know your friends and family are protected with the products they are using, and they have been well-trained. I'm willing to do that training for you for nothing—because I believe in empowering women to make good choices for their families. YOU will get the paycheck from it, to cover the cost the kit you buy today. If we get them on Essential Rewards, and they start swapping their toxic products out cabinet by cabinet, you'll get a check every month and can your family's NingXia, Thieves cleaning products, supplements and <u>oils for free</u>. Let's get a date on the calendar before you leave."

It doesn't need to come off like a sales pitch. My favorite line is "I believe in empowering women (or men if you are male) to make good choices for their families." That's what this whole lifestyle is about: education.
Tapping into friends of friends is one of the most powerful vehicles you have to grow your team. Speed isn't as important as momentum. You keep momentum going by scheduling classes. If you run out of people, <u>never forget that your people haven't run out of people</u>. If you have a team of five or six, that's easily enough distributors to build to Silver with their friend circles alone. Just ask.

I love to tell my growing distributors that if we can get 10 people signed under each of them on their first level, that would be enough to cover their family's toothpaste, Thieves cleaner, dish soap, and laundry soap and more on Essential Rewards. A handful of classes can save their budget. Always word it in ways that show the blessing is for them.

Let's recap. My 4th mojo method to re-energize yourself is to tap into friends of friends. Also, keep naysayers at arm's length. And never forget to tease the business in your classes—even if it's just handing out the Gameplan mini and leaving it on each seat of those that walk in the door, or in their purple bag. You never know who needs hope.

Overall, these four tactics are my quick-start guide to get my head in the right place when it's been too long since my last kit sale: **utilize your warm market, hand out purple bags** to strangers and non-strangers alike, **do vendor events** (especially if you think you don't know a soul), and **tap into friends of friends.** One friend's friend circles could take you to Silver. Keep your feet moving and always look forward. Let your actions show the success of your business.

You have what it takes to do this!!!

If you've tried all those things and still see no results, or just don't feel like you have the energy to move yet, let's pause and do a little mindset training in Part 2 of Unstuck before I take you through all the classes I've seen in Young Living. I have compiled all I know about sharing oils into one place: mojo methods, mindset, visual layouts of 15 types of successful classes, and how to talk to strangers. We're going to tackle your objections one by one and get your business off the ground!

Sign Your Circle.

One of my favorite writers is on the move! You go girl! Just to give you more steam, your books have given me and my team in Jakarta, Indonesia (yes, it's on the other part of the world with 12 hours' time difference) to run our business and regularly share. Thank you!!

Rina Amalia

I am so excited for this book! This is the answer I have been looking for.

Malinda Mackie

Sarah, I have been homeless for over 1 year. Tonight I had the opportunity to help the desk clerk in our hotel by giving her a PURPLE BAG. She is really interested in the business. Last night you talked about FEAR and there was no fear when I talked with her. Thanks to you I had all the information I needed to give her. I can't thank you enough. I couldn't have done it without you. She said to check in on Sunday night when she works again. I am praying she will get on board! If she signs up, she will be my first one.

Ruth Wetherbe Webb

CHAPTER 8

IF ALL YOUR MOJO METHODS FAIL

Talking to your family and friends can be incredibly frustrating. But if they are the only voices you hear on this journey, it's going to be hard to get off the ground. That means you're at a fork in the road and have to make some tough choices about who you allow to be close to you. No matter how hard I teach and how many purple bags I hand out, if I come home every single day to a nasty message or a crude comment, it takes the wind from my sails.

Some of my closest family members have been the last to sign to my oils team. They will second guess business decisions because network marketing has a bad rap, or because of a lack of education on how the business model works. They will think the research behind the use of oils is quack science, even though you have tried and true recipes that have changed how you care for your family. The truth is, they just want the best for you. They are in the same place where you stood before your kit arrived. They are in darkness.

Honestly, some family members just need to see your paycheck. They need to see you are ok. And for many, that will be enough. Others will fight even when you are a Royal Crown Diamond with a huge house and a giving heart that helps thousands. Keep those family members out of your inner circle so you're not torn down emotionally– and keep walking toward freedom. Their freedom and your freedom are not tied together. If you listen to their words and let them tear you down, you give up on your own release. Keep your family and friends close, but not in your inner circle if they are naysayers. Surround yourself with people that give you joy, move you forward, and believe in you. One of the things I did when I got involved in Young Living was to decide who my "five" were. Those are the five closest people that you text regularly, hang around and do life with. Everyone else was special, but not at arm's length. If you're mind is toxic emotionally, it can be just as traumatic for your business as being physically ill. You can't move. And that includes toxic family members and close friends.

With all that said, there are a few facts you can toss at those close to you to try to get them on the same page. And if they don't get it, kick the dust off your feet and move forward with your business until they cannot deny where it goes. You show them what freedom looks like.

Fact sheet:

- Young Living is 25+ years into network marketing (most network marketing companies fail within seven years)

- Young Living does over 2-billion dollars in sales annually

- Customers return because the products work

- There are 6 million distributors globally

- network marketing is a viable business model (watch this: https://www.youtube.com/watch?v=zZiw15VgWoI Type in "Pat Petrini Pyramid Scheme in YouTube)

- Young Living has 3000 global employees, 50 highly trained scientists, and more than 20 international markets

- You can visit the farms. The company is transparent. (Enroll for a farm visit online at younglivingfarmtours.com)

- Young Living's oils library of plant constituents is unparalleled in the essential oils world. We have been keeping records for 25+ years on 300 singles and blends. That's longer than most oils companies have been in existence. In addition, our distillation methods are copied all over the world.

- No one else has Seed to Seal. That's the protocol we use to make sure our oils are unsprayed, non-GMO, grown on virgin untainted soil (including no mercury, arsenic, lead, or other things in the ground), harvested at the peak of their plant power, and distilled in a way that preserves the benefits so the oils work when you use them.

- And if that list fails you, I love this tidbit:
- Young Living is in the top 10 on the Direct Sales charts for all network marketing companies in the entire world. That means the business is successful and thriving (Direct Selling News, 2019).

If you're still meeting resistance, another thing to consider is that some of your friends and family simply may not be on board with a Clean Living lifestyle. They may not see the value of Young Living's products. Young Living President Jared Turner said this on September 18th, 2019:

"When the cost of our essential oils is seen as a challenge by our customers, I like to describe for them the work required to run farms around the world without using herbicides or other toxic chemicals.

It costs us around $12,000 per acre to weed our Mona, Utah Lavender fields by hand, using manual labor. Do you know how much "weeding" costs other companies? $60.00 per acre. Spraying cheap (and toxic) herbicides is faster and much cheaper. Thank you for this information, Jason Barnum, Mona farm manager. #SeedToSeal"

That is what we pour out to make sure every drop you pour from a bottle of oil is pure. That's why Lavender is over 20 dollars a bottle instead of 4 dollars online. I realize that your family may not want to put that much into chemical-free products. No matter how many times you speak with them about dangerous ingredients, they only see the cost. What's the solution? You go out and be your best you, and when they see the health of your family, it will speak for itself. When the window opens and their family is sick and you have a small space to speak without a condemning comment in return, pour out. Until then, sometimes the best words to use with naysayers are no words at all. Let the results of your lifestyle speak for itself.

They only see the cost.

Your family may be stuck in poverty mode and not willing to grasp that if they have a team of five to 10 friends or family under them on Essential Rewards, their products will be free, even if they are not "running" their own business.

You know what? All of that is ok. Sometimes no now is not no forever; and if, Lord forbid, they or someone near them gets a health scare, they may be more willing to open up and have a discussion with you. Sitting with them repeatedly, having the same conversation over and over again is going to tear your mojo down, make you feel like a failure at your business, and possibly lead you to believe that network marketing (used by hundreds of thousands around the world daily) is not a viable way to build your future.

None of that is true.

It's just not viable for those that don't see it. It doesn't make them a bad person, they just live in the land of doubt and fear... and that's ok. Walk away. Kick the dust off your feet and move to the next person. I said this in the full *Gameplan* book: *Be so busy focusing on new people that you don't have time to notice the no's.* That includes your own family.

What if I were to tell you that 98 percent of my business is not built on family members and friends? How big would your customer base be if you considered every person outside your door, not just those in your circle; and if there was no one that was "untouchable?" Stop focusing on the people that have told you no. Wait for the opportunity; but don't wait on your business to share. Move on, for now. Those family members and friends become distractions that will cost you everything, including your mindset, which is the most important thing.

What is it that I want you to consider from this chapter? EVERYONE outside could be on your team. Every single human you see. If you focus on that thought, it's a wide open field. There are no barriers except the ones you place in front of yourself. You must simply learn to talk to people you don't know. That's a skill that can be mastered by memorizing a few mantra's: replace fear with confidence; replace doubt with hope; and get outside your warm market. You have to expand your vision if you want this to work. You have to dream as big as Gary Young.

Their freedom and your freedom are not tied together.

PART TWO

CLEAR THE WAY: DITCHING MENTAL ROADBLOCKS

Sarah, your work has given me a standard, a foundation, a reason, and an excitement to do Young Living!!!!

Julie Ann Berry

Find a plan that works for me, then rinse and repeat. You gave me the courage to break out and do this business my way.

Tonya Dwire Peterson

I thought it was me. I thought that I just wasn't 'good at' talking to people. Sarah's books taught me how to talk to people and my whole life changed: business, marriage, kids. Be quiet and listen to the people.

Theresa Messner Yeager

A high school English teacher with zero business experience, I went from starter kit to Silver with Gameplan! Unstuck is the next level!

LaRona Crane Ezell

Sarah's book changed my whole strategy to business building. She lays everything out in an easy to follow, step-by-step format that will help your business soar. Her books have been an absolute game changer for my business!

Danielle Strunk

CHAPTER 9

You Are Not Forgotten

Have I scared you off? Listen for just a moment, even if you are shy. As I write the words on this page, my eyes are welled up with tears for where you are. I have cried over and over again with each new paragraph in this book. It's because I know the place where your mind is. I have heard your stories! My own mind was there just moments ago! It feels like yesterday that I started my business, and truly didn't believe I had it in me to go all the way. I believed this was something that worked for other people, but not for me. Your stifled hope and deflated dreams are raw for me! It is because we shared the same mindset when I first started.

I spent 36 years in poverty. 12 years in the projects, with cockroaches and tile floors. I was mattresses-on-the-floor, Salvation Army birthdays, food pantry and food stamps *poor*. I was a kid living-in-my-garage-with-sheets-for-doors poor. I was eviction-notices-every-month poor. I was come-home-from-work-with-no-power poor. I understand desperation. I know hunger. I know what it feels like to collapse from physical exhaustion from working too hard, to sleep at a gas station in my car on the drive home from my second job because the last 30 miles were too hard to drive. This book has been the most difficult for me to write, because it is as if you're speaking right to me, crying out. I am still there beside you, unable to fill some of my own classes. I have only been in Young Living a little over five years! I am a baby at network marketing, and a baby to oils. Maybe that is why I can speak to you, because I don't have the head knowledge of a multi-millionaire. I am just a mom with a 3-page script who shared from my couch and saw results, even when I didn't believe where it would go; and my "why" was tiny. The Lord has taken my simplicity and my disbelief and has done amazing things with it; and He can do it for you, too. That soil is still wet on my own feet, and that journey not yet finished.

Now, when I speak on stage or stand in book signing lines, in whatever country my feet are in—Malaysia, Indonesia, Australia, Europe, Mexico, the United States—it all comes back to the same question, again and again: "I can't get this thing off the ground. I am STUCK. I have no momentum. No one will listen. No one will come to class. I NEED this business. Help me make it work!"

I want you to know that I have heard your questions. I have written you back and have addressed you in person, online, and from stages all over the world. If you take away anything, take this: <u>you are not forgotten</u>. When I tell you that you are a Royal Crown Diamond, I don't say it lightly. I say it because I know you can walk the same steps of the Diamonds before you. You CAN get out of where you are. You are a #diamondrising. You have it in you to break free, but you will have to fight! It will not be easy. Nothing that's worth having ever is.

I see your struggle as if it pops right off the page at me. I bore the same hurt and frustration and rejection to build my own Diamondship. You are pleading for help, coaching, a leg up, release. You need the escape from poverty, stress, or exhaustion so bad that you can hear a Diamondship knocking on your door. You can see it and touch it, but can't reach it. You've tried every method, every book, and every training; and yet year after year, you have no results. You are frozen.

Let's dissect exactly why you are frozen. For Chapters 10 through 15, I'm going to shred your excuses and pull you out of the muck in your mind. We're doing to tear apart exactly why people don't respond to you. I will shred the theory that you have reasons why you can't build as effectively as the Diamonds that hold rank right now. I will train you how to genuinely listen to people and hear their needs in a way that leads to growth in a network marketing business. I'll train you how to get the contact information of total strangers in a way that's not even remotely uncomfortable. I'll train you how to fight fear at its root. And then together, hand in hand, we will closely look at each type of class in Young Living that gets results. We'll get there when your head is ready to run. We'll get there when you know in your heart that you can do this business. We'll go there when you're ready for fire all over again, as if your kit is in its box on your front doorstep. We'll go right back to that place and those emotions all over again. And you'll have a hundred new ideas to try to grow your business by the time you read the last page of this book. Because it's time for your OGV to move. And it's time for you to rank. This is your HARVEST YEAR.

Let's go.

There are a lot reasons why people don't respond. It's not always because they are saying no to you.

Thank you, thank you, thank you for Unstuck! I had a table at a health fair today. For introverted me, this is a big deal! I handed out purple bags like candy, with either the 101 or the Toxin free classes on CD, and Fearless and Minis in them. I had real conversations with people. And the results are phenomenal. We had less than 75 people show up, and I have 5 people wanting classes (4 willing to host!) 2 people wanting kits and on of them wants info on doing the business! I can't wait to get my hands on the full Unstuck and the workbook!

Jenny Hafner

CHAPTER 10

WHY DON'T PEOPLE RESPOND TO YOU?

You need a tangible answer because you want to try to fix it one last time before you walk away from network marketing. Every time you hear another success story, you pause and want to wait before quitting, because there is a piece of you that sees yourself free. You know that how you're spending your time now will not lead to freedom. You question your "why" after you hand out oils sample after oils sample, only to see them never engage, purchase from someone else, or worse yet... do *NOTHING*?

There are actually a lot of reasons why people don't respond. It's not always because they are saying no to you. They may be legitimately busy. They may be distracted. They may be overwhelmed. They may be amid a major life event. They may not see the value of oils yet. They may not be emotionally or physically in a place to learn something new, though the desire for clean living is there. There are ten thousand reasons for silence. I wrote in "Gameplan" that in network marketing you have to emotionally detach yourself from the sale of the kit, or this business will eat you alive. You cannot take every "no", "not yet", or silence as a personal affront. Yet, though we know it in our heads, we still live in a place of fear or rejection. This is why we don't confidently ask people about oils. Without confidence, you are dead in the water. People will only follow what they want for themselves. They will not follow fear.

How do I personally get over rejection? It's simple, really. I can answer that question with one word: **volume.** Be so busy teaching classes, reviewing your warm and cold market lists, and handing out purple bags, and doing vendor events, that you truly don't have time to notice the no's. You don't wince at the six people that checked "yes" to come to your event and it was a no-show. Those people aren't even an afterthought to you. Just rinse and repeat with the people you meet and the ones you already know. Stay focused on new faces every single day. You won't have time to tally those that aren't responding. You won't have time to wear the pain of the message that was not responded to or the hurt of a friend that skipped your class with no explanation. **That is the evil one messing with your head**. Don't give him ANY space. Focus on the next person every minute you're running your business. Always look forward, never backward. Backward thinking leads to backward business growth.

I know I called you a Royal Crown Diamond and a piece of you said, "maybe someday, maybe not. Maybe Silver is enough. Executive would pay for my oils and NingXia." Until you get over that mindset, that rank will never be attainable for you. Those thoughts actually make me angry.

Being satisfied with Senior Star means that you're living in your own world, unaware of the needs of others. It means you're happy right now taking care of you. What if *your work* could impact thousands of lives? I have only been in Young Living a little over five years; and our team is well over 10-thousand members. I am your average run-of-the-mill Diamond, a homeschool momma of five in upstate New York with every excuse, every time limitation, and financial limitation in the book. I'm not the youngest Diamond or the oldest Diamond; nor am I the fastest or the smartest. I'm not tech savvy and I had nothing to start with. I had never run a business before and I've never worked in sales. My friends were 750 miles away in Chicago, because I'd moved across the country. I'm just right in the middle somewhere on the list of Diamonds. No bells and whistles on this momma. That tells me that <u>the Lord loves to use little people to do big things</u>. If I'd never said yes to that Premium Starter kit, and if I'd never fought for freedom, I would have never written "Gameplan" or "Fearless". 1.5 million people have read those books in one year; and it all started with a tiny yes on a living room couch. Nothing special, nothing big. Just a yes.

Where is your yes?

Yes means you fight. It means you don't give up. It means you expect no's and keep moving despite them. It means you're in for the mountain climb. It means you know where it goes. It means you commit to speaking life over yourself. It means you put action to dreams. It means you ditch excuses. It means you run the marathon even when it hurts and even when you're tired. It means you keep running when doubt creeps in; and you run even if you have moments, or days, when you don't believe. Yes means you are IN.

For two years, I've shot a 20-minute Facebook Live every Tuesday night at 8:30pm eastern on the Oil Ability with Sarah Facebook page. Anyone can get on from any team. I take all business questions. One night, a woman wrote me on a roundtable and told me that she didn't dare allow herself to dream anymore. She said she'd lived in a land of lost hope and incredible poverty for so long, that she didn't dare allow herself dreams anymore. Do you know what you do from that place? You move. You move even when you don't believe. Anyone can move. It does not take a dream to put one foot in front of the other. Convincing yourself is harder than convincing your spouse, family, and friends. If you're in the place of lost dreams, you can still do this. You get the script and you read it. Those dreams will start to form all around you like snow in a snow globe. You'll start to believe in yourself again, kit after kit. Move even if you don't have it in you to think big. Move until you're standing on a Diamondship. I didn't even see the business until I was almost a Platinum! God can show you big things even in your disbelief. Passion for oils is different than big dreams. You'll find as you rank up that it gets easier and easier to dream bigger and bigger, because God can do ANYTHING. He loves to show His kids His awesomeness. You have so many adventures ahead of you! If you don't see them yet, that's ok. It does not take the biggest dreams to walk. It just takes a sprinkle of possibilities, enough to keep your feet a walkin'.

This is a story about a big God that loves to use YOU. You can either be a worker in the fields, or you can watch from the bulrushes. I want to be USED. You'll only be used if you move and do hard things. I challenge you to put that Royal Crown Diamond goal right in front of your face and prepare for the platform the Lord **will** bring you to pour into thousands of families; because you know who you are: you are a hope-bringer and a world-changer. Stop goal-setting for only Star and Senior Star. The impact is too small. Stand out and look at the stars in the sky on a big clear night, and set your sights on that volume. Pray for Abraham volume. Pray for that influence. You can pray while you are building the size of your dreams! You know the story of Abraham, the man that had no kids? God told him to look up into the sky, and take note of all the stars; for he'd have more kids than the stars in the sky. Pray the Abraham blessing over yourself. That is a blessing of a platform, the blessing of a legacy, and the blessing of influence. Those families untouched, (the widows, the sick, the poor, and the hopeless), those are the people that need you. There are people that only you, no one else, no other Diamond (not your upline, not your friends) can reach. It will take your gifts, your talents, and your creativity to get to their hearts. Do not put yourself down and do not focus on the negatives. Do not make excuses. Just lay out a dream and say YES. Then put action to the vision the Lord has given you over your business.

I have mentioned before that if you have a 3-page script and a starter kit, that's all you need to get to Diamond. You don't need a bid old upline placing people under you. You don't need gifts and recognition. You don't need leaders that live in your town so you can teach together. You don't need lots of knowledge or aromatherapy certifications. You don't need a retail storefront. You don't need bless and whistles and pretty folders packed with photocopied oils science. You don't need Cricut labels for your Thieves glass bottles and Peppermint Vitality brownies in class. All of those things are time-wasters and they delay the start of you moving. They are distractions that will cost you rank up time. If it's just you, your script, and your kit, you have what it takes to fly. Just as important, your team can copy you. Keep it simple and move your feet. Ditch the excuses and leave them at the back door. That's baggage and drama you don't need.

How do I personally get over rejection? It's simple, really: volume.

Your labor of love is about to bless everyone's socks off, especially mine! I've been a baby Star for almost two years. I'm ready to get Unstuck. Help me, Sarah!

Andrea Berry

Sarah Harnisch. honey, your passion has pulled me through some pretty dark times. You looked me in the eye and said, "I believe in you". Somedays, the Moses prayer is all I have to hold on to. I want to be you when I grow up!

Tara Nichols

CHAPTER 11

TONGUE, HEAD, FEET

Is your mind taking you down? Speak life over yourself until you believe where you are going. Are you a realist? Let's take that on too! Just look at the profiles of the Diamonds and let's start kicking some of your self-doubts to the curb. I am going to throw a lot of facts at you in one page. Brace yourself.

You may be saying...

I can't do this because I don't have money.

I can't do this because I have no friend circle.

I can't do this because I live in a small town.

I can't do this because I am too old.

I can't do this because I am too young.

I can't do this because I am not pretty like that Diamond is...

I can't do this because I don't have a business to pull from.

I can't do this because I'm not an aromatherapist.

I can't do this because I don't have time.

I can toss every single one of those sentences out the window in less than 60 seconds. You want a Diamondship, right? Look to the Diamonds for your answers. Look at the profiles of those that have success. Study them and only them, because that is where you are going. Always look where you are going.

There are more than 450 Diamonds in Young Living right now. There are Diamonds that started from extreme poverty and some that started from significant wealth. There are Diamonds that began their organization in large cities, and some that began in towns of 600. There are Diamonds that moved across the country, or across the world, and left everything they knew behind, including all their friends and family. There are Diamonds teaching in the small towns they grew up in. There are Diamonds that are missionaries living in isolated locations. There are Diamonds that were famous before they ever got a Young Living starter kit. There are Diamonds that built entirely on social media like Instagram and Facebook; and there are also Diamonds that built with cassette tapes of 101 classes on horseback (both ways work, by the way, and neither is wrong). There are Diamonds with 15 children, and Diamonds that live alone. There are Diamonds in their 70's and above, and Diamonds that have just broken into their 20's. There are Diamond men that built without a spouse; and there are female Diamonds that built without the support of their husband. There are husband and wife Diamond teams that are also wildly successful; and there are single Diamonds that enjoy the exact same amount of success. There are Diamonds whose spouse is still working because they love their job, and have never been to a Young Living event. There are Diamonds that are quite shy, and Diamonds that love the biggest crowd they can speak in front of. There are introverted and extroverted Diamonds. There are Diamonds from Malaysia, Singapore, Australia, Indonesia, Mexico, and Europe; as well as Diamonds from America. Each one found a way to share in their own place.

There are Diamonds with phD's in various fields who have won the respect of their peers at their prior jobs and had very gifted skills outside oiling. There are Diamonds who have been stay at home moms and dads for years, with no title, and no letters after their last name, just "momma" and "daddy." There are Diamonds that are battling a major health crisis, or have struggled with weight and hormone issues for years; and there are Diamonds that are running gyms. A Diamondship is not based on how you look or what the scale says. The majority of the Diamonds have had no formal aromatherapy training, and have never been to school for network marketing, sales marketing, or business. I can safely say that nearly all the Diamonds didn't have the time to launch their business when they did. Many were "accidental" business builders that got in just to get the product for free. They infectiously shared, and found freedom through it. There were also some who started because of the business opportunity. They were dedicated and focused from the get-go. They planned strategically. Both got a Diamondship. Some had Royal Crown Diamonds that knew their name and cell number by memory. Others never met their Diamond until their first Diamond retreat. Many do not even have an upline Diamond. There are Royal Crown Diamonds with senior star or inactive uplines.

Do you know what that means? None of that stuff has anything to do with what it takes to be a Young Living Diamond. It's true! If you are holding out until you know more people, or your kids get older, or you lose weight, or get more certifications, or more network marketing training; it's costing you rank up time. You don't need any of that stuff. It's not a qualifying factor for what it takes to go Diamond.

I can tell you what is. There are only three things that grow your business: teaching classes in whatever form that looks like for you (I am about to wipe your fears away on the many methods of sharing in the coming pages); getting your team on Essential Rewards; and training your leaders.

I will tell you that **all** the Diamonds did all three of those things to rank: taught classes, got people on ER, and trained their leaders. They did them with tenacity and consistency. The amount of cash in their bank account or how many friends they had did not impact their rank. Their fight sure did, though! Start with very first step: teaching. Then you'll be in a position to learn the other two as the team grows underneath you. Don't worry about not feeling like you are a leader yet. Leadership does not happen by accident. Leaders grow into the role. That growth for you is an ongoing process. There are things to learn from every single rank. I actually prefer not to rank too quickly, because you miss the growth opportunities at that level. As I sit here on the cusp of a Crown Diamondship, I feel like there are thousands of things I still have yet to learn. You'll make a lot of mistakes, but mistakes make the best leaders. The greatest leaders are those that handle mistakes with humility and a teachable spirit.

You may be telling me that you're too soft spoken, not just to lead a team, but to even approach people. Here's the thing: even soft-spoken people have fight in them. They will go to the end of the earth to care for and protect their families. Personality does not matter; so do not use that as a crutch to avoid sharing oils. You just need to share in a way that's comfortable for you. There are 61 Silvers and up on my team right now. 36 of them are soft spoken. There are truly only a handful of leaders on my team that talk as much as I do! That, too, tells me that being outgoing simply isn't a requirement to rank. Fight... that is a requirement. Every person I know has fight deep down inside them. That means you have what it takes to go all the way; but only if you see it and go for it.

You know you need mojo. They did this with tenacity and consistency. We have slayed the concept of mindset and the way you speak about your business, your rank, and where you are going with it. We have conquered beliefs, dreams, and goals. You speak it until your head and feet follow! You know what to do! You know how to listen to your words and speak life ONLY. You are ready for this, but how do you get people to listen to you?? There is no business without an audience. The good news is that drawing people in is easier than you think, because it does not depend on them. It depends on you.

The greatest leaders are those that handle mistakes with humility and a teachable spirit.

Sarah Harnisch. you are being prayed for right now in Australia. This book is going to be a huge blessing for many people.

Andrea Donaldson

I love that you share the process of writing Unstuck online! You have such an authentic heart to ask for prayer and support. I'm praying for your stamina with gratitude of how God uses you to inspire, bless and connect.

Angela Marie Eidenmiller

CHAPTER 12

THE ART OF LISTENING

You get them to listen by listening to them.

What?!??!

I am going to repeat that because it's the key to unlocking classes for you.

You get people to listen to your love of oils by loving on them, by listening to them, and meeting them where they are, without judgement.

You have just reached the inner chambers of network marketing. When people tell you network marketing doesn't work, it's usually because they can't get past this first step: getting their message in front of faces. Here is clear instruction on what to do: <u>stop making every conversation about you</u>. Look for opportunities to serve them. Here is a stat that will blow your mind: One "on-fire" oiler can fill class after class for you. One "on-fire" oiler, that you have poured into, knows 2000 people by the time they are 20, just like you. I told you earlier that the average Silvership has 100 people in it. That means with one "on-fire" oiler, you could build 20 Silverships. It's simple math. Invest in people and they will build your business for you, even if they are not an active business builder. They will build it with their excitement and their experiences and through the conduit of the relationship and the trust you have built with *them*. When you invest in people, you invest in your business.

Every single way of sharing has to have the element of relationship in it somewhere to be successful, whether it be at vendor events, online events, Instagram, in-person classes, textable classes, purple bags, or dozens of other ways. Without the relationship, you might have a lot of kit sales, but they'll all go inactive in a year and drop off your team. There is no longevity without relationship. Those that are successful at this have mastered the art of loving people and meeting them where they are.

But how??? How do you do it with total strangers? Here is the entire secret: if you ask leading questions, stand silent. Usually within two minutes, the person you're speaking with will give you more than enough information about themselves and their families for you to suggest an oil or start building a relationship.

How to Build Relationships 101

What does that conversation look like? Begin by asking leading questions, then stand down. Wait for them to respond. I have found that when I ask about a person's child, their spouse, their activities (maybe we share a love of running, gardening, kids, faith, or sports) what they do for work, their passions, their health (any of those topics), they will run with it. I rarely get an "I'm good" response, and nothing more. Start the conversation, then let them add the flavor to it. Watch and take mental notes on how you can help. If you become a good listener, it makes it easy to meet needs. Meeting needs leads to passionate oilers. Passionate oilers will lead to full classes. It's a process, but it works. It works online; it works in person; it works at vendor events; it works with people you know, and people you do not know. It's the art of the relationship. It even works if you are soft-spoken, because quiet people are often some of the most compassionate people I have met. They long to make a difference in others' lives. Keep that as your focus, not your fear, when you make contact. You are changing lives.

Case in point: I asked an acquaintance at a basketball game how their son was doing after practice. He had been sitting on the bench. She said he'd torn his rotator cuff when he'd fallen a few days earlier. As I stood there, just listening, she shared another half dozen facts about her family and how they were doing in under two minutes. I learned about the stress at her job, how they had been down with the flu, and how she wished she could get a weekly date night in with her spouse. For her son, I responded with, *"I don't know about rotator cuffs, I have never had an injured one before, but maybe you could try this oil tonight and see how he feels."* She left with my oils in her bag. She signed for a kit the next week because of good follow up. The secret to success is to ask leading questions, then stay silent.

Let me repeat the steps again.

1. Ask leading questions about their life.

2. Wait and let them talk. Don't respond with your own stories. Don't steal time on the clock that you need to get to know them.

3. Take note of the things they are saying; and if the chance arises, get oil on their body on the spot, or at least loan an oil, or an oil and a diffuser.

4. If the chance does not arise, then don't shove oils down their throat. Keep building the relationship. You may have three or four conversations before oils ever even enter in. That's completely ok. If you force it, you are a hunter. Do not hunt people. Bless people with knowledge and wisdom. If you are tense, they will be tense.

5. Always smile. I know that seems trivial; and it may seem fake for a while, but you are generating a warmness that will get them to be open and share with you. If you give them a blank stare as they are speaking, you will generally get short curt responses.

6. If there is an opportunity to talk oils, don't try to be the expert. Don't diagnose disease; and don't pretend to know what you're talking about. I actually get better results when I say, "I am not sure about that. I've never had that before; but I LOVE this oil. Would you like to take this home tonight and see how you feel?" If you pretend to be the expert, they will always come to you for questions. Worse yet, you'll scare away all your leaders, because they will think they need to be an expert to build their teams as well. Train people how to research. Do not offer suggestions for them. The reality is that because of biochemistry and what we are exposed to on a day to day basis, your suggestions may not be right for them, even if they have worked with you forever. Their body will tell them what they need. Let them learn it on their own.

The secret to relationships is silence. For most people, a two-minute conversation is long enough to get more than you need to recommend an oil. The trouble is, you don't ask the right questions ("how is the weather?" Does not cut it!) or you do not wait for the answers.

You already have a love and passion for oils. Your mountain is to develop eyes to see the people who have a need for oils around you. Casual conversations are not awkward. They happen in every room, in every building, around the world every day. You just need to direct them in a way that helps people and blesses your business. Master the art of the leading question and being a good listener. They will tell you what they need.

I can give you two great stories of the power of recommendation from last week. I was speaking in Stuart, Florida, and a woman entered the room with a pile of French Fries. Two other women walked in with the same fries from the restaurant a floor below. I looked at them from the stage and started salivating. For 30 seconds, I told the room of people how good French fries sounded. At the book signing line, after I spoke, more than 30 different people told me they were going to get fries.

Story 2: The next day, my events team and I went into Panera to get breakfast before getting on our flight home. I recommended an organic fruit juice that I really like when I am up for a treat. All I said was, "oooh... I really like that drink." When we got to our table, three out of four of them had picked up the drink and added it to their order. They did it from a single sentence recommendation.

Why? There is effective marketing and ineffective marketing. Network marketing is built on relationships. That means your chances of selling a Premium Starter Kit are dramatically higher if you make a personal recommendation, over stapling a poster of your class to a Salvation Army wall, running an ad in a newspaper, or putting your ninetieth Facebook post up. It's better than sending a text, sending an email, or mailing a flyer. Network marketing is built by a friend of a friend of a friend. You share your love, you oil those near you, they develop fire and share. That's how this works... word of mouth advertising. It is the most powerful tool you have.

Let me give you a few more examples about how to start a conversation with a total stranger, because I can still feel your hesitation through the pages of this book. I promise you, once you do this a few times, you'll get the hang of it, and it will be far less scary. Here are a few leading sentences:

- *Your baby is so cute! How old is he?*

- *You look like you have had a rough day! I worked in retail for 11 years. I can't imagine how tired you must be.*

- *That has got to be the funniest t-shirt I have read all day! There must be a story behind it!*

- *I see you at every single basketball game. You are such a good parent!*

- *That is a pretty good cough! Are you ok?*

- *You have your hands full! I raised __ kids. I remember the exhaustion!*

- *Your cart is full of gardening equipment! I LOVE gardening! What are you putting in this year?*

- *I see you in here every single day. How long have you had this job? (at the hardware store, at the Post Office, etc..)*

Step one: Keep an eye on what's going on around you. Their clothing, what's in their arms, their kids, their grocery cart... There are so many things that can start a conversation! I once sold four starter kits from a single bag of popcorn. I am not kidding! I had a large bag of popcorn on my lap (picture Sam's club size), and the woman sitting next to me roared with laughter when she saw it. That one bag struck up a seven-hour conversation on our flight. Then she signed; and she signed her three adult children when she got home. It all started with a single bag of snack food.

Once the conversation is moving, pick from these categories: what they do for work, their spouse or kids, what they do in their down time, where they live and why they live there, how their health is, if they have any pets, or anything unusual. I have been a news anchor for 22 years, so that usually comes up in conversation, because it's an oddity and sparks laughter, unique stories, and good conversation. Quickly though, I get off of me and ask them what they do for work.

The goal is to gather information so you can lean in and bless them. **Step two:** Offer an oil. You do this gently by just making an offer. "I'm not sure about that, but maybe you can try this." "If I give this to you, would you try it?" "I LOVE this product. Take it home and see how you feel." "This has really helped me. Would you like to try it? I have some you can take for free." "I am all about chemical free living. This is what I use when I am at home. Oils have no yuck. I have some here, would you like to see how you respond?" Bam! Now you're off and running. If you don't have the sample with you, get it in the mail the next day, and then check in with them to make sure it arrived. Many a time, I've had no problem collecting mailing addresses just from the promise of a sample. People are more likely to give that out than a phone number or an email address. Listen to their needs and meet them in that place. If you are not sure what they need, gently and honestly say, "I'm not sure about that. Let me look it

up and I'll write you back tonight. I may have something you can try."
Remember, you don't need to know it all!

Step three: Collect their contact information and leave a purple bag
with them, so they always have a class in hand, and a way back to you.
If you do not collect their contact information when you leave, you have
wasted time and money.

How do I collect their contact information? Isn't that... creepy? Not at
all. It's because you have already found a common bond with them. You
have listened, and it's amazing how that one act can impact a life. So
many people just want an ear. They want to know someone is out there.
Build trust; then find a way to maintain the connection.

---

*Stop making every
conversation about you.*

Every time one of my business leaders gives me an excuse, I show them the pictures of how your family started. They are speechless. Remain humble Sarah, but never forget where you came from. Your story is always a reality check for my leaders.

Jenny Stephany Gracia

CHAPTER 13

HOW TO COLLECT CONTACT
INFORMATION

You're ok talking to people. You're even ok handing them an oil sample and a purple bag. When it comes to asking for something back, though... "WOWSA"! That's where it starts to get uncomfortable. That's when you start to feel like you're in sales, right?

Let me take you back to the beginning of this book when I reminded you that you're not in sales. You're in the "changing lives" business. People get involved in oils and never, ever look back. They don't stare down their old cough drop with four dyes in it; and then look at Thieves cough drops and say, "boy, those dyes sure were a better choice." They have the same response to Thieves cleaner or Cool Azul pain cream, or any of the oils. Every oil you are using is replacing a toxic chemical you have kicked to the curb. As you learn how to use the oils by experimenting and looking things up, your entire mindset shifts on how to care for your family. Young Living really is a lifestyle change. You're facing one direction when you start, you begin the simple swap from room to room, and you never look back. I can count on two hands the number of people and the experiences that have completely changed my life: my

Lord and Savior (in a category all His own), my husband, my kids, family, and friends, my radio and homeschooling mentors, some Dave Ramsey financial training, Weston Price and the GAPS diet, and Young Living. I never looked back after my starter kit arrived on my doorstep. We care for our family in a completely different way. I am facing 180 degrees in the other direction with the personal care products in my home, how I clean, the supplements that we use, and the oils we have incorporated. It's a whole new life. If you want to take a peek at what the inside of my cabinets look like right now, check out the "Scavenger Hunt" video on my website for free, at oilabilityteam.com, "share", and "free stuff". I live what I love. The people you come into contact with will as well. This isn't a "sale" to them; it's hope.

When you look at the fact that this is a game changer for those that you talk to, it strips fear out of the conversation. You're simply making sure you can connect with them so they get the resources they need to grow. Carry in your mind the image of them returning to products that poison their homes and their kids, and the urgency to share becomes much more prominent. Every day they wipe their counters down with products that say "poison" or "do not consume" on them; or they take supplements made of fillers and chemicals, or use creams and other products laden with toxins. It's another day their liver grows more and more tired, and their immune system more and more weary. You can train them how to make a shift in how they view every product in their home; but not if you don't collect their contact information.

I mentioned above that if it's someone I have never met, I am much less likely to ask for a phone number (or share mine). However, I am comfortable "friending" them on Facebook so I can touch base from a distance. Another tip is to immediately text yourself their Facebook name or screenshot their page. You may not remember it in the sea of the names of your friends just by adding them.

Here are a few leading sentences you can use to get to the part of the conversation where you add them as friends online:

☐ *I want to make sure you are ok. Is it ok if I add you on Facebook?*

☐ *I was so inspired by your story of how you overcame ____. I can't imagine having gone through that. I don't want to lose touch. Would it be ok to add you on Facebook?*

☐ *I want to check in with you and see how you liked the oil I loaned you. Would it be ok if I add you on Facebook?*

☐ *I have a book called "Fearless" that I'd love to mail you. I think this is the answer you have been looking for, based on what we just talked about. It's a little tiny book that has had such an impact on me. It's given me so much hope. Would it be ok if I add you on Facebook?*

☐ *I really admire how long you have held on with such a high stress job! I hope you enjoy the Gameplan mini. That's completely changed how I view work. Would it be ok if I add you on Facebook? I have another resource called Gameplan that I really think you'd like.*

☐ *I have a sample of Stress Away (or Thieves, etc...) that I'd love to send you when I get home. Would it be ok if I add you on Facebook?*

You get the idea. If you have taken the time to listen, the majority of the people I speak with are completely ok with me adding them. There's a safety level on social media by being able to unfriend people that usually makes them comfortable. When you get home, send them a short message. Something like this:

"It was great meeting you today! (recap your conversation in a line or two). Oils have completely changed my life. I'd love to send you a couple more things in the mail. Would that be ok? Shoot me your address and I will hook you up. I think this is what you have been looking for."

If the conversation has not built a strong enough relationship yet, keep working on the relationship before offering oil. Each relationship is laying a seed that will grow your team into a big old oak tree. It takes time, effort, patience, tenacity and consistency to pull it off.

Many have asked me how to apply this same technique at the end of a 101 class, because they are not confident in their close. I have written two different closing scripts that can be tacked onto the end of any class you teach in the Appendix of the *Gameplan* book. I don't want to rehash old topics, but let me give you a couple of lines that really may help you if you're trying to end your class with confidence. Tweak it to fit your needs.

"The Young Living Premium Starter kit is the best deal on the website. I am a frugal momma, and I love discounts. This kit is worth over $400, and it's offered for $165 on the website. When you start with the kit, you also get 24 percent off your oils for life. This is where I started my Young Living journey; and it's where I recommend you begin yours. This comes with 12 bottles of oil and a diffuser, so you have a whole playground to learn to oil. I have freebies and gifts; but only for those that get their kit today. There is a laptop in the back of the room, and I'd love to help you navigate the website. Thank you so much for your time! You have survived Essential Oils 101!"

One of my tips is always to make sure you pass around a clipboard and collect all their contact information at a live 101 class. Contact them one by one if you did it online, and use the technique above. Contact any person that liked or commented on a post. Tell them that they have given their time to come to this class, and you want to make sure that they have the tools they need after it's over to continue to grow.

Here's a script to use when you are contacting someone cold from an online class that liked or commented on a post:

Thank you so much for attending the class today! Are you already oiling? Do you have a kit with Young Living? Tell me what your favorite part of the class was, and what you'd like to learn more about. What did you want to learn? What are areas of concern for you in your family? I am so glad that you were there! This has changed the way that I take care of my family. If you're not already oiling, I'd love to come alongside you and hand-train you myself.

Then you begin to build the relationship with them, even if you have never known them before. Follow up is critical in an online format. It will save you.

If you are not collecting contact information the first time you meet someone, either in a grocery store aisle, in a live class, or online, you are handing your paycheck to someone else. *You have sowed seeds that someone else is going to harvest.* My leaders will come to me, frustrated, that one of their inactives signed on another team. My response is always, "do better follow up." If they harvested the seed you planted, that falls on you, not on them. If you are not collecting information to touch base, you have invested time that you cannot get back. Tackling fear is the number one way to avoid this. You are afraid of coming off poorly to the person you are speaking to, or getting a negative response. Just use the scripts. They work!

One sentence gets me almost everyone's contact information: "I think this is the answer you have been looking for."

This is my first time posting on your page. I am one of the quiet sponges of your information. But after all the encouragement you have given me this past year, I could not pass up the opportunity to give some back to you. With great appreciation for all that you do Sarah, thank you for all that you have blessed me and my team with. I bet Gary is smiling upon you.

Alice Grob

CHAPTER 14

You Are Telling Me to Do Things I Have Already Tried

"Sarah, I have tried everything you're telling me to do; and it just doesn't work. I've tried it all. I am truly starting to think network marketing is a farce."

Here's the deal: If it were truly a farce, Young Living would not be doing over two-billion dollars in sales annually. I am going to throw some more facts at you. Let's look at Young Living as a company for just a moment to see if the quote above has true ground. The average network marketing company fails within seven years. As of 2019, Young Living has surpassed year 25 and is growing by leaps and bounds. There are 50 highly-trained scientists in their labs. There are 20 corporate farms and partner farms. There are 3000 global employees. There are 6-million global members. There are 20 international markets and 13 worldwide offices. That's what it takes to keep up with the orders that are coming in; because the oils work, and they are easy to share. It's not a fad. Oils have been around since the book of Genesis.

Young Living is easy to share because you have 100 percent market share. Everyone needs oils. It's not the same as sharing books, pans, or clothes. Men and women need oils. The mature and the young need oils. The wealthy and the poor need oils. Anyone who wants toxins out of their home needs oils. Anyone who uses personal care products, makeup, or supplements need oils. People with kids, and people without kids need oils. Every human you make contact with is a potential oiler. Animals are potential oilers. People that detail cars for a living can be oilers. Your mailman, your pastor, your doctor, and your kid's teacher can be an oiler, if only you will share with them. If you step outside your front door or get on the internet, you have the whole world at your fingertips. In every store, at every ballgame, at every volunteering opportunity, at church, at work, at school, at your kid's schools, at the gym, in the park, in every building, and on every street; every face is another opportunity. Your task is simply to see their need, and to have the courage to meet it.

I truly believe your greatest struggle is not that Young Living or network marketing is a farce. Your greatest struggle is in your head. If you can put passion and fire back into your business, you will be unstoppable. Practice some of the tactics I have shown you on mindset and speech. Practice some of the scripts above with people that you know, and people that you don't know. See where it leads. Randomly talk to the next store clerk, person in line, or person who sends you a Facebook instant message. Test the scripts.

If the only people you have spoken with are your closest friends and family, it is time to branch out. It's hardest to preach in Nazareth, but we stay there because it feels safe. Sometimes those closest to you are the last to join Young Living. My father, sister, and son are not even members. Several of my best friends have gone inactive, despite repeated attempts to train them to oil. My other sister is Gold; my mom is nearly Platinum; and my brother is Executive even though all six members of my immediate family, equally, have seen our success up close in Young Living. Don't use your family as your gauge as to whether or not you can run this business.

You DO have it in you, just as those before you. If you feel you have tried every nugget of wisdom for holding classes, and deliberately have focused on every type of market; and you are still getting zero results, then it's time to pause on classes and focus instead on personal development training to become a leader that will attract people to you.

What the heck does that mean, Sarah?

It means the way people perceive you is not good. You are scaring them away before you have a chance to connect. It may be your tongue: negativity, sarcasm, despair. It may be your demeanor. You may come across as indifferent. You may have no fire. You may be putting your potential distributors to sleep when you talk with a lack of passion. It may be weariness. No one wants weariness in their life. So when they see it on you, they'll go with another oiler that seems to have what they want. It may be drama. You may be sharing oils confidently, but posting political or controversial posts on your social media pages. It may be a total lack of confidence. "You may not like these... I don't think you'll buy anything, but here's something for free just in case... If you can't make it to this class, I have three next week..." Keep this in mind: people won't follow indecision or weakness. You get around that by using scripts and training your brain for confidence.

If you are in that place where leading questions and building relationships with people isn't working (i.e., you have handed out 170 samples and have had no starter kit sales), we have to train your brain in the right language and facial expressions so that you magnetically draw people to you. For that, I rely on the network marketing gurus.

Even as a Diamond, I commit time each week to training my brain and filling it with things that are good. You will only be as good as what you surround yourself with. That includes friends, how you spend your time, and what you choose to fill your head with. Are you spending too much time on mindless television shows or on social media? Are you training your brain with good business knowledge? When you pour truth on yourself, you live in truth. When you listen to lies and disbelief and focus on all that's wrong, you will start to spew that. Live in a place of truth. You CAN do this.

Some of my favorite trainers are Jim Rohn, Brendon Berchard, Dale Carnegie, Eric Worre, John Maxwell, Tony Robbins, Hal Alrod, Stephen Covey, Richard Bliss Brooke, Robert Kiyosaki, and **ANY** Young Living Diamond. I mean that! As a Diamond myself, I am constantly gleaning wisdom from the other Diamonds. One of the first questions I ask a Diamond I have never met is how they got success. You want to follow someone that has results. Look into the training you are using and check out its source. If they are not running a successful multi-million-dollar international network marketing business, you should not be listening to their training, because they don't have the experience to back it up. My husband and I built an international multi-million-dollar Young Living business in just over two years, from ground zero, with virtually no resources and no business background. We built it while we were in the pit of poverty. The *Gameplan* series, this book, *Fearless*, and anything we produce has results. It's based on our mistakes and our successes; and it is tailored specifically to a Young Living audience. If you follow it closely, it is designed to shave months, and in some cases years, off the time it takes you to rank.

In the same breath, I am just as likely to advocate for other Diamond's training, and I use it myself to grow. Why? Because I want to see you rank. My goal is not book sales. It's your freedom. Some of the other Diamonds that have phenomenal training are Jodie Meschuk and Sarah Lee's 3 Pillar Coaching (speakupbuttercup.com), Jim Bob Haggerton's Essential Oils Club (EOC) Facebook page, Oily App, and the books JB has written with Andy Jenkins (doctorjimbob.com), Doctor Oli Wenker's work is incredible (doctoroli.com) as well as his must-not-miss yearly Essential Oils Symposium with dozens of speakers, Melissa Poepping's Basi6 program is wonderful (mellissapoepping.com), as is Eric Walton's Downline Leadership program (downlineleadership.com). Vicki Opfer's "Essential Sharing" and Debra Raybern's "Road to Royal" are Young Living pillars, check out Amanda Uribe's "Grow" series (growinghealthyhomes.com), and Jordan Schrandt's yearly Diamondbound event is electric (diamondboundevent.com). These are treasured friends who have developed resources that work. The list is far from a compilation. Visit sites like growinghealthyhomes.com and discoverlsp.com to see more Diamond resources.

If you resonate with *Gameplan*, use it. If you resonate with other training systems, use them. Whatever gets results, use it, and rinse and repeat until you are on the Diamond stage and have generational income for your family. We have a saying with *Gameplan* that has become dangerously famous. **I want to raise so many Diamonds that Gary Young needs a new stage at convention!!** He won't be able to fit them all on one stage! After bootcamp, people started hashtagging their social media posts with #breakthestage. That got back to corporate; and at one of my #ylunites rallies, a corporate representative said, "Sarah, I've gotten word that you want to damage or destroy property at convention this year?" I was thinking that I was about to get fired. They went on, "We have a screenshot of you telling people to 'break the stage'?" I was like... "Ruh Row". This is not going well! Then they told me, "we have a message for you. Gary says BRING IT. He has reinforced the stage." Young Living is ready for you! Get out there and SHARE.

Whatever you do, do your work heartily, as unto the Lord. Pick your system and your method, and sprout with it. Don't jump to ten other things, or ten other leadership training programs. Keep doing the same thing that got you results. That's your place of growth. That's your way of sharing. If your head isn't in a place where people listen to you, train your brain in the right language until you're getting a response.

Even though I am known for leadership training, I will also tell you that no network marketer is successful without action. You need to gauge the point you're at in your business. If you're in despair and have not had results in a long time, focus only on training your brain until you notice a change in your speech, perspectives, and vision. If leadership training is slowing you down, **teach classes**. A growing leader will be doing both in a good balance. There is a Facebook page called "12 Days of Diamonds", where over 100 Young Living Diamonds shared their business advice. It's a fantastic page that I fully support, especially if you need to get your head in a positive place and want to follow results. But if you watch fifteen videos and never teach a class, the page becomes a distraction for you.

My favorite post on that page was from Royal Crown Diamond Adam Green, who titled his video, "Is 12 Days of Diamonds Hurting Your Business?". It was brilliant! Sometimes we get so captivated by training and systems that we never move. In the newsroom, we call it paralysis by analysis. If you take training and apply it, and get results, then go train. If you use training as a crutch to avoid holding classes, stop training and start teaching. Though we have different methods on getting from point A to point B, (and none are wrong), all the Diamonds will agree on one thing: you need no degree or certification to take a 3-page script and read it to a few people on your couch. You need no degree or certification to share oils in the way that you were uniquely gifted to share... (whatever that may look like). Follow great leaders for passion, mindset, language, and vision, not for a certification or "enough training" to do a Young Living business.

Don't jump to ten other things. Keep doing the things that got you results in the first place.

Sarah. I got three Contact Me cards filled out today! I LOVE having those little babies - they are so handy!!!

Robyn Sanford

CHAPTER 15

FEAR

Your biggest problem if you are stuck is not a lack of knowledge about oils, or a lack of network marketing training. It's fear. Once you find a way to break through fear, you will build a legacy income that will last for generations for your family. As stated earlier in this book, Young Living is like baking a cake one time, and your great-great-great grandkids benefit from the sale of that one cake. That's how network marketing works.

If you put all your time into training, and none of your time into implementing classes, you will not see growth in Young Living, <u>or in any other network marketing business</u>. Jumping to the next network marketing company will not solve the problem, because you are still carrying the fear with you that you had when you tackled Young Living. It's not an issue with your upline, saturation, friend circles, time, training, or any other reason; because you, and you alone, dictate the growth of your business. If I could give you one tip that I KNOW will help you rank this month, it would be to fill your calendar with classes. If that is the only thing you get from this book, my time will have been well spent. It doesn't matter what type of class; and it doesn't matter what you call it, or how you deliver it. **Get oils in people's heads and on people's bodies. That is**

how you grow this business. If a week goes by and no one outside your home has been oiled; or you've not had a single conversation online or in person, I can usually directly link that to no-show classes. You are not building the relationships necessary to draw people to class.

Back to fear. What's my message for you?

Do things that scare you. Do them deliberately because you know that's what you need to do to get over your fear of sharing. That's the one skill you need to master to build an empire that will bless your family, and change thousands of people's lives. If your fear is speaking, speak. If your fear is closing, close. If your fear is rejection, get rejected a hundred times until it does not hurt anymore. You have it in you to build this business. You have done harder things than grow a Young Living business! Most of you have birthed a baby! That's a watermelon coming out of something the size of a lemon! That's MUCH harder than building this business. Stop saying this is hard, because that falls into the category of excuses. It's not too hard for you. You are just paralyzed by doubt and fear.

Can I tell you a story?

I was afraid to start, too. I was the accidental business builder. My husband saw this business a good six months before I ever even considered that there was a business. I had significant Young Living paychecks in my hand and STILL didn't see it. I just wanted to get my oils for free.

When I first started, I knew that if I sold three kits, I would make back what I spent to buy my starter kit. I wanted to get on Essential Rewards so I could get rid of all the yuck in my cabinets. We only had 20 dollars a week to live on after we paid our mortgage, student loans, vehicle payments, and utilities. I didn't make enough to cover my oils order and build our savings account at the same time.

My husband said if I taught a class and had a few people sign up under me, my oils would be free. I followed his advice. I went to Amazon, I bought a bunch of aromatherapy encyclopedias, and read them cover to cover. I wrote a compliant script based on what I would want to know about oils: Were they safe? Does purity matter? Can I just go to the grocery store and buy oils? Where did they come from? Why does all the stuff online contradict itself? Are oils a fad? Can I use them on my kids? How do they work? It's the Who, What, When, Where, Why, how of essential oils. It's in the back of this book, along with three new scripts. I read the 101 script to a bunch of women on my couch. Six of them got kits. MY starter kit was paid for.

I read that script once a week and hit Silver twelve weeks after getting my kit. I read it some more and hit Gold five months after that. It was about that time that John approached me and asked, "What are you doing, *selling the fountain of youth??*" I said, "no, I only taught so I could get my oils for free." He said, "You know that your check has surpassed your full-time job? The job you have had for 18 years? The job that you wake up at 4 a.m. for, every single morning, 52 weeks a year? The job that you come home tired from every day, and then try to homeschool our five kids, when you have nothing left?"

Now I was at a fork in the road.

You see, I never wanted to leave my job. I had a pretty cool job. I got to be on a morning show with a radio network that reached five million people. I was not wealthy, but I was famous. I had prayed for that job for 11 years. It was a job I moved my family across the country to take. I left everything I knew for that job. Now, I was at a standstill. The Lord had opened every door for oils, and I was standing there staring the choice down.

I told myself radio was all I knew how to do; and that I wasn't good at "selling oils." I told myself that I'd lose my identity. I told myself a lot of things; but the reality was that I was afraid. I have written over 140,000 newscasts in my career, on 39 different radio stations in Chicago and New York. I have interviewed Presidents, Senators, missionaries, and actors. I can write news in my sleep. I was comfortable. I didn't want to stretch outside my comfort zone. Oils were scary to me. I had to talk to people I didn't know. When I went to anchor news, I talked to a wall all day long, alone in my studio. I did not have to look at the five million people listening. It was just a microphone and me. It was a dance with the craft of researching, writing, and performing. Every 25 minutes, I started the dance all over again with the next newscast. Rinse and repeat.

I am actually quite afraid to speak to people in person, and definitely terrified to stand on a stage. I get sick every single time I speak. It seems quite funny, because I have been in 31 cities the last six months, speaking in front of thousands of people all over the world. God has a sense of humor when He's trying to stretch you! Before each speech, I still get sick. I think it's the Lord's way of keeping me humble. I have taught well over 800 101 classes. I taught one this week and still got butterflies. Being afraid means you're doing it right.

Do you know how I made the decision to leap from anchoring news to sharing Young Living? It all happened because of a bold intern. I was in the newsroom one morning. It had been months since my conversation with John. In fact, I was nearly to Platinum by then; and still not even considering Young Living as a business. It still scared me. My intern was shadowing me that day. It was a morning that I had very bad writer's block. Every time I tried to put something to paper, I wrestled with the language, and every word was deleted. Finally, it was a couple of minutes before 7 a.m. when I was to go live. My intern was breaking out in a cold sweat as she looked at the white sheet of paper in front of me. I look up at the t.v. monitor with a news station on it, got some inspiration, and started writing. Two minutes later, I had ten stories written with seven fresh soundbites; and the stinger went off as I typed the last word. I read that newscast top down, for the first time, cold, with no mistakes. I turned the mic off and got a smug look on my face.

When I looked at her, she had a completely different expression. She said, "You're not where you are supposed to be." I said, "What do you mean?". She replied, "I just watched you put a newscast together in two minutes; and it would have taken me at least three hours. You're not being stretched. You're not where you are supposed to be."

I could not get her words out of my head. For two weeks, I tossed and turned. It was like a knife in my back. I was mad at God. I was mad at Him for moving my family across the country when He had plans to take radio away. I was terrified at trusting Young Living for my sole income source. I was still nervous that network marketing didn't work. All the fears you have about the business, I had when I was nearly a Platinum! I was listening to all that play out in my head, even though the Lord had already amply supplied a replacement income.

Do you know what happened once I trusted the Lord? I walked in and quit my full-time job. I still anchor once a month, or so; because it's in my blood. Now I do it for fun, not because I have to. I do it out of sheer love for news and for the news team. Eight weeks after I walked away from an anchoring position that some work a lifetime for, I made Platinum. A little over a year later, John and I went Diamond. The *Gameplan* series has sold 1.5 million copies. That's 1.5 million families given the hope of the business with the strategy on how to pull it off. None of that would have happened had I stayed full time anchoring news. None of that story would have taken place if I lived in fear. It's not a story of my personal success. It's a story of submission and obedience to a great big God who loves me more than I can put on paper. He loves you, too!

Sometimes our fear gets in the way of the plans the Lord has for us. His plans are SO much better. Picture your biggest dream. I guarantee you God can outdream it! He is the one that, with a breath, created life and the stars in the sky! He can carry your Young Living business. He can give you the strength to keep pursuing it. He is already moving chess pieces on the board in your favor as you sit here right now, pondering whether you even want to do this.

Maybe you are afraid of a loss of identity. The truth is, your identity is in Him, not in anything that you amass; and not in anything that you're good at. It's not even in something you may have spent the last 18 years of your life doing. Your identity is not in how others see you, how they describe you, or how you describe yourself. If you keep Christ as your focal point, it really doesn't matter how you generate income or spend your time. There is no loss of identity; and there is no fear when you're walking through an open door that the Lord has put right in front of you. It's a door that leads to freedom.

So what's my advice?

Jump.

Walk away from your comfort zone. Step into something that scares you just a bit. If you're not scared, you're too comfortable. Step out of habits and routine. Every day that you are frustrated, He is still faithful.

When I was at that fork in the road, I dared the Lord to take me to a place with oils where I could still use my writing and speaking. I'll tell you, I stand corrected on that one! I had no idea when I penned *Gameplan* that the Lord would do what He did with it. Even now, after an entire year of awe, the Lord keeps telling me that I have seen nothing yet; and that the best is yet to come.

You just have to trust... and jump. His plans are always better than your plans.

How do I get over fear? I live every day knowing that that my future isn't contingent on me. It's ordained by a God that loves me more than anyone else I know. It's easy to move when you know the future will be brighter and better than where you are now, if you stop holding so tightly to who you are comfortable with. The leap is worth it.

What does my life look like now? I am no longer up at 4 a.m. 52 weeks a year. I get to travel with my teenagers and see them build relationships with people who have the right mindset, speech, and focus. I have time for personal development, self-care, and time with friends in countries all over the world. The stress of finances is off my plate. My husband and I are closer than we have ever been. I get to spend the rest of my life watching miracles every single day, especially the miracle of my leaders, and you, ranking up. I get to hear your stories of freedom. It's the best job in the world. I am so glad I took that leap.

I would have missed it all had I stayed in fear. I would have missed it all if I thought my only identity was as a news anchor. I would have lost everything, had I not let go of my ego. I would have never met my leaders, or you, if I let my mind and my insecurities dictate my business.

What's my advice? Just walk. God will handle the rest. Don't overthink it. Just share. God brought this business to you; and He's not about to leave you now. Do the things that scare you. That's the exact place God has for you to grow, so He can bring you to the next place in your business. You are out there gathering testimonies and stories that you will need for later. You are gathering experiences that you need to lead, and that your leaders need to rank. Tribulation is good. Every experience has a purpose. It is the cornerstone and rock that you need to do this well. Don't live in fear! Step out of that place and let God grow you. He'll only do it if you let go of what is so tightly in your hands right now. What He has is so much better! I promise.

What Happens Now?

I have done all the mindset training I can. I have pointed you in solid directions for more training if you're in a state of desperation, or are close to giving up. The rest of this book will be dedicated to tools. Now it's time to train you inside out, and upside down, on every form of sharing oils that I've seen since I started Young Living. I am sure the list is not comprehensive; but you will have many options and many new ideas. I asked the *Gameplan* fans how they shared; and they gave me 81 pages of ideas on Facebook. All of that is consolidated in the following chapters of this book. If one way of sharing does not produce results for you, try another; but never give up. The only ones that don't make it to Diamond are the ones that walk away.

I will give you checklists on how to be prepared for each main type of class, and what the biggest mistakes are in each environment. There is an Unstuck workbook to customize this training and help to keep you on track. The workbook tailors all this training directly to you and your team. I will end *Unstuck* with four Young Living Starter Kit scripts, including two that have never been published; so you can tailor your training to the core of Young Living, the products that speak to who we are. You'll hear me speak of these classes as the Core 4, because I believe heartily that if every member on your team was trained in the Core 4, your Essential Rewards totals would go up exponentially. Most people on your team have likely had a single oils class. The bulk of them don't return for a second class statistically. What if they learned oils, Thieves, NingXia and Savvy in their first few months of oiling? They'd have endless ideas for restocking their kit and learning about the power of the oils, for cleaning, for whole food supplementation (I am convinced that you can get to Diamond on NingXia classes alone), and for makeup. Those are the four starter kits that Young Living offers for a reason: they encompass what we're all about: lifestyle. A tease of nearly all we do is tucked away in those four kits. They are also the only kits that lead to a Wholesale membership. That's where you need to start everyone. No retail. Not one oil. Not a basic membership for $40. Start them with one of the Core 4 to train the lifestyle. That's how you find active, lifelong oilers.

I will give you every single tool I can think of to help you succeed in this. The first step is up to you. You have to want it. You have to be willing to fight for it, and not rely on others to do the work for you. Get out of the mindset of "winning the lottery" with a rockstar distributor that carries all the volume of your business. You need "rockstars" (or many steady committed builders) on six different legs to hit Royal Crown Diamond. That means you need to work. You have to work when you are tired. You have to catch the vision to see where this goes, and hold tightly to that vision, or you'll forget why you are doing this. If you forget why, you don't fight. That vision will change several times over the course of your business; so constantly revisit it. You have to set your goals high and not give up when plans don't pan out. You have to take the word "no" or "not yet" on the chin, and keep moving.

You also have to have some strategy to know your game and where you are placing people. You have to be willing to go places where you are scared. You have to be willing to grow. You have to speak life over yourself, even in your greatest moments of frustration. Then, my friend, you are ready to lead a team. You are ready for this business. The practice comes in the classes.

You are not building the relationships necessary that draw people to classes.

PART THREE

FUELING CONNECTION

You inspire me as a single Mom of two boys working full time and stuck in this business! I love. love, love the oils and products.

Karen Francis

CHAPTER 16

THE KEY TO GROWTH

It's time to jump right into the meat of the book, which is about how you actually get people to listen to you. You see though, I have tricked you; because that training actually came at the beginning of the book. You get people to listen to you by listening to them. That's the secret to the whole thing. You build strong relationships by overcoming fear. If you don't like where you are right now, either for emotional reasons like stress, physical reasons like finances, or simply for the relationships you will build along the way, CHANGE IT. You have to want freedom more than the fears that hold you back.

What you actually need to know is which type of teaching will reach your soon-to-be-oiler so you can get them on your team. For that, we need to look at different ways to share. Your personality, gifts, fire, talent, interests, and desires weigh far more in how to teach than anything else.

This little book, the *Gameplan* series, anything I write, or any training anywhere... none of it will get you to Diamond. They are just books. The true talent is YOU. The trick is finding the way of sharing that best resonates with your gifts. That's what the second half of this book is wholly dedicated to.

Stop believing that you can't approach people. That's another lie that the evil one has planted in your head. Your upline, the Diamonds, all the people that you put on a pedestal... none of them can reach that person that is right in front of you, because the Lord already picked them for your team. It's a done deal. All you have to do is walk the steps and share your passion.

Stop putting yourself down! Stop spewing a list of reasons why you're not as good as those around you or above you. It just means they are a few steps ahead of you in network marketing. It absolutely does not mean they are better than you in any way. You are a fresh slate, with no prejudices, no bad habits, no poor strategy, and no messy mistakes. If you have a small team or no team, and a list of a hundred no-show classes, you are in the perfect place to explode. You just need to see what you are capable of. 99 percent of the reason you're not filling classes is because you don't believe you can. The minute you start to know it, to truly deeply know that you are a Royal Crown Diamond inside, that's the moment people start to listen to what you have to say. It's because you are confident. Anyone will follow confidence.

I have five kids with five completely different personalities. The littlest guy, Mr. Noah Justin, talks more than the other four put together.

What always gets everyone's attention about Noah is that he's confident. He may have absolutely no idea what he's talking about; but he will convince you that he does. This little guy could likely get you to try almost anything. It's because he's not afraid. He is so certain that "his way" is the right way, that he will talk you into some of the craziest things. For instance, I am up all night working on this book tonight; and everyone is tucked into bed. They have been asleep for hours. Everyone except Noah, that is. The little bugger convinced me that if he did a load of dishes, and brought me unlimited water and NingXia, he could read a book he wanted to read. With a spotless kitchen at 5 a.m., my 12 year old is deep into his book; and I am deep into mine with a full glass of NingXia beside me. That's the power of confidence. He met my need, and got his wish... or maybe I'm just a sucker for a really cute 12-year-old face. I challenge you to have Noah's confidence.

You know oils are the better choice. You know it deep in your gut. If you don't, and you're just starting, there are four audio classes you can listen to for free on my website to get some oils education. Go to <u>oilabilityteam. com</u>, click on "share" and "101 audio", "Toxin Free Life audio", "NingXia audio", or "Savvy Minerals Makeup audio" textable classes. Yes, the Core 4 are now available for free as textable resources for your growing team. Copy the link and send it off– and inspire the next generation of leaders and product users in your

organization. It costs nothing. They will rock your world! The task now is to get you to communicate with confidence. The easiest way to do that is to pick a way of sharing that makes you confident.

The good news is that there are many, many ways of sharing oils. If it works for you, no way is the wrong way. If you get starter kits out of it, it's a viable method. However, let me give you five quick tips that apply to nearly all classes before I dig in.

No book will get you to Diamond. They are just books. The true talent is YOU.

Sarah taught me that I am worth Diamond!
Gina Foerster

Your book taught me not to procrastinate or nothing happens. You have to have dates on the calendar and start the month before filling it up! Once I put dates on the calendar I went to Silver in 5. It works.
Leigh Perkins

CHAPTER 17

How to Get People to Respond 101

Tip 1: I want you to ask yourself what would get *your* attention. What was it that got you to get *your* kit? Who got you to class; and how did they do it? Begin in that place as you reach others, because it may be the key to you finding your way of sharing. Speak from your place of passion. If it's Savvy makeup, start there. If it's the oils, start with the Premium Starter kit. If it's Thieves, begin there. No way is wrong.

Tip 2: Remember where you were when you first got your kit? You knew NOTHING. You were overwhelmed when that Starter Kit showed up on your doorstep. Start from that place when you speak. What would overwhelm you? What would encourage you? Take baby steps; and don't give too much information as people are starting. It's one of the reasons that I discourage against making folders loaded with information for classes. These people don't even have their kit yet! Give them a break from aromatherapy training. Just meet their needs.

Tip 3: Go where the people are. I mean that. If you have friends three hours away, put your Young Living paycheck in your gas tank for six months and forget it exists. Don't spend more than you are making. Be a good steward of the new income the Lord is building; but go where you know people as your income grows. I forgot I even had a paycheck when I first started; and I invested every drop of it into going where I had friends. It made all the difference in the speed of my growth; and it will for you too, if you are teaching in-person classes.

Tip 4: Go where you know people with large friend circles. Write down your friends that have a large sphere of influence and start building relationships with them first. An on-fire friend that knows a lot of people is a huge asset to a new Young Living business builder. If you don't know any friends with large circles, or you're living in a new area far from all your friends, don't sweat it. There are still many different ways for you to build successfully.

Tip 5: Don't undermine your chances of finding leaders, even from the very first class you hold, by doing things that can't be copied. You scare away your leaders when you put a lot of time and money into making pretty Thieves bottles with Cricut labels, having huge posterboard signs filled with science, knowledge, and studies, doing make and take classes that require lots of prep with jars, labels, and supplies, handing out folders loaded with information that took you a lot of time to photocopy, or showing off all your aromatherapy knowledge, making yourself the expert from day one. Your long-term goal is a Diamondship, and that takes leaders. Do not scare them away with your actions. They should look at you and say, "I want that". They should NOT look at you and say, "that's too much work", or "I can never be that." For my 101's, even the one I taught this week, I don't even have a powerpoint. I literally walk into the room with my 3-page script (that same one I have used since my first class in July of 2014), and my Premium Starter Kit. That's it! There are no bells and whistles. Just me. My classes would probably seem pretty anti-climactic if you attended! I promise, though, they'd be full of passion! I am just a homeschool mom of five from upstate New York that hates toxic chemicals on my kids. That's my story. And THAT is duplicatable.

I want you to ask yourself what would get your attention. What was it that got you to get your kit?? Begin in that place to reach others.

I'm having a rough night, and I'm sitting here crying. You're so dang inspiring! I'm watching you never give up on Unstuck. Thanks for keeping on. You got this.

Kelsey Parton Ronan

CHAPTER 18

PERFECT PERSISTENCE: 7 TO 15 CONVERSATIONS

How do you bridge the gap between the beginning of this book and the point we're at now? How do you go from listening to someone, offering an oil and a purple bag, to physically getting them to come to your class? Isn't that a massive jump? No. It's not as big as you may think. You have already stepped into their personal realm by oiling them, putting a sample of a product in their hand, or loaning out your diffuser. You listened; and that's more than most of the people around them do. You offered hope and a solution. The next step is actually much easier. The hardest part is opening the dialogue; and you have already done that.

Usually, if you're offering something they need, and have loaned out an oil, or given a sample, there is an interest. You are filling a need they have. My next statement usually is, "It worked for you! That is AWESOME! Would you like to learn more? I have a FREE 101 class coming up in a week and a half that I'd love for you to attend. This is the class I start all new oilers in, and requires no background knowledge. My passion is education! I'll train you how to use this stuff." You can use my favorite sentence, which you know so very well now: "I think this is the answer you've been looking for." "You just had rotator cuff surgery? Pan Away and Cool Azul Pain cream... they are *the answer you have been looking for.* You have a mild headache? I believe Basil *is the answer you have been looking for.* You have a cough? I believe Thieves Cough Drops *are the answer you have been looking for"*. Meet their needs. THAT is how you get people to classes. It may require a reminder text the morning of the class, or a quick note the night before. They may need three reminders the week of the class; and they may still miss it. Then, you follow up after class, find out what went wrong, and haul your 101 script and kit to a one-on-one with them the next week at their convenience. Chase people because they are worth fighting for.

They won't see what you see in oils yet. It's ok. You did not start with a knowledge base before you had your kit, either. Leading them to training is your job. Lead them with your story, your passion, and most importantly, with your love for them. That's the secret to stopping no-show classes. If you are missing this part, it's likely the entire answer to your business being stagnant. You've either stopped sharing, or you are not persistent enough. You give up too soon. You give up before they have a chance to see the hope you have for them, and the answer to their problems.

If they say no to attending a class, I usually gently ask "Why?". More often than not, it's not you. It's a scheduling issue or personal conflict. If you have offered an oil to them that has helped them, rarely do I get a no. Like I mentioned at the start of this book, don't take the "no" as a personal affront. It may have absolutely nothing to do with you, and everything to do with timing or something outside your control. You get them to class by finding their need, offering relief to them through an oil, and through perfect persistence, never giving up on them, no matter how many conversations it takes. People show up to classes because you see their needs and meet them, and for no other reason. They have to have a reason to give up their time. If their tush isn't in your class, their reason to show up wasn't strong enough. Other things were higher on the list than you. If you have no-show classes, the missing element is always the foundation of relationship and the persistence to see their needs.

If it is awkward for you to ask why they did not come to class, my next statement is usually, "I am sorry I caught you at a bad time! I'll check in in a few days and see how you're doing." Then I catalogue their name, write it down in my *Gameplanner* to touch base in the next thirty days; and I am off to my next contact built through relationships. If your love for them is greater than your fear of speaking up, compassion will ring through that conversation. They are not numb to your intentions. Even someone totally unfamiliar with oils can feel if they are being hunted. Gauge their state of mind when you start the conversation; and if it's not a time to invite them to a class, continue building the relationship and wait. That means you keep gently doing the same steps you did: asking leading questions, listening, and offering oils. That investment will pay off. I like to call it the gentle touch. You're always prospecting, but it does not need to feel that way in your conversations. You're prospecting to drop hope on someone. Hope is not always welcome when they're in a place of stress; so wait for the moments when you're able to speak into them and they will listen.

If you are too timid to touch base after the first initial contact where the relationship was launched, the chances of that person making it to your class is pretty remote. Get over the fear to get them in a seat. Fear is the enemy of freedom. It keeps you chained. It keeps them from learning about one of the greatest things the Lord has created: essential oils. You bless them by being bold. Keep the distributor as your center, focus on their needs, focus on education, and fear melts away.

I will say here: the woman that signed me asked me for **seven straight weeks** if I would get a kit. You read that right. She asked me SEVEN TIMES. The average person can only say no seven times. I fit perfectly into that statistic! Every week I'd tell her, "I am interested, but not this week." She'd say "Ok! I will call you next week!" She did, week after week, with the same sweet gentleness. I did want the kit, (I was not totally convinced that oils worked, but I was willing to play with it). What I was too timid to tell her was that I was in such poverty that I needed two months of grocery money and my birthday cards to afford it. Her tenacity put a Diamond under her a little over two years later. Imagine if she'd not called back, and gave up after the first week or two of "no's"? It is said that the average person requires 7 to 15 moments of pursuit. That's 7 to 15 contacts. 7 to 15 conversations. 7 to 15 gentle drops. 7 to 15 times of asking their needs. 7 to 15 times of engagement. 7 to 15 moments of listening.

I think this is the answer you have been looking for.

Are you giving up too soon?

In the *Unstuck* workbook Appendix, I have a "7 to 15" tracker. Write the name of the person you're working with; and each time a conversation occurs, put a check in the box. You don't need to write every nugget of the conversation down, just don't ever walk away too soon. You may be on the verge of signing up a Diamond, someone who desperately needs the freedom Young Living has to offer, but isn't aware of it yet. Everyone needs oils. Don't leave the conversation until that door is shut. Even then, I'll still pursue the relationship and wait for the door to open a second time... by them, when they are ready.

There is a second half to this story on the other side of the spectrum. It's a story that is painful. In that same moment that one of my friends was blessed the night I got my starter kit, a second precious friend lost three quarters of a million OGV (750,000 OGV built over four years) because of fear. A few months before I got my kit, a good friend of mine, a friend I'd had for ten years, had considered asking me to join her Young Living team.

She never did.

Life got busy. She wasn't "officially" doing the business; she had no Young Living business training; and she thought I'd be too busy to pursue it. She had a dozen reasons to stay silent; but that silence cost her beyond belief. The woman that signed me is an Executive who makes 20,000 dollars a month because of the OGV of my team. My friend has given up 20,000 a month for the last five years—or about 1.2 million dollars—(and that doesn't count the next 60 years of my business)—because she was too afraid to ask me. Is silence worth 750,000 thousand OGV? Think carefully about the possible repercussions when you allow fear to own you. Walk it out a few steps in your mind if you need boldness.

She knew I was a news anchor, and I loved my job. She was sure that I'd never walk away from being famous and my love of news writing. The Lord has a weird way of using your passions in different fields that you may have never thought of! I didn't think *Gameplan* would do what it did. I didn't think that God could restore writing for me with the loss of full-time radio through the conduit of oils. What is the purpose of a gift of writing when it comes to sharing oils?? Every time I think God can't do something, I get caught again in my own doubt and fear! I stand corrected. <u>No talent you have will be wasted with Young Living.</u> I can assure you of that. God is not the waster of talent. He is the designer of it. It will be used, likely, in ways you never comprehended.

After my sweet friend did not ask me about Young Living, I got approached by someone else, another friend. I signed on with them (someone who was not on her team). I had no idea she was even using oils. That sweet friend who never asked is now my personal assistant and holds Executive rank. She tells people at every single *Gameplan* event we do, "I could have had SARAH HARNISCH under me if I'd JUST ASKED HER!" I know she replays the conversation she didn't have in her mind all the time. It's a decision she can't un-make. It would have blessed all four of her kids financially for the rest of their lives. It would have blessed her kid's kids, but she never spoke up! She is a rockstar and can get to Royal Crown Diamond without me; but her journey would have been faster and simpler if one conversation had happened. A single question... seven times. That's what freedom looked like for the woman that signed me. Be bold. Let me walk this forward just a smidge more and blow your mind again. What if you're considering dropping off Essential Rewards, or possibly going inactive because you can't afford the 100 PV order you need to place to get your check monthly? Maybe there are only a few people under you, and it doesn't seem worth it. Oh friend, it may be so much more worth it than you realize. What if just one person under you catches a fire and builds? And what if that one person signs an up-and-coming Diamond? And what if YOU miss out on 1.2 million dollars over 5 years—simply because you never stayed in the position of their upline? You didn't even need to sign another person... just being in the place where you were placed by God would give you lifelong generational financial blessing, if you did the one step of staying at 100 PV to get your check. You have no way of knowing the future of your organization. Pray it through before you go inactive. (By the way... these are true stories of real people. Lean on their wisdom and don't let the blessing of Young Living be robbed of you, too.)

Half the battle is simply asking. One of the worst feelings is to see a close friend or family member go to another team simply because you never opened your mouth. Who would you cry over if they were on another team? You need to start fighting for them right now. Pick up a pen and make a list of their names, and be relentless. Never, ever give up on them until they see the vision. Be the first to ask them. Be the one to war on their behalf and pray for their eyes to be opened to oils and to the business.

Most people do not understand that network marketing is a family. Where you end up is your team for life. If you want your team to include the rockstars of your life growing up, don't be too timid to approach them. Sign all your friends and take them with you to Diamond. Sign your circle, even if they have no interest in the business. Carry them with you. What other job can all your besties get freedom at the same time?? This is the most incredible company on the earth. It all starts with your questions and your persistence. Silence is not golden, persistence is. Literally.

Seven to 15. Never, ever forget those numbers.

If you had a no-show class, the missing element is always the foundation of relationship and the persistence to see their needs and meet them.

I struggle with the "starting an oily conversation with a stranger" thing! But my purple Young Living sweatshirt got the ball rolling with the Costco membership rep on Saturday. I handed out a purple bag and collected his contact information on Facebook. Thank you Sarah for Unstuck!

Penny Sorokes

CHAPTER 19

DIAMOND RISING DECKS:
FOLLOW UP AT IT'S BEST

It might seem odd that I'm talking about how to get people on Essential Rewards before we train on how to get them signed for their kit, but there is a method to my madness. Essential Rewards is the key to your rank advancement. Without it, every month you reset to 0. A healthy ER number is 35 to 40 percent. If you're above that, you're doing incredible. If you're below that, you have a bit of work to do. With many people that don't rank up, this is their Achilles heel. They can get the sign ups. They can't train the lifestyle. In Unstuck, we're going to work on both of these things—because I believe if you could master those two core concepts, you have the most important tools for laying the cornerstones to your business. Leaders will find you in 101 classes. I never hunt for them. But if you're not prospecting and training the lifestyle, there's no way to build a Young Living business. It requires both of those things.

You need to go into every single class prepared for the dialogue. You need training on how to speak so it rolls off your tongue effortlessly, without appearing as a sales pitch. That process starts well before they're even on your team. It starts when they are a prospect and continues through aromatherapy training as they become a lifelong distributor. The way I do this is through a funnel.

Until now, Young Living business builders have not had a simple system for tracking our teams. We have oodles of tools to hand out and get someone interested in oils, and even to train them after their starter kit arrives—but what about our end?? How do we know what was given to them so we don't send the same tools again? How do we know what their health goals are? How do we remember as our team grows which members have had the Core 4 classes—oils, Thieves, NingXia and Savvy? I'm convinced if they had all four, our Essential Rewards totals teamwide would skyrocket—because these are the core products of Young Living. Everything centers around oils, Thieves, NingXia, and Savvy makeup.

What if you had a funnel, a system, that you used without fail every single time—and all you had to do was run them through the steps? I've already told you it takes 7 to 15 times for a person to say yes to a kit on average, and the same amount for them to say yes to Essential Rewards. Some people may get it right away, but they are either in the minority or someone else has already been dropping seeds of knowledge into them before you showed up with a class.

One of the toughest parts for me has been to keep up on repeated follow up. I'll touch base once or twice, but after that, I feel like I'm pestering my friends. However, if I had a system where, after a 101 oils class, I immediately signed them up for a 102 Thieves class—then a 103 NingXia class and a 104 Savvy class the months or weeks following, I now have four opportunities to get them a starter kit and get them on Essential Rewards. I have four face to face opportunities to meet their needs. And suddenly, it's not so awkward anymore.

If my aromatherapy funnel includes training on how to order, a run through of the reference guide at Life Science Publishing, and simple training on how to label read and look things up—those are also all opportunities for 7 to 15 conversations and seed planting instead of picking up a phone and saying "are you going to get your starter kit yet??" It's not obtrusive when you follow a pattern. It feels natural because you're just doing the next step that you always do when you're working with a prospect, a new member, or a leader.

Enter in the Diamond Rising decks. I have been developing these for over a year to be released with Unstuck, because we needed a simple system for tracking the funnel. In Gameplan I released a script for teaching classes and a leader training system. With Unstuck, we now have a follow up system. You already know the core 3 activities that lead to direct OGV growth: teach classes, get people on ER, and train your

leaders. You have all three tools. I used these decks on my S.
up first and they went bezerk for the concept, then we broke it ⌐
all the leaders and hustlers on the Oil Ability team in August 2019,
my Essential Rewards has been increasing by 1000 to 2000 a day sin⌐ ⌐
we trained the team in following up. You don't have to overthink it—just
follow the card and cross it off.

There are three 4x6 cards that follow each person: a Contact Me card, a
Distributor card, and a Diamond Rising Leader card. It's all done through
a checkmark system that's fast and easy—no journaling. It literally takes
minutes a day. If you have 15 minutes for follow up, you can reach into
the deck box and just grab a few Contact Me cards from your last class,
or a few Distributor cards that are tabbed with post it notes to mark
those not on ER yet, and contact them exactly the way they asked to be
contacted on their card. They have already told you their biggest health
struggle, what classes they have had, if they are a member on someone
else's team, what they want to learn next, and how to contact them. And
they are expecting you to touch base. The hard work of uncomfortable
personal questions is already done for you when you hand these out in
classes, at vendor events, or pick up a phone and run your pre-existing
team through them. Each leg is color coded for more organization.

The Contact Me card

Runs your people through a prospecting funnel. It asks all the tough
questions for you. They fill out the front of the card, and you fill out the
back as you follow up with them. There are checkboxes just for touching
base—for building that relationship with no strings attached, without
oils conversations. You are laying the foundation with that person and
building trust. Their personal information is not hard to collect because
of social proof—the entire room around them is effortlessly filling out the
same card. It's private and they don't have a stranger (you) asking them
about their health struggles face to face, which can get uncomfortable.
This is how I start all my classes.

The Distributor card

Is what you use after they sign up. It runs them through an aromatherapy funnel. They will walk through the Virtual Office so they know how to
order again, unbox their kit, get a sign up link with their member number
so they can share oils immediately, get Fearless trained to learn to label
read and research, and get funneled through the 101, 102, 103 and 104
classes, with tailored targeted training and a 3-month Essential Rewards
wish list to start trying products based on their wellness needs.

The Diamond Rising Leader card

Is a full business funnel. The first half of the card is for new leaders, someone who has signed a single person up, or has an interest in the business. You take the card as slow or as fast as they want to. It may take an entire year to fill up the front side. They will start with the Gameplan mini prospecting book, morph to the Teacher Training in Gameplan, get coached on teaching their first 101 class, how to do follow up, Ignite, Gameplan, Unstuck, and more. The back of the card is advanced training with rank mapping, coaching, Oily Tools, and stat tracking. You track them from Star all the way to Royal Crown Diamond, coaching them every three to six months so they never throw their hands in the air, frustrated that no one is listening to their troubles. You catch the troubles before they give up. And you know exactly where you left off in the training every time you pick up their card.

Got all that?

Contact Me card: prospecting funnel

Contact Me

Name: _____ Phone number: _____
Email: _____ Facebook/Instagram: _____
I've been to these classes: ☐ 101.Oils ☐ 102 Thieves ☐ 103 NingXia ☐ 104 Savvy
Biggest health struggles: _____
Looking for more information on: (check all that apply)
☐ hormones ☐ sleep ☐ stress ☐ pain ☐ colds and flus ☐ cleaning ☐ supplements
☐ natural personal care products like shampoo, toothpaste and deodorant ☐ a whole health wellness plan ☐ makeup ☐ kid's and baby care ☐ oils in the bedroom ☐ oils of the Bible ☐ oils in the kitchen ☐ oils for fitness ☐ oils for animals ☐ skin care ☐ oily nutrition ☐ oils as a business ☐ cleansing and detox with oils ☐ Fearless class (next step in oiling)
Why I came to this class: _____
When contacted for aromatherapy training, I prefer:
☐ phone calls ☐ texting ☐ email ☐ social media: Facebook or Instagram
☐ I am already a Young Living member (check if applicable)
Please fill out the front of this card only

Distributor card: aromatherapy funnel based on Young Living's top products

Diamond Rising Leader card: business training funnel

That's how the deck works. Store them in a 4x6 card box and you're off and running. I am praying this revolutionizes how you track your team. I want so much for it to be a huge rank up year for you! If you have questions about how to organize the cards, what to do with large teams or teams that are just starting, the color tracking system of the cards, or anything else, there is an FAQ and samples of the Diamond Rising Decks here: https://oilabilityteam.com/product/diamond-rising-deck/

I ask myself every month—why do people go inactive? How can they not fall madly in love with Young Living? I had been losing anywhere from 500 to 700 people a month on my team, so I started investigating. For every 8 in 10 people I spoke with, it was not the cost of the oils or the cost of the products--which is what I had assumed. It was a lack of a support system and feeling overwhelmed at learning something new. They did not know the next thing. They did not know why they needed oils. It was not the answer to their problem. And because of that, the kit stayed in the box and collected dust and they moved on to the next thing. What if the next thing was the Core 4 classes? What if it was training on the reference guide? What if you tailored that kit to exactly what their needs were—and gave a homework assignment of sitting down with their reference guide and the catalogue that comes in their kit side by side and finding the five oils or oil-infused products they need next?

If we can stop the process of being overwhelmed by aromatherapy and show them WHY they need oils in their life every single day by being there for them and training them to stand—it changes everything.

And you keep your team.

Track your team, keep your team. That's how relationship building works.

If you're not prospecting AND training the lifestyle, there's no way to build a Young Living business.

Track your team, keep your team. That's how relationship building works.

This book has changed more than my business. The strategies for communication have changed my life. As an introvert, I never felt comfortable talking to people. This is just the roadmap I needed to engage with people in all different types of situations!! Thank you, Sarah!!

Theresa Messner Yeager

PART FOUR

15 Classes to Move You Forward

The chapter on Perfect Persistence, 7 to 15 conversations alone did it for me! Don't. give. up. It takes an average of 7 times to expose someone who keeps saying no, and if we give up on the 7th, that may be a huge loss for us! Sarah spells out how to not give up even for the most discouraged. This book lifts the heaviness and turns it into the light at the beginning of the tunnel. Get this book in your hands!! Your 8th time could be your Diamond leader in disguise.

Nettie Bancroft

CHAPTER 20

METHODS OF TEACHING

We have done a lot of head training up until this point, but everything I write requires action. I did not pen *Unstuck* to fill your head with good thoughts. The goal of this book is OGV growth, momentum, and rank ups. I want to start a movement to show every person they have it in them to rank. That ONLY happens with action.

Here's a quick check of the *Unstuck* system to make sure you have tried EVERYTHING if you're still finding yourself in a plateau. This is the exact format I use when it's been too long since a kit sale: I am having trouble making contacts; or am I just generally discouraged? (Discouragement happens to Diamonds too)! The Diamond in the rough will pull themselves out of a rut and never give up. The strategy below is how I back myself out of a corner. This type of freedom, the freedom Young Living offers, isn't offered in a 9 to 5 job. You're gonna have to fight for it (possibly harder than any other job you've fought for in your life). Network marketing is hard because it's emotional. I'm going to train you to set those emotions aside to the best of your ability, and do actions that will get you back to a place of movement. If you let emotions own you, fear stops you. Let's train how to dig out of the state of "stuck."

How to Get Unstuck

Unstuck has never been written before. It's completely new. With this book, we're trying a different approach if your OGV is stagnant. You're going to play until you find your gifts, especially if all of your OGV is your own personal order. I'm helping you to find your niche, your way of sharing. I am going to lay out the most common types of classes (after speaking with many Diamonds on the ways they built their organizations over the past two years) and collecting research and data on classes that actually work.

Here's my advice: try one type of class several times. If you have kit sales, it works for you, even if the pace feels slow. If it does not lead to any kits, try another method. If you try three or more class methods, and you're still not seeing results, drop it all and focus on one person; and build a relationship with oils. If you don't know anyone, try one of the four mojo methods at the start of this book. If that still gets you nowhere, spend a month working on you. Do personal development training until you have built up confidence and trained your tongue against negativity. Play with the products and gather stories as you train your mind. Then go back to square one and try one type of class all over again, once your head is out of the gutter. Got all that?

- **Step 1:** Try one type of class several times (at least 4-6 times). If you have kit sales, it's your way of sharing. Rinse and repeat to Diamond, and skip all the other steps below.

- **Step 2:** If you have no sales during Step 1, try another class style from the 15 types of classes.

- **Step 3:** If you try three or more methods, and still have no kit sales, focus on one-on-ones, or one of the four mojo methods to build your confidence.

- **Step 4:** Spend a month working on you if all the above methods fail. Do personal development training until you have built up confidence and trained your tongue against negativity. Consider an emotional release session, vibrational raindrop session, or neuron-auricular technique session (google each technique to learn more!) At the very least, order the Feelings kit, and simply start diffusing the oils one at a time, not missing a day, for 30 days. Get them on the back of your neck, on your brain stem, and over your heart. Pray, and give your business to the Lord. Ask for protection against a spirit of negativity. That spirit is keeping you from freedom. You CAN do this!

- **Step 5:** Go back to square one and try it all again. Once you find a way that works, don't jump ship and try something new. Stick with the same class type until you go Diamond; even if it's 288 101 classes to Diamond, and another 400 101 classes to Royal. Just because you've heard the lecture doesn't mean those in your class have been exposed. It doesn't need to be new to you to be new to them. Rinse and repeat to freedom.

You **need** to hear me on this.

When you find something that works in network marketing, the secret to the rank is to keep doing it. In everything else in life, you're told to keep growing, keep pursuing, to change up your game; but not in this. In this, you need a system. Your system is to find what works and use it to get you to Diamond. Rinse and repeat is the mantra. It may sound boring, but I swear to you, it works. Of all the Diamonds that I interviewed, not a single Diamond said they had success at one method, jumped ship, and tried to learn a totally new skill over and over again. All pursued education and personal development; but that's not the same thing as changing a strategy that works. Their stories were the same: "I taught a lot of classes, then I ranked." "I went to a lot of vendor events, then I ranked." "I posted on social media five times a day for three years, and I ranked." There was a system in place that they stuck to that yielded results.

Do you know what happens when you stop doing the thing that got you the rank? You lose the rank. I see it with Diamonds all the time. They hustle and sign kits. Some of them are super recruiters, knocking out 30 plus kits a month; but when they rank, they slip into leadership mode and focus on training their team only. Then one leg dips below the volume they need, and they are again a Platinum. Rank loss has become such a problem that Young Living now recognizes Diamonds in the monthly Essential Edge newsletter only on the months that they maintain their ranks.

The Best Piece of Advice in this Book

I swear it to you, if you highlight nothing else in this book, this paragraph needs to be in bright yellow with arrows drawn all around it, so you never, ever lose it. <u>When you're picking the type of class you want to teach, look at what you've already done to be successful.</u> If you're a Star, how did you sell those four kits to start with? Was it a textable class? Was it a vendor event? However you made your first, second, third, fiftieth, or 150th kit sale... that's likely your gift and way of sharing. Don't try blogging if you've never used Wordpress in your life. Don't try make and takes if you hate creativity, but someone else had success with it. You have to look into the deep part of yourself, and find what works, based on your unique set of talents.

What are you good at? Do you like social media? Consider Instagram. Do you like events? Consider vendor events. Are you terrified of face to face contact, but you can whip out a text in no time flat? Try textable classes or DVD teaching. What are your gifts?

If you have not had a kit sale yet, 70 percent of distributors build with in-person classes, class style 1. Start there. We tend to avoid that type because we either want fast growth (we think building another way is quicker), we see other's success in different methods, or we REALLY don't want to look people in the face. It can be just as tedious using another method to grow your team. Other's success does not necessarily mean you'll have success at that type of class. Sitting in front of someone is one of the fastest ways to find their needs and build relationships. It's a lot harder for them to avoid you or not answer when you're three feet from their face. If you need a starting place, I'd say start with class 1. If you need to know your niche, and you're frustrated, go take a hard look at the kit sales you've already had; and repeat the method you used to get those sales. That's what you need to continue doing until you are a Diamond. For me, it was 288 in-person 101 classes to Diamond. As a push for Crown, I've clocked another 250 classes already, over and over again. It was the exact same script with new faces. No cool title, no bells and whistles, just the same thing over and over again, with new relationships, and new people to love on. Some people I knew, most I didn't. All of them started with building a relationship and meeting needs.

Look at what you've already done successfully, and that's your way. Go back to the method that got you your rank in the first place. No distractions.

Let's move on. Aside from the style of class that you choose, there are three things that grow your business: teaching classes, getting people on ER, and training your leaders. If all your time is spent in training your leaders, you're not teaching or getting people on ER. If you're not teaching, bye bye rank. It's a matter of time before your leg volume starts to dip. Even Diamonds must teach. They don't have to hustle as hard; but that's also a danger zone, because they can lose rank if their hustle slows to a crawl. 1 in 2 Diamonds in Young Living do not maintain their rank monthly. That means as of 2019, with 450 Diamonds, only 200 hold rank each month. It's not because they are incapable. They have the gift of sharing that got them the rank! It's that they get comfortable and stop teaching. If you want to maintain, you need to continue sharing. Sharing is the one skill that is most critical in your entire business.

Can I challenge you to take an honest self-assessment of how you're spending your time? Make a quick pie chart (I'll help you with this in the *Unstuck* workbook). For a week, every time you do something work related, jot it down. Then look at the minutes spent, and plot it out. Just once. How much time is spent prospecting? If the answer is less than 80 percent, you're upside down in your business. That's why people aren't coming to classes.

If I could give you just one tip, and you would follow just that one thing from this book, I'd tell you to fill your calendar with 4-6 classes this month. Make sure you've clocked 7 to 15 conversations per person, and have taken the time to build the relationships to make sure those classes aren't empty. Empty classes are a waste of your time and talent. If the relationship work isn't done ahead of time, you'll be speaking to an empty room.

That schedule of at least one class a week is how many of my upper leaders went Silver in six months. If you do two a week, you'll rank faster. You'll see so much fruit from it, and your mojo will skyrocket. Don't bite off more than you can chew; but if you look at your planner and the calendar squares are empty, I can pretty much say with certainty you're not looking at a rank up month. If you put action to your goals and teach, it's the number one way to blow up your OGV. Teaching is the only way to find leaders. It's the only way to build an Essential Rewards base. If there are no people, there is no business. This is the starting place.

We tend to overcomplicate things. Before you spend months doing network marketing training, and reading all you can out there on this style of entrepreneurship, just grab the script and get three people on your couch and read it. You will be blown away by how truly easy it is to grow this thing with that simple action. Sharing saves your business above all else out there. The months you don't teach, you are in a holding pattern. The months you get out there, you will watch your volume grow. When you get frustrated and feel stuck, it's from a lack of teaching. When you can't find leaders, it's because you haven't taught enough classes yet to find them. When you are starting over at 0 again each month, it's because you didn't train the lifestyle. Teaching = direct income growth. You have growth months; and you will have hustle months. There should never be backsliding months, unless it's after something unusual like a Black Friday sale. If it's a trend for you to have backsliding months or holding months, you have stopped the simple act of sharing.

If you are frustrated with the pace you are growing, the secret is in your calendar. It's as easy as that. It took two and a half years from the purchase of my starter kit to diamond. I didn't re-invent the wheel each time I taught. I did not give the class cool names, or integrate make and take supplies, or teach on different topics. I just kept doing what got me results from the beginning of my business. You don't need cool titles for your classes, you need new people. You get new people by building relationships with them. If it sounds overly simple, it was. Three pages built a Diamond income for my family.

I regularly hear, "no one is coming to 101 classes anymore. I need fresh ideas to get them in the seats." I have seen so many diffuser bracelet classes and succulent plant classes out there, but guess what? You have to buy tools to do the classes. That costs money. Classes that cost money scare away new leaders, because they can't duplicate the cost of the supplies. If you want to rank, keep it simple. The issue isn't the title of your class, or the cool ways you come up with showing off the starter kit oils. The people around you still have sore throats, coughs, and headaches. They don't need a bracelet class to get cough relief. They need to know you have a solution to their problem. Be the solution finder and you'll have full classes, without plants, beads, pretty stickers, and cool titles. You'll pick up leaders that see how simple you keep it, which is even more important, because then your OGV grows even faster.

If I'm being straight with you, I didn't build terribly fast. My business was built brick by brick, piece by piece, over a period of years. I had many no-show classes and poor relationship building. I have made ten thousand mistakes, yet I taught enough classes that I did eventually end up at Diamond. My goal is to shave some of that stagnant time off your clock, so you're only focused on doing the things that will get you the rank. My experience is that beads and plants will cost you time. You may pick up a new member or two, but you will lose your leaders. Don't scare away the next generation of your business.

The class structure where I flourished most was in-person classes, usually five to ten people at a time. Sometimes, I only had 2. Sometimes, I had 40. Most my classes were ten people or less. Of those ten people, typically at least half, (sometimes just one, and sometimes all ten) would get a kit. Half of the kit sales led to Essential Rewards and longevity on my team. Those are my stats. If you do the math, that doesn't mean starter kit to Diamond in twelve months. However, with repetition and consistency, it does equal freedom. If your pace is an area that hits you hard mentally, don't close this book before you read the chapter on expectations. I'm going to lay out some benchmarks that will put your mind to ease on how efficient you think you are, and erase some negative programming on the speed of this business.

The most common type of class is sitting on a couch and sharing. That's the place I will begin. I do want to tell you that I have nothing against specialty classes (Oils of the Bible, Oils and Emotions, etc...); but I'd like you to keep a three to one ratio: teach three 101 classes for every specialty class.

Why? Because that's what leads to kit sales. If you're training on Inner Child and Release oil, that doesn't lead to a starter kit. Start with one of the Core 4 starter kits, so you can funnel to a wholesale membership that gets 24 percent off their oils for life. Then teach the specialty classes when they need ideas for Essential Rewards. 80 percent of your time should always be spent prospecting. That means if you're not funneling all the attention to the Premium Starter kit, the Thieves Starter kit, the NingXia Starter kit, or the Savvy Minerals Starter kit, you're going to end up with a retail customer that doesn't get the perks and doesn't reorder. Don't focus on one oil. Don't even offer retail as an option. Always funnel to wholesale memberships. That leads to longevity. They can't learn to oil with one bottle of oil. Oils are a lifestyle, not a one-hit wonder. Twelve bottles are the training playground. If you feel like you're "selling" them a kit they can't afford, instead of offering a single oil, consider this: when you walk into your family's home and you see Thieves soap on the counter, is your first thought, "Oh my GOODNESS, I can't BELIEVE I *SOLD* them that!!" Or is your first thought, "what a relief that they don't have that blue dye soap on their counter anymore that smells like birthday cake!" Your first thought is their protection. Walk that sale out a few steps further, and you'll see the motive behind the conversation. That means the reason you offer only one oil instead of the full kit is because of fear, not because you're "salesy." Stand above fear to reach your motive of protection of their home.

You might still feel like you're pressuring them to buy something they can't afford, but not if you look at the numbers. The cost of the diffuser and two oils, PanAway and Frankincense, are nearly worth more than the value of the entire kit ($147). By the time they buy oils separately with the diffuser, they could have owned 12 oils, Thieves, NingXia, and more. You just have to train your tongue to never offer retail oils and always go for the wholesale membership; and it will roll off of you effortlessly. You'll also have peace of mind knowing you saved them the most money. The starter kit is the only thing on Young Living's website that is more than half off: a $412 value for $165 means they save $247... more than the price of the entire kit! Get them the most for their money.

Premium Starter Kit
cost breakdown

LAVENDER	$15.79	THIEVES	$19.41
FRANKINCENSE	$40.13	VALOR	$39.75
PANAWAY	$47.70	STRESS AWAY	$9.92
RAVEN	$15.70	PEACE & CALMING	$34.75
CITRUS FRESH	$7.50	DIFFUSER	$83.88
LEMON	$8.22	THIEVES CLEANER	$2.20
PEPPERMINT	$13.49	NINGXIA RED	$5.80
DIGIZE	$18.42	THIEVES HAND PURIFIER	$5.00
		MEMBERSHIP	$45.00

Total: $412.66  $165

Let's Talk Ratios

Why teach a three to one class ratio? Because the newbies on your team have unlimited resources to learn. If you use *Fearless* and habit train them to look things up; and they have access to the internet and a reference guide, the sky is the limit for them. Get them plugged into #ylunites rallies all over the world four times a year. Open your ER box online in front of them each month to give them ideas. Point them in the direction of books and websites where they can learn. Make sure each of your new members get the Core 4 classes: oils, Thieves, NingXia and Savvy ; and that's likely enough to create a lifetime oiler. Then move on and let them take the reins of their own education.

If you put all your time into the people that are already on your team, you're not bringing new people in. Only commit 20 percent of your time to that audience, and with the rest of your time, find new faces. That's how you grow much *faster*. **Your new audience needs you more**. They don't have access to oils yet; and they don't know why they need them. Your team members are capable of standing on their own two feet and researching. Get them started, point them in the right direction, and let them fly. Then put the bulk of your time into new people.

A word of caution... I am also talking about losing time on social media. Some of us are so caught up in the time it takes to run our business groups, that we get to the end of our week and don't have enough energy left to teach. As a Diamond, I work about 10-15 hours a week. One hour a week, I train my business builders on our training page. Usually, twice a month, I ask my Silvers (and up) to stand in for me, so the team gets to see new faces and hear new stories of success each month. I'm not even committing a full four hours monthly to training my own team. How am I on the cusp of Crown Diamond? I prospect for new oilers and use the $1 *Gameplan* mini: *Build A Life Beyond Survival Mode* for each attendee. It does the talking for me. Let the tools do the work. Just funnel to tools and keep them moving to the next thing. Then your time is free for other things. If they express an interest in building, I hand them *Ignite* next, then *Gameplan*, the *Gameplan* workbook, and bootcamp videos. They stand on their own two feet. Then they duplicate it like crazy; and their leaders duplicate too. That frees up my time to teach 101 classes and pursue my warm market and leads. Always continue to pursue new people. That's where most of your business lies.

To put this section together, I spent over two years going from Diamond to Diamond, asking them how they built their organizations. I did not hit every Diamond; but many generously shared their struggles and their triumphs with me. This list, even though it's probably the longest compilation out there, is still not comprehensive, because there is so much creativity in Young Living! There were about 80 different subset types of classes, but I compiled them into the top 15 categories you see above.

This list of 15 categories of classes is not comprehensive, but it covers 95 percent of what is out there. Most that did not make the kids are variations of the classes listed, versions that just have a catchier name but similar content, or a type of class that doesn't lead to large yield when it comes to starter kit sales.

Many other types of "classes" are structured the same as the list above, but given a catchier name. I am sure, because I have not spoken with every Diamond, that there are classes I have missed. It should still give you a good starting point if you need fresh ideas. It's not meant to overwhelm you, but just to show you how others have successfully made headway at growing their OGV and their downline.

We will begin at square one, the most common type of class out there... the in-person class. One of the simplest ways to teach is to pick a friend or two, grab the 101 script in the Appendix of this book, and read it from your couch.

Let's take a closer look at the style of class that built most of Young Living to what it is today. If all else fails, return to class one. Here we go!

If you're not teaching, bye bye rank.

I have not read this book, so I have no review. But what I do have is a hard core respect for Sarah, and all that she pours into her written works. She tells it like it is, uses her story to lead people to their own truth as God intended us all to do. So when I commented earlier that I was praying for this to be finished sooner than later, I meant it with all my being. I know the love, and dedication, and hard work that goes into every Sarah does. And I know it is worth every penny and more.

Rebecca Chrisman

CHAPTER 21

CLASS 1: THE IN-PERSON CLASS

Before the class...

I'll start by walking you through what my classes look like. I will promise you one thing though: it's unimpressive. The simpler you keep your 101 classes, the more business builders you will attract. I could easily lay out $200 in food at each class I did when I first started. I would have pretty make and take stations with Cricut cut stickers on the bottles; but it's not duplicatable. Always ask yourself if what you're doing can be copied. If the answer is no, you're likely scaring away potential leaders with your own actions. For this class, I use the script, a starter kit, and humans. I do like to keep a cheap brand of Lavender on hand to showcase purity against Young Living's oils. I also use the Powerpoint on the oilabilityteam.com website; but if you're not tech-savvy, and putting something on a screen is intimidating, don't sweat it. Many people have enjoyed powerful 101 classes that don't have Powerpoints.

I do occasionally like to have a couple of giveaways for this class; but I never spend more than $10. My favorite giveaways are a roll on of Peppermint oil, a Thieves cleaner packet, a NingXia packet, a Life Science $1.50 mini reference guide, a sample of the Thieves Whitening Toothpaste, or three Thieves cough drops, and a little tiny travel sample of Cool Azul Pain cream. I toss each giveaway in an organza 10-cent purple bag off Amazon, put them in the front of the class and say, "once I start the lecture, if you can be the first to answer a question, you can pick something that grips you the most (something you want to learn about) off the table." It keeps the class focused on what I'm saying; and I don't get a lot of people clocking out on cell phones. I also never pay to rent a room. I'll use a friend's living room, a library, a firehouse, senior center, or VA, before I pay. Simplicity keeps this type of class duplicatable. 99 percent of my classes were in church gyms or living rooms. 100 percent of them were done for less than $10. All of them used a script, a kit, and some humans. For the first six months of your business, forget that you have a paycheck; and put it in your gas tank to teach classes. Go where you know people.

This is a good place to tell you that for each of the Core 4 scripts, (101 oils, 102 Thieves, 103 NingXia, and 104 Savvy), I'll be generating a few tools to make you look good. These are not costly items (in fact they're all free); but they make you look like a pro when you walk into a room. When I first started sharing, I used torn off pieces of lined paper and broken clipboards to collect contact information. This is definitely a one-up on my initial presentation! First, I use the Contact Me card from the Diamond Rising deck to collect a LOT of personal information. It's the information I need without having to awkwardly ask for it—like if they're already on another team, or if they've already had classes I'm offering them, how to contact them, and what their biggest health struggles are. Asking those things of a stranger can be awkward—so let the card do the hard work for you. Second, I like to have a printable to keep them accountable after the class. For the 101 oils class, I use the $1 *Fearless* book and the free *Fearless* calendar for simple aromatherapy training to get them off the ground researching, reading labels, and looking for poisons in their home. It sets up a lifestyle of oils. There are also free 30-day printables for the Thieves challenge, NingXia challenge, and Savvy challenge on my website. Each of the Core 4 classes (101, 102 Thieves, 103 NingXia, and 104 Savvy) also have a free textable class that you can send each person later to listen to the class again on their cell phone. There's also a professionally designed Powerpoint if you choose, that's free and on my website. None of these resources cost a penny; and we put a lot of time and effort into using a professional design team to make you look great in class. Use what you like, toss what overwhelms you. My goal is your rank up.

Before class, I will assemble purple bags to hand to each person (it has a *Gameplan* mini for the business opportunity, *Fearless* and the *Fearless* calendar, a flier with a photo of the starter kit, instructions on how to order the kit (that's free on my website), a cover photo that lists the contents of the bag (free on my website), and my business card and information. I also toss in a 101 or 102 (Toxin Free Life) cd, so they can listen to the class again after it's over, or pass it to a friend (which effectively doubles my class size). We will go over purple bags in depth in the next chapter, because it's an entire way to teach a class.

This is what I take to class with me in a "101 Class in a Bag." Some like to call this their portable office. It's everything you need to teach in one simple place. I leave it packed all the time and restock it after each class so I'm already ready to teach.

Class in a Bag/Portable Office Packing Checklist:

☐ 4 or 5 **giveaways** (Peppermint roll on, Thieves cleaner packet or a capful of Thieves in a plastic spray bottle, a mini reference guide, NingXia packet, Cool Azul sample, Thieves Whitening Toothpaste sample, Thieves cough drops sample, etc...

☐ **Purple bags** for each member of the class.

☐ **Contact Me** 4x6 Diamond Rising deck cards, a clipboard, and a pen.

☐ 30-Day **Challenge printables** (for accountability after the class. This is under the *Unstuck* tab at oilabilityteam.com and is FREE for the Core 4 classes. Look for the Fearless calendar, Thieves calendar, NingXia calendar and Savvy calendar).

☐ My **starter kit** with a diffuser, 12 bottles of oil, Thieves cleaning packet, Thieves hand sanitizer, and NingXia packets + EO magazine and starter kit literature.

☐ Life Science pocket **reference guides** for each person that gets a kit.

☐ **Cheap Lavender oil** to compare to Young Living's lavender.

☐ If needed, a **laptop** with the Powerpoint that corresponds to the lecture you're giving (101, 102, 103, or 104) and an HDMI cable to plug into their television.

☐ **My script** (I usually just bring the *Gameplan* book or *Ignite* or *Unstuck* and read straight from the book to show potential leaders how simple it is to share).

☐ **A cheap tablecloth** to lay over a table to display everything in the bag ($1 at the dollar store).

☐ All of the **Essential Rewards promotions** for that month, to show off what they get for free if they place an order over 190pv. You are more likely to successfully promote this if they can see the items, pass them around, and smell them, and if you talk about what they do.

☐ As you rank up, you can also pack **a couple of tablets** and a **hot spot**, or a couple of $100 laptops, so that there is more than one station for people to sign up after class. People are more likely to sign if there is not a long line. Make sure they are all on the internet before you begin the class. Only do this if you have other leaders in the room to help check people out. If your average class size is 1 or 2 people, this is unnecessary. I'd only do it if you have the income to pour into this. If not, don't stress about it!)

Speaking oils

What are speaking oils? They're oils I slather on myself before I speak. Over the last year and a half, I've been on stage in 45 cities; and 45 times, I've thrown up. Most think that because I have a background in radio as a news anchor, that it's an easy slide to the stage; but that's simply not the case for me. I spent eight hours a day for the past two decades talking to a wall with a microphone in front of me. Transitioning to a thousand people staring at my face on the *Gameplan* book tour, or ten people staring at my face in a 101 class was quite scary. I do NOT have a natural knack for speaking. It comes with a lot of practice, a lot of tears, a lot of vomit, and a lot of forcing myself to do hard things. I used an entire bottle of Valor on my body at my first 101 class. Valor is what truly got me to do the business. It's the courage oil; the oil the Romans wore before battle. Without it, I likely would not have continued. I was terrified.

Maybe you're thinking you can NEVER stand in front of someone and read a script. I get that. That was me. I also knew I was worse at blogging; and my ADHD was too severe to stand still for eight hours at a vendor event and man my booth. That means in-person classes have been my go-to. I am extroverted, so that helped; but I'm also quite self-conscious standing in front of people and having them stare at me for long periods of time. I will tell you this: getting over that fear of sharing built an incredible Diamond income for my family. It's changed everything for us. Without that script, faces, my kit, and a lot of Valor, I'd still be sitting in the radio studio making $2200 a month (an income I can't leave for my kids). I'd have an income that would be gone within months after I was gone, even after deliberately saving for more than a decade, and a fantastic 401k matching program. It took staring down my fear to protect my kids. Even though I still get sick when I speak, the oils have helped my nerves tremendously. Practice your script so you're confident. Douse yourself in oil. Start with people you know that will encourage you as you read; then move onto a group of more unfamiliar faces. Always keep the prize of the rank up in the forefront of your mind; because as I look back now, in our Diamond home, all I can say is that I'm so grateful I never stopped. I'm so grateful fear never took such a gripping hold on me that I quit. I could have been a quitter. It is easy to continue doing what I knew how to do, to stay in my "safe" zone. I was so close to quitting so many times; but the taste of freedom was worth the tears and the stress. Those feelings are fleeting. This new life is forever.

What speaking oils do I use? You can use any combo or any oil that really speaks to you. These I've found really help me to focus on the script, get over myself, focus on the crowd, avoid rabbit trails, and have fun in the process. I put them all over my feet, especially on my big toes (where the nerve endings come out of my brain), on my brain stem, the back of my neck, and generally slather them all over my hands and arms for good measure. It helps me act as a human diffuser to myself. I use at least 50 drops of oil, sometimes more, on class days.

My favorite speaking oils are:

- KidScents GeneYus
- Northern Lights Black Spruce
- Cedarwood
- Valor
- Brain Power
- Frankincense
- Believe
- Abundance
- Gathering (if you don't like people)
- Grounding (for introverts)

I want to make a quick statement here, that no matter which of the scripts you use, and no matter which of the 15 types of classes you prefer, the foundation of relationship must be there. You can't use online classes to avoid people. You may not have face-to-face contact, but you most assuredly need to find that sweet spot in their heart for a lifestyle of oils; and that only happens with conversation. I find that many times with online classes the follow up is much longer. Online classes are easier to teach, but the work afterword is very time consuming, building relationships without that person in front of you. That one essential element of "why do I need oils personally?" has to be under every single class you teach, or no class will be successful. You may have kit sales; but if they don't see why they need oils, they will fall off your team without the rock of a relationship. Always ask yourself why you are picking the type of class you're picking. If it's to avoid people, you will not see success in any of these methods, because all classes require relationship.

None of these classes are "better" or "worse" than another. They are just a different way of sharing. Thousands of leaders have seen success with every single one of these methods. My advice to you is that you don't hop, skip, and jump through them. If you have no results with make and takes or vendor events, consider coming back to this very first class type: in-person sharing. Why? It's not necessarily the best, but it is the most-used. I said earlier that at convention 2018, corporate said that 70 percent of all classes are built with in-person, face-to-face relationships; and 30 percent of all other classes are the rest of the types listed here (the other 15 classes). That means 7 in 10 builders in all of Young Living are seeing success with class 1. That means going back to the basics: script, kit, human, will likely yield you results. It does with nearly every type of builder out there.

In each of these classes, I'll give you the structure, the supplies lists, and step-by-step instructions from people who have used each method. For the words of what to say, grab one of the Core 4 starter kit scripts in the back of this book; and then follow a simple format that I've repeated in my last 500 classes: share your personal story, read a script, and end with the bold close. That format is bulletproof for a few reasons: 1) You're using a script, which is duplicatable throughout your team, and takes the fear out of sharing. 2) Your leaders can customize the script, the bold close, and include what they feel is most important (yet it still has their flare). 3) Facts tell stories sell. That means by starting by starting each class with your story, you're pulling the room in with the power of what Young Living has done for you. Each time a story is told, you carry the torch of getting oils into every home in the world. It is our stories that will turn Young Living into a 10 and 20-billion-dollar company. If you cut that element, you dice out the most important part of the class. This goes for every class out there: online classes, make and takes, etc.... Even vendor events can have a 15 or 20-second version of your story to catch people's attention. That is where the power is.

Mary In Alaska

I just got off the 2019 Global Leadership Cruise to Alaska a day ago; and I had the honor of hearing Young Living founder Gary Young's wife, Mary Young, teach for a good hour on the boat. She shared her personal daily lineup of supplements, and what she does for building strong bones. Side tip: Look into AminoWise, Mineral Essence, MegaCal, Agilease and BLM, and do your own research on their ingredients!

Any time you can get yourself in front of Mary, you'll walk away inspired. As she shared her story, she talked about the importance of telling your story. This company was founded on the principles of storytelling. Mary said, "we are giving you permission to get your voice back! Go share your story!" Maybe you aren't sure how to do that, so the Unstuck chapter "How to Craft Your Personal Story" in this book will give you the most comprehensive lay out, to date, of how to get people's attention with YOUR words and YOUR personal oils journey. I'll walk you through line by line, and give you a worksheet to help you plot out your story.

A question I frequently get is, "I don't really know enough about oils yet to talk about them. I don't have a story." I love what Mary said on the boat: "the oil does not need your instruction to work. The oil will do what it needs to do whether you know what to do or not." Use them with confidence, and share the results; because sharing our stories is how we constantly learn from each other about what these incredible plants can do. This is a photo with Mary, my team, and I on the boat:

Mary said, "One man cared enough that he gave his life for what we have today." Gary spent decades studying how to grow and distill the plants so we would have the purest form of the plant that God designed. He was amazed at the benefits, and was always surprised when he heard from a member about a new thing the oils had done that he'd not thought of. Because of his work, we have access to the purest oil on the planet.

Mary said Gary knew more about oils than anyone in the world. He certainly distilled more than anyone else! No other company can boast 300 singles and blends, and 600 oil-infused products. It's incredible what he did in such a short time. How did he know so much about the plants? Well, first he went into what he called, "God's living room" (the mountains,) every time he was stumped with a question. He went into the hills to pray to talk with the Lord. Part of his knowledge came from what he tediously studied. However, part of it was God-given. The Lord gave Gary the gift of being the oil whisperer.

Because of Gary's work and legacy, God is the foundation of all that we do at Young Living. The knowledge of the plants, the distillation into oil, the heart of all the oil wisdom... it all came from the Lord. Instead of fretting that you don't know enough to teach, lean on the legacy that this man has given us; and trust that the Lord knew what He was doing when He created the plants. Share what you know, and tell them to look the rest up or experiment, just as Gary did. That's how we get oils into every home in the world. That's how we keep walking for Gary. We share.

That is a good enough reason for me to sit on a couch, pass oils around, and share my story. If anything, it's to keep Gary's story alive; but also to protect more families. Gary fought so hard for the people we've not reached yet. Don't give up on them because you don't know enough. The oils will talk for you. They'll talk when you pass the kit around in the class and you get the oil molecules in their noses; and they'll talk when your new distributor learns to play with the kit themselves. Your job is to start the conversation.

I personally teach more oils classes than NingXia or Thieves classes; but there are people on my team that have grown to Gold solely by sharing Savvy Minerals and NingXia. Those scripts have their place, too. If I have tried several times to reach someone with oils and they are not there yet, that's where the 102, the Toxin Free Life (Thieves) script comes in. Most will switch their cleaning supplies when they are aware of the dangers. I believe every person on your team needs training on the first three months on the Core 4: Oils, Thieves, NingXia, and Savvy Minerals. Once a new member has been through one of those Core 4 classes, be deliberate about teaching the other two to them to build longevity in them; and set them up for understanding the lifestyle.

I am very careful not to put down other ways and methods of teaching and sharing, or ways of strategizing your organization; because the truth is that there is more than one way to get from Point A to Point B. One way isn't necessarily more or less successful than another, or faster, or slower. Where you run into trouble is where you see someone have success with a way of sharing that you have no gifting at, like blogging. You might decide that is the only way for you to grow. Maybe you really want to avoid face-to-face conversation, so you decide to build solely on Instagram, without having a good pow wow in your heart. You realize that you're still going to have build relationships; but it will be via messenger instead of face to face. That conversation still has to happen. It's important that you're setting realistic ideas of how to build from the get-go.

I am a tomboy, so makeup really isn't my gifting. My sisters and good friends dress me for the stage; but there are women on my team with twenty and thirty years in skincare and makeup, and they fly with the Savvy line. They have exploded their businesses in ways I never could with that script. Why? Passion. It's what they care about.

Find the thing that you care about most and start to share from that place. The only way you won't find success is if you're not listening. If it's solely about your love for the products, and not about their needs, it won't work. If you always keep it on their needs, you can succeed in anything. I do recommend you start with the Core 4 instead of an Animal Aromatherapy (or other specialty) class. It's not because Animal Aromatherapy isn't a great way to share; but because there is no Animal Starter kit. You always want people to come in at the entry level with 24 percent off as a wholesale member. If you are not driving toward that, you'll end up with a lot of one-hit wonders that get an oil or two for a need, and never order again. You can drive to the starter kit, and then add on oils for that type of a class in an Essential Rewards or One Time Order; but you'll only have success in that way if you are good with follow up and have a strong close. If your passion is animals and that's your sharing place, then find uses of the 12 oils in the Premium Starter Kit for animals and start with that above the oil-infused animal products. Always steer them toward a PSK. It gives them a playground to learn oiling that a single product can never do. If you want to direct them to the Animal Scents line, have them add the oils to their first Essential Rewards order. That's great for the second conversation. The first one should put them in a place to get 24 percent off their orders for line with the starter kit.

Now let's walk through what the anatomy of a 101 class looks like in detail.

Many ask me where I hold my classes. Honestly, I clean a room in my home and have classes in my living room. When I traveled to speak for friends, I held it in their homes or in a church gym 95 percent of the time. I have never, ever paid for a site. Not ever. Maybe for a rally, but not for a 101 class. That's a good way to put yourself in debt; and it's not duplicatable for leaders on your team. You'll have a lot of leaders drop out if they have to pay for a site from the get-go. Do your research and find places near you that offer rooms for free if you are not comfortable with people in your home. Honestly, I just shove everything in a closet and keep one space clean that we can meet in if it keeps it free for me. I have five kids and 2 grandkids. I get it on the presentation-of-the-house thing. But your freedom is at stake here. 20 minutes of straightening is better than delaying my business, or scaring off my leaders with pricey room rentals. You want everything you do to be able to be copied. You set the tone for your team.

If your home absolutely isn't an option, (one of my leaders has a non-verbal autistic son who would be uncomfortable with new faces in his home), then start to get creative. Try churches, community centers, senior centers, fire halls, Y's, VA offices, or Moose Lodges. I even taught at Gameplan event at a funeral home once, when I spoke in Beaumont , Texas just after a hurricane. This is a photo with host and Young Living Platinum, Lorene Allen, in front of the hearse. Yes, our teams had to walk past that to get into the event!

The goal with your class sites is *free*. Do some legwork, pick up the phone, and start calling. Some of my leaders have had classes in Michael's Craft store rooms, in family or friend's empty businesses after hours, and even in parks if it was warm enough and not raining.

One of my leaders said people weren't comfortable coming to her house; but she had no problem drawing them to a public site. I disagree. If you are taking time to build the relationship, they will feel comfortable coming. The bigger issue is that *you* are not comfortable with it. If having people in your home takes you too far out of your comfort zone, take the time to find a free site, and use it again and again. If you are not comfortable, that will come out in your teaching. Just know that all your leaders will try to do the same legwork you did; and if it costs them too much time, or they cannot find a free site near them, you may lose them. I live in a pretty rural area (40 minutes to get to Walmart, rural); so option two for me if my home was not available was a friend's living room.

Once you have a site, start inviting. Go through your warm market list and build relationships, just like I trained you at the beginning of this book. Get oils on people's bodies. Meet their needs. Have eyes to see the needs around you. Listen for a cough in a store, or offer Cool Azul to a woman with a limp. Pay attention to what's going on around you. Loan your stuff out. Be an oils megaphone. Be an oils diffuser. Wear your oils everywhere you go, so it causes people to say, "Wow, what's that?" Get their attention. Then offer an invite. Tell them the class is FREE and FUN; and it will completely change the way they care for their families. It is the answer to what they are looking for. I have pages of pre-written invites for you in the full *Gameplan* book, book 1 of 3 in this series.

When you have a guest list, even if it's a list of one, it's go time. If you've never used the 101 script before, you'll need to modify it. Always begin by sharing your story. Facts tell, stories sell. They need a personal connection with you, the host. They need to hear why you love these things so much. It need not be long, but at least 30 seconds to a few minutes.

Then I want you to grab the 101 script from the back of this book, find a mirror, and read it through, top down, ten times. Grab the Bold Close, and read that through ten times too. If you're still uncomfortable, grab your mom, sister, or best friend; and ask them if they'll let you read it aloud to them. Be as authentic as you can. Don't look like you are reading the script.

I still have not memorized my own script; and I've given it over 500 times. It's because I don't want my leaders to feel they have to memorize it. If you can't be copied, it's all moot. I did highlight a couple of lead sentences; and I go off script a lot, sharing stories and inserting my own flavor to it. Lauren Crews Dow, a good friend of mine who is a Diamond, gave a demo of her 101 script on the 12 Days of Diamonds page. It's my script modified to fit her, with her story. If you want to see the two side by side, it will give you a good starting place on how to share. She did an excellent job.

By the way, my feelings are not hurt if you make changes to the script. I penned it just to give you a leg up... a starting place. Tweaking it for your own use is completely ok. I want you to make it yours! I also just wanted to save time for those that needed the words to use. There was an entire thread on whether or not to use scripts on a leadership page. Let me tell you why I think scripts serve a purpose.

First, look at what the greats are doing. There are some that have built without the use of a script, so it's not the ONLY way to share. My own sister doesn't use my script. She just reads right out of the catalog and passes the kit around. She reads a couple of pages on Seed to Seal, where the farms are, a smidge on purity, and then she moves on. Others have built just by their own story and sharing Seed to Seal.

May I make a case for the script? You take all the fear out of coming up with the language. Any leader can print three pages, sit on a couch, and read it; but not every leader can grab a catalog and ad lib. Not every leader is comfortable sitting there for thirty minutes and sharing stories. If you give them the words, you empower them. They don't have to reinvent the wheel. They have a starting place that has results. For me, that script built a team of over 10-thousand in four years, and an OGV of more three quarters of a million dollars a month. Follow something that has results.

If you look at the top people that have been successful in network marketing, Dani Johnson, Eric Worre, and so many others. They advocate for the use of scripts. It's because it's simple and duplicatable. Keep it as simple as you can, no matter what you are capable of. If you have passion, that is enough to pique their interest. Peppermint vitality brownies are not required. Always ask yourself if you are stepping too deep into your personal skill set. If you're a scientist, and you're sharing all the science, you'll scare your team away. If you're a teacher, and you have so many printables and handouts because you love visualization, you're going to scare your leaders away. They don't want to drop 30 dollars on photocopying before every single class they teach. Are the things you're doing copyable? If not, stop. Even if you're a rockstar at it, stop it! Leaders are the most valuable part of your business. They lighten your workload exponentially; but not if you scare them all away.

Now that you have a site, a crowd, and a script, the real fun begins! You need to make sure you're marketing the tar out of that class, and not just a day or two before, but at least two weeks before. I like to get all my events up on Facebook to market them at the end of each month for the next month. I'll have all my events up for the month of June by the last week of May. I ask three that commit to coming to go into their friends list and invite 50 people. Then I fill that Facebook event full of teases, nuggets, and good things to encourage them to come. It may be a picture of a giveaway, a sentence or two from my script, or from my close. Before I personally add anyone to an event, I have built that relationship, and they know the invite is coming. I heard the sneeze, I handed out the cough drop, and they're ready for a sign-up link. Lay the foundation so your classes are successful. Don't rely on others to do all the work for you. That's how you end the no-show frenzy.

Then it's D day. What do I do to prepare for class?

Nothing.

Seriously, nothing. I make sure my kids haven't run off with a bottle or two from my starter kit; and I always make sure my portable office bag is stocked right after the last class ends. Outside of that, I just get the script ready and lay out my kit. No bells and whistles.

When the doors open, get a diffuser going. My favorite "smell" in the kit is Stress Away; but I don't want to put them to sleep, so I usually diffuse Peppermint, especially if the class is at night and they're coming from a long day at work. I have a table set up at the front of the room with the kit displayed, the ER promos for the month, the giveaways, and my purple bags. My *Unstuck* book is close with the script.

I take time to welcome them and get to know them until everyone arrives. Then sit on your couch, share your story from your heart, read the script, pass around the starter kit, and make sure everyone gets oil up their nose. Have a laptop open and ready for orders. Go into the class anticipating orders, and your sales will be higher. If you go into the class thinking nothing will happen with it, that's all you'll get out of it. The script takes me about 30 minutes top-down to read; but I always block out about two hours for class so I have time to share my story, sign kits, and to get to know those that came. Relationship is everything. If you are cold, they will leave and look for someone they want to follow, even if they like the oils. You're selling yourself as much as your selling oils. Passion matters.

the Close?

no need to be timid or shy when you come to the sale of the kit. ot pushing people to buy something they cannot afford. You are leac g them to a lifestyle that will protect and guard their families. You are training them on wellness. It's one of the most precious gifts you can give them. There is a closing script at the end of this book that will help you tie it all up at the end and give you the words to say; but it need not be scary. If you are scared, they will feel it. Just practice your script until it rolls off your tongue, and you'll sound like a pro.

Let's go over the order of operations again.

1. Find a site.

2. Invite people by building relationships with them.

3. If it is your first time, or if it's been a while since your last 101, practice the script.

4. Make sure no kids have run off with oils from your starter kit.

5. Make sure your "portable office in a bag" is stocked and ready to go.

6. Get the diffuser going with Peppermint.

7. Display the kit and the ER promos, purple bags, and giveaways on a table.

8. Open your door and build relationships as they arrive.

9. Have them fill out the front side of the Contact Me card from the Diamond Rising Deck. You will fill out the back in the days after the class as you run them through the prospecting funnel.

10. Share your story.

11. Read the script.

12. End with a powerful close.

13. Hand out the 30-day *Fearless* calendar and mini book, as well as purple bags.

14. Have a laptop and working internet where they can order on the spot.

Once you get good at this, it looks more like this:

1. Throw the kid's toys in the closet just before people arrive.

2. Douse yourself in Valor as a deodorant because you didn't have time to shower.

3. The doorbell rings, welcome them in and ask their needs.

4. Realize that your darn 5-year-old took your Lavender out of the kit AGAIN.

5. Share your story, read the script, close powerfully and point to ordering the PSK.

6. Love on people after class. Practice listening, and sign 'em up.

7. Rinse and repeat next week; but perhaps sneak that shower in. The house is still trashed.

8. You can do this with virtually no prep and no frills. The simpler you make it, the more leaders will be attracted to your organization. It's just you, your 3-page script, and your kit. That is duplicatable.

One other thing I will do, depending on whether or not I'm teaching alone, is to make sure to include my leaders in the room. If I am working with a leg (a person and a team), I'll have them introduce me, give my biography, and edify me before I speak. Then when I take the floor, I immediately edify them. I talk positively about their personality, their background, their rank, and their character. As I wrap up the class, they are in the back with a tablet or laptop ready to sign; and we both work through the people in the room together. Edification is a powerful tool that gives you credibility with the people in the room. Use it when you are not teaching alone. This is called tag-team teaching. And it's extremely powerful, because you're using the social proof of each other's stories before a room. Every leader on your team can't have a piece of you as your organization grows and you must move to build new legs, but when you're in a season of hustle in certain areas of your team, doing your class shoulder to shoulder with your other leaders will strengthen your presentation.

Common Mistakes In 101 In-Person Classes:

There are a few mistakes I see when I watch those around me teach. I am a blue/red personality, so loving on people is my jam. Blues love fun and people. They love leadership and successful classes that lead to kit sales. For some, the art of hanging with relative strangers is truly uncomfortable, especially people they have never met. Just keep it about their needs. If you saw someone hurt in the mall, you wouldn't hesitate to go over and see if they need help. That's the place you're teaching from. You are not the creepy-buy-my-oils-person. You're the change-your-life-forever-these-oils-are-awesome person.

Here are some big errors you can make when doing in-person 101's:

Dry Reading

Don't read the script like you are reading a technical manual. You have to have passion, or people will tune you out. Bullet point the script out, highlight the first sentence of each paragraph, insert your own little stories along the way; but have personality when you are reading it. That's what draws people to you. If you are not able to do this, I'd recommend you use the 101 DVD instead. There is training on that in a few pages, but the gist of it is that it releases you from having to read the script; and you play the role of host instead.

Being Impersonal

When people come to your door, greet them warmly. Listen to their stories. Get to know them. Use all the leading sentences, and find common things between you and them to talk about. Get to know their stories. If you are cold, they will feel it; and the chances of them signing on your team drop dramatically. If they are going to trust you with their insecurities in learning to oil, or with the stories of their health journey, you have to be someone they can connect with. You do that by asking leading questions and listening.

No Close + No Option to Order at The End

This will destroy your classes. I once had a woman on my team teach twenty 101 in-person classes with an average attendance of 24 people, and she never sold a single kit. I finally went and sat in the back of one of her classes, because she was about ready to throw the towel in on her business. She read the 101 script to a T; and she did a great job! She had passion and enthusiasm. Then she ended and said, "You've survived Essential Oils 101!" That was it. She never passed around the starter kit. Getting oils in their nose and on their body is critical before they leave your teaching space. If you leave that part out, you have lost them. They need to have an experience with the oils; and they do that by getting oiled. Even if it's a single drop of Peppermint in the middle of their palm, everyone gets oil on their body before they walk out my door. Many times, they come right back to me and say, "WOW! What was that!??!"

After she ended the script, people started to leave. She never told them about the starter kit; and she had no laptop set up for them to make a purchase on site. I went from person to person and asked what they thought of the class. They loved it! However, several mentioned to me that they had no idea she was running a business. They just thought it was a class on oils; and she was freely giving of her time. You know what happened? Many went on to sign with someone else. She planted a seed that she never watered; and someone else went in for the harvest.

Why did she do it that way? She was afraid to sound "salesy." Friends, PLEASE listen to me. You are running a business. It's the best business on the earth. When you give your samples out, and give your time out, it's poor stewardship not to expect something in return. Your business is not a handout to people. It's your livelihood! It's like handing out purple bags and not getting their contact information. You have given and expected nothing back. You would not purchase inventory for a storefront if you were running a retail store, and just hand it out to people who walked in, expecting nothing back. You'd expect them to pay for your service. Do the same with your home-based business, or you will put yourself out of business.

If you read through the closing script, it does not sound "salesy". It sounds like education. You are equipping them to make better choices for their families. It's a better choice than where they are. Always go into it from the education aspect. Run your business with good stewardship, and the Lord will bring the harvest in. If you're uncomfortable, just read the script. It will take you where you need to go without sounding like a sales rep.

Not enough time marketing

Another mistake I see is that you pop your events up or start to market them without giving enough lead time. People need a heads up. Don't wait until two days before the class to tell people it's coming. Give them a good two to three weeks, with several reminders. People are busy. If you don't give them lead time, you're going to have a lot of no-show classes. That includes relationship building with people. Some people take a large, long investment of time before they will get a kit. Others you'll meet in a Panera shop, and they'll show up at your house for a class that night and sign up (true story!). You have to be willing to make the investment, no matter how long it goes. Put the time into your people. One of the best investments with your clock that you can make the morning of your class is to send a personal text to those you have personally invited with a gentle reminder. Customize the message for them. "Remember that sniffly nose we were talking about last week? I will run through all my go-to natural health secrets tonight. I cannot wait to see you! I think this is the answer you've been looking for." No show classes are because they have no reason to come. Make their reason so loud it's like a megaphone in their face. They CAN'T miss the class. It's their answer. That text or call may be the thing that draws them to your door. You cared enough to check in! A simple text, 90 seconds of your time, can change the entire attendance list in your favor. Include their solution in the message and make it about them for the best results.

No-Show Classes

"Sarah, I gave enough lead time. Why did no one show up?" If you're having class after class, and no one is showing up, nine times out of ten, the issue goes back to relationships. We hit on this earlier in *Unstuck*; but it's such a key point of this book, that I'm going to put a little exclamation point on it in this chapter by emphasizing it again.

If you had a no-show, you didn't take the time to invest in them; and they didn't see the value of giving up their time to learn. They didn't know why they needed the product. Their time is one of the most precious things they have. If you meet a need they have, you will have their attention, because they see a reason to sacrifice their time. Your product solves their problem. Keep your focus on helping them; that's how you open class contacts. If you're not filling classes, you still have to master the art of the relationship. Go back and re-read the first half of this book on relationship building each time you are discouraged. Apply the principles and make the investment in those around you. Your love and compassion will be the key that unlocks your business.

If you stood in the presence of Gary Young, all you would feel is his love. It didn't matter if you were a farm worker in Ecuador, or a Royal Crown Diamond, he loved you. He built Young Living without judgement. If you were Jewish, Muslim or Christian, or any other religion or belief system– you were precious. Gary befriended the Sultan in Oman (not only the Head of State, but the Head of Government) to secure the best Frankincense fields in the world—and we still have access to those fields, because the Sultan was so deeply respected and honored by Gary. He believed the best in people. Somehow, this whole sharing thing is so much simpler if we live by his example. It was never about what Gary could get; it was always about meeting the need. He was a master listener... a master at loving people.

This is a shot of Gary and I in 2016 in Hawaii. Cheek to cheek, he told me that the secret to full classes was building trust. It's how he began Young Living, by being there for people. It may lead to a kit sale, or it may not. They may sign with another team. They may sign with you, and blow your OGV up as they ignite a fire across your organization that is unstoppable. Who knows where a conversation can go? Go in with no expectations, and you will not be disappointed. If your core message is love, you change the game on relationships.

We're nearly at the end of the hardest chapter in this book. Let's say you've conquered the in-person class. You've built the relationship, opened your home, shared your story, taught the class, and ended with a fiery close. Now what??

Now it's time to bring in the harvest of your time and love.

In a nutshell, what does it look like when I am signing someone after an in-person class?

1. Give the bold close from the *Gameplan* book, (and in the Appendix of this book,) and offer to help them "navigate the website" as they get their kit in the back of the room. If they get their kit today, they get an education bundle which includes a full reference guide, and coaching from me to learn how to use the kit. If they get the

kit today, they get an education bundle, which includes a pocket reference guide, coaching from me on how to use the kit, and a full aromatherapy funnel of the Core 4 classes, as well as training on how to get your Essential Rewards order for free each month. (You teach classes for them and give them the sponsor and enroller by tapping into friend circles.)

2. Sit next to them; but let them fill everything in. Then you do not have their credit card information or password; and they learn how to log into the Virtual Office and reorder on their own. Set up their ER on the spot; and set a date where you can meet to change their order for the next month.

3. Once they are done, I gift them *Fearless* and a *Fearless* 30-day calendar, and encourage them to accept the challenges. If they screenshot the calendar and send it to me once it's filled out, I will then gift $25 toward their Essential Rewards order as soon as it processes.

4. Set up a date, while they are in front of you, to touch base to help them get every drop out of the starter kit. Tell them you want to explain how to use their diffuser and the products. If they did not sign up for ER the day of the class, I use this as my second chance to explain the benefits of ER. If you pick a date when they are in front of you, they are expecting your call, or expecting you to show up. You'll get a much better response than if you try to contact them randomly after the fact. This is also a good opportunity to invite them to the next class... NingXia, Thieves or Savvy.

From writing *Gameplan*, I have had a unique vantage point to hear the stories of tens of thousands of business builders in Young Living. That series landed me in book signing lines around the world. Last year, I had an opportunity to speak in Malaysia, Indonesia, and Singapore.

I love the story of Francis Fuller from Singapore. Her story is one of my favorites in all of Young Living. She is a beautiful Royal Crown Diamond that took 14 years to hit the rank of Silver. You heard that right... 14 years to *Silver*. When she caught the vision, she was the definition of class volume. She told me she taught 101 oils classes on Tuesdays and Thursdays, and four classes a day on Saturdays. That is commitment!

She has a heart to work with the poor in Bali. She has opened a wellness center where she offers free massages for the poor, and so much more. Her story is powerful. She is chasing her dreams! One of the things I love about her is there is no fear—just humble, raw passion. She is a trailblazer. Francis single-handedly tore the Asian market wide open with her passion for sharing. She began when there was no Young Living in Singapore. She now has an organization of over 150,000 members. Many other incredible Diamond leaders have followed in her footsteps in Asia. Her fight made it easier for all of us to share.

How did she do it? She followed the model of class 1: lots of 101's. She is the definition of persistence. Frances created a market when there wasn't one; and she didn't accept no. She kept the calendar full. She buried excuses and always looked toward the next relationship. She left emotions on the doorstep. I see the same characteristics no matter how many Diamonds I interview. They all build slightly differently, but the core spirit is the same. When Frances reads this paragraph, she'll blush, because she's humble. That's one of the things that makes her so amazing; she's approachable. She has no expectations. The center of her entire business is love. Love on people like Gary did, and you won't go wrong.

Ask yourself how bad you want this. I can tell you, volume matters. If you're teaching one class a month, your rank up **will** take more time. You'll get out of this what you put in. You can take decades to get to Silver, or you can fight and build this thing brick by brick. Continue to gather stories. Keep your passion fresh. Share with fire. Don't clock out on your business, or you're treading water. Treading water = no rank up and no momentum.

That wraps up my top tips for in-person classes. Let's move on to class 2! I laid a foundation in this chapter that we'll build on in the coming

, so they'll be much shorter. I pray this gives you the confidence
forward!

took me a year to research and write this single chapter in Unstuck.
You have just survived 20 full typed pages on the single topic of how
to teach a successful 101 in-person class. It's the most comprehensive
published write up of an in-person 101 in all of Young Living history. Take
every line of wisdom, customize it to match your flavor and gifts, and get
out there and the tell world about Gary's greatest secret—the purest oils
on the earth.

---

*I was so close to quitting so many
times, but the taste of freedom
was worth the tears and the
stress. Those feelings of fear are
fleeting. This new life is forever.*

Pros & *Cons*
TO THIS STYLE OF TEACHING
IN-PERSON CLASSES: CLASS 1

70 percent of successful Young Living business builders use this method. 30 percent are all other types of classes combined. That means if you figure this way out, it will likely work for you!

It requires you to stand in front of people, and to do the relationship work necessary to get them in the door.

The chapter on Perfect Persistence, 7 to 15 conversations alone did it for me! Don't. give. up. It takes an average of 7 times to expose someone who keeps saying no, and if we give up on the 7th, that may be a huge loss for us! Sarah spells out how to not give up even for the most discouraged. This book lifts the heaviness and turns it into the light at the beginning of the tunnel. Get this book in your hands!! Your 8th time could be your Diamond leader in disguise.

Nettie Bancroft

CHAPTER 22

Class 2: Purple Bags

What on earth is the famous purple bag??? Why do I keep hearing about it??

It is an organza bag (of any color) that connects a person interested in oils to you. 80 percent of your business is simply being prepared. Have the tools on hand when a person shows interest. If you are prepared, it's much more likely that a conversation will end in a kit sale.

What inside the bag?

- Purple bag contents

- A cover sheet with the contents of the bag (a free printable at oilabilityteam.com).

- A photo of the starter kit (available at discoverlsp.com).

- A class in a bag: a 101 cd or a Toxin Free Life cd

- Instructions on how to order from you (a free printable at <u>oilability-team.com</u>)

- Your contact information, so they can reach you

- *Fearless,* so they know why they need oils in their life + the *Fearless 30-day calendar* to get them oiling right out of the gate

- Your *Gameplan,* the mini, because I always give the business opportunity at every encounter

"Why, Sarah, would you have me take time making purple bags when you don't advocate for me to make pretty folders loaded with aromatherapy content for my classes?" It's because they serve two different purposes. One is cost and time effective as well as duplicatable, and the other is not. I spend about two hours a month putting these together.

How do I use them? I make them up at the beginning of the month (about a hundred or so), because that's how many people I make contact with in a single month through chance meetings in hallways, on ball fields, in church, on walking paths, and in the places where I live. I carry five in my purse. I carry five in the glove box of my car. When I run out, I restock them from my stash of pre-made bags. When I get an oil on someone's body, or when they spark an interest through conversation, they get one of these little nuggets in their hand.

Why??

They need to see the kit to know what's coming. Your sales will be much higher with a visual. They need to know how to order if you are not standing in front of them to walk them through the process. They need to have your contact information, like a business card. If they missed your class, I put a cd inside with a class, and tell them to listen to it while they are dropping their kids off at school. This is one of my favorite tools to use for people who keep telling you they will come to class, but never find the time to show up. It's because it's simple to pop the cd into their car and listen.

If they attended a 101 class, and I have not heard much from them, I gift them a purple bag with the Toxin Free Life cd inside, so they get some new content; and it catches their attention on the dangers in the cabinets of their home. If they are not ready for essential oils yet, like to start with the Thieves line. It's simple, easy, and everyone a clean house. That's the Toxin Free Life cd. *Fearless* follows the thread. Tell them why they need the kit. Then tell them why they need the lifestyle.

Tools are powerful. You won't always be standing in front of someone the minute they decide they have an interest in oiling. They say a lot more in a small space then you can ever say. They point people to the next step. They can be read and re-read and listened to when you are not standing in front of them. They can be handed to friends to double the size of your influence. They are powerful. If you have connected with your prospect, built the relationship, hand them this bag; they will have everything inside it to place an order without you standing over them. It works.

The good news is that many of the items inside the purple bag are free. I am committed to helping you run your business without going into debt. You should never, ever spend more than you are making. The cover sheet and the instructions on how to order are a free downloadable on my web-site at <u>oilabilityteam.com</u>. The cd's, mini's and *Fearless* are a dollar each. I can print that cheaply because I don't print in color; and because Young Living Platinum Leader, Steve Sheridan, generously offered to open a publishing house to keep the tools affordable for you. I know what it's like to be a Star with an 80-dollar paycheck, and want to spend 300 dollars on resources each month. Don't do that. It will create animosity between you and your spouse; and it will put you in debt. You don't want to drive a wedge in your marriage.

What did my business budget look like when I first started Young Living? I was so poor that I could not afford business cards, so I typed my information out, printed it, and cut it out on strips of paper to hand out. I did not drop 20 dollars on business cards before launching my business. Don't spend more than you get from Young Living. If you are on that type of a budget, print off the printables, type out your contact informa-tion, offer the free textable class on my website (I'll go into more of that later), and save yourself money. As your business grows, you can invest more. Be faithful with the small things, and the Lord will make you ruler over more. Re-invest your check into your business each month and

see where it goes for six months. Make sure it's the best use of your check (not pretty glass bottles, expensive mailings, or non-duplicatable folders). Gasoline. Purple bags. Those are good tools.

All the elements of the purple bag are up on my website and are hyperlinked to make it easy for you to find things. Many of the tools inside were not developed by me. The printables are free and were made by a gifted graphic artist on my team named Jayme Kuenkel. Mary Jiminez, a treasured friend, makes the starter kit photos for Life Science Publishing; and they are knockout good (and only about 10 cents a piece). The organza bags cost pennies each on Amazon. When you go to oilabilityteam.com, click on "Share," and then "Purple Bags;" and you'll find what you need.

How Do I Use Purple Bags?

- I gift one to every person in an in-person class.
- I carry them in my purse and my car for chance meetings.
- I send them out to people who I've connected with a while ago, but have not heard back from.
- I send them to friends that are far away (if they're not able to attend a class)
- I use them at vendor events; but only for those willing to host classes (not every attendee).
- I send them out when people respond to my Facebook posts and want more information.
- I keep them at my desk at work when my co-workers ask what I am using.
- I hand them out to people that have a need for the business.

It's an extremely efficient tool. Most of my new sign-ups are cold market people (those I have never met) that I connect with on airplanes, in hotels, restaurants, and in lines when I am traveling. Before I traveled, I met people in homeschool groups (and if you have public schooled kiddos, PTA's), sports, all the places where my feet walk, and in all the places where I see people. I have Silvers on my own team who built their entire rank using purple bags. They work.

The Act of Passing Out the Bag

How do you hand out the purple bag? Walk through the exercise at the beginning of this book on asking leading questions. Then simply be silent, listen to their stories, and meet the need. Be where they are. If you are starting from a place of compassion for their needs, the passing of the bag is not hard, because you are helping them. Then I collect their contact information when I walk away; even if it's simply a "friending" on Facebook. Facebook is a safe place to friend someone because they rarely say no. If they feel uncomfortable, they can easily unfriend and block you; and there is no harm done. It feels "safer" to a stranger, rather than offering a personal cell number. However, I have had success getting cell phone numbers as well from total strangers, especially if I'm sending a textable class.

There is another use for the purple bag. It's when you're in a season of life that you truly can't have people at your home to teach. In-person classes do not work for you right now. Some moms are raising special needs kids, or working two full time jobs with only overnight hours free in their schedule. They may be juggling college and work. Some are taking care of aging parents and it would be a burden to them to have a home full of people. Some are in abusive relationships, and their home is not a safe place. I am broken for you! However, there are still ways to share around your mountains.

If you have 30 seconds to talk oils with someone in a Walmart line, you're likely not going to give the full business opportunity. If you hand them a *Gameplan* mini and Facebook friend them, they can read that 60-page mini over lunch, see the income disclosure guide, and gain some hope. You can't give all the information in that tool in the few moments you're checking out. However, when they're in that still small place, weary from their shift, their feet aching, and they pull it out of their pocket; it makes a huge impact and opens the door for your follow up conversation later. Tools are extremely powerful.

"What do I do if they don't look at the tools"? I'll press them gently two or three times; and if they still 'didn't have time to look', then the problem really falls on me. I haven't made the solution clear enough to their problem. It's not high enough on the to-do list. If I've asked more than once, and they are still not moving, I'll usually offer them a sample with a gentle reminder of the problem. "Do you remember telling me about your rotator cuff? I slipped some Cool Azul pain cream in the mail to you. I think it may be the answer you're looking for. I'll check in in a day or so to see if it came. I hope you feel better for your next shift! I remember how it felt when I had xyz... and I just wanted pain relief!"

Do you see how the flow of the conversation goes? There's compassion, and you're meeting a need. You make it about them, even in the context of a purple bag. Lean on all those relational skills from earlier in this book; and the bags work as long as you have the contact information to touch base a second and third time.

I will tell you, though, to avoid follow up burn out, if you have asked two or three times, and the bag has not even been opened, and you mail a sample that also remains untouched, it's time to move on to the next person. Don't hand off unlimited resources if they're unwilling to sample. By the second or third encounter after investing in tools and investing in them, I'd kick the dust from my feet and move to the next person. Most people though, if you're fixing a problem, will be willing to take a look, especially if you speak to their need.

Purple Bag Follow Up Structure:

- Hand out the bag and collect their contact information.

- Touch base online a day or two later to see if they've looked at the book or listened to the cd.

- If the answer is no, try one more time a few days later.

- If the answer is still no, offer a sample.

- If the sample goes untouched, move on.

- If they have taken a look at any point above, move to the next tool: an in-person class, an online class, a textable class, or writing up a wellness plan for Essential Rewards and discussing the starter kit, if they are at that point.

Let me end this section with one fun thing that I do with purple bags that makes this a training tool for leaders. I always love to demonstrate acts that will help with business growth to my leaders. One of the things I do are purple bag stuffing parties. I will hold a contest team-wide (if you do it for a single leg, that's against Policies and Procedures). I base it on number of kit sales, or number of people added to Essential Rewards that month. The winners come to my home, and we have a purple bag stuffing party. I have all the supplies printed and ready to

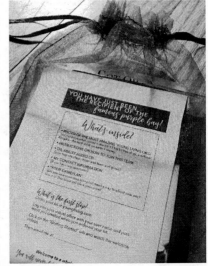

go in stacks (cd's, *Fearless*, mini's, all the printu together. I make a crock pot of Santa Fe chicken anu crank up the music and enjoy one another for a few hours away with whatever gift I have budgeted out, (10 bags, maybe 1u each). If your check doesn't allow for this, then have them bring their ov. supplies and do it together at least once a year with your top leaders. It's great for bonding. Then take photos of your party and put them on your business page so leaders see it and duplicate it.

In *Gameplan*, I gave you my favorite smoothie recipe, so this is a good place to pause and give you Santa Fe chicken for team gatherings! (Not for 101 classes!) This is one of our favorite family recipes of all time!

The Famous Santa Fe Chicken Recipe

In my crockpot:

- 6 shredded chicken breasts
- 3 16-ounce glass jars of mild salsa
- 1 pound of frozen organic corn
- 1 can of organic black beans (strained)

Stir it all up and set your crockpot to low for 2.5 hours. Don't lift the lid. After that, add **a brick of organic cream cheese** (8 ounces) and stir well until all the cheese is melted. Serve with your favorite tortilla chips. Be careful... it's addicting! My team goes crazy for this stuff, so we have it whenever they come to my home.

A word of caution: the biggest mistake you can make with this method of teaching is not collecting contact information. Hear me on this: if you hand out purple bags and are too timid to collect a way to contact them, you are giving away your paycheck. If you spend $100 on purple bags, picture taking that money and putting it into a fireplace. You have wasted it. It could be spent in much better areas! Make sure that you're always walking away with *something* for investing in that person.

If you are prepared, it's much more likely a conversation will end in a kit sale.

Pros & *Cons*
TO THIS STYLE OF TEACHING
PURPLE BAGS: CLASS 2

The tools in the bag do a lot of talking for you. They say far more than you can in a few minute conversation or even a full class.

Without good follow up, this method can be worthless. People will toss the bag in the back seat of their car if you're not checking in. If you incentivize them to check it out (a free spray bottle of Thieves cleaner for listening to the 101 cd, etc...) you will see stronger results. Meeting their needs will yield the strongest results.

Your tools WORK! I am so excited to be writing you! I used your Ignite book to enroll 20 new members. I also received the good news that I am GOING TO HAWAII!!! I was 2nd top enroller in Canada! You have gifted me oh so much confidence!! #Diamond Rising! I am also running a mini Ignite boot camp! Each participating member will receive a copy of Ignite as a congratulations for completing the bootcamp. Thank you for always being there! I hope you truly know how much I personally appreciate you, your time, and all you are pouring into me and so many more! May God truly bless you, your family and your business 100 fold! Thank you! Thank You! Thank you! for all you do!

Carmel Florizone

CHAPTER 23

CLASS 3: TEXTABLE CLASSES

This way of sharing is new, unique, and EXCELLENT! Whenever I develop a tool, it's always after listening carefully to what the needs are out there. You may be very shy. You have an amazing online presence, or can text like a boss; but when you are standing in front of someone, no words come out.

I developed two tools to help shy leaders (because I believe you have what it takes to go all the way to Royal Crown Diamond). This takes the fear out of the process of standing in front of someone and sharing. The elements are the same: leading question, meet the need, offer an oil, share the class script in some way, and lead to the starter kit. Rinse and repeat. All of that can be done online or by phone. Now, you can teach a class that way too.

In this method, and in the DVD classes that I will show you next, you don't have to physically stand in front of them and read the script. One of the blessings of this type of teaching is that it's probably the most duplicatable format out there. Anyone can text a link easily. Anyone can hit play on a DVD. I believe anyone can read a three-page script, too; it may just be in front of a mom or a friend instead of a room full of 50. If you're truly not to that place, this is a stepping stone that will keep your business from stalling as you gain a level of comfort. If you find this is YOUR way of sharing, I have Silvers on my team that ranked with textable classes. It works.

"How do they work"? About a year after I started my business, I went into a 100-thousand-dollar radio studio, took the three-page 101 script, sat down, and recorded it with the bold close. Then we saved the audio, uploaded it to my website at oilabilityteam.com, under "share"... and BAM! You can now text that sucker to anyone. The 101 class is up, as well as the Toxin Free Life class, based on the Thieves line. NingXia and Savvy are coming. You are about to have all of the Core 4 for FREE.

> *"I was thinking of you after our conversation, and I really think this would help."*

How Do I Do It?

You still need to make contact with prospects. Make a list of your warm market, the people that you know, and start there. Watch their needs online or in person. Ask a leading question and connect with them. Offer an oil, if you are local, and have the option to. Then use Eric Worre's, "if I will you" principle. "If I text you this class, will you listen? I will check in soon. I really believe it will help you!" Go to the website and copy the URL once you're on the 101 or Toxin Free Life page. Then just paste it into a text with a message and hit send. You just taught an entire class with a single click.

What message should you write? Maybe something like this: "I was thinking of you after our conversation, and I really think this would help you! Take a listen. I'll check in tomorrow." Then simply click the link on their phone and listen in. The 101 runs about 45 minutes; and the Toxin Free Life class runs about 30 minutes. If it takes them 15 minutes to take their kids to school, they could listen to the whole thing in one round trip.

One of the benefits of a textable class is that it goes ANYWHERE. Many of my leaders, especially those that live in urban areas, said that every-one was so busy they could not commit to an actual class. It took them too long with traffic to make it; and they'd lose three hours of their night. This is a simple solution for busy moms that have no free time, people with tight schedules, or people who have a fast-paced life and aren't likely to sit through a 101. They can listen on their phone while they are doing dishes, and make use of parts of their day that typically wouldn't be used. It's a great way to train their brain.

Once they listen, you still have to do the footwork. This is where I'd offer an oil and see where it leads. Loan your stuff out. Show them how to purchase the starter kit. Mail them a purple bag. Text and touch base. The follow up on these types of classes is harder, because you're not in person. You may have to make contact more than once. The average person, generally, only says no seven times. Don't be afraid to engage.

Another way I love to use this type of class is for what I call, "second-chance listening." In my in-person classes I say, "Hey, don't feel like you need to write everything down as I'm speaking. Sit back and enjoy the content. When you leave, I'm going to give you a link to listen to this entire class on your phone again as a podcast. You'll have a full copy of all the content." I always see a collective sigh of relief across the class. I do this either by printing the web link to the class on my business card and handing it out in purple bags, or by offering the class on cd (the 101 cd) in my purple bags. Both ways are effective and work well. If they are listening a second time, or passing it to a friend, you have an engaged an almost-oiler that is prepped to ask questions and start making changes in their life. The 101 class is a great conversation starter and conversation continuer. It's a powerful tool that has results.

But they're not responding—now what do I do?? Funnel them to the next thing. It may be an in-person class of one of the Core 4. It may be loaning out your diffuser to meet their need. It may be a listening ear and continuing to build the relationship. Track your work on your Diamond Rising Deck cards and continue the funnel. They are worth fighting for.

I want you to keep this one sentence in mind: "everything I do has to be copied."

Pros & *Cons*
TO THIS STYLE OF TEACHING

TEXTABLE CLASSES: CLASS 3

If you don't have time, this class is your best friend. Once you come up with a good leading sentence to get their attention, you can re-use the same texts over and over again with different people. You can teach an entire class in the time it takes to send a text.

The hard work is done after the text through relationship building, meeting needs, and running them through an aromatherapy funnel using the Diamond Deck cards. Because you don't see them face to face, connecting can be tricky.

Sarah, thank you for each and every one of your tools. I have used them all and I have propelled my business forward. But now I am completely out of ideas and my circle has been oiled so to speak. I know there are more humans out there, please help me become Unstuck to I can reach these humans!

Peggy Ward

CHAPTER 24

Class 4: DVD Teaching; Playing the Role of the Host

This class is very similar to textable classes in that you have no responsibility to read the script. My sister and mom are dyslexic; and it's very hard for them to stand in front of a room and read words off a page. I told you that my sister modified it by simply grabbing the catalog and flipping through the pages, and using them as bulletpoints to explain Seed to Seal, and essential oils. I take a step back from that because you have to be really good on the fly; and it can hamper your ability to find leaders that aren't comfortable without words to say in front of them. In her case, it truly was her strength to share with her own mouth. She has almost built her way to Platinum with it.

For those that really don't want to read *anything*, there is a second way to do this without reading the script.

Enter in DVD teaching. I took the 101 script, rented a camera crew, and recorded the whole thing with the bold close in my living room. Then we sent it to a professional studio to be produced.

What does the class look like?

The elements are the same as the in-person 101. Invite to the class. Open your doors. Get to know them. Share your story. Then pop the DVD in and let me do the teaching. At the end, pass around the kit, and have a laptop open for sales. You're playing the role of the hostess. There is no pressure to teach.

One of the perks to this type of class is that you don't come off as an expert to anyone. You're just playing information on your T.V. When they come to you with health questions, say, "I don't know about that; but why don't you take this oil and my diffuser home tonight, and see how you feel". It's easier to find leaders when they don't feel like they have to be aromatherapists.

The DVD already has the close on it; so you don't need to feel pressured to get them to "buy the kit". You just have to end the class by passing around the oils and get them in their nose. Then say, "I have a laptop in the back of the room; and I can help you get started. Anyone who orders tonight will get a free copy of *Fearless* and a *Fearless* map, and some coaching on your new journey." Have the laptop up and ready to go.

Let me pause for a moment and give you one more idea on how to invite to classes. This is something that I covered in the *Gameplan* book; but I'd like to hit it again briefly here too. I truly believe if you get one person on fire with oils, their friend circle is wide enough for you tap into. Once you have a downline, you can contact them (person by person) and ask them to host as well... (or at least open their friends to you so you can host their friends in your home). I started my business going where I knew people, by asking my closest friends that would support anything I do, and by asking friends I had that knew large amounts of people. It grew from there, one brick at a time.

Another tool I like to use for inviting is: "ask three to invite 50." This works REALLY well because all your marketing is done online. When it's online, people can tap in at will, when they choose. If their day is power packed, they may see the event at midnight when they are home, and you are asleep. The internet never sleeps.

Create a Facebook event about 2-3 weeks before the class; and pick people you have never asked before to go through their friends lists and invite 50 people each. Then market inside the event for the class you will hold at your home. If you have invested in the three you asked to invite, this yields very good results. It's because once you learn to oil, you don't want to go back. You don't swap chemical cleaning supplies for Thieves cleaner; and then return to the chemicals. So if you have invested in those you ask to invite, their fire will get people to come.

Hostess Gifts

For those that invited friends to the class, or that offered to host a class for you, I love to give gifts. This is a list of things I have given in the past, based on my Young Living income. It is not in any way comprehensive; and many people have had cooler ideas! I just like to keep it simple and duplicatable.

- Thieves Cleaner undiluted roll on "stain" sticks.
- Oils that aren't in the starter kit in Share It bottles or roll ons (my favorites are Tangerine, Grapefruit, Highest Potential, Northern Lights Black Spruce, Valor, Believe, and Release.) *You can get creative with these if you are artsy, and put a plant sprig in the bottle. I have slipped in organic lavender sprigs, pine needles with a bit of the branch, and even Frankincense and Myrrh resin with gold micah powder before. This one is NOT something I do regularly, just for close friends and family that are hosting.*
- The 101 cd or Toxin Free Life cd.
- *Fearless* and a *Fearless* calendar.
- A spray bottle of Thieves cleaner with a microfiber cloth.
- A Peppermint roll on (if they do not have their kit yet).
- A Young Living chapstick.
- Your *Gameplan—the mini.*
- A sample of Cool Azul pain cream.
- A sample of Thieves laundry soap.
- A sample of Thieves cough drops.
- A sachet of Mindwise.
- A sample of Pure Protein complete with a smoothie recipe.
- A glass water bottle and a vitality oil (like lemon).
- A wolfberry crisp bar, chocolate coated (I LOVE this in my baskets).
- A can of Zyng.
- A packet of NingXia.
- A tube of Nitro.
- A bar of Young Living soap.
- A sample of Copaiba Vanilla shampoo.

- A baggie with Wolfberry Granola.

- A sample of OrthoEase massage oil.

- A bathroom sampler with the tiny travel toothpaste and floss.

- A purple bag.

- A diffuser bracelet with a few drops of oil (I love citruses or the emotional oils like 3 Wise Men or Magnify Your Purpose).

Now I know you read that list and got all excited. Keep in mind, **your time matters**. Don't get so carried away with the time it takes you to make these things up that you aren't out there teaching. It can be as simple as getting a dollar store basket, putting some Wolfberry Crisp bars and NingXia packets on your ER order, and tossing it all in with a *Fearless* book and a piece of tissue paper; or it can be a complicated process that takes you ten hours a week to put together. I want you to keep this one sentence in mind... "everything I do has to be copied." If you're going to Hobby Lobby and buying pretty chalkboard mason jars and hand creating signs; you're going to scare your leaders away. The goal here is to say, "thank you"; not to have them look at the basket and think, "I might have done this as a business, but I can't put all this work in." The simpler the better.

Another thing to keep in mind is that I only make these for hostesses, and I give it to them in secret. If I do it publicly, I am scaring away leaders in that room that feel they cannot duplicate. You also have to decide what your budget can handle. Don't get in over your head with hostess gifts. You can do them as cheaply as three or four dollars if that is what your budget allows. When I first started, my budget was five dollars per hostess. I use these any time I am asking someone to tap into their friend circle for me, no matter what type of class I am teaching. It's an investment in them. When I was teaching 4-6 classes a month, I made about 8-10 little gifts. I like to put them in dollar store cellophane baggies with a piece of tissue paper instead of baskets, because there is less to space to fill.

What I *don't* do is make these up in advance and gift samples to people. I don't make up 20 Thieves Cleaner stain sticks and keep them in my bag. Why? Because it's expensive; and it's not duplicatable. You are not meeting them where they are. That falls under the category of "hi! My name is Sarah Harnisch! I am a Young Living Distributor! Please buy my starter kit!" I do get oils on people; but it's not through pre-made sampler kits. It's through what their needs are, and it's a tiny amount. keep it simple.

Pros & *Cons*
TO THIS STYLE OF TEACHING
DVD TEACHING: CLASS 4

This is a phenomenal way of sharing if you're truly too timid to read the script, sound dry reading a script, or get such severe anxiety that you don't communicate your love of oils effectively. This takes all the fear out of sharing. Simply play hostess, love on them, collect their info with the Contact Me Cards, get the oils in their nose, and have a laptop ready when the DVD ends,

You still need to do the footwork to get them to come. That requires relationship building, which is face to face contact. If that part of the business scares you, it will be tricky to build, because it's required in network marketing. Following up is easier with this method because you have had time with them in front of you.

I am a corporate VP executive and there are literally 500 people fighting for one position of CEO in my corporate job. When I think about what that looks like long term, it's daunting! I was headed for Gold, now I am barely maintaining Silver. I want the freedom and the ability to do great things for others and be present for my family by becoming Unstuck!

Chrissy Kelly Buechler

CHAPTER 25

Class 5: Oils on The Body: The Personal Loan; Informal Sharing

One of the downsides of this type of sharing is that it will take longer. I am always of the opinion that you should embrace your pace. If this is the way that gets you results; and you know you're not stopping until you get to Diamond; and you're not going to compare your rank or the speed of your results using this method, then go for it! Many a Diamond has built through informal sharing, building relationships, and meeting needs.

How do you do it? The same way that you invite to a 101 class. You meet people where they are. This woman was helping me pick out clothing at a Nordstrom's store for the Diamond gala last year. She'd had a rough day and was intimidated. I pulled out a Stress Away roll on and loved on her a bit. Within three minutes, she had three other store clerks wearing Stress Away, giggling, and sharing how much they loved the oil. I left with her card and contact information. I had built a relationship with her, because I started with her needs, not my kit.

We have already discussed in depth where this type of sharing takes place: in hallways, stores, your own home, on the sidewalk, with your garbage man or postal worker, or even with your kid's parent's friends. How do you spend your time? Start in that place. That's where you know people, even if you don't know them well.

You know that, right? You don't need to know someone well. I had never met the women in the Nordstrom store before; but I met a need. They were tired. They were ready to get off work. Meet the people you talk to in *their* place. Ask a leading question. For the photo above, my leading question was, "you look like you have had a long day!" They were all wearing Stress Away before I even finished checking out. It wasn't because I talked; it was because they talked. It wasn't because I knew them or had a history with *them*. It wasn't because I was outgoing. I simply listened to the need and was there for them. If you love to care for people, you will LOVE this job. It's all about making a difference in people's lives. And you get a front row seat to do it forever.

What about samples?

I'm not walking around with an entire chest of samples everywhere I go. I don't keep extra oils in the car because it gest too hot, and the heat will break them down. I usually just carry on me what I use for myself. I use Stress Away pretty much every day (I have five kids, and four of them are sons), so I had it in my bag. I'm not making up sampler packets. I'm listening to needs. If I have it on me, I share. If not, I go get it and loan it out. If I can't meet up with them again, I mail it, or I return to the store a day later. Making up hundreds of samples will cost you a lot of time and a lot of money. Just share your stock.

Getting Taken Advantage Of

One of the reasons I don't advocate for making up dozens of samples and carrying them around is because it's easy to get taken advantage of. I have lost count of the number of people that have told me they gave out hundreds of samples and never ranked up. It's because they were missing the art of the relationship. It was always about handing out what they had on hand, not offering what the actual need is. Samples usually end up in the bottom of a purse or a desk drawer, or in the trash. And that's a lot of work, time, and money on your end... gone.

What I do instead is meet the need. In the case of the Nordsrom lady, I offered an oil I knew I had in my bag so she could experience it. Usually it's a drop in their hand or on their wrist. It's not a pre-made sampler bottle that I had to order with a pretty handmade label and ten drops of an oil that I had to purchase. When you are offering something custom tailored to their need, I recommend to just do it a drop at a time out of your own bottles; or if they need it for the night, loan your bottle out and expect it back.

I met a woman at an event that had been sharing oils for 14 years and never hit the rank of Star. She had literally given out thousands and thousands of samples over that time. It yielded no blessing to her. Why? First, she wasn't giving them what they needed. Second, she didn't build a relationship with them, hear their story, or meet them in that place. Third, she never collected contact information and touched base a second time to see how it worked.

Those are the three critical ingredients to sharing in this way. You have to touch base after, or you just loaned something out or gave something away that you'll never see a return on. You are running a business; and you need to run it with integrity, even if your heart in the whole thing is to take care of people. It's an act of stewardship.

The Lord is not going to bless the work of your hands if you have poor stewardship. He has brought something amazing to you through Young Living; but it still needs to be well managed. Poor stewardship means spending time, money, and resources and expecting nothing back. Let me put it into more realistic terms. If you were to walk into someone's store, would you take something off a shelf and walk out with it? That's what you're doing when you hand out samples and don't collect contact information, or expect anything back. You're handing away part of your business. It's stealing from the bounty the Lord is giving you. Be smart about how you loan out your oils, and always, always expect something back. It's not cruel or mean, its wisdom. You are planting seeds. Water them and give them some sun and they will grow. Walk away and never touch base and what do you have? A seed and some dirt, not a big oak tree.

Does getting oils on people's bodies work? Absolutely. I have built most of my business by sharing the 101 and oiling people, and gaining many a rank through a drop in a hand. However, do it in a smart way, where you're not giving your business away. Go into it with the expectation that if you're not teaching, the process of them developing fire for oils may take a bit longer. I'd chase a sample with a purple bag and a class on cd or a textable class to get faster results. Getting their information is harder when it is your cold market instead of your warm market; but start with a Facebook friend request when you are standing in front of them, and see where it goes.

Compliance: Updated with New Young Living Regulations Enacted in 2019

Before I wrap this section up, let me just say a word or two about compliance. It is a good place to put this, because when you are meeting needs, you may end up with a lot of health questions.

You are not a drug store; and Young Living is not a drug company. It's a wellness company. With that said, if you offer oils to treat disease, you can get in a lot of trouble. You may be frustrated with the FDA and the regulations you encounter; but it's only there to protect us and to protect you. Making claims without having science to back them is a dangerous place that can cost you your business.

Let me give you a few words that will take the pressure off of you having to answer health questions. Start from this place, and it will take the fear out of sharing oils compliantly. "Gosh, I don't know about that. I have never dealt with that before. Why don't you take this home and see how you feel?"

If you paint yourself as an expert, a few things will happen... you'll chase off leaders. You'll get asked questions about everything at all hours of the day and night. You run the risk of losing your business, because it is illegal. I don't need to know the science of the RC in my diffuser. I just want RC in my diffuser. Start from that primal place and keep it simple. You'll save yourself a lot of drama down the road if you train your team the same way. You don't need to be the expert. That's what the scientists at Spanish Fork do at our Seed to Seal testing site. They are the ones with degrees in chemistry. Your job is to be a mouthpiece. To share. The rep at Starbucks doesn't know about the sourcing of the coffee beans. We don't expect them to! You're not the distillery! You're a mom, or a dad, or a wife or a passionate oiler. That is enough. Always share from that place. If they require more, say, "I don't know! That is completely new to me; but here's a place where you can start your own research." and offer them a guide to look it up. Then stand down and let them tackle their own wellness. You introduce, listen, oil them, and stand down. They do the rest.

My favorite guides for the Core 4 Premium Starter Kits

- The Essential Oils Pocket Reference (<u>discoverlsp.com</u>).
- Essential Oils Integrative Medical Guide (by Gary Young, <u>discover-lsp.com</u>).
- NingXia Wolfberry: Discovery of the Ultimate Superfood (by Gary Young, <u>discoverlsp.com</u>).
- Thieves: 350 Ways to Use the Thieves Product Line from Young Living (<u>discoverlsp.com</u>).
- My favorite Savvy training tools are on Royal Crown Diamond Erin Rodger's website, (<u>oilsupplystore.com</u>).

Outside of ref guides, what *can* you say? You can share your personal story. In fact, Young Living encourages it. If you think it's non-compliant, keep it to the in-person classroom, and out of the online realm. No one can take your story from you. Be a bit more careful if you're sharing other people's stories, especially online. Let me tell you what the FDA is looking for. They want to make sure you're not steering people away from medical care, and potentially endangering their life. "I used this oil for my blood pressure, and haven't been to the doctor in four years!" Those kinds of sentences will land you in trouble. If someone forgoes medical care because of your post and is injured, you are in a place of danger. That's #1 on their radar. Some of the buzz words they keyword search are: cancer, MRSA, ebola, depression, and anxiety.

The FDA is looking to see if you are diagnosing and prescribing. Don't do that! Instead, you can say "I've never had that before. Here's a reference guide. This is how you use it. This is where I'd start my research." If you open the guide, point to page 52, and send screenshots of how to "cure" disease, you've crossed the line. The FDA is looking to make sure you're not practicing without a license.

What are words you can say? "Occasional". "Mild". "Everyday". For example, "Occasional headaches." "Minor head tension." "Occasional runny nose." "Everyday stress." Those are things you would not need to see a doctor for.

You can say the word "support"; in that you are supporting your respiratory system. You can't say that you are preventing, treating, mitigating, or curing. If someone delayed critical medical care because of something you shared, would you want that responsibility on your shoulders? Always ask that question before you post. Slapping a disclaimer on it doesn't free you from trouble. Share your personal stories, encourage them to look it up and do their own research. Say that everyone's body is different; and your results may not be their results. That's how you keep yourself safe. If you're ever unsure of wording on a specific oil or product, go pull it off the Young Living website. That's a place that's been vetted, and the wording is more secure.

I do want to say here that the Lord has not called us to live in spirit of fear. Sharing nothing because you're afraid of the consequences is taking it too far in the other direction; and it's not going to lead to oils in every home in the world. Your personal story needs to be out there; so start from that place. Don't live in fear. Start with a beginning place of passion, train to research, train the lifestyle, and you can build a viable business. Train your distributors to stand on their own feet and take hold of their health. If you do that from the beginning, your entire way of sharing is completely different, and safe.

The Lord is not going to bless the work of your hands if you have poor stewardship. Your business needs to be well managed. You are stealing from the bounty the Lord has given you."

Pros & *Cons*
TO THIS STYLE OF TEACHING
OILS ON THE BODY: THE PERSONAL LOAN, INFORMAL SHARING: CLASS 5

They get their "wow" moment before they ever get a class. Many people will get a kit just after experience Peppermint! That can lead to impulse buying without the "why" behind oiling.

Essential Rewards can be trickier with a lack of education. Make sure you funnel them to the Core 4, even if they purchased the starter kit for one oil for one need.

I cannot wait till I can read it. I feel like I have been "stuck"
spinning my wheels for months now. I am doing the IPAs but not
seeing the results I want. I need a refresher for sure!

Cheri Hakese

CHAPTER 26

CLASS 6: ONLINE CLASSES: VIMEO, ZOOM, & YOUTUBE

Now we are going to switch gears and tackle a completely different type of class. Up until now, it all mostly relied on the 101 delivered in person; either on your couch or via a method like purple bags, textable 101's, DVD's, etc...

For online classes, the method of delivery is entirely different. Let's talk about the perks and the pitfalls of online sharing. This is a VERY powerful tool! It's likely the most powerful available to you today! I remember having a conversation with Royal Crown Diamond Teri Secrest, who had primarily built her business on horseback, delivering oils content on cassette tape. There is a high level of respect for the first Diamonds in the company, who have had to forge the way to make the words "essential oils" common household names. I am grateful when I think of how much easier it is now to share simply because of the internet. It has given our world a closeness that didn't exist even ten years ago.

You are living in an extraordinary time in global history to run a network marketing business. If delivery by horseback is your jam, go for it if it gets results! Many busy moms have been relying on social media; and have had dramatic results. There are many Diamonds in Young Living that hit rank before their 30th and 40th birthdays by sharing online in some way. How? I'll take you through it step by step. The biggest success stories are just in the power of the internet itself. What are its perks? Volume. I have 5,000 friends, and 19,000 followers on my Facebook page. I have 16,000 on Instagram and 65,000 on the Oil Ability with Sarah Facebook page. That's a lot of influence. Before Young Living, I still had hundreds of friends on my Facebook account. It's easier to put a post out there and have hundreds see it than to teach a hundred classes in your living room. Your advantage is the power of numbers. Your downfall is the screen between your faces, and being just another name on the internet (someone untouchable and not real). Relationship building is a trickier task.

You do have the power of time on your side. When you put something online, someone can view it and comment whenever it's convenient for them. They can watch your class at 2 in the morning, if that's when they are free. You can't always cater to every schedule in person. However, every schedule is compatible with online content, because it works with and for you. When I shoot a *Gameplan* roundtable as a Facebook Live, 4-thousand people may view it that night. The next morning, it may be up to 10 or 12-thousand as people around the world tune in; and early risers catch it before work.

I learned the power of social media right after I wrote *Gameplan*. It was a complete accident. I put the book to paper, had a friend upload it on Amazon; and I put four posts up on four different Facebook pages. We sold 45 hundred books from four posts. I was blown away. I told my husband I'd like to shoot a bootcamp off the 25 chapters in the book. I went on Facebook, started the first live video thinking that maybe 200 people would get on; and the numbers started climbing and climbing . I did not run a single ad. I didn't announce anything. Because one person was on, and they "liked" it, it popped up in their feed to all their friends; and the next thing I knew, 107-thousand people were on that first night. The largest "live" I had ever done was about 200 people. I was sitting there kicking kid's underwear under the couch, and turning the phone away asking someone to tell the kids to be quieter (with tens of thousands watching). I learned my lesson! I was better prepared the next time! I am completely convinced that *Gameplan* sold 1.5 million copies because of the power of social media, not because of a single thing that I did.

You can use it to your advantage, too.

1 in 9 people on the earth are on social media. If Facebook were a country, it would be the third largest on the planet. 1 in 8 U.S. couples met online. My own sister met her husband on christianmingle.com!

There is something to be said for the power of the web. If you ignore that power, even for the marketing of your own classes, you are missing something large.

For the scope of this section, I am not talking about sharing on social media. That's a completely different category of class that I will hit on next. Let's start with some simple online classes on Vimeo, Zoom, and YouTube. Then I will train you to use social media to drive to those classes.

Vimeo

This was a tool first introduced to me by Royal Crown Diamond Joanna Malone, a precious friend that I met the first year I started my business. She picked me up off the ground when I didn't have a single friend. Joanna is *really* media savvy. If you don't have a strength, study someone who does. Joanna is definitely a pro, and has about a thousand gifts I don't have. Talking to Joanna is like talking to my teenagers at home. She has likely already experimented with sixteen other media formats and she's been successful with them, as I ask her to show me how to log into Instagram. I am always impressed when I have a conversation with her. As a matter of fact, by the time I print this book, I am pretty confident she'll text "Vimeo?? *Really* Sarah?? Are you going to start training on MySpace and AOL next??"

Well, in the spirit of Joanna, let's move on.

What does my Vimeo class look like?

I set up a Facebook event. I invite people and market the class. When it's the morning of, I get really excited about the class and show off some giveaways. They can be very simple things, like a roll on or a Thieves cough drop. You cannot gift more than $25 to someone who is not signed to your team, according to Policies and Procedures, so watch your gift sizes and make sure you keep it legal.

When it's time, I like to give a little countdown that we are about to start. I have all my videos loaded and ready to go—and all the links saved in a Word document so I can just copy and paste. I also write a little intro to each video (a sentence or two) to tease it. For example, for the paragraph in the 101 on where oils came from, I'd write, "think oils are just a fad? You will not BELIEVE the first time they were used!" For purity, my lead in paragraph might be "I used to buy all my oils at the grocery store, until I learned more about what's in grocery store oils. This video will blow your mind!"

I have all my write ups and video links ready to go before the class starts. Why? Because I want to spend my time interacting, not trying to come up with witty lead ins for the videos. The neat thing is that you only need to do the footwork once. Save it all and use it again and again—the lead ins, the videos—all of it. You'll have a difference audience every time.

When it's go time, I paste the first lead in right in the Facebook event, with the link to the class. Then I wait two or three minutes longer than the video takes to play, interact with the posts underneath (you always want to encourage them to post), and post the next lead in and video. At the end I post all the winners.

The kick with this kind of a class is that you have to get really good at online interaction. When people are not in front of you, it's easier to say no. You can't pick up on body language. Therefore, you really need to pay attention to what is going on in your class.

For example, if someone likes a video, I write them right away after class and ask them what they like, and see if they are interested in more information about oils. I may say something like, "thank you for coming to the class! I saw that you liked the post about purity. Tell me if you have oiled before!" Off you go. You just asked a leading question. It's now time to work on building the relationship.

I do the same thing if they comment on a video. During the class, I make sure I am replying to every single comment. The ones that are really interested usually get an Instant Message from me after the class is over.

In some ways, it's more work than an in-person class, because I can be on the computer for an hour or two after an online class building relationships, and getting names and contact information to mail samples or purple bags. Your follow up has to be knockout good in online classes, because you don't have them in front of you to build the relationship.

Here are a couple of tips to keep in mind with Vimeo: the information is there forever. Make sure everything you are saying is compliant, the videos can be seen by the FDA, and they can be shared, unless you password protect them. Vimeo is easier than doing a Facebook Live if you are easily distracted, because you're not responding in-person to the long stream of comments. If you're constantly pausing to answer questions and respond to comments, it can be really distracting for both you and the viewer, and can cause you to go off on rabbit trails. On the downside, if the videos are pre-recorded, it can be harder to tell when people are finished watching them. You control a Facebook Live, so you know when everyone is done. With Vimeo classes, some people can "fall behind" as you're posting the next link.

When the class is over, for those that could not watch it live, I like to put all the links at the top of the page in one pinned post (in order). Then, if people are commenting on them in the Facebook event, it's still bumping older posts to the top; but everyone can find all the links because they are in order, and pinned to the top of the page.

Last but not least, know your out. Know what your last sentence will be to get out of the class. Have it written out and ready to go. End by smiling and holding the camera for a few seconds after your last word. You have GOT this! You are a diamond RISING!

YouTube

YouTube classes are almost identical to Vimeo, except that you can't password protect them. They are out in the public for the world to see. What you can do is create a channel that people can subscribe to and build a following that way. Because of the public nature of YouTube, I have found you'll pick up a lot of people who already have Young Living accounts with other teams. They are looking for good educational material; and you'll be training them instead of pouring into new faces. That's an advantage of Vimeo over YouTube.

One efficient way to use YouTube is basically as a hosting site. Record a class, upload it to YouTube (it's free), and then save the links, and time release them in a Facebook event, just as you would with Vimeo. That gives you the freedom to control your audience and to respond to them in a way that's simpler than their YouTube comments under the video. You can run it exactly like your Vimeo classes, for free and you can shoot the video in one sitting, rather than in small pieces, if you choose. However, small videos that are time released seem to yield better audience interaction.

A Bit More on Video Length

The top ten most popular videos on YouTube on any given day average somewhere between 42 seconds and nine minutes. You can get away with a bit more because people are expecting longer than a nine-minute class. However, I wouldn't have any individual video go longer than five minutes. The average video length, overall is four minutes, 20 seconds. I find that interesting, because there are always exceptions, like the 30-minute-long Kony 2012 video that surprised us all by getting millions of views. There's also the fact that people are getting more accustomed to live-streaming entire shows, and even movies online. Netflix is booming online; and so is Hulu. You can even watch movies via Amazon now. This is something that's grown tremendously. When I first started uploading videos five years ago, Snapchat was in its heyday, and 8-second "Vines" were all the hype. I think our attention span has lengthened somewhat!

When you first sign up with YouTube, they'll limit your account to videos under 15 minutes; but if you follow the 5-minute rule and shoot several videos, it's still not a problem as a new user to get an entire 101 class uploaded. That limit is only in place until your account is verified. Once verified, you still can't post any video that exceeds 20GB (but that would be over an hour long).

Viewers favor short videos with lots of energy and important stuff at the get-go. We'll talk more about that in the chapter on Facebook Live classes. Your audience will start to disappear over the length of your video, but that's normal. For a video of 4-5 minutes, fewer than 60 percent of your viewers will still be with you at the end. 75 percent will stick around for a 1-2 minute video. That means you don't want to do your call to action at the end. Do it at the beginning. I actually open my online 101 classes with my powerful personal story. Then in that first video, give a quick teaser of the Premium Starter Kit and how to snag it. I hit it again at the end during the Bold Close; but I want to make sure no one slips through the cracks by becoming part of the 40-percent that likely don't stick around until the end.

Let's run through the steps of an efficient YouTube class again...

1. Record your class into bite size chunks and upload each section to YouTube. Keep each section under five minutes each.

2. Set up a channel so people can find those videos when you're not hosting a class.

3. Open a Facebook event and invite into it using the relationship training earlier in this book.

4. Market the class inside the Facebook event.

5. The night of the class, count down the time until you start. Build energy in the event. Show off any giveaways you have. Ask where people are from and what they want to learn (leading questions).

6. When it's time, begin posting your YouTube videos. Simply post each link with a leading sentence. Just like with Vimeo, it's easy to break the 101 into paragraphs and record those. You only have to "teach" (record) the class one time; and you can use it over and over again. If you get into the 20-30 minute long category per video, even with your personal story, you will see a huge dropoff in the number of people that stay for the whole class.

7. As you post each video, engage. Respond to their questions. Laugh with them. Like their comments. Have fun with it. This is the easy part of the class.

8. Afterward, make sure you post a link where they can sign up immediately. Offer to coach them through the process if they get stuck (I like to use Facebook video chat in an instant message for this). Offer a photo of the education bundle gifted to new sign ups at the start of class, so they see it right at the get-go.

9. This is when all the legwork starts. Make a list of all the people who liked or commented on each post. Instant message them and ask the following questions:

   • "What oil did you most want to learn about, and why?"

   • "What are your top three health struggles?"

   • "What did you like best about the class?"

   • "I saw that you "liked/commented" on XYZ post. What struck you about it?"

   • "May I invite you to an oils/NingXia/Thieves/Savvy class later this month?"

   • "For tonight only, I'm offering an education bundle with your starter kit. I believe this kit is the answer to what you've been looking for. I'm going to send you a link to snag it; and if you run into any trouble, I'm right here to answer your questions." Always make the assumption that they will get the kit.

- "These are the free ER promos for the month. If you're close to any of these benchmarks...190, 250, 300pv, toss a toothpaste or a Thieves cleaner bottle in your cart, so you get all the freebies."

- "Thank you for coming to the class! Oils were one of the best health decisions of my life. I'm honored to join you on this journey. This is my personal cell number. Please feel free to call or text me. I know this was an online class, but our team loves giving educational training and support. You're welcome to touch base any time."

Most of the legwork is in the follow up after that class is over. Systematically check in with each person that attended and make sure their questions are answered. Voila! That's a successful YouTube class via Facebook.

Zoom

Now let's talk about the last online class type for this book: Zoom. There are many other formats similar to Zoom; but I picked it because it is most commonly used. Once you get the hang of a new app or program, most of the online classes will follow the similar format (either time released or live videos). There are a couple of online formats that absolutely don't work in the context of a 101 class: Snapchat, because of its very short videos that disappear quickly, or Twitter, which limits each post to 140 characters. They're just not conducive to the length of time that you need to get the message across.

Zoom, however, is a fantastic online vehicle to get your viewer to the message of oils. You will need to set up a Zoom account (don't worry, Zoom doesn't start charging until you exceed 15 people). The basic package costs nothing. The second package is $15/month, and that gives you space for 100 people, which would be an unusually large 101 class. For all the legwork you have to do after, it's not a bad idea to stay away from a massive online class, because people will get lost in the sauce and slip out unnoticed. That's a lot of relationship building for nothing.

In the Zoom format, everything is live. You'll set up a class, and it will email the link to each participant. A few minutes ahead of time, you'll log into zoom.us, and make sure your webcam is on. Pay mind to the fact that Zoom can't be done on a cell phone, only a laptop or computer. Make sure your volume is up, and then you're off and running. Just like with any video, it's really important that you have good lighting. This is a really simple fix. You'd laugh if you saw my setup; but I talk to tens of thousands each week with a $7 Walmart desk lamp that has a piece of paper taped over it to make a soft, white light. I pride myself in finding the cheapest possible method to look good. Remember, avoid business debt, save your marriage. Get that light right in your face, turn on any overhead or ambient lights in the room, wait for everyone to join the Zoom, and you're good to go. There's also a record option on Zoom that will allow you to send a link after the class to everyone. This is nice if a couple people miss the class, or if someone wants to watch it again later.

How do you teach it? Do the same thing you'd do if you were in an actual living room. Share your story, read the 101, and give the bold close. Because people's faces are on the screen in a zoom call, they are less likely to hop off. There is a chat option; so I usually ask everyone to mute their microphones at the beginning to avoid barking dogs and screaming kids during the class. I also keep the chat window open in case anyone has questions while I'm speaking.

The class is interactive and fun. You'll get a lot of engagement on your giveaways, because it's as if everyone is sitting in a room together, even though you may be all over the world. Just as with all the classes we've already trained on, make sure your follow up is outstanding after the class. I like to connect with everyone on Facebook Instant Messenger or Instagram, rather than an email (which can be a much slower process). Ask them to share their Instagram handle (i.e. @sarahharnisch) in the chat window, before the end of the Zoom, so you can give them a "free textable class". I love using those textable classes as leverage to have a second conversation with classgoers. It opens the door in a non-awkward way. Make sure your close is powerful! Provide the signup link in the chat window, just like in a conventional class, and you're ready to rock.

That wraps up our online formats. Now we're going to dig even deeper with social media classes. Outside of the 101 in-person class, this is the most powerful way of sharing that I've seen. Even if you're not tech savvy, you won't want to skip the next chapter.

The advantage of building online is the power of numbers. The downfall is the screen between your faces.

Pros & *Cons*
TO THIS STYLE OF TEACHING
ONLINE CLASSES: VIMEO, ZOOM, YOUTUBE: CLASS 6

Shoot it once, let it go. Unlike with Facebook classes where you have to go live again and again, you record this bad boy one time and use the link again and again and again. Time saver.

It is impersonal, and sometimes people do not watch, especially if your videos are long. Make sure you build the relationship and lead them into the class with purpose. Then have strong follow up with a funnel.

Sarah is an amazing speaker and educator! She is unlimited.

Barbara Fiske Weiland

CHAPTER 27

Class 7: Social Media Classes; Facebook and Instagram

Featuring Diamond Christie Rose

Facebook is my jam; so that's where I'm going to start this chapter. Then we'll move into Instagram; and I'll have one of the gifted Diamonds that built in that platform step in and do some intimate training with you. Her name is Christie Rose. We'll lay it out in a way that's so simple to understand, that even if you struggle with social media and all the changing technology, you'll still have a massive leg up in using Instagram for your business.

Facebook Lives

Facebook could be its own country. No seriously!!! The size of it is ridiculous! If you ignore appealing to that market, you're missing something critical. If you're anti-Facebook, or a person who takes "breaks" from social media; let me make a strong case for why that's not a good idea.

You wouldn't take a "break" from the building where you work, would you? You wouldn't tell your boss that you need some space, and you'll be working from home. In network marketing, your network is your place of work. By going off social media, you've shut off your voice. Instead, turn off notifications, or opt to only run your business a couple of hours a day; and then make the rest of the day a phone-free zone...but I wouldn't disappear. You lose the ability to connect with your team; and more importantly, to build relationships and be seen as an oiler in a public space.

Let me throw a few statistics at you, if I still haven't convinced you that this is a worthwhile place to spend a little time. A Zephoria study from 2019 listed the top 20 Valuable Facebook Statistics. I'm not going to list all 20, but here's a snapshot of the power of the world's largest social network.

Facebook by the Numbers

- Facebook has 37,773 employees.

- Worldwide, there are 2.38 billion active users. That's an 8 percent increase from 2018. China has 1.34 billion people, and India 1.2 billion. This means if Facebook were a country, it would be the largest on the globe.

- 1.65 billion people log in daily.

- "Like" and "Share" buttons are viewed across 10 million websites daily.

- 25-to-34-year-olds represent 1 in 3 users. It's the most common demographic. That younger demographic is good for your business.

- 5 new profiles are created every second.

- The highest traffic occurs from 1-3pm daily; though if you're shooting classes, the best time to be on is between 7 and 9pm.

- 300 million photos are uploaded daily.

- The average time spent per Facebook visit is 20 minutes, which means you have a short time period to make your impression. Use it wisely with relevant, interesting, and unique posts.

- Every 60 seconds on Facebook, 510-thousand comments are posted, 293-thousand statuses are updated, and 136-thousand photos are uploaded.

- 4.75 billion pieces of content are shared daily.

- 16 million business pages have been created since 2013, which is a 100 percent increase. Facebook marketing has transformed how business is conducted.

Source: https://zephoria.com/top-15-valuable-facebook-statistics/

What do these numbers mean? Well, if you're looking for humans, this isn't a bad place to take a peek. Even if your close friends are not interested in oils, friends of your friends might be. When they like your post, their friends can see it. You have massive marketing and relationship building ability on Facebook.

Good lighting and a smile can dramatically multiply the power of a Facebook Live.

One of the most powerful vehicles on Facebook is the Facebook Live. I use it several times a week to train my own team, run with my hustle team, teach aromatherapy classes to them monthly, and lead *Gameplan* roundtables every Tuesday to tens of thousands of people. We've already mentioned Facebook events, which allows you to add people to a time-released class; but you can also "Go Live" on your personal page, business page, or a page you've created for product education. This reaches a lot of people in a short period of time.

To engage with your audience, you want to connect emotionally right out of the gate, or you'll lose them. On Facebook, most stick around for only 20 to 90 seconds. Though, if you're doing a class, the stats are more like 20 to 30 minutes, if you keep the class moving swiftly. A person will decide if they're going to watch you within 15 to 20 seconds of tuning in. Don't waste any time. Don't wait for people "to get on and watch." Just start the video. The majority of your audience will be watching after the fact; and if they have to sit there for two minutes waiting for you to start, you've lost them. Speak as if they're already in the room. They can go back and replay.

If you are shooting a video on your personal page because you want to gain a large audience, typically nine percent of your entire reach is able to view. If you have 300 friends, about 20-30 people will actually "see" the video online. If they like it, nine percent of their friends will see it. If they leave positive comments, and hit the like or love button, Facebook will boost the viewership. I can prove this is the case. At the Diamond retreat in Spain this year, I shot a 15-minute interview with Lauren Walker, who is in charge of sourcing all of Young Living's oils. I asked her what set us apart; what made Young Living different from every other oils company in the world. She explained. Then I asked her to dumb down the language (more than just "Seed to Seal"). It ended up being the most powerful interview I've ever recorded. Within a couple of days, Facebook had boosted the views because of all the positive comments. On a page of 60-thousand, I shouldn't have had more than 5-thousand views. That's not how the Facebook algorithms work. They favor: "likes", "loves", and positive comments. After the video was shared 1,200 times, 121-thousand people engaged! A Young Living video went completely viral on Facebook. (You can find this interview at Oil Ability with Sarah on Facebook under "videos", or on the oilabilityteam.com website). Let's keep it going and get it to 1 million views!

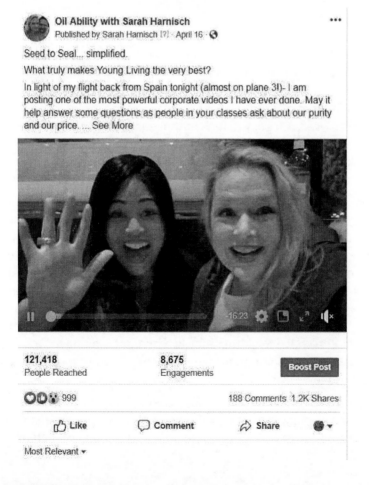

Why are videos more successful than posts? They're more "human." The movement more closely represents life than a GIF, photo, or emoji. One tech writer said, "when it comes to content, Facebook Live is the king of kings, the best player on the field, and the colossus of clout." Your face on that video gives off emotional cues that viewers can identify with and understand.

With all that said, and now that I've got your attention, let me give you a super simple explanation of how to get every drop of goodness from a Facebook Live.

How to Pull Off A Knockout Good Facebook Live Class:

1. Tap "Post".

2. Tap Go "Live".

3. Write a brief description. Less is more. Keep your words tight and powerful.

4. Tap to switch between your phone's front and back camera lenses.

5. Again, PLEASE make sure you have good lighting on your face, and open with a smile.

6. Don't sit too far away. This is intimate. If you were having a conversation with someone, would you be 10 feet from them? No. I like my lives VERY close (about 12 to 18 inches), because I want to be in your circle. If you don't believe me, shoot a video 10 feet back with poor lighting and no smile; and try one again about 18 inches away, smiling, in full light. It's a night and day difference, and I promise you, it will help build trust with your audience. You're not afraid of them. You're close.

7. Tap "Go Live" to start a 3-second countdown to broadcast.

8. You have 10-15 seconds to grab their attention. Write your open and close on a little piece of paper and have it beside you, so you always know how you're going to open your Live and how you're going to close it.

9. I also like to bullet point my notes. It may be 10 words, but I have a good idea where I'm going and what I'm training on. In radio terms, this will help you stick to a tighter clock.

10. If you're teaching a 101, give a quick tease of the kit, start sharing your personal story within the first minute, read the script,

end with the close, and occasionally interact with the people that get on and comment.

11. Don't obnoxiously over-respond to comments. What do I mean by that? The other people in your class will get irritated and leave if you pause for each response, squint, or continuosly look at the screen to try to read the words. You get the point. If you can respond without stopping the flow of the class, go for it. Have fun during contests. However, be aware of the flow of your class, keep it on point, and be respectful of people's time.

12. Watch the length of your class. You obviously don't need to keep it to 5 minutes for a full 101; but a Live really shouldn't go much over 30 or 45 minutes, even if it's a class people are expecting. Statistics show people will watch these while they are doing other things, so keeping it shorter will yield better results for you. Even my *Gameplan* roundtables rarely go over 25 minutes weekly. I want you to stick around; and I want to provide powerful concise content.

13. As you're ending, peek at your "out", the line you wanted to end on. Read it off, make eye contact and smile. Wait about 5 seconds to hit "finish", or it will cut your words in the video off at the end due to a time delay in what you say and when they hear it.

14. Hit "Post", and boom—it's up forever, unless you choose to take it down. You can go back in and respond to questions by typing out responses to the comments. It's a great way to interact.

Know your out before you start.

As with any Facebook Live, because this is an online class instead of an in-person class, the hardest work is done after the class. Go back through the Live and make note of every comment. Make note of all the people that liked the overall video, and start Instant Messaging them, one by one, using the question list I gave you in the last chapter.

When it comes to Facebook posts, my best advice is to avoid overposting on oils. Keep your ratios one oils post to four other posts. Create posts on your family, posts on what you're doing, emotional posts about how you feel and why you feel that way. Take people with you your life. Don't make every single thing you post be about a of oil, or you're going to lose friends fast. Even in this format, people want to feel like you're always selling them something.

Also, don't post things that are political, negative, or divisive. If I can shoot straight with you for a moment, and create a safe zone around this one paragraph in *Unstuck*, I'd like to share openly. I have some pretty intense views on vaccination. I opened this book with the story of my autistic son. My husband I believe Gabe is autistic because of his vaccines, which he had a severe reaction to. He was speaking in 10-word sentences before his 18-month-old vaccinations. He spiked a fever within hours after the shots, and stopped talking until he was 7 years old. He started hitting his head on walls, and had to wear a helmet for his own protection. We had 27 people working with him when he was in high school after four mental health diagnoses. We have no family history of serious mental health issues; and none of my kids have a single diagnosis. It has been a nightmare for my husband and me. Nonetheless, I deeply believe that everyone should have a choice as to what goes in their body. Despite our road and our story, I don't post much of that online. Why? It interferes with the burden the Lord has laid on my heart. My mission is to raise as many Diamonds as I can before I die. My mission is to spread hope into dark places where there is little hope. My mission is to free people so they can pursue what they were called and created to do. If I post my thoughts on vaccines, or anything else of that nature, it makes my page a war zone. Then I have lost my voice to speak into others. By sharing the few sentences above, I likely have already lost some of you; but I share it to train you and to protect you. Your Facebook page does not belong to you when you are in network marketing.

You are building a business. So whether you like it or not, your personal page is going to be watched, both intentionally and unintentionally. You are a spokesperson every single day for Young Living. It doesn't mean that everything you put up is oils related; but it does mean people are watching your tone and your voice. They are looking for negativity. Are you someone they want to follow? Do they want you in their circle? Choose wisely how you use that voice, especially if you want an audience that will listen.

I've given you the best tips I have for reaching that massive audience on Facebook. Now let's switch gears. I'm going to talk about something I know nothing about. It's ok! When I don't know anything about it, I research, or I ask someone who does know something about it. In this case, you're going to get Diamond, Christie Rose, who signed 100 people in 100 days on Instagram. In fact, she personally enrolled 250 people

. That's nuts! Many people go a lifetime in
.ve that many personally enrolled. There are
or 40 personally enrolled for all time.

.iree years to learn Instagram. Even now, I only have
. a high Instagram user. You'll laugh at me, but I made
.n forgot how to use it for about two years. I logged in
ag.   a year ago, and had over 15-thousand followers. Oops! I
guess   ime to start providing valuable content! Let's take a look at
the format that may very well be the next Facebook. Instagram is already
boasting 77 million users in the United States alone. One in every four
Americans has an account.

Instagram Instruction

I'm going to start by showing you one of my favorite faces in Young Living, Miss Christie, whose smile and heart light up an entire room. Don't
let her gentleness fool you though! She's tenacious with her business
and hit Diamond in record time.

Let's jump right in. It's Instagram 101.

How to Effectively Share on Instagram:

1. Post 1-3 times daily on both your personal Instagram page and
    an oils Instagram page that you create.

2. Keep your personal Instagram mostly personal, and only occa-
    sionally share about oils.

3. Give tons of tips on your oily Instagram page.

4. Keep your pages looking very uniform. Pick a theme and stick with it. For instance, if it's Clean Living, post on green topics. Christie really likes white backgrounds, so her images follow that theme.

5. Every day, Christie would comment or like 100+ profiles, and would message them immediately when they followed her.

6. She says to keep conversations really personal and ask them lots of questions.

7. If they follow your oily page, ask them if they've ever used essential oils.

8. Host daily online classes and invite people constantly.

9. Send out samples weekly to people who are really interested. Use the samples as an excuse for a phone call.

10. Occasionally, offer incentives to join the team and share them with every person you've connected with so far. It helps people on the edge to join.

11. Add your Instagram friends on Facebook to get to know them on a personal level.

12. Eventually, you will get to the point where they will chat with you on the phone. It seems like a big jump; but not if you're having regular conversations, not seeming creepy, and not being too pushy with oils. Ask a lot of questions and keep the conversation on their needs. Remember, you help solve problems!)

13. Utilize Instagram to educate your team. Share often about the business opportunity.

What does it all come down to? Building relationships. What starts off as a simple "like" by scrolling through random pages, becomes a conversation. What starts as a "follow" becomes a friendship. It branches to Instagram messages, then to Facebook, to some samples, and a phone call. The system works. 250 sign ups in a year is unbelievable! Don't think that if you have an issue with face to face contact though, that you'll rock this method. You won't avoid the relationship by building on Instagram. It starts a little differently through clicking in an app, but the outcome is the same. There's a human being that needs their questions answered, their problems solved, and another real human at the end. Network marketing is the art of the relationship, no matter which way you build.

Christie's Warnings When Building on Instagram:

1. Don't send samples to people that you don't get to know well enough first.

2. Charging people a few dollars for shipping will wean out those who aren't really serious.

3. Posting too much about oils on your personal page will decrease your friend count. The days Christie posted too much she lost a LOT of followers.

4. Not following up well will cost you distributors and leaders. Follow up is the KEY to consistently enrolling. You may not be bold in person, but you need to be bold behind the screen if you want this method to work. (Remember...7 to 15 contacts, even with Instagram!)

There you have it! If you want an even more in-depth training, Christi has put together a phenomenal 10-day Instagram online video class at: http://theoilysquad.com/instagram-101/.

To end this chapter with a punch, I pirated three of her Instagram posts to show you what a powerhouse looks like. The key word when using this type of class is "engage". Engage your audience. You want to learn about them. That's what leads to a kit sale. Post about your life to build trust, but ask leading questions to grow your team. If you get off track, and it's all about you, or if you're too fearful to talk to total strangers, this will be a very slow way to build. This is because you're not doing the activities that lead to a rank up using Instagram.

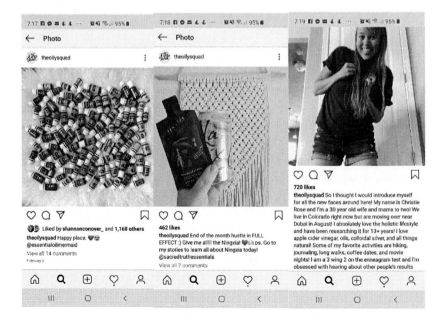

Pros & *Cons*

TO THIS STYLE OF TEACHING

SOCIAL MEDIA CLASSES: FACEBOOK AND INSTAGRAM: CLASS 7

There are larger audiences and friend circles online. It's simpler for you to set up and tear down. You can literally teach these in your p.j.'s, because no one knows what you're doing on the other end of your cell phone. (This is the place I don't tell you how many times I've anchored news to millions of people in pajamas–even in Chicago!) This teaching style is a great option for busy moms. Pop a movie in for your kids, step into the next room and have at it with your social media platforms. Wrap up, read your kids a story and put them to bed, without leaving the house.

Follow up is HARD. We tend to walk into these so excited that we don't have to see people face to face, forgetting that the relationship building still has to be done for online classes. For longevity, IM them right away, plug them into the Core 4, and meet their needs. A lot of work is done on your cell phone and computer after these types of classes are over.

What starts as a 'follow' becomes a friendship.

Sarah does a great job of educating in easy to follow terms!
Deborah Rose Yeager

CHAPTER 28

CLASS 8:
LUNCH & LEARN, SIP & SNIFF,
SIMPLE SWAP, DITCH & SWITCH

Are you tuckered out yet with the wide variety and intense creativity of Young Living business builders? I am a simple Joe. I grab a script, I sit on a couch, and I read it. I'm always blown away by the various ways people have found to communicate the need of one of the four PSK's to unaware bystanders. Let's talk in this chapter about interactive classes: kinesthetic learning and active participation. Here we go!

With all of these class types, there's some extra prep work involved. It's not as simple as a script, a kit, and a human; but if you keep the focus on the four Starter Kits, it can still be very effective. Keep the class as simple and as cheap as possible; and you won't drive away business builders. Let's look at these one at a time.

Lunch and learn: This is a 101 class that's given over a corporate lunch break. Sometimes it's within your own office; and sometimes you're a speaker that's invited by a company to teach health and wellness to their employees. I've done both. Because the class is often rushed (a lot of the time I'm given a 30 or 60 minute time limit), I don't have a lot of time to share my personal story; so I keep it to 10 minutes or less, and rely on a quick make and take to drop a wow moment in the room. Most often I go to the dollar store and grab spray bottles and have them all make a $1 bottle of Thieves cleaner to take home. They're challenged with wiping down their kitchen counters and texting me a photo. That gives me an opportunity to funnel to the starter kit, and have a second conversation. Many times, the companies will not allow sales on the property; so I'm not allowed to take purple bags unless they contain only the cd and *Fearless,* and no instructions on how to order the kit.

Using the Contact Me cards from the Diamond Rising deck will really save you in a class like this and make it worth your time, because there won't be sales on the property—but there for sure will be sales when you get home with all phone numbers on your cards!

Sip and Sniff: This class carries the same type of premise, but it also incorporates the element of NingXia. Attendees get a mini 101 class (I usually focus on purity and share my story); and then they also get a few paragraphs of the NingXia script. They sniff the oils and get a 1-ounce serving of NingXia. Because of the cost of the NingXia, many hosts will charge $3 to $5 for the class. Sometimes they let them make one roll-on of an oil in the kit, and then take a shot of NingXia before the class is over. I use the 101 script and the NingXia script to teach the class. It's different than a straight 101 because of the interactive nature of drinking NingXia and making a roll on. You can also have a little fun with it by adding some of the starter kit Vitality oils to the NingXia and making your own concoctions. (One of my favorites is Citrus Fresh and Lemon (2 drops each per shot). If you like something a little spicy, a drop of Thieves and a drop of lemon is also fun!) Many leaders have taught this class a lot like a Speed Oiling class, with multiple stations around the room, and a single oil or product from the starter kit at each station. If you have many people that are able to speak, that can work quite well. If it's only you, you may need to rely on little cards at each table that tell them what's there. Then have them do a "scavenger hunt", where they pull a fact off the card, jot it down, and return to you at the end with notes on each station. Usually this is a timed event with five minutes or less at each station.

Simple Swap (*Fearless* Class)/Ditch and Switch: This has been taught in many different ways, by many different teams effectively. It may be an oils or a Thieves class. All three titles allude to the same type of class (a class where you're training that the products in their home are dangerous and need to be swapped with pure Young Living products). I like to use *Fearless* as my Simple Swap class. I've also included that entire class script in the Appendix of this book. It's a good tool because it doesn't just train the starter kit, it trains the entire oils lifestyle and gives the "why" behind oiling. *Fearless* encourages them to go home, pick three cabinets, pull bottles out, and check the labels. If they don't know what a chemical is, type the words "dangers of" in front of it in Google to take a closer look at the products they're using in their home. *Fearless* takes them room by room; from their kitchen to their living room, from their cleaning closet to their laundry room, and bathroom. It shows them the most common places where poison may be hiding. There are also *Fearless* Powerpoint and media elements to make you look good. I end this class making a $1 bottle of Thieves cleaner, and handing out the 30-day *Fearless* challenge calendar, which is free as a printable on my website. If they screenshot their 30-day calendar and send it to me via text (another way to get ahold of people in the class if they are on a business site that doesn't allow sales), then I will gift them $25 off their first Essential Rewards order. This is a great class for people that aren't totally warmed up to the idea of oils. You can usually get their attention if you show them the science that the products they're using are dangerous to their kids. A great tool I love to use in these classes is the Scavenger Hunt video, where my kids run through our home and show what a Clean Living house looks like, after it's been swapped with Young Living products. Check that out here: oilabilityteam.com

Beauty School: For this class, I'd caution you not to do the traditional Young Living Beauty School with cream masques, Renewal Serum, and Sheerlume brightening cream. Instead, focus on the Savvy makeup line. You can demo the ART Gentle Cleanser to help them wash their face before application, and the ART light moisturizer to lay down on their face before they apply the makeup. For dry skin, offer both of those items as an "add on" to the Savvy kit for Essential Rewards. Once their face is clean and the moisturizer is on, put all your attention to makeup, do a makeup demo, and follow the Savvy script in the back of this book. You always want to lead to one of the four starter kits; so doing a Beauty School that features spa products that aren't in the kit would not lead to longevity on your team. Start with makeup.

The nice thing with each of these classes is that you already have the words to say. To keep it duplicatable, use the scripts in *Unstuck*, and keep the cost for supplies at $1 or $2 per person. I usually don't charge because you'll dramatically cut the attendance numbers. In addition, you'll lose your future business builders if you start going all crazy with the cost (like having them recreate the entire starter kit in roll-ons with expensive sticker labels and pretty chalkboard stations, with hand-held mirrors for the Beauty School). Watch your budget. That's how you ignite leaders. The more complicated you become, you may as well not teach. You'll burn yourself out, and the results will feel like you're swimming against the current with your business.

I tend to give the lecture part of each of these classes before we do the tiny make and take, because once they start, they're not paying much attention to you. The room gets noisy, and there's no point in giving a lecture if no one is listening. Share your story, read the script, give the bold close, have the stations set up after to make cool oily things; and then funnel them to a laptop to sign up if you're in a location that allows it. If not, at the very least, bring your contact form on a clipboard so you walk out with leads. That's how to have a successful interactive class.

If you make this complicated, you'll burn yourself and will feel like you're swimming against the current of your business.

Pros & Cons
TO THIS STYLE OF TEACHING
LUNCH AND LEARN, SIP AND SNIFF, SIMPLE SWAP, DITCH AND SWITCH: CLASS 8

These classes are FUN. They draw people in that don't like boring lectures. They may bring people in that have no interest in oils simply for the sake of getting together.

Watch your cost for the events and make sure what you're doing is duplicatable. Also, because the crowd you're drawing may not necessarily have a lot of background knowledge in clean living (but came for the diffuser bracelet), you may need to do more product education and lifestyle training with this fun bunch. Make sure your connecting time with them is regular and solid as a rock.

I don't have strong enough words to say how much value Sarah has provided free of charge to the entire Young Living organization! Her generosity is unsurpassed.

Tricia Deini Lopez

CHAPTER 29

CLASS 9: SPEED OILING

This class is quite different from anything else I've trained on so far. In the last set of five classes, the attendees are relatively stationary, then move at the end to do a simple make-and-take. For this class, there is movement during the entire lecture. It's set up like speed dating. The emphasis isn't on one person standing in a silent room teaching; it's on exploring.

A station is set up for each component of the starter kit: the two NingXia sachets, the packet of Thieves cleaner, the 12 bottles of oil, each at their own stations, and the Thieves hand sanitizer. At each spot, you can either place a card with a bit of the lecture on it, or you can have a leader stand there and teach for 2-3 minutes on the topic at the table. How do you pull that off? Use the paragraph on Lavender from the 101 lecture for the Lavender station, and pull a bit from the 102 Toxin Free Life lecture for the Thieves station. Pull a couple paragraphs from the NingXia 103 lecture for the NingXia station. You have all the tools in the back of this book to pull off an amazing Speed Oiling class. You pick and choose which details you want them to know. I'd open the class with everyone collected in a circle. Share your personal story, and the power of purity. Then release them to explore, setting a timer. Instruct them to switch stations when the timer goes off.

If you want to up your game, create a little scavenger hunt card, or a page for collecting random facts from each table that you can reuse with each class. Then see who collected the most facts and can spout off answers the fastest for a few giveaways. This is a very fun, interactive class that can be just as powerful as a 101. Make sure you end the class with the Bold Close and have a laptop where they can sign up to get their own kit before they leave.

One of the biggest mistakes I see is the cutting of the close. It's because you're nervous about the sale. Don't give yourself a chance to be nervous. Just practice the script and fall back on your training. Then it's a matter of doing what you already know (not sounding "salesy" or trying to come up with the right words on the spot). In *Gameplan*, book 1 in this series, I told the story of a woman who ended every class with the phrase, "you've survived Essential Oils 101"; but she never told them how to order the starter kit. You're not going to have any kit sales if you never open the door. Many in her classes never even knew she was doing the business. Read the close, let them know that if they'd like to get started, there is an education bundle they can take with them as they leave. Then direct them to the laptop at the back of the room. Run this class just as you would a 101. End it the same way, or you'll teach a lot of classes for no reason, because it isn't to build your business. Stay focused on the actions that will lead to growth. It's ok to have fun, just make sure that the critical elements of a 101 are still present.

One of the biggest mistakes I see is the cutting of the close. It's because you're nervous about the sale.

Pros & Cons

TO THIS STYLE OF TEACHING

SPEED OILING: CLASS 9

You will draw people in that don't have a lot of time simply with the name. You can train on many things in a short period of time. If you have several leaders manning stations, the people working their way through the room will get to connect with many oilers and get lots of social proof that they work.

The set-up time can be significant for this, as well as the duplication factor. Always make sure you're not scaring your leaders away with your setup. If you keep these simple, people can copy what you're doing.

I can't begin to tell you how helpful and inspiring Sarah's free Bootcamp (Gameplan, Ignite, Unstuck) classes are. I've been struggling with the whole compensation concept. I feel like I understand it much better now since listening to the videos. There is more for me to learn, but I know I am on my way to Diamond thanks to Sarah Harnisch and Bootcamp. Thank you, Sarah.

Peggy Snell

CHAPTER 30

CLASS 10: MAKE AND TAKES THAT WORK

I have a vendetta against make and take classes. I'm coming clean. You see, my predominant personality is blue (I am also an Enneagram 7 wing 8). That means I love fun, people, adventure. You would think I'd love a fun, people-filled adventurous make and take class. My secondary color is red (wing 8), which loves the shortest point from A to B. I love efficiency. I love to get a lot done and cross things off the list. I see make and takes as a lot of work and a lot of cost; many times from several different stores (none of which yield OGV for my business) with little return.

My fears were confirmed at Beauty School in 2015, when one of the speakers said that 70-percent of those that attend Make and Take classes never purchase the oils and never make the craft again. That means you're only getting (at max) a 30 percent yield on your time and investment to do the class. I want 100 percent yield! That is not very efficient!

While I was walking around sulking at this class type, pretty confident it was a total waste of time, a few of my precious Diamond friends showed me how it could be done correctly, and still lead to kit sales. It's simple to put down another person's way of doing something if you don't see success at it yourself. Always remind yourself that there are lots of ways to rank, and another method isn't necessarily wrong. It may be wrong for *you*, because you don't have the skill set, character type, or gifting to slip into the requirements to do it well, but that doesn't mean it never works. I was pretty sure in my head that there was no world where make and takes would yield steady business growth.

This is also a good place to tell you that a Young Living business is quite a bit of work. I think you've figured that out by now, because we're 10 classes into 15 different class types, and I'm hundreds of pages into this book. That's many pages of work! Thinking that network marketing comes easy is a farse. Every single job that you do requires work and effort, and this is no different. All these different class styles are just different types of bricks to build your castle, but each style requires a foundation and walls and has to be laid relationship by relationship and class by class. For some, it's a process that's many years long. For others, it comes faster. No Diamond will tell you that they didn't roll up their sleeves and put in a lot of effort to get that rank. We'll talk about honest expectations a little later in this book, because I don't want you to set your mind up for failure when you don't hit your own personal benchmarks. Speed does not dictate success in this line of work. It's consistency and the right actions that led to growth. Nothing that you work for comes easy.

Back to make and take classes.

As I was sulking, Young Living came out with two products that flawlessly fit into a Make and Take model: the Thieves Home Cleaning Kit (#20421) and the DIY Kit Collection (#21625). The Thieves kit comes with Citrus Fresh essential oil, Lemon essential oil, Pine essential oil, Purification essential oil, Thieves essential oil, Thieves Household Cleaner, a carrying case, a stainless-steel bucket, an amber glass spray bottle, a cleaning cloth, and a cleaning recipe booklet. The DIY collection comes with supplies for three different crafts for six people, including: lotion base, spritzer base, lip balm base, containers for each project, a scoop for measuring, a funnel, labels, a presenter card, recipe and social sharing cards and organza bags. The DIY kit does not include essential oils.

Now all my excuses were gone. You get OGV (organizational group volume) by purchasing both kits. All the supplies you need are in one place, right on Young Living's site. That means you're not ordering labels and bottles and stickers off different websites and expending money and time that doesn't move your business forward. By not having the oils in the DIY kit, you can make all those lotions and lip balms with the oils in the Premium Starter Kit, thus driving to a kit sale, and not one random bottle of oil that doesn't lead to a wholesale membership. All my frustrations were repaired in two small bundles labeled 20421 and 21625. The Thieves bucket came with a little recipe book that taught you how to make your own scrubs and yummy smelling mop water with all the various oils already in the bucket. Again... OGV.

So how I would I run these make and take classes?

Exactly like an in-person 101 class, but with a craft. Follow all the steps from Class 1. Build relationships so it doesn't end up as a no-show. Get your diffuser going before they walk in. Have the Diamond Rising Deck Contact Me cards ready to go so they can fill them out as they take their seat. Deliver the whole 101 script, or part of it if you want to keep the class shorter. Remember, the two most important components of the 101 class are your personal story and the purity section (where we cover grades of oils), otherwise they'll go out and buy cheap oil at the grocery store. When you're done with your bold close, tell them how to order the kit and have laptops set up. Then start the Make and Take. Make your luscious lotions, sassy spritzers and brazen lip balms, but put a few drops of Lavender, Frankincense, or Stress Away in them and drive to the PSK.

You can teach the Toxin Free Life class (the 102 at the back of this book) then break out your bucket, give the uses of Thieves cleaner and make some cleaning concoctions right out of the Thieves recipe book. Make sure you close your class. Make sure you have a laptop for people to order Thieves and the 101 oils kit. Make sure you have their contact information so you can touch base after class. Just like that, a Make and Take class can have a closing rate that's higher than 30 percent. You also filled a need for fun and fellowship with friends.

Pros & *Cons*
TO THIS STYLE OF TEACHING
MAKE AND TAKES THAT WORK: CLASS 10

The people in the class may have no knowledge of oils at all, but you draw them in with the excitement of a craft. You can reach people with these types of classes that a "101" may never be able to touch, without some serious listening-to-needs skills.

They can get pricey. And you can scare away your leaders. If you charge a lot for supplies, your attendance size will go way down. It takes time to gather and prepare for the class. Watch the system you set up and put in place for doing these; and ask yourself if someone who has $20 a week after bills could pull it off. If your answer is no, rethink it. Ask yourself if someone working two jobs and going to school could handle the time commitment of your system. If the answer is no, you're scaring away leaders. There are ways of doing make and takes without lots of prep and cost; stick with those ways.

Great training with the heart it requires for people to receive it easily. Sarah empowers others to share it as well.

Sherry LaMarche

CHAPTER 31

CLASS 11: SPEAKING AT EVENTS

"Ok Sarah, all the other classes so far have been pretty fun. In fact, I could see myself doing most of them. Speaking at events though?? That's weird! It's already rough enough speaking in my living room to strangers. Now I'll have to do it in a larger venue??"

Well, it's just one way of teaching. If you don't feel you have enough lead time at a vendor event to build the relationship and train the lifestyle, and you can't seem to get anyone to show up at your house, go where the people are. You'll hear me say that more than once. There are lots of opportunities around you for a chance to speak at events. Look at your local chamber of commerce and see what festivals are happening near you with tents for speakers. Look for county and state fairs, and farmer's markets with special event days for speakers. Look for men's or women's conferences in the area on health. Local gyms or the Y will host wellness fairs several times a year, and will look for speakers. Large companies host health fairs for their employees. See what churches are putting on seminars in your area (many host events for women or families). At the very least, host a #ylunites rally in your town and use it to attract people that may not have come just to your home. Collaborate with other leaders near you, and build relationships to get people there, just as you would for a 101 class.

What would this kind of an event look like? I'd definitely prep ahead of time and make sure you have plenty of purple bags. You could, at a vendor event, make up a giveaway basket that they have to leave their contact information for to try to win. On that contact card, ask them if they're interested in attending or hosting a class; or are they looking for extra income as a business. Have that table near the stage, and man it before and after the event. Hand out purple bags to everyone who fills out a card to win the basket. When they invite you to speak, gauge the crowd. If it's some type of a wellness fair, it would be just fine to teach any of the four starter kit classes; but I'd probably go with the 101, since oils is what we do. If I ever have the choice, I always lead with oils, because we have 600 oil-infused products. It's our foundational product; and it leads to hundreds of other products in the Young Living lineup. Sometimes they'll allow a speaker to close, but not end with sales. If that's the case, do your entire bold close, and end with, "if you'd like a second aromatherapy class for free, come see me at the table."

Then when your speech is done, hand out purple bags with cd's in them from the class you didn't teach. If you did the 101, put the 102 cd's in your bags, and vice versa. Use those bags as an opportunity to gather their contact information. Never, ever, give away your business tools without expecting something back. Seek out a Facebook or Instagram contact, a phone number, an email, or best yet, an address to host a class.

The secret to this kind of event is leads, or walking away with names you can call afterward. Also, have flip kits (extra starter kits that you have on hand at the event that they can purchase and walk out with). I'll go into more detail on flip kits when we go through vendor events; but suffice it to say, having a few on hand (as well as a laptop with internet access for them to order) is not a bad call for this type of event.

Also, have eyes to see the people around you. Some of my best contacts at these types of events didn't come from the people I was speaking to. It came from the other vendors in the hall. It came from the other speakers and the hosts I befriended backstage. It came from the tech teams running our lights and sound. Always have an eye for the people around you and constantly be scanning the room for needs. If you're in a place with people, you have a window of opportunity to build your team. If you don't make a contact, it's because you stayed silent. They will not come looking for you. You must hunt opportunity. If you pay attention, God will always open a window to a conversation, but it's up to us to have it. If your head is down in the sand, and you're afraid to speak, it's going to be very hard for you to build a business in network marketing. We're in the business of helping people. If there are people around you, there's a market for what you have to offer. Go share. The issue isn't a lack of people. It's that we've already crossed them off the list before we've even begun. Our lists of what we can and can't do and who will and will not grasp oils cripples our business. It's our own self-doubt and fear that keeps this business from us... nothing else.

Go where the people are.

Pros & *Cons*
TO THIS STYLE OF TEACHING
SPEAKING AT EVENTS: CLASS 11

You can reach a totally different crowd here. If your warm market has dried up and you're really discouraged, and not used to making cold calls or picking oilers up off the street, this can be really effective. I just did a class this past weekend for a women's retreat and ended up with 47 Contact Me cards of people interested in more learning. (Core 4 baby!)

They have no idea who you are. Follow up will be uncomfortable. (Remember the high when you read the sentence "I don't have to pick oilers up off the street?" You're basically doing that.) Stick with it. These guys have an interest in natural health because they pulled up a chair and listened at the event, usually willingly. They didn't skip your session and get lunch. Keep that in mind when your hand is shaking as you pick up the phone. This is where the line on the Contact Me card that asks which way they want to be contacted is very valuable, because you'll touch base perfectly on their terms. You'll also know if they're already on a Young Living team and if you should invest in them or not.

The way Sarah opens her heart and let's it ooze out, and then pours in bite size morsels of hope, light, and real tools. Wow.

Terry Martineau

CHAPTER 32

CLASS 12: TEACHER TRAINING CLASSES

I just revamped the entire teacher training to a double-sided page that you can pull off in 30 minutes. It's POWERFUL and hits the core of what you want your new builder to know: comp plan, simple strategy, how to rank up, the "why" of doing this, and action steps on what to do. *Check it out in the Appendices!*

If Make and Takes and I don't get along, teacher training classes are my bestie. I could spend all day with a business builder that gets what we do; someone who's willing to roll up their sleeves and do the hard things. One of the top things I hear when I run *Gameplan* Roundtable each week on Facebook is that it seems to be very hard to find business builders.

I sat and thought about that for a long time. Do you remember what I told you at the beginning of *Unstuck*? You have to teach classes to find your builders. If the average Silver has a team of 100, and 92 percent of Young Living is made up of product users only, then the average Silver has only 7 or 8 business builders. Most of them are likely Stars or Senior Stars that haven't caught the vision of what Young Living is, and what wellness, purpose, and abundance mean. That means the top 1 percent of this company, the Silver rank, might have one, or possibly two, people running beside them. And they are in the top 1 percent!

The top one-percent of this company, Silvers, likely have only seven or eight business builders!

It's easy to look over our shoulder and think we have it pretty bad, and that no one understands. If we could only find that 1 person, that one rockstar, this business would take off for us. The reality is that you have to roll up your sleeves not once, but six different times, to build all six legs you need for Royal Crown Diamond. You don't need one strong builder. You need builders on all of your legs. Once you hit Silver, the reality sinks in that all the hard work you did to build two teams, you have to do all over again for a third leg. Then it happens again with your fourth leg for Platinum, and your fifth leg for Diamond. That issue you have of finding builders... even Diamonds struggle finding leaders on their legs with the lowest volume. Instead of looking around, start digging out. Instead of waiting for the rockstar, BE the rockstar.

What does that look like?

Well, there are two tools that I use pretty consistently when I'm hunting for builders. If 1 in 6 people are looking for a new job in the next 12 months (statistics according to a careerbuilder.com survey in 2016), then I have a pretty good shot if I'm teaching four to six classes every single month. In fact, I'd have to put effort in to NOT picking up builders, if that many people are actively frustrated with where they are and are looking for a way out.

How do I find builders? This is going to seem overly simple all over again; but I teach classes. 101 classes, over and over. I don't lead with the business, because on a team of 10 thousand, I've only had three people come to me wanting to build because of the business before the products. I think you need a healthy love of the products before you can share them and generate a viable business. If you're leading with you (your business) instead of leading with others (your future team members), it's opposite of the mission of Young Living. The mission is to serve those around us, love them deeper (so deep we can stand above fear to talk to total strangers, and meet their needs where they are, without judgement). Of those three that came to me asking for the business, five years later, none are higher than Executive rank. I think it's because that initial passion was missing. If you come into this hunting for a paycheck, you can find it if you fight. If you come into it looking to take care of families and train yuck out of their homes to protect them; that's a different mission. It hits you on a spiritual level. Anything that hits that deep stays.

How do I find builders? I do my 101 classes faithfully (4 to 6 a month). At the end of the class, I say a single sentence. It's the same sentence I've used over and over again. It goes something like this:

"If you want to learn how to get your oils for free, stick around after class and we'll do a thirty-minute teacher training."

If you have time constraints and are limited on getting out on time, this is a backup:

"If you want to learn how to get your oils for free, there is a book in your purple bag that looks like this... It's called, *Your Gameplan: Build A Life Beyond Survival Mode*. It's a lunch time read. Check it out. When I pass this form around, check the box that says you're checking that book out; and I'll touch base with you in the next two days."

What did I just do there? I led to a tool. Tools speak to that silent place when your reader is alone, to the places that hurt in their heart. Tools offer hope. Give them the tool (that's the *Gameplan mini*, by the way); and then check in in two days and see if you can get them to a teacher training. That little book has the income disclosure guide in it! It is powerful!

What about method one, a 30-minute teacher training? I'm always surprised if I start a teacher training right after a 101 how many people will stay in the room. I'd love to believe it's inadvertent, but it seems to happen quite a lot, that most just stay put once I start. What will I cover in a teacher training class?

- I'll tell them how to teach a class.

- I'll show them how to log into the virtual office so they can place an order; and, so they get a full paycheck if they have a kit sale.

- I show them the rank qualification buttons so they know what they need to do to hit the first few ranks.

- I share a 2-minute compensation plan training with them, so they understand how they are paid.

- Can you guess the last thing? I share my story! My business story! If you don't have a business story, share one from your team. It may be a momma that's cut their hours back or was able to increase their grocery budget. It may be something crazy like an early retirement. It may just be hope, and the promise that they are moving toward something better. All of those are good stories to share. I do all of that in 30 minutes, then get them out the door with an *Ignite* book in their hand and a mission to share.

I just revamped the original *Gameplan* teacher training, and it is POWERFUL. You now have a bulletpointed, intensely visual and insanely simple way to train leaders in under 30 minutes, without overwhelming them with facts, details and numbers. Oh—and it's FREE. Check it out in the Appendix of this book, then print the sheets at no cost for you and your leaders at oilabilityteam.com.

That little teacher training script and the mini book have set a vision in our team that's unique. It raised leaders where I did not see them. If you never mention the business in your classes, no one knows it is there. Those one in six that may have said yes will likely say yes to someone else. The someone else who brings them a little hope. BE BOLD.

It's hard to believe, but we have just three types of classes left: corporate classes to business owners (think of your chiropractor), blogging and vlogging, and the famous vendor events. Then I'm going to walk you through classes that won't work that will cost you quite a bit of time. If you need a quick printable page to do a teacher training, I put together a double sided resource with the Income Disclosure Guide, a strategy Graphic for placing people and the four parts to your check (how you are paid), and the Rank Qualifications tab. Print that off, run through the sheet and show them how to log into the Virtual Office and place an Essential Rewards order and you are off and running. It's a 20-minute teacher training. The cheat sheet to train them is free at oilabilityteam. com under "Unstuck."

Instead of waiting for the rockstar, BE the rockstar.

Pros & Cons
TO THIS STYLE OF TEACHING
TEACHER TRAINING CLASSES: CLASS 12

This is all pro. No cons. I'm just going to leave the 'cons' word below, blank, so you know there's never any reason to avoid training a leader. This is the power of your business. Your greatest tool in all of Young Living is the power to be copied. If you teach a class on a Saturday, and you have five leaders teaching on Saturday, you just taught six classes in the same space. Duplicate. Get oils in every home in the world. You do that by setting a fire in people. Hand out the mini, touch base, gather their why, and start a flame 'a burning.

Ope, my mind is blank. Oh well. No cons.

Sarah has inspired me more than anyone ever has. She cares about people so much and it really shows. Every time she talks I feel like she's talking directly to me. I am blessed to have found her.

Stephanie Hudson

CHAPTER 33

CLASS 13: CLASSES FOR BUSINESS OWNERS

I feel like everyone at one time has had the thought, "my business is going to explode if I sign a chiropractor; a naturopath doctor; a nurse practitioner; a pediatrician assistant; a health food store owner; a gym..." (you fill in the blank). "If I can just get that business to sign, they'll stock all the oils in their office, place a $2000 dollar order each month; and I'll kick that leg over with one order and get the next rank."

If you've taken a peek at the Table of Contents for *Unstuck*, you'll see that I've divided this book into a few sections. There are 15 types of classes that work; but then there's also a section with a list of classes that, for the most part, will cost your rank and cost you time. Run the other way from those classes! If corporate classes didn't work, I would have placed them in Chapter 38. They do work. There's a really specific way to go about it to see growth in your business, though. I've had many leaders flop; and I've had many leaders do quite well if they follow a few general rules.

First, signing a business still requires relationship. Someone in the office/clinic/store/gym needs to be in love with Young Living. Every single class type, no matter what it is, requires a person recommending our products. If you just pop a diffuser in a waiting room, most people are gonna walk right on by. If you have a nurse saying, "you need to come to the class we're holding on oils in this office on Thursday, the woman teaching it is incredible. I believe it's the answer you've been looking for". That changes the ballgame. When someone has had their oils encounter, and is all-in, during their 9 to 5, you won't have no-show classes when you haul your portable office out to teach. Classes for business owners can cost you a lot if you haven't made that investment in at least one person in the office that will rally on your behalf, and draw people in.

Second, it's not wise to play the retail storefront role. You see, the paycheck from your business isn't predominantly locked up in single orders. It's found in your leaders. If you sit down and look at the breakdown of a Diamond check, the fastest way to spike your check is to collect Silvers. Generations pay is much higher than your Fast Start, your Starter Kit bonuses, or even your Uni-level pay, based on the OGV of your top five levels. That means as you build, collect as many Silvers as you can. Sign in sets of two under your level 1's, and raise them up with you, even if they're not building. You get anywhere from 128 to 140 dollars per Silver, plus a percentage of their OGV, depending how deep they are in your organization... (Yes, you're paid on them twice). That means the better idea with a business is to sign the person who loves oils in the office. Then sign every person in the office under them; and then every person that comes to a class under them, forming two legs to take that oil lover to Silver. You'll get so much more in your check from their rank than you'll ever get from the 8 percent (at most) that you get from their order each month.

Here's another word of caution: The money is in your downline, not in the fleeting rush of a retail storefront. Stocking oils on a shelf in a store isn't where your best check lies. Always look ahead, not at the immediate temporary benefit to your OGV. The greatest blessing you can have is a team. It's duplication. Spend the time developing relationships in the office, signing patients, clients, or office workers, and building your organization. That pays a thousand-fold more once it's established. The value of 10 people ordering on Essential Rewards,then turning around and signing their friends and family, far outweighs a single large oils order.

The Heart of Nearly All Failure in Network Marketing

I truly believe the root of failing at every single type of class is always the same root symptom, failure to establish relationships. If you love on people and meet them where they are, whether it be in a vendor event,

in a one-on-one class, on a blog, or in a chiropractor office, yo
something special and sacred that goes beyond oil. You build trus.

The miracle of this business starts by being your genuine, auth c
self, no matter what type of class you find yourself in (even a random
classroom or on a sidewalk with a stranger by your side). Stop looking for
faster ways, ways of dodging face to face contact, ways of hiding behind
a screen or behind a storefront, ways of dodging the bold close that will
lead to a kit sale and a new life for that family. The blessing is in the people. This whole world of network marketing is in the people. That's the
skill you must master to rise to the top. Quick fixes and fast money don't
last long in our world. It's the people that glue this business together. If
you're looking for the missing piece, I believe you have just found it in
this chapter. Stop trying to find simpler easier ways around the things
that scare you. Reach out and do hard things. Take the time to invest in
the lives of those you know, and those you don't. The payoff is more than
you can imagine.

How to Grow A Successful Team in a Business Environment:

1. Invest in one person deeply until they fall in love with oils. Do a
   one-on-one.

2. Let them be the megaphone in the office.

3. Equip them with purple bags, a diffuser and oils for the office, and
   an offer to teach for them.

4. If you can't fill classes right away, use that one person in the office
   to lead you to other people in the workspace, and sign them one at
   a time. Then incentivize them to invite to a class.

5. Utilize those connections to branch out into clients and friends of
   friends.

6. If the office has a specialization, don't be afraid to teach on it.
   I had a masseuse once who really wanted to learn the raindrop
   technique. I taught it; and that ended up being the doorway to a
   massive NingXia class for his work buddies. Then it was a Thieves
   class. Ultimately that leg grew by 2000 OGV over the next eight
   weeks. It's not because of a single order, but because of targeted
   aromatherapy training and investing in multiple people. Use caution
   that you're not teaching *only* specialty classes that don't lead to
   starter kits; but if it opens a conversation you've been waiting to
   have, go for it. Then drive to the PSK.

7. Always put an effort in to try to funnel to the starter kit. If they want
   to talk about pain, then bring up PanAway and Lavender (or Deep
   Relief). They may have many other interests, but the goal is always

to start with a wholesale membership, and build from that place. If you have no success, then revert back to #6, appealing to their specialized interests; but always keep a goal of a 101, 102, 103 or 104 class in your back pocket.

8. If the worker in the office is the one that invites other staff members or clients, as long as they are placing a 100PV order, I give them the sponsor and enroller number so they get the paycheck. I want them to see what's possible with Young Living. I already get it...I'm going all the way! I want to spread vision and hope, not just oils, across that office.

9. It is ok to set up a professional account if the office wants to stock a few products that they believe will be gateway products they can use to get people to classes (like Deep Relief roll-ons or Cool Azul Pain Cream). I would first sign the one person in the office that loves oils, and put the professional account under them. Any time someone buys anything oily in the office, they always get a purple bag. It has the sponsor and enroller information of the office oiler, not the professional account (because professional accounts forgo their paycheck to get oils at a discounted price). As people sign, build in sets of two under the office oiler to get them to Silver, because that's your best check.

10. Be persistent. It can be hard to break into an office. The employees are busy; and time for conversations is short. I once pursued a prominent doctor for my team for about two years, but he never signed with me. Then, a few years later, one of my leaders asked me to teach a 101 class; and when I went, the doctor's son was there. He ended up signing, as did his dad; but it wasn't because of me, it was because of the leader under me that never gave up. She had been in his office a dozen times over the course of two years before he signed. The funny thing is that after he was on our team, at least five other leaders came to me and said, "he signed??!! I tried forever to get him on my team!" Well, you stopped at least one conversation too soon, because he was ready. Now, someone else got the harvest. That is not their fault. It was your fault for not being persistent. You have heard it before, but it bears repeating: the fortune is in the follow up.

11. Avoid burnout. If you've been to the office and hosted several no-show classes, don't keep returning. You need the foundation of a relationship before you'll see those classes filled. It does not make sense to keep showing up to empty rooms. Pour into the staff one by one until you have someone's ear before you return and attempt to teach a class there again.

The money is in your downline, not in the fleeting rush of a retail storefront.

Pros & *Cons*

TO THIS STYLE OF TEACHING

CLASSES FOR BUSINESS OWNERS : CLASS 13

These guys have massive networks. One chiropractor on my team has a client base of 10,000 people. He puts fliers up when I'm going to speak, carries starter kits (not individual oils) and purple bags right in his office, has an on-fire assistant that always talks me up when people are scheduling their next appointment, and we have packed classes once a month when I pop in.

Getting their attention is hard. With the chiro above, I approached him over and over again and seed planted for five years. It was actually one of my Silvers that signed him, not me. Her follow up was better! Getting their attention and getting them to promote your business at their business is your greatest task. That will only happen once they have some "wow" moments with the oils. Oil them up. Fire doesn't just happen. You have to start it. If you want a mouthpiece in them, be the mouthpiece to them.

Sarah offers real nuts and bolts dynamic training to accommodate many learning styles and many levels. She funny, honest, generous, and inspiring. There is nothing else like it out there for Young Living distributors.

Anne Gianacakes Burke

CHAPTER 34

CLASS 14: BLOGGING
AND VLOGGING

We are in the home stretch! There are two different types of classes left. There's blogging and vendor events; and then I've given you all the research I've collected over the last three years about the systems in place across Young Living that get results. There are real people behind each of these chapters. In many cases, thousands have used these methods to rank. You have in front of you a compilation of the best of the best. It's almost time for you to take all this knowledge and wisdom, (25+ years of hustle), and put it to work on your own team. How are people building? You have all the research right at your fingertips.

I am entering this chapter with a bit of caution, because I am always looking at the duplication factor when it comes to network marketing. You need your team to replicate what you're doing. I have been writing since I was in 4th grade when I penned my first novel, *Star the Horse*. 30 years later, and 60-thousand newscasts in two of the nation's largest cities, I still can't write a blog to save my life. I do not have the technological savvy to grow in that way. I am also not gifted at pulling in a large audience online; though I have tremendous respect for those that can. I am just a homeschool momma of five that likes to research and talk a lot, and sometimes puts those words on paper. Gifted people around me make it look nice. Whatever miracle happened with *Gameplan*, it was all the Lord and His grace over our family. I'm not sure I could do it again, because it wasn't purposeful or strategic; and it wasn't because of my talent or gifts... it was all God.

Please hear me here. It doesn't mean blogging isn't a viable way of building the business—because there is more than one Royal Crown Diamond who has built using this method. If you have the talent and the know-how to build an online audience—this is a viable method to hit rank. It is the hardest of all the class types to duplicate though, so even the most famous bloggers in Young Living will tell you to train your team in other ways. Most of them go back to class 1, (in-person classes) by building relationships.

With that disclaimer at the head of this chapter, let's look at how the master bloggers built their audiences. There are two on my own team who are nearly Platinum that are extremely gifted bloggers with massive 100,000+ audiences. This is how they did it.

There are six steps to starting a blog.

1. Choose a name for your blog. (Some of my favorites are: theencouraginghome.com, trinaholden.com, and kaylahoward.com)

2. Choose a blog platform (the most common is wordpress.org)

3. Choose a hosting company (Bluehost and Siteground are common.)

4. Choose a domain name (oilabilityteam.com)

5. Choose a logo .

6. Create great content. Write at least 10 posts before you launch your blog.

With vlogging, (video blogging) it's the same type of deal, but instead of writing you're shooting videos. You'll choose a place to host (a Wordpress site has video capability) and your content will be delivered primarily through short three-to-five-minute videos. Follow all the rules with blogging and utilize social media to drive your audience to your content.

Here are a few other important things to keep in mind:

1. An email list is mission critical. That's how you connect with your audience. Make sure you have a capture page from the get-go. This is something that a webmaster can design for you when they get your blog built. You don't own the platform you are posting on, which is why you need an email list. Those are your followers. You can create a list in your email service and place a box on your blog. People must opt in. I am so glad I had this ready right at the start. We picked up over 60-thousand people just in the first few months *Gameplan* was launched, and that has been the driving factor for sales for all of my books since *Gameplan*. It's how you communicate all things to your fans, because they may not see every blog post.

2. The goal is to use the blog to sell Young Living, but remember that people aren't coming there to buy a product, they're coming there to buy you. Make sure your posts are giving insight into your daily life and your passions, without the constant drop of oils. Your posts should be positive and encouraging and spread joy and knowledge. Provide value every day. If every post is about oils, it will be hard for you to grow. Make sure they are getting "you", not just your business. What are you an expert at? What do you love? Decide on your niche. You need only post once or twice a week. Having a wider variety of content will draw more people to your site.

3. Use social media as a vehicle to drive to your blog. Whenever you put a post up, send it out in your newsletter and tell people it's there. Write a catchy sentence and put it on Facebook and Instagram with your blog link. Your audience is on social media, but your business is on your blog. Drive to the blog. Market you.

4. Make sure you're staying compliant in everything you do. Every watchful body out there. (The FDA and Young Living's Compliance Team are watching online.)

5. Have fun and don't stress about finding ways to connect with your audience. If you feel like you're running out of topics, pause and get fresh ideas by just being you. Be still and watch your environment. Catch the pace of what's being discussed online. What do people care about? Be there for them. What about your own home? What are your kids talking about? What are you dealing with on the soccer field? What are you struggling with as a mom or dad? What are you processing emotionally? How can you use that content to encourage other people? That's your starting place. You have endless content just by living life.

6. Throw your mistakes out there for all to see. If you are a master oiler and got Oregano oil on your hoo-ha, or drove with four packets

of NingXia on your van roof for 10 miles and it was STILL THERE, share it. That's what makes you real and relatable. (I'm not saying any of those things happened to me... but if they did happen, hypothetically speaking, they would be good things to write about. Hypothetically.) People don't need your perfection. They need to know they can make mistakes too and it's ok. You build a blog by doing life together, not by having every answer.

That is the framework of a powerful blog. With great content and marketing on social media, it can lead to serious results. I do have one final thought, though, and it's the most important thought of this chapter. It takes time to build an audience. A lot of the bloggers that saw huge success in Young Living in a short time period did so because they had already put the work in to build the platform. They already had a voice that was followed. If you're feeling that none of the other 14 class types will work for you, and you have the gift of blogging, go for it. (Just recognize that your results may not be as fast, because you need to build the audience before you can sell to the audience). One blogger built her site for seven years before starting Young Living, then rose through the ranks quickly. It was because the trust was already there between her and her followers. Go into blogging with realistic expectations. Don't forget, even with blogging, the relationship has to be there, or you'll see kit sales but no lifestyle changes that lead to Essential Rewards. They see your post on the starter kit and snag it because you said to do it, but for long-term growth you have to connect off the blog and explain the "how-to" and the "why" of oiling for them. Otherwise, they'll be one-kit wonders that drop off your team a year after signing. The heavy lifting of relationship building is still required, even with blogging.

Always look at the duplication factor when it comes to network marketing. Can you be copied?

Pros & Cons
TO THIS STYLE OF TEACHING
BLOGGING AND VLOGGING : CLASS 14

Simplicity! Oh, do I have dreams of building an audience of 1 million and writing passionately with research and knowledge every week on a new topic! (Maybe when I have no kids!) But seriously—if you have the audience, use it! Just live your oily life and post what you do. Many an oiler has had a video or a post go completely viral. Share your life. One of my sweet blogging friends, Mary Clendendin, signed over 50 people in one month using her blog. It can be a powerful way to express your lifestyle and connect with people, if you have an audience already and an understand of how to work the blogging platform.

You need an audience. And you need to know how to use the platform in a way that leads to starter kit sales. If you are lost in this area and tech isn't your thing, run. Run far away. The learning curve will cost you too much time that should be spent teaching classes.

Sarah has the best network marketing training!

Ingrid Glenn

CHAPTER 35

CLASS 15: VENDOR EVENTS

We wrapped up class 14 with one of the toughest ways of sharing, and now we're going to wrap up this entire section with what I consider to be one of the simplest ways of sharing. In fact, it works so well and is so duplicatable that this is one of my main mojo methods for getting your confidence back when it's been a long time since you've had a kit sale. If you feel like you've not been successful at any other method, vendor events will usually bring results (especially if you follow a few rules).

The hardest part about doing a vendor event is FINDING a vendor event. Vendor event season is usually spring, summer, or fall, sometimes lasting through Christmas. In cold weather states, it can run May to October, so you'll still need to find a way of building in the off months, or you'll lose over a quarter of a year of work for your business. In those months, it's best to do weekly one-on-ones so you are still growing. Develop relationships with those that signed during the last vendor season and train them on the lifestyle to get them on ER (teach an in-person 101 with them, or 102, 103, or 104). Then spend the rest of your time lining up venues every weekend for the upcoming spring through fall vendor season. Put deposits down to hold your tables.

Questions to Ask When Booking a Site:

1. How large is the event? How many people attend?

2. Does the event cater to wellness groups, or is your message opposite of the audience's?

3. What are the fees to set up a table? Is it worth it for you financially?

4. Is there electricity? Can you plug in a diffuser?Do you have wifi access so you can sign people up for kits right in the booth?

5. How early can you come, and how late can you stay for set up and tear down?

Make sure you have your ducks in a row so you can decide if you want to be there. Doing the legwork in your off months to make sure your calendar is booked solid with at least 1-2 events per week is the only way this works well. If you have one vendor event a month, you're going to have extremely slow growth. It might be so slow that you think network marketing doesn't work. If you're putting the right kind of work in, the results don't lie.

One of the beautiful Gold leaders on the Oil Ability team, Theresa Yeager, has quite a story with vendor events. She tried many times by contacting Chambers of Commerce in multiple towns, hitting up state and county fairs, and she grew one event at a time. It was slow and steady and required a lot of legwork to get into events. However, one rainy afternoon, we walked into a flea market-type venue called "The Windmill" in upstate New York. She auditioned in front of a panel of jurors and showed off the oils. She was awarded a booth. Every Saturday, faithfully from April through December, she has run her table at a rental cost of $40 a week. That event has 10-thousand people through it daily. Theresa, (the one who built from 8,000 OGV to 43,000 OGV) in two years through steady, hard, consistent work. Theresa is the best example of success at vendor events that I've found, so I am basing this chapter on her, after multiple interviews. Here are her tips.

Top Vendor Event Tips:

1. Make sure you have a starter kit on the table and the diffuser is running. Of everything you bring with you, this is the centerpiece. The less you have that distracts from that kit, the better. Gussy up the kit. Put each oil in a jar of Epsom salt for them smell with pretty labels. All of that is fine. It's also fine just to display the kit. Don't travel with the Seedlings line, the Animal Scents line, charcoal bar soap, KidScents oils, business building tools, and five different reference guides. Those do not lead to wholesale accounts. It's

information overload for someone who will be at your booth for 30 seconds to 2 minutes. How much could you take in within a two-minute window? The only thing they need to know when they walk out of the booth is that a starter kit is on its way to their house. Any other message you send is too much information. If you're not having success at vendor events, four times in ten it's because you have pulled their attention in too many directions. The other six times it's because you did not find and meet their need.

2. Have flip kits for sale. I cannot reiterate this enough. Outside of showing off the starter kit on your table, this is literally one of the only ways we've seen success at this type of class. Having a giveaway basket and touching base later isn't enough. You have to know your audience. Your audience at a vendor event has come specifically to make a purchase. They are walking through your oils store. It's a great type of "class" because they are already coming with the intention to buy, whereas in an in-person format, they may just be coming for the information. Vendor event attendees don't want a lot of information. They want to impulse buy, and they have set aside cash to do it. Give them the opportunity. What is a flip kit? When you log into the Virtual Office, you'll see the option to buy an entire PSK (oils, Thieves, NingXia or Savvy). It will look exactly like the one that comes to a new member. Buy it and stock it in your booth. When they express interest, have it in a bag ready to go. They get on your laptop and place the order for their own kit, but ship it to you to replace the one they just walked out with. (That gives you a reason to call them later, to change your address out of their Virtual Office once it ships, and talk to them about Essential Rewards.) Flip kits are completely legal. They're one of the only viable ways of building with the vendor event method, because follow up from vendor events is notoriously difficult (especially if they're not on your team yet). Don't miss the opportunity in front of you by going with no flip kits. In an average event, depending on the size, I will have 4-6 kit sales. If you are doing an event a week with those numbers, that's 16 to 24 kits a month. That's rockstar status!

3. You only get those kind of results by knowing how to talk to people. That's the one skill laced throughout this entire book; but I'm going to customize it for vendor events to give you some ideas that work in a high-speed high-traffic environment. Check out the customized scripts at the end of this chapter to help you with this part of the vendor event process.

4. In a vendor event, you need a 30-second script memorized (something that catches their attention and hooks them in long enough to fill out a raffle ticket or leave contact info for later).

5. I love raffles at these types of events. They catch people's eye from a distance. I have seen some pretty creative things at vendor events that don't detract from the starter kit. One woman even had a wheel you could spin for a free roll on! Genius! You want them to walk over to you. People who never would leave their info will leave it to get something free. They won't fill out their information for just anyone it has to be something they want. If oils are something they want, then you want their contact info. You're collecting the right people. I usually get a basket from Walmart or the Dollar Store and fill it with a pre-made bottle of Thieves cleaner, a Fearless book, a 101 and 102 cd, a Peppermint roll on, and anything else that I usually give as hostess gifts, (like a $1.50 reference guide). They have to fill out a contact form, so you can touch base after the event. Tell them you will call so they are expecting it. Set up a time with them before they walk off if you can.

6. Make sure you have a laptop with internet access so you can sign kits. That's so very important. No one walks out with a flip kit unless they have ordered their actual kit. That can't happen if you don't have a computer on site.

7. If it's not knockout busy, ask them about their health journey. I love that as a lead in question. You don't have to answer it. Just say, "oils may be what you're looking for. I'm willing to have a quick call with you so we can take a look at how this can help you. Would you leave your info so I can check in when it's not so crazy, at your convenience?"

8. This is up to you, because depending how many events you do it can get pricey, but I like to make up 20 $1 bottles of Thieves cleaner. I give them to people who enter the raffle for the basket that check that they are interested in hosting or attending an oils class. I want them to go home and wipe their kitchen down and fall in love. I only make the investment in serious prospects, not everyone that enters the booth. These people also get a purple bag, as well as those that sign up for kits in the booth.

9. And finally this from Megan, on the Oil Ability team:

"Diamond Rising Deck Contact Me Cards are CRITICAL for vendor events! They are a complete game changer! Today I am filling out Distributor cards, following up with my Contact cards and asking folks to let me teach their circles. What are you doing today??? Let's rank together. Let's pray together."

Why are these cards mission critical? They ask questions you have NO time to ask, like "are you already a Young Living member", "what's your biggest health struggle", "what classes have you had?" etc... You can't ask that stuff in the 30 seconds they are at your booth. But now you have a record of all the things—even how to contact them afterward, because they gave you the information. I ask them to fill out the cards before they can win my raffle basket. At my last event, I went away with 52 Contact Me cards and 44 people that were interested in attending a class. THAT was worth my time invested in the vendor event!

If you want to read more, Theresa has written an ebook to chronicle her journey with vendor events. You can find her book here: heresayeager. com/vendor-events-demystified/

I WANNA KNOW MORE ABOUT OILS!

Name: _____

Phone: _____

Email: _____

CHECK A BOX:

☐ I am interested in having you come teach a FREE class for me and my homies, at any location.

☐ I am interested in showing up to a class that you teach. I will bring my friends!

☐ I would LOVE to get my hands on a Premium Starter Kit and start oiling!

☐ Please... please... please... Teach me how to use oils! I can't make a class right now; but just contact me and give me information!

☐ If you call or contact me, I will likely not answer. But... I do want to win that gift basket.

☐ I am already an oiler on another team, but I'd love to get more oils resources.

☐ I get oils from someone else, but do not have a starter kit.

☐ I am interested in the business opportunity.

This is the address where you can mail the raffle basket if I win:

_____

30-SECOND SCRIPT TO DRAW PEOPLE INTO YOUR BOOTH:

"Hey there! The average person puts 300 chemicals on their body a day; 80 are before breakfast. Essential oils are a better way. They are 1 ingredient: lemon, lavender, peppermint. They have no toxic chemicals. I can train you how to use these to protect your home and your family. *(Add in two sentences of your personal oils testimony)*. What's your biggest health struggle right now? I'd like to point you to some resources and put free tools in your hands".

Then, as always, the hard work begins when you get home. Now you have to build relationships with all those people. Some got a kit. They need *Fearless*, the *Fearless* calendar, and a follow up call on how to use their diffuser. Some filled out a form, and are interested in hosting or coming to a class. Call them and ask them about their health journey. Then, tailor the follow up call to address their needs. That's the best way to get them to a class. They have to know they need oils. Someone won that basket; and that alone is a good tool for a follow up call. Some just wanted information, but can't come to a class. They are a good candidate for a follow up call and a textable class. There are so many resources at your fingertips to reach every single person that walked by that booth. The fortune is in the follow up! Relationships are the cornerstone to every single type of class. Now let's end this section by talking about what doesn't work when sharing oils. My goal is to protect you and save you time. I want you to avoid the things in Chapter 38 like the plague. Here we go!

Diamond Rising Contact Me Cards are a GAME CHANGER for vendor events. They ask questions you don't have time to ask.

Pros & *Cons*

TO THIS STYLE OF TEACHING

VENDOR EVENTS: CLASS 15

These are one of my mojo methods! It's because they work! Pop a table up, lay out the starter kit, give away a gift basket so people fill out your Contact Me cards and you're off and running. These require little prep and set up, connect you with a lot of people if there's enough foot traffic at the event, and are wonderful if your head is in a bad place. If you think you can't do this business, I challenge you to sign your mom and best friend first, then go do a vendor event. They are wonderful for resetting your mindset and showing that you CAN do this and it IS worth fighting for.

Getting people on Essential Rewards is hard after the fact. Many won't answer their phones or connect with you, because they saw you for two minutes in a booth; and don't even remember your name. Make yourself memorable. Then meet their needs. Tell them you're going to call them this week about their son's breathing, their back pain, or the cough they can't shake. Then they're waiting for you. If you meet needs, even strangers who think you are semi-creepy will listen.

PART FIVE

A Bit More: Talking to Humans 102

Sarah is gift from God. She inspires us, upholds Gary and Mary's vision, she tells it like it is and is a FEARLESS leader!! Truly bootcamp is one of my top three ALL TIME FAVORITE Young Living events. Sarah I am Blessed beyond measure to have you in my Life. Peace and grace to you and your family.

Nina Cowell

CHAPTER 36

THINGS THAT DON'T WORK

This is a hard chapter to write, because many of us want to re-invent the wheel, and find new, creative ways of ranking. If we are honest, some of us just want a faster way rather than rolling up our sleeves and doing the hard work. We don't have a lot of time. Most of us are afraid of talking to people, so we search for other methods. We are also natural entrepreneurs at heart; and we organically have our hands in many pots. Please hear my heart, because my only purpose in putting this chapter together is to save you stress and frustration. The 15 types of classes listed in *Unstuck* are all tried and true and have worked. The things below are <u>dangerous</u> for network marketers. They could cost you everything. They will definitely hurt your mindset, and without that, you're a lost ship at sea. I am begging you, turn the other way and don't waste your time on these things.

Your freedom does not lie in anything in this chapter. Every month, I make five times the income with my Diamondship than I make with *Gameplan*. I never wrote that book for money. I wrote it so my team was on the same page. The book got leaked; and we made it available to Team Young Living after several leaders asked me to publish it. Then it exploded without any professional marketing. But after that—when the speaking requests came in, and a massive audience formed online-- it consumed too much of my time. I needed to get back to what started it all for me: teaching. Writing books did not take me from starter kit to Diamond in 2 years. Sharing oils did. As much as I love *Gameplan,* and it has blessed me unbelievably by hearing your stories, it cost me dearly. I went on to write *Unstuck* because I saw so many people trapped and not doing the things that lead to freedom. I could not leave you behind when I know you have what it takes. It's the distractions that made me want to go back and leave a warning letter for you before I take a writing break and get to Royal. The freedom for my husband and my five kids is in my downline. It's in my team—not in anything else. It's the time I invest growing my OGV and doubling the number of enrollers under me. And it is the same for you.

Stay focused.

There are hundreds of Diamonds, thousands of Platinums, and thousands upon thousands of Golds and Silvers. The numbers do not lie. If you work this thing, it can be a huge blessing to you. But there are tasks that absolutely won't grow your team. They will cost you a lot of time and money; and you'll be sitting at the end of the project, a little older, more tired with a bit less money in your pocket, and no rank up. You may not like the things I write below, but if you can avoid these pitfalls, and focus on one of the 15 classes listed in the previous pages, it will keep you out of the danger zone. At the very least, if you learn to talk to people with a few leading questions and give one-on-ones with total strangers. That can build a Silvership. Just that one action is enough. That one action will do more than everything else put together in this chapter. You don't need to be a rockstar. You need one skill: talking to people.

It's humiliating, but I'm going to lay it all out there by listing some of the things that I did that cost me a TON of time. Ask yourself with every minute you spend on your business—is this building a legacy for my kids right now? If the answer is no—STOP! Run from it like Joseph from Potiphar's wife. Flee the room. Then focus. You know what to do.

Sarah's Distractions:

- Write the books on your heart when you're a Royal. It's not because you're a better writer then, but because you are a better steward of your time and resources. You are disciplined. Every word you put on a page is stealing food and financial protection from your kids. It's taking from their future. If you haven't put the time in yet to build their willable, generational income, your priorities are out of order. The desires of your heart are good and were meant to be pursued; just wait until you have protected your family first. God, spouse, kids, work; your life should be in that order. Pleasure and dreams are #5. (For me, that was my full-time job of radio. That's why radio happens a couple of times a month and Young Living is nearly every day.) I see so many people chasing things they love and leaving their kids and spouse in the dust if anything were to happen to them. I think there's a place for all those things, once you've put the time in to make sure your family is safe. Steward the dream.

- I made recipe books for my team. I had them laminated and I print-ed hundreds of them. The reference guides are WAY better. Don't re-invent the wheel. Don't lose time generating unnecessary tools.

- I found my favorite aromatherapy printables, articles, and graphics online and made 60-page folders for every person that attended a 101 class.

- I gave most of my oils away, sometimes by the bottle.

- I made rank up gifts that were really time consuming, expensive, and cost a lot to mail. With 500 new Stars a month, I have had to re-evaluate what I do. Now they all get an *Ignite* book. It's simple, easy, they're well-trained, and I don't spend a lot of prep time. I order and ship Ignite books from Amazon and spend my time teaching classes rather than making roll on bottles and hand-written labels for dozens of leaders. I love giving business tools as rank up gifts, because it helps them pursue their dreams in a tangible way with tools and action.

- I played around with oils. I'm not talking about looking things up in reference guides and trying them. I am talking about ordering lots of DIY supplies, making pretty stickers, and crafting. Crafting is fun; but if I took that time and poured it into teaching, the rank would come faster.

- I spent more than I made and created a wedge in my marriage because of it. If you want your spouse on board, show them the check. Don't spend the check before you make the check. What did I spend it on? Food for my classes (sometimes more than our weekly budget for groceries.) I'd spend it on taking my leaders to the spa. God to the park instead if the money is not in your check yet! Do a $10 Panera salad or a hot cocoa hangout instead of pedicures. I would spend it by buying oily things that I liked from stores online and on Amazon (I admit it, my name is Sarah and I am an Amazon junkie!) I have a massive aromatherapy library of books that did not honor my husband's need to balance the budget.

- I paid for **6** different aromatherapy certifications, including an international certification. **YOU DON'T NEED A CERTIFICATION TO SHARE OILS**. People will trust you because you are authentic. They will trust you because you help them; because you loan out your diffuser and help them breathe at night. The certification doesn't matter if you love on people. We are programmed to think we need certifications. I think it's pretty amazing that D. Gary Young, who didn't even have a college degree, became millionaire. How? He built trust. Do you want the check, or do you want a title? I am running for the check. A title is self-serving. It's just to give me honor and status that isn't required in this field. A check takes care of my babies. They are more important to me.

- I made an entire oils store and hauled it to <u>every</u> <u>single</u> <u>class</u>, selling my own roll-ons, creams, prays and salves. First off, it's against Policies and Procedures to open Young Living oil, put it in your own concoctions, sell it, and say it has Young Living oil in it. More importantly, THEY WON'T GET THE KIT. They will walk away with your pain cream, and spend money in your homemade store. Instead, have them get a kit and let Young Living do the hard work at the distillery. Let them handle the shipping and payment. You collect the check. That's a lot easier than hauling around an illegal store. For the first time, I'm going to post a photo to show you how far I took this. When I stopped doing my store, my business absolutely exploded.

Embarrassing, huh? That is for ONE class! There could be a serious flogging from compliance in that photo! Don't waste your time trying to be Young Living. They do a great job of it without you and me. Just lead people to the kit and to the lifestyle. Then relax and enjoy the check.

Stay focused.

Those were my biggest blunders. Let me list a few others that I see out there that break my heart. All I want you for is a Diamondship. It doesn't come when you invest in other things. Focus.

1. **Investing in more than one network marketing company.** You will be jack of all trades and master of none. I'm going to say something quite sharp and pointed here: I do not have a single Silver or above on my team that's in two MLM's as a business builder. Why? Because it takes a lot of work to do one MLM. If you attempt two, you succeed at neither. Then you're stuck at a 9 to 5job the rest of your life. Zero successful builders out of 10,000 people are pretty stark numbers. The odds are highly against you if you dip from two pots. You will confuse your business builders. You will divide your time and your check. You will pull from the same pool of people to build in two places, and confuse your distributors (who wonder what your "next" MLM will be.) You lose your authenticity.

2. **Building a storefront.** Do you remember what I said about Young Living being excellent at being the storefront? They handle the website, the ordering, the payment, the shipping, the development of pure products that work. Why do you need to stock oils in your garage or shed or family business? This also goes for stocking single bottles of oils at vendor events. It's unnecessary, and it will ultimately pull from your business. If your family or a friend has a pre-existing business, or you're at a vendor event, stock the premium starter kit and lead people to a wholesale membership. Then tap into their friend circles and build a downline. When you sell a bottle of Thieves to someone, you're training them to order from you instead of online. If they are not on your team, you're taking someone else's OGV. If they are on your team, they are losing ER points and ER bonuses. You are literally robbing them. You are reaching into their pocket and taking their 10, 20, or 25 percent in

ER points and their free products that month when they don't hit the PV for their order. Drive everyone to the website and enjoy the simplicity of what Young Living has set up for us to thrive.

3. **Running side businesses linked to oils.** Running side businesses linked to oils. These include ideas and projects such as: making oils racks, designing graphics and classes, oil-infused soap, giving massages with Young Living oil, charging for Raindrops, making diffuser bracelets and necklaces, setting up an Etsy shop and making bottle labels, creating cool oily things with your Cricut cutter and selling them (or not selling them and just wasting time). THAT DOES NOT LEAD TO FREEDOM.

4. **Doing classes that cost a lot and don't lead to a starter kit.** The big craze lately has been succulent classes. The plants act as tiny diffusers, and you drop essential oil right into the rocks or the soil. How does that build your team?? The time it takes to order the plants, set up the stations, get all the printables and stickers ready-how does that grow your OGV? When someone comes to that class, what oils are they ordering afterward? If they get a bottle of Lemon, does that mean you make 80 cents for all that work, if they are a level 1 and you get 8 percent of their order? Walk your actions forward and ask yourself what it does for your growth. I know that every action does not need to lead to OGV for your business, but most of the people I have met have very little time to do this. If you have two hours a week, and you spend your time in a class like that instead of building a relationship and teaching a 101 or 102, you have given your business hours away that week. It's not always about the financial investment that you're making. It's also about your time.

5. **Recreating the starter kit.** It's called a mini kit. You order little drams and take a starter kit, disassemble it, put a few drops of each oil into several bottles and hand them out as sample mini kits. What do you think happens after that? They don't order. Why would they need to? You have just given everything away. If they are going to play with 12 bottles of oil in a little kit like that, they would have played and explored with a full kit too. Mini kits are extremely costly and can't be duplicated by your leaders. For every 10 kits made, less than 1 person gets the actual starter kit. Those are stats from 30 different leaders on my team that did the mini kit challenge for several months. Put money and your time into places where it will grow.

6. **Charging for business training.** This one really irks me! There are plenty of Diamonds that are willing to give their things away for free.

There are so many sites with freebies on it. Just the <u>oilabilityteam.</u> <u>com</u> site alone has interviews to excite your team, textable classes, free powerpoints and scripts, *Gameplan, Ignite* and *Unstuck* bootcamp, printables. Don't spend time trying to make money on a side business by charging for training for your team or for other people's teams. Just build your organization.

7. **Putting ALL your time into personal development.** Personal development is a good thing, especially when you need a good firing up. Get to a Go Pro event, invest in a coach if your check allows, get to Diamondbound, absolutely go to convention and #ylunites rallies. Don't do any of those things INSTEAD of building your team. If the time you're taking in personal development leaves you no time to share oils, you are upside down in your business. If the cost of personal development is taking too much of your check, you're not running your business in a way that honors the Lord. Never spend more than you make. If you want to go to more events, teach classes and build your check so you can go. No event is going to save your business. You save your business by sharing oils. It does not take an event to learn that. It just takes courage. I don't go to events to learn to share. I go to events to get my head out of the gutter and be around like-minded people with a positive energy and outlook. The event is the reward for the work.

That chapter was a thorough whooping! You know what to do. You know what not to do. You have everything you need to start wrapping up this book, leave you with some tools and some fire—and let you be you. You have everything you need to move forward. Don't second guess yourself. Just find humans and oil them.

You are a powerhouse. When I am feeling down about my classes, I just listen to you and I have motivation again!

Marion Ford

CHAPTER 37

LEADING SENTENCES THAT START CONVERSATIONS

This is the hallmark chapter of this book. It's the skill you have to know to grow. I'm going to walk you through exactly what I do when I'm talking to someone I don't know. Then, I'll walk you through how I talk to someone I do know. I'll give you a massive list of opening lines to start conversations, all bullet pointed. Pick one and start the convo. Find the need. Meet the need. Sell the kit. Rinse and repeat to Diamond.

Talking to Someone I Don't Know

Part of this may be because I am a blue personality and just love people; but I am always on the hunt for a conversation. My husband always jokes around that I am well-paid to talk. It's true! 22 years in radio, and now oils! Admittedly, there are days when my kids have pushed me past my limit and I am peopled out. For the most part, though, I have no problem striking up a conversation in a random Walmart aisle or Barnes and Nobles café. My goal with this chapter is not necessarily to get you comfortable, because not everyone will get to that place. It's just to give you some words that you can fall back on (a mini script to open the floor for you). I want to crack the door open so you can funnel to a tool. If we can get that far together, we can get you over one of your greatest fears. Then this business is wide open for you.

Truly.

Do you believe me? Do you see how very close you are once the conversation has begun?

Visualize something with me for just a moment. I said this in *Gameplan* bootcamp; but let me reiterate it in print form. If you open your front door, what do you see outside? Humans. A lot of them. Even if you live in a small town, there are humans at the soccer field, and humans in the next town over at the grocery store. If you live in Alaska, and there are no humans; when you get online, guess what? Humans!! Talk to the humans.

What if you weren't afraid at all? What if you were a toddler all over again, and you could approach anyone? Could you imagine what would happen if every single human was on your team? *Every* human outside? Just the people in the grocery store would build you to Diamond. Just the people in your cell phone could equal a Gold rank. It's not that there aren't enough people. It's that we're too chicken to talk to them. Stop telling yourself that you can't do this, or that there aren't enough people, or that everyone already oils, or that your town is too small, or that you're not getting upline support. Those are lines you pop out that have nothing to do with the real problem at hand. YOU are afraid of people; and THIS is a people business. The good news is that you can still do it, even if you're afraid. In fact, I think it stretches you and brings you closer to the Lord when you do hard things that require you to lean heavily on Him for confidence and favor.

I have found that the green personalities on my team (those that are analytical problem solvers that see the world through a lens of what is practical and logical) can really struggle with this. (Though I don't believe that reds, yellows, or blues always find it easy to talk to complete strangers.) May I offer some encouragement here, no matter what your color is? My sister is a super-green. Her OGV is 100,000. The head of my 4th leg is a green personality. Her OGV, built primarily through vendor events, is 45,000. The head of my Diamond leg just built her team from 12,000 to 24,000 in a summer. She is the greenest leader on my team.

Don't use your personality as a reason to avoid engaging with people. The truth is, any skill can be learned if you are teachable. It doesn't mean you'll have an outgoing in-your-face super people personality by the end of Unstuck; but it does mean we can train fear out of you, and get you in front of people in a way that makes you look confident, just by learning a few key sentences that open the doorway. May I challenge you to forget your "I can't do this" sentences, your "I'm not good at that" sentences, and your "my personality type doesn't do that" sentences; all the things that exclude you from having to talk to people (because that's how you build this business); and just hear me out on this chapter? You can do anything you set your mind to. You can achieve what you choose to achieve—if you stop telling yourself what you can't do. Your personality has no bearing on your success. Your decision to fight equals your level of success. Stop using your personality type as a crutch to avoid your business. You can't build a viable business that way. Freedom over fear.

Let's get a good poker face for you! If we can kick off that convo, the door is cracked, and you can fall back on your training for the rest of it.

When I am approaching someone I don't know, I size them up. Do we have anything in common? Do they have kids? What kind of shirt are they wearing? Is it athletic wear? Does it look like we have any sports in common? Are they wearing anything with a sports team? What are they talking about with the person next to them? What is in their shopping cart? Is any of it organic? The contents of my cart alone started an entire conversation with two 85-year-olds. That landed me a 30-person class. You are a CIA spy. Find something to kick off the conversation after you do your 15 seconds of investigative research.

Here's a list of sentences I used to kick off conversations with my cold market:

- Are you a Cowboys fan? My husband grew up in Dallas! (Come on. Why do you have to put down the Cowboys? I know that's where your head just went!)

- How many kids do you have? They are so cute!

- You look exhausted! I just got off work and I'm wiped.

- That is a nasty cough. Would you like a Thieves cough drop? This helps me SO much.

- You look like you are in pain! I have XYZ... I use Cool Azul Pain Cream for it. I think it's the answer to what you're looking for. It will help you get through this shopping trip!

- Your kids are so well behaved!

- Can you believe it's almost 70 out in November?

- That is my FAVORITE type of spaghetti sauce! (I sold a kit once from this one sentence! It led to putting Oregano Vitality in my sauce... and you can connect the dots.)

- How are you doing today?

- I love your purse! Where did you get it? (Maybe guys shouldn't use this. It may sound like a pick up line!)

- I used to work in retail for 11 years. How long have you done this?

- If you can pick a topic related to work, hobbies, or family, that's a big score. Usually they'll talk much more if it's something they are passionate about.

Here are a few more:

- What's your story?
- What personal passion project are you working on right now?
- How long have you done that?
- Has this been a busy week for you?
- Having fun? (I love this one at Walmart! Especially if there are kids in their cart!)
- What are your favorite restaurants around here?
- Are you local?
- Is that a charitable organization you support? (If they are carrying something with the name of it, or mention it).
- What's the best thing about working here?
- Do you have any insider tips for getting out of this store faster?
- What's your New Year's resolution? (I totally used this one last year and got a guy's contact info!)
- How does your family celebrate the holidays?
- What are you making for dinner? I need an idea!
- Do you have a ___? Me too! (I used this when I was in a parking lot, and we were comparing Dodge Caravans).
- Hey, you're a ___? Me too! That sounds really interesting. What's your favorite thing about your job? (I used this also in a parking lot with the guy loading my groceries. He had a radio shirt on; and I told him I had done radio. It turns out he was going to school for Broadcasting.) This could apply to any job. Maybe the person in front of you has something identifying on them that marks them as a construction worker, or the greasy hands of a mechanic. You can ask, "do you fix cars?" My dad was a mechanic for 40 years. He'd always laugh when he was asked about his hands. It's a talking point. Find something identifying on them, that's not embarrassing, and use it to open the conversation.
- How is your week going? (I like to use this if the conversation stalls and I REALLY want to get their contact information).

- If they are carrying a book, ask about the title. I have sold at least 20 kits just by carrying *Gameplan* with me, and using it as a talking point. One lady got a kit from me after she saw it sitting on the floor under my chair; and it led to a 30-minute conversation about her job frustration. Another guy joined my team after buying it online, thinking it was a book about chess. Oops. (For the record, I've never played chess in my life. I'm not kidding. I just thought it sent a neat message about strategy and preparedness.)

- "Are you ok"? (This is one of my most-used lead ins.) Scout around you for people with seeming ailments. This works so well. You can find someone just about anywhere you are. Then sometime in the conversation, slip in my favorite line: "I think this is the answer you've been looking for."

- You don't have to skip the small talk. Station yourself somewhere where you can start a conversation, like a Starbucks or a Panera. Never underestimate the power of, "the weather is amazing today!" "How is this rainy day treating you?" From there, talk about what you did yesterday when it was sunny.

- Start a conversation with an open-ended question. People like sharing their opinions, especially when it's something they care about. If the cover of the "National Enquirer" in the checkout line says, "Man Claims To See UFO", you can say, "Do you think he really saw a UFO?? What do you think it could be?"

- Comment on something you have in common. If they are carrying a yoga mat, you could say, "where do you do yoga? What type of yoga do you do?"

- Give your stranger a genuine compliment. I use this ALL THE TIME. "Wow, I love your bracelet!" "You are an incredible mom. I don't think I've ever seen anyone's kids so well behaved!" "That is the best mermaid hair I've ever seen! Where did you have it done?" "Your floral printed pants are LEGIT. Where did you get them?" "Your Clark Kent spectacles are awesome. I was looking for some for my son!" Everyone loves a compliment. Edification is a very effective way to kick off a conversation.

- Ask questions about your surroundings. For example, if there's music playing, say, "this is a great song! What song is this?" If there's a game on the tv at a restaurant, say, "which team are you rooting for?" If you're at a friend's birthday party and your friend is singing terrible karaoke, say, "Susan is ridiculous, but I love her! How do you know her?" Open the conversation by being observant.

- Ask for help. This may sound cheesy; but it's our human nature to want to feel useful and necessary. Ask for directions. Ask the time. Ask the forecast. Ask for the best nearby restaurant. Ask for advice.

- Just say hi. That seems pretty simple; but it's amazing where it can go. Break the ice. Get 'er done. If you are alone, and they are alone, they probably want someone to chat with also. Humans are generally social creatures. You may not like being in a room with 50 humans; but most of us don't like being totally alone, either.

Sometimes they start by asking me a question; and I turn it around on them, so I can form them and learn more about them to get them into my business funnel. When I was on my way home from the Young Living Gold retreat, a TSA worker asked me about my swag bag that I got as a backpack. It was bright yellow. That led to why I was traveling and Young Living as a company. He told me he had used Frankincense before. I gave him a purple bag and challenged him to listen to the 101 class on his way home from work. When I got off the plane 5 hours later, he had already signed up on my team. He asked me a question, and I used it as an opportunity to learn more about him. If you keep the conversation on them, you'll have more data to ask leading questions. If you keep the conversation on you, it will fizzle out, and you'll be left standing there with no forward momentum. Get good at asking good questions.

Another time, I had put some Peppermint on at my son's basketball game. The parent next to me asked, "what is that smell?" That's an easy conversation to transition into oils. She did all the work for me! She is now on my team, after I shared my personal Peppermint story, loaned it to her, and she had her own oils experience. I had never met her before.

The goal of this chapter is just to get the conversation started. Here's a homework assignment for you now. Remember when I told you to go to Starbucks or Panera, or somewhere similar? I meant it. I want you to go and try to have three conversations this week with total strangers, just to prove to yourself that you can do it. Your goal is to walk out, having added three people as Facebook friends. You may not mention oils for a month. Just be chatty online for a while. That's completely ok. Just prove to yourself that you can open the dialogue. Try to sneak in the words, "I think this is the answer you've been looking for." Then offer an oil, if the conversation allows. If not, build trust and wait for the window.

How to Talk To Your Warm Market, Those You Know

Obviously, any of the conversation starters above will double for this as well; but it's good for you to go a bit deeper. Make the goal of the conversation to address an ailment. You want to forge a wellness plan.

The people that know you don't need small talk. They need solutions. Be their solution.

Talking to your mom, sister, or bestie about oils can be really intimidating, because they carry a judgement zone about you and your behavior everywhere they go. It may be a kind judgment zone, but there's always something under the surface with those you're close to. They may be much less ready to try what you have to offer. Don't take it personally. Let them see your success. Saturate them with your stories. Be there for them without judgement. It took me two full years to even have a conversation with my brother about oils. His hand always went in the air, blocking me out, when I started. It took a need that he had (getting rid of the smokers smell in the basement of his new home) for that window to be opened for me.

You may have to wait a long time for that window. Gently drop seeds. Don't allow yourself to be hurt. When the time is right, offer. I call it the gentle drop. My husband got it after he personally witnessed my bathroom experience and a bottle of Peppermint. Now he's a bigger oiler than I am! It's ok if they don't get it right away. Oil them up, loan your stuff out, talk about wellness, meet their need, look for the window to speak into them. Above it all...never give up!!!

Any skill can be learned if you are teachable.

I like the honesty and open book way of Sarah's story. Thanks for sharing your ups and downs so we can all improve ourselves and our businesses.

Micah Robledo

CHAPTER 38

EXPANDING YOUR CIRCLE: HOW TO TAP INTO FRIENDS OF FRIENDS

We are going to take a step away from opening cold discussions for a few minutes, because I believe I have put the fear of God into you; and that's enough for right now. Just practice. Talking to strangers is not as terrifying as it first appears. It's like the 101 script and the bold close. The more you do it, the easier it gets. When you take time off, you have to remember how to do it again.

I want to speak to those of you who ran out when you started your business, signed everyone you knew, and are left with a small pool of people who have already told you no. Your whole church is signed, and everyone has been to nine Oils of the Bible classes. Your 101 classes are dwindling or nonexistent; your mom spends 50pv and complains about it; and you're tapped out. You've been chasing this dream for a long, long time, and the rank just isn't there.

If you have a team of 20 or less, this chapter isn't for you. You haven't even begun to tap your warm market yet, nonetheless your cold market. Practice the tactics from the last chapter at a few sandwich and coffee shops and sign your family, your friends, and everyone in your cell phone that will listen. Then return to this chapter when you're truly burned out. Go get this thing off the ground, then return here when you need encouragement.

If you have a team of 20, you can easily build to Silver with your pre-existing team. It's actually simpler than talking to your cold market from the last chapter, because the people under you already gotten a kit, and even if they're not on Essential Rewards, they have made an investment. That means your knowledge is valuable to them. You can help them get everything out of that purchase.

In *Gameplan*, I told you that the average person knows 2,000 people by the time they are 20 years old. The average Silver has about 100 people on their team. If you have 20, and each of those 20 host a single class with 4 people in it, you're there. Silver is done. When you crunch the numbers, it's not as far fetched as it may seem. Your task is to get in front of them, fire them up, and sign their circle.

How on earth do you do that?? What if you weren't the one that signed them in the first place?? Isn't it a little creepy to get a phone call from a random stranger? Well, in my opinion, not as creepy as talking to a total stranger about the Cowboys, or Oregano on a hoo-haa. (You knew I was gonna drop that one more time in this book, didn't you?) If you EVER talk to a stranger about that topic, by the way, you're fired. That was NOT on the list of conversation starters.

Systematically Befriend Your Team

What I want you to do is to systematically befriends your team (even if you didn't sign them.) Start a conversation with them individually, even if you have to use the talking points in the last chapter. The goal is to get to their health. Find out where they are at. What do they need?

Here is how I open the call:

I want to show off a Senior Star leader on my team, Jessica Yasin. She is just raw joy. She has no problem connecting with people, but she doesn't want to appear "salesy" when talking to friends of friends. When she first started her business, she would sign her circle, then get stuck and not know who to talk with next. She felt like she'd tapped out everyone she knew. Once she became bold in approaching friends of friends, her whole dynamic changed, and now she is solidly running for Executive. She started a texting campaign and gave me permission to use her brilliant words. Let me share a little Jessica magic below.

Jessica's words: *My script is working, so wanted to share it! I now have 10 classes booked this month!*

I'm reaching out to my close-knit circle and those who say they can't afford oils but want them. I ask them, **"Hey Stephanie! May I ask you for a favor? I can really use your help...."** *and then I follow that sentence with this copy/paste script:*

"I was wondering if you could help me reach a goal. Before the end of this year, it is my mission to teach 200 people the dangers of toxins in their home. I want to show them evidence of how the things they purchase everyday can cause sickness in their family down the road by sharing science, truth and fact.

I'm reaching out to my dear friends and asking them to help me.

All I want to do is educate. I know the impact of chemicals, and what it's done to my family. I want the chance to share my story to help others.

If you choose to help me reach this goal by hosting a class for me to teach, and if you can get five friends (or more) in a room to hear me out, I will gift you a hostess basket with wonderful goodies that I know you can you use to protect your family.

Beyond that, if any of your friends decide to get a starter kit and say YES to a better lifestyle, YOU get the $50 commission. I don't want it. It's a thank you for helping me show someone a better way. You have been to my 101 classes and have already fallen in love with oils and with Thieves. My goal is to help you get those for your home for free. There are no strings attached. You never need to "sell". I just want to help you afford the best oils on the earth. You are a precious friend, and I know what it will do for your family to have each person drinking NingXia every day, to get your laundry soap, dish soap and Thieves cleaner for free, and to be able to use your oils generously, without worrying constantly about the cost. If that's as far as this ever goes for you—free oil and pure products for your home—then I feel like I've made an impact on your family. And every day, you're protecting them with each chemical you have kicked to the curb. YOU are why I teach.

Sooooo, can you help me? And do you know anyone else who would be interested a toxin free home? Together we can train our closest friends and family to protect them. Thank you for helping me. I am so passionate about the care of my friends and family!

Much Love.

Sincerely,
Jessica

I then follow with a "you're awesome" GIF.

BAM. Jessica had thirteen people in her first class. Seven got kits. She responded to a few of those people in the days after that class and booked ten classes for the next month. THAT is how you go Silver in Six: friends of friends. Sign your circle, then sign their circle. There is power in the strength of numbers.

Hi, I'm _____, and I'm part of your Young Living support team. You got a Starter kit, and I'm calling to walk you through that kit. I want to make sure you get every drop out of your investment. What do you love most about it?

Here are a few other questions:

- Have you had a "wow" moment with any oil?

- What's your favorite oil?

- What have you tried so far?

- What's your favorite oil to diffuse?

- Where were you when you first got your kit?

- Why did you go to the class initially?

- What made you want to buy the kit?

- Do you have a reference guide? (If not, get one in the mail).

- One of the first things I do when I get my kit is make a list of health goals for my family. Then, I open the catalogue that came with my kit, open my reference guide, and put them side by side to make a wish list of oils for certain health goals. I'd like to demo that for you right now. Is there anything you're working on?

- What are your top three health goals?

- I am going to send you a copy of *Fearless*, which goes through the entire starter kit. It also shows you how to start swapping each room out, systematically (room by room), so you kick dangerous chemicals to the curb. I am also sending a *Fearless* calendar. When you accept the challenges in the book and fill out the calendar, I'd love to gift you $25 off your first ER order. This is going to give you basic aromatherapy training in minutes a day .

- Have you attended a 101 class? 102 Toxin Free Life class? 103 NingXia Class? 104 Savvy Minerals class? I'd like to get you plugged in. Tell me what your schedule looks like. (If it's busy, suggest a textable class or a one on one with them. You will build a stronger bond if you can meet face to face at least once.)

- What products do you see in the catalogue that you'd like to learn a little more about?

- Let's come up with a 3-month ER wish list. I'm going to call you back next month and check in to see how you're doing with your goals and answer any questions. This is my personal cell. If you have any questions, you can always text me.

That's a really long list of questions for one phone call. What I want you to do is gauge where they are at. If you get through one question and they're done, offer them *Fearless* and set a date for another call. Use the tools, because they will do the speaking for you. Maybe you get through five questions, and can save some of the others for another call. The goal is to get a tool in their hands, discuss Essential Rewards, and point them to an event, a class you're teaching in person or online, a #ylunites rally, a business building event like #diamondbound, convention, or a team event. Get them plugged in. Events lead to OGV.

Also, signing their circle has another added benefit. They are 90 percent less likely to let their account go inactive if someone is under them and they know it (especially if it's a family member or friend). If you can't get it in on the first call, with the second or third call, try to see if they'll host a class and bring a few friends. I like to say, "hey, if you can't make it to a class, that's completely ok. Let me bring the class to you. I'd love to teach you and your mom about NingXia; it's my favorite supplement." Always sneak a personal story or two in each time you connect with your team. They love seeing results. One picture, one personal story, can be worth a thousand words, or at the very least, an ER order.

That is how I start the process of signing their circle. Tap into friends of friends. Sign your friends that know a lot of people. They may never build the business, but at least you can teach their friend circle, and they can get their product for free as they cash the paycheck. You might feel a little disgruntled at doing the work; but ask yourself... why? The goal is to increase the number of people on your team and find business builders. You'll increase the number of people on your team by signing their circle. You'll find business builders by teaching classes. One of your friend's friends may be the one that catches the vision and runs. Either way, it's a win-win for you. Go into it with a good attitude and a grateful spirit at the Lord opening another door for your business. All you need are faces. You can do the rest. You have the script and you have fight. (You know how to ask freakishly weird questions to strangers. That's a triple win!)

Co-Teaching to Help Your Leaders Lead

Let's talk about roles for a moment. When a person first expresses an interest in the business, very rarely do I have them tell me from the get-go that they're ready to teach 4 classes a month and go straight to Royal Crown Diamond. It is quite unusual. The vision takes time to set in.

Most of the time, the initial goal is small: to make a little extra to increase their grocery budget; to afford a monthly oils order; to save for a vacation; to get one of the kids into a private school; or to take on a second car payment. Not many can see a Royal Crown Diamondship from the vantage point of a Distributor or Star. I didn't even see Diamond until I was a Platinum. I was pretty confident that I would NEVER do the business until I was Gold, nearly Platinum. Then the whole thing hit me over the head like a box of rocks and it all clicked.

About two months ago, I was invited to teach a class for one of my Silver leaders. In that class, was an incredible leader named Nikki, who had a heart for women considering abortion. She started a ministry called *The Red Egg* on Facebook. Nikki had no desire at all to build a Young Living business. She was up to her neck with multiple other successful businesses, and was a mom and wife on top of it. She came to the class to tell me about her ministry.

I was pretty bold with her, and challenged her as we talked afterward. I said, "what if it was not a mistake that we were supposed to meet? What if God intends for Young Living to be the financial vehicle to fund your ministry?" This poor woman had just attended her first 101 class. She did not even have a kit yet. I knew deep down that she was a rockstar, and the Lord would do incredible things with her. Not only was she humble; but she was gifted, God-focused, and she had integrity. I prayed hard for leaders like Nikki on my team. She gave me a bundle of ministry information, and I thought I may not see her again at another class.

Then I got word from the Silver leader above her that Nikki would like to host a 101 class herself. I was blown away! This was a woman whose plate was overflowing! I went out and taught that 101 for her. I told her, "Nikki, if you can put faces in front of me, I will teach forever for you. My goal is cash for your ministry. Let's do this together. I need faces for my team. You need income for the work the Lord has laid on your heart. Let's work in tandem. Put people in front of me."

Then Nikki, who was not building a business, built a business. I was teaching (though in all truth, she is an expert in natural health and can slay a 101 class herself), and she was getting the check. I was getting the OGV in a leg I needed to maintain Diamond. By teaching classes, we were picking up leaders all over the place. The progression looked like this:

Nikki's Team:

April 2019: 298 OGV

May 2019: 2,638 OGV (Senior Star in 1); held 2 classes this month

June 2019: 3,654

July 2019: 5,644 OGV

August 2019: 6,870 OGV

This is a perfect example of speaking to friends of friends. Nikki tapped into friends of friends in her friend circles.

Do you see, too, how you can become blessed by serving others? I was not sure what my role would be in *"The Red Egg ministry"*. The Lord made it clear over eight weeks. This woman is anointed. People trust her because of her integrity that existed long before she got involved in Young Living. Now her gift of serving others is coming back to her, as the Lord gives her the desires of her heart. All she wanted was a red egg in my pocket when she came to that 101 class. All I wanted was new faces to get that leg to a solid place. By working together, and me not being a stickler about giving her the check for my teaching, we were both blessed.

The moral of the story? Serve your leaders. Whether they are building or not (whether they know it or not), put them first. Do everything with their best interest in mind. Teach for your leaders, and tap into their friend circles. Let the check go. You don't need the $50 in your account for the starter kits and fast start, because you see the vision. You know where you are walking. Pass the vision to someone else, and spread a little hope. You may end up with an accidental business builder.

Systematically befriend your team.

I have never been so pumped! I wish I had started Gameplan bootcamp a year ago when my leader gave me Sarah's book. The sky is the limit. I am a #diamondrising!
Vicki Fierro

CHAPTER 39

HOW TO CRAFT YOUR PERSONAL STORY

Telling your story is, I am convinced, the most powerful part of your class. It's where your passion lies. It's how you decided to do this whole thing. It's what changed the course of the wellness journey for your family. It's what's given you vision, purpose, and hope. When you speak from that place, others will get excited, because it hits them not on a physical level, but on a spiritual level. You are truly changing lives. You are spreading wellness, purpose, and abundance, Gary Young's mission. You are serving the man who cared enough to spend his life building what we have today.

Gary was a master storyteller. If you could spend some time with him, it was like sitting in a room on your grandpa's lap. He threw off times at convention during the general session with other speakers lined up during the day. Diamonds have told stories of old Diamond retreats where Gary would talk for 12 or 13 hours, well into the night. He was the first up in the morning aand the last to go to sleep, (the hardest worker on the farm!) He knew how to push and he knew how to have fun. He lived every drop of his life, never wasting a single adventure. Gary always had the best stories!

A good story has three critical components. First, a story has to have an exciting incident. I love to open my classes with a personal story of running to the bathroom at 5am with an overactive stomach. You need a conflict to make it interesting. Something goes wrong. I assure you, something went quite wrong in the bathroom for me. It was like Armageddon in the toilet bowl. The smell alone woke my husband up from REM sleep through two closed doors.

Second, a story has to have a personal transformation. Both my husband and I were oils skeptics when my kit arrived. I'd been eyeing oils for years but never jumped on them because they were snake oil to me. I believed it was all a farce to get my money. I absolutely didn't want anything to do with MLM's. My grumpy and tired husband, bitter that he had to use my birthday money to order my starter kit, said, "well, we got the stupid kit. Is there anything in it that will help?" I said I had no idea. He told me to look it up. I told him I'd look it up, then go make his breakfast without washing my hands. That's why my sleepy husband googled stomach discomfort and oils; and sure enough, Peppermint oil popped up.

I'd never used Peppermint in my life. I had not even opened the bottle. My thoughts were, "Peppermint patties and candy canes aren't going to stop what's happening in this bathroom." Still, my husband snagged the oil out of my starter kit, and I topically applied about 15 drops on my stomach. (That's a LOT more than I needed, but I had no idea what I was doing). I love to share that part of the story in my classes, because it empowers people to play and to look things up. You don't need to be the expert. You just have to pop open your reference guide and look up "ear" or "knee", and see what it says.

Within 2 seconds, the gurgling sound stopped after the Peppermint was applied. 18 seconds later, the spigot that appeared to be attached to my tush also turned off. I sat there unbelieving for a few minutes, not willing to move from my place of safety on the perch of the toilet bowl. I finally stood up and realized I was just fine. I had undergone a personal transformation. Peppermint, the snake oil, had eased my occasional digestive discomfort. It was the first time I'd ever seen an oil do anything. I played with the rest of the oils in that box, while John got the sleep he desired. I went out to play with the rest of those oils that had sat in the box since the day they arrived.

The third element to a good story is a life lesson. Rocky Balboa, Luke Skywalker, and Kate Winslet's character Rose in "Titanic" all underwent a major life lesson. Make sure you include yours. Mine was that one episode with Peppermint. It forever changed my view that oils were useless plant liquid. Because of that lesson, I went on to share what I'd learned;

and two years later, the stuff inside the cabinets of my home, the way I cared for my kids, and even my finances were radically different. They were changed from 15 drops of Peppermint, a smelly bathroom, and a grumpy husband.

That is my oils story.

Now let's work on crafting yours.

I find it easier to plot out my story if I answer a few questions. There is a neat worksheet for this in the *Unstuck* workbook that fleshes it out even more than I do in this book. To start, here are some things to ponder as you put your story together:

1. Who invited you to your first oils class?

2. Why did you initially set foot in the door? What drew you there?

3. Did you believe in oils?

4. Did you get the kit right away?

5. If not, what got you to get it later?

6. What was your "wow" moment? If you haven't had an encounter with oils yet, it's ok. Tell your upline's story. Tell a family member's story. Tell me why you oil.

7. Are there any other oils in the starter kit that got your attention?

8. Why do you believe in Young Living?

9. Was there a transformation for you?

10. What about a life lesson? Did you learn anything in the process?

11. What do you want that room of people to know about oils? Why do you give up your time to teach to them? Why does it matter so much to you? Spill your passion.

Once you have your words jotted down, try crafting it in story form. Then get in front of a mirror and practice it. Read it to your mom and best friend. See if you can get your story to 10 minutes or less. Then practice a 60-second version of it (something just long enough to get someone's attention). (You know where I'm going next with this, don't you?) Remember Starbucks and Panera? Go test your story out there. Go find a skeptic. Open the dialogue like you so expertly can now with a total stranger, and share your oils passion.

When you teach your 101, 102, 103 or 104 classes—never, ever leave your story out. The people in that room came to connect with you. By sharing, you are giving a piece of yourself to them and walking with them on their journey. It's the personal part of the class. If you hit someone on a spiritual level with your why, they are much more likely to stick around. I tell people, "just a few years in, I cannot imagine my life without oils. We use them every single day. It's completely transformed the way I take care of my kids. I now have one-ingredient plants to run to, instead of a chemical cesspool of dyes, preservatives, and sugar. I will never look at the protection of my family the same way again. We are forever changed because of a bottle of Peppermint."

Hit them on an emotional level. Share your journey, your doubt, and disbelief. Train them to fall in love with oils just as you did. That's the power of a moving story.

Now go tell the world.

Share your journey, your doubt, and your disbelief. Train them to fall in love with oils just as you did.

Sarah your script is with me in every class. Your passion comes out of me in every class. I have all of your books. This is just what I need at this point in my journey.

Angie Kimble

CHAPTER 40

Essential Rewards 101: ER Without the Sales Pitch

You might be wondering why I included how to share your story, how to train on Essential Rewards (ER), and how to close your classes together in a tight little cluster of chapters in this section of the book. It's because this trio of knowledge-packed goodness is mission critical for you to know before you walk in and teach. If you have done this business for a while and have not had results, it's likely one of these three things; not the *type of class* you choose to teach. Study the various classes, settle on how you want to grow (or return to what you were doing initially that had you growing, but that you stopped doing)—and then remind yourself how to do these three things effectively. You are on track to explode your business prolifically if you walk through this list of knowledge. **These are the specific skills needed to grow a Young Living business.** In this chapter, I'll give you language that takes the creepy sales feel out of it so you're more confident and start asking the right questions.

Of the three, Essential Rewards is the only way you can **rank** successfully. Without training the lifestyle, there is no business. You can sign 100 people this year, and if none grasp the concept of what Clean Living is, they will all drop off your team within a year, and it's as if the work you did never existed. You can sign as many leaders as you want and they can duplicate everything you do, but if they have no training on ER, all of you stay at Star. You have to go into every class with ER right in the front of your mind. You have to offer "yes" or "yes" options. You have to offer "good", "better", "best" options— (190pv, 250pv, 300pv, etc...) instead of never mentioning ER at all. When you feel it's too expensive on top of the starter kit, you have already shot yourself in the foot before you've started the class. That's bringing your prejudices into the class with you. You're peppering the class with doubt before you start. **Don't do that**.

The way you train your budding oiler is by using specific language. **You are saving them the most money by offering Essential Rewards.** Consider this:

1. If you buy oils for them, <u>you are stealing their ER points and their free oils.</u>

2. If you allow them to buy one oil instead of the entire kit, <u>you are stealing their wholesale membership</u> at 24 percent off. That's taking money out of their pocket.

3. If you never train them on ER, then they never train the few people they sign (their friends and family) and they never get their oils for free. *You have now stolen their paycheck.*

Instead of looking at the initial cost, look at the long-term cost to their family when you stay silent. I have lost count of the number of people that have told me "Sarah, if you told me about ER at the beginning—I would have done that!" Your silence is because of FEAR, not because of them. Your perceptions of what they will think of you is costing your new oiler money. Stop sabotaging your business and stop sabotaging them!!"

There are a lot of tools to train ER, and all are phenomenal. I can't see a reason to discourage you from using any tool that's been generated for Young Living. I use a specific set of tools, but it does not mean they are the best—they are just what I use. I did design the Diamond Rising Deck around the tools I personally use to help you keep track of how you're training your team, and the Distributor Card is my secret weapon for ER training, but you can customize that card for your own tools. We'll go through that deck card in a few paragraphs, because it's a game changer for running your new oiler through an aromatherapy funnel and remembering where you left off. Knowledge is power. If they know that burning their candle for two hours is the equivalent to the toxins of smoking a pack of cigarettes, they are a lot less likely to go home and burn candles in their home. 40 percent of all candles have lead in their wicks; the same lead that is poisonous to you and your kids. Education happens piece by piece, conversation by conversation, and class by class.

If you have to have 7 to 15 conversations to get the point across to a new oiler, how do you do that without coming off as a salesperson? It's simple. **Keep the focus on education, never on sales.** I get most of my personally enrolled on ER through continuing education. I don't pick up the phone and say "did you get your kit yet? Did you get on ER yet? Why are you not on ER? Don't you understand how much you save?!??!?!!? 10% 20% 25%! 190, 250, 300!!!" The conversation NEVER happens like that. I just start by making sure they have the Core 4 classes: oils, Thieves, NingXia, and Savvy. (You can teach a Savvy class without the makeup; don't sweat it. The videos are powerful enough to keep you from stocking a thousand dollars of Savvy and giving it all away in makeovers. Though if you like teaching that way, that's fine too.) They can color match with the Savvy Minerals Swatch Cards (item #21840) in the Virtual Office and order their own product to play with it.

Just educate. If they have had the 101, funnel them to the 102. If they have had the 102, it's time to funnel them to the 103. Usually by the time they've had the first three classes, they're ordering NingXia for themselves and their family (that alone is over 70pv a month)—as well as stocking the Thieves ER bundle regularly, and ordering oils. They will have fifty ideas in their head for ER just from those classes, not to mention the 3-month ER wish list you build with them. The fortune is in the follow up and the funnel.

You see, you're not "salesy" when you train. You have been given a supernatural gift of wisdom. And you need to share it with the world. I truly believe if most people understood what was in their cabinets, they would make a conscience effort to start cleaning them out. They just don't know. So that's your task. Train them. Don't beat them up over their ER order—just train. Run them through the funnel.

Let's talk about the funnel.

Once a person becomes a member on my team, I start a distributor card for them. I paperclip that card to the Contact Me card in the Diamond Rising Deck, and I can track their entire Young Living journey on a couple of 4x6 cards. You've already been trained on the Contact Me card. Here's what to expect from the Distributor Card.

If they are not on ER yet, I put a little Post-It Note sticky tab on the top of the card. When I have ten minutes to do follow up, I grab the cards with the post it tabs and get to work. The Contact Me card will tell me exactly how they prefer to be contacted.

This is what the funnel looks like:

1. Walk through the starter kit together, showing them my favorite uses for each product

2. Put a pocket reference guide in their hands (discoverlsp.com) and train them how to look things up

3. Complete reading *Fearless* and fill in the 30-day Fearless calendar (the calendar is downloadable for free at *oilabilityteam.com*). Why *Fearless*? It trains the lifestyle. Don't train the starter kit, because they already have it. Train the lifestyle. By working through the 30-day Fearless calendar, they now know how to unbox and use every oil in their kit, to get their diffuser going for 30 straight days, to read labels and look for poison in their home, they engage in the 3-cabinet challenge to swap toxins, and so much more. It's the most comprehensive checklist out there for fully training a new oiler. Just print the calendar, accept the ten challenges and oil on!

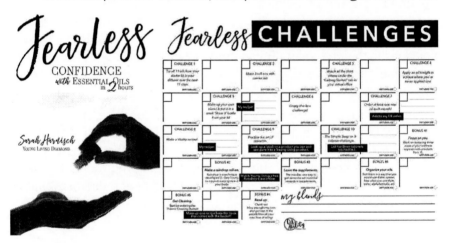

4. I also use the calendar as a tool to get them on ER. I tell them that if they text me a screenshot of the completed calendar, I will gift them $25 toward their first ER order once I see it process. You can do that by sending a check or by putting a credit on their account. You may feel like you are giving a lot of your check away, but the early investment of a reference guide and completion of the challenges so they are using their oils and drinking their NingXia and cleaning with Thieves is worth it. It sets the stage for 100, 250, or 300pv orders for years. The payout monthly is far more than losing $37. If they are a level one to you, and you are paid eight percent on their $300 dollar order, you'd make $24 dollars in month one alone, and $48 dollars, more than your investment, in 8 weeks. Invest in people.

5. Draw up a 3-month ER wish list with your new oiler. I love to sit with them for one session and have them break out the catalogue and their reference guide side by side. Pick five oils that are not in the starter kit and write down what they do in the margins of the catalogue. How would their family use that oil? Train them how to start researching. I love to use the line: *"I'm not a doctor, and I never will be. I'm a mom. I'll never be able to diagnose you. Calling me at 2am for an answer is the same as calling a friend. I have no medical knowledge! But I can look things up. If my knee hurts, I look up "pain." If my ear hurts, I look up "ear". 90 percent of what I have learned about oiling was simply because I played, just like we're doing right now. I played around and it worked. You can call me, but we're going to be doing the same actions; we'll be looking things up in this book. Let me teach you how to fish instead. You are about to see what God can do with the plants He created!"* (Never paint yourself as the expert! That's the way to have a low-stress job!)

6. In that same session, show them how to log into their Virtual Office and place both an Essential Rewards order and a "One Time order." Tell them you can only place one ER order monthly, so I save all the items I want and put them on that one order to get the most points and free items. You can put anything you want in the cart, but it must be at least 50pv (100pv if you want a full paycheck).

7. Show them how to generate their own link to sign their mom and best friend. You can find the link builder tool under the "Member Resources" tab in the Virtual Office and "Link Builder." Simply type in their member number and it will generate a link you can send them via text or on Facebook or Instagram messenger so anyone can sign under them. It autofills their number for sponsor and enroller. Tell them if they sign 10 people under them and get them on ER, they likely will not be paying for their oils, NingXia, or Thieves for their family. That may be as far as the business goes for them; and that's ok. Could you imagine what it would do to your OGV to have 30 members of your team sign 10 people just to get their own products for free? If they all spent 300pv, your OGV would be 9000 every month—nearly a Silver, just by training your oilers how to use their link. That is a simple duplicatable exercise that I do right away.

8. Now they're ready for continuing education. If they still aren't on ER, it's time to get them into the Core 4. If they started with a Thieves class, get them into a 101 oils class, or a 103 NingXia class. There are textable classes, free Powerpoints and scripts, and 30-day

challenge calendars and graphics at oilabilityteam.com under the *Unstuck* button. Get them trained.

Advanced Aromatherapy Training

9. At this point, it's good to invite them to a #ylunitesrally, team event, or (after they have had the Core 4) a specialty class or refresher class that you or one of your leaders are doing. Getting them plugged in will keep them focused on oils.

10. Are they interested in the business? I always give a business tease right at the beginning, because this is where Young Living has made the biggest impact on my own life. It's time to put the $1 mini in their hands, *Your Gameplan: Build A Life Beyond Survival Mode*. They might be part of the 92 percent of Young Living users that never go beyond the starter kit. And that's ok. Your business needs them too! But maybe… just maybe… they will be the next Diamond on your team. You don't know if you don't do a little business drop. Be a hope dropper!

11. Perhaps they are not open to teaching their own class, but they will open their friend circle to you so they can get their products for free. They don't want to tell their mom about Thieves, but they want their mom using Thieves. If you could be that person for them, they'd open up. Most of my business was built this way. Remember, it's not about who you know. That's amateur network marketing. You need to ban that thought from your head, or you'll stay stuck at Distributor. Think outside the box. This is your freedom! It's worth fighting your fear.

12. Ask your new oiler if they are on your aromatherapy training page or business page. Make sure they are plugged in to your social media updates and are following you.

13. After three months, sit back down and revisit their wellness goals. This can be a 10-minute Zoom call. (zoom.us is free if your videos are under an hour). Lay out some new products based on their goals. If you're touching base with your personally enrolled a few times a year, you keep them engaged. You can speak to your leaders all over the world with that service. The Marco Polo app is good for this too.

14. Make sure you're building the relationship. That means talking to them or responding to their social media posts on multiple platforms without talking about oils. Build trust without being a salesperson.

Is all this a lot to remember? I figured as much! That's why I put it on this Diamond Deck card in a series of simple checkboxes so you can track your progress and remember exactly where you left off.

Check it out:

Distributor

☐ on Essential Rewards ☐ not on Essential Rewards

Member name: _____ Member number: _____

Phone number: _____ Email: _____

Mailing address: _____

Date they joined ER: _____

☐ Walked through the kit together and trained on essential rewards
☐ Showed them how to generate their own link to share oils with friends and family (under member resources, "link builder")
☐ Got a virtual office tour
☐ Watched the Getting Started videos
☐ Gave them a pocket reference guide and trained them how to use it (get it at discoverlsp.com)
☐ Completed reading Fearless and filled in the 30-day calendar
Taught them: ☐ 101 oils ☐ 102 Thieves ☐ 103 NingXia ☐ 104 Savvy
Checked in on 30-day challenge calendars for: ☐ Fearless ☐ Thieves ☐ NingXia ☐ Savvy
(Find all four calendars for free at oilabilityteam.com!)
☐ Made an oils wish list (showed them the "Build My Oils Collection" checklist in Fearless)
☐ Broke down their wish list into 3 months of Essential Rewards orders
☐ Invited to a #ylunites rally, team event, or another class
  Dates invited: _____

This is my aromatherapy funnel. This is the training I use <u>without being a salesperson</u> to instill the value of a chemical free life. There is no timeline for working through the card. Some oilers may take much longer, some may be through it in a couple of days. Pace doesn't matter. Freedom does. Make it a goal to help your personally enrolled get all their orders for free. If you make it about them and not about you, you have changed the game when it comes to Essential Rewards. It's the same principal we've trained on since Chapter 1 of *Unstuck*.

As I was writing this page, I **just** got this question on the Oil Ability Facebook page from Patti Cushing:

"This all makes sense. The people I have introduced to ER have used it, but not all the time. And people have said 'no, I just want to try the kit first.' How do I let them know that it's a lifestyle change without sounding too salesy?"

Patti, it happens organically and naturally through training, but with a lot of sweat and exhaustion too, as I teach over and over and over again. The secret is teaching. The secret is relationship. The secret is making it about them. Make the investment of your time. You either sell or you invest. I choose investing.

I pray the funnel gives you some new ideas to approach people. It has worked very well for me! I asked a team of missionaries I was working with if I appeared "salesy" to them, and room of 45 women shook their heads 'no.' They just wanted the information. Missionaries can be a tough crowd to crack because most of them are on missions support. The last thing they want is a sales pitch. They need to see your heart and they need to see your passion and they need a way to make it work. What did I do? Well, I come from a missions background, so I understand the mindset. I gave them the information and let them make the choice. If they can figure out how to get their order for free (and you have a funnel on how to do that above with the link builder and your scripts), they will more often choose the route of oils. They need fact and they need finances to make that decision. Give them both and build your team.

They will move if it's their own decision. That's why no one likes to be hounded by a salesperson. They feel bullied into the decision. Don't bully, educate. Then stand down. (Or, in Sarah style, invite to the next class).

Transfer Buying

One other thing I want to mention here is transfer buying, because it is a huge talking point for you. Your team is already buying certain products from the store. Why can't they buy them from themselves? They will save it in their budget elsewhere, and they can apply that cash to their ER order instead, buying the same products. They'll get 10 percent back on ER right away, 20 percent at 4 months, and 25 percent after 25 months. With oils, a little goes a long way. A single concentrated bottle of Thieves laundry detergent lasts me half a year, even with five kids and two grandkids. If they order from themselves instead of giving their money to the local store, and they train their team to do the same, they'll also find it easier to hit the 190, 250, and 300pv tiers. I'm not just ordering oils I want to mess around with and see what they do. I'm ordering supplements my family needs; including first aid supplies like Mineral Sunscreen, Lavaderm, and Insect Repellant; cold and flu supplies like Inner Defense and Super C; personal care products to keep my teens from stinking, like deodorant and shampoo and toothpaste; cleaning supplies like Thieves Cleaner, dish soap, laundry soap, hand soap, Thieves spray, Thieves hand sanitizer, and veggie wash; OTC medications Young Living Acne Treatment and Thieves Cough Drops and Cool Azul pain cream; supplements like Life 9 and MultiGreens, and even food, like Einkorn crackers and Einkorn flakes for breakfast cereal. These were all things I purchased before Young Living!Instead of spending $50 or $100 a week at the grocery store, I invest in my family business and train my team to do the same.

But the laundry soap on Young Living's site is SO MUCH MORE expensive then what I buy locally!

It seems like it costs more then what you're spending right now, but not when you factor in free oils and oil-infused products on ER, all the free ER points you accrue, the 24 percent wholesale discount, the 10 to 25 percent Essential Rewards discount, and the multiplication factor of every member of your team doing the same thing and seeing it in your paycheck. Suddenly, $29 laundry soap that lasts six months isn't so expensive. I'd spend at least $10 or more on cheap, toxic laundry soap in that time frame (and because it isn't concentrated, it's actually $20 because I need to buy twice as much as what I get with Young Living). I definitely don't get 25 percent off either bottle (that alone takes my Young Living laundry soap cost to $23). I don't get a paycheck from my friends when they buy cheap toxic laundry soap. I also can't use points accrued from my cheap laundry soap to order my toothpaste for free. Oh—and I'm poisoning my family with toxic soap. That is a BIG deal.

Young Living makes sense.

One of my crossline friends, Young Living Platinum Kelly Underwood, had the best write up I've ever seen on Transfer Buying. I asked her for permission to reprint it in this book to bless you, because she is a genius. It's kind of funny, but Kelly was actually at Target when I wrote her for permission to use her writing in Unstuck. She even sent me a photo! You can't make this stuff up! Kelly is LEGIT!

This was her Facebook post:

"OMG! OMG! OMG!!!!!! You guys!!!! Guess what just happened???

I walked into my local Target 🎯 (Surprise, surprise, I know...) and all these flashing lights went off and Usha (my favorite Target cashier) congratulated me and handed me a REDcard with a 24 on it. I asked her "what was the 24 for? Did that mean I got $24 off my purchase today???"

She shook her head no and told me I would get 24% off today. AND EVERY DAY FOR THE REST OF MY LIFE!!!!! 🙌🙌🙌🙌

"Wait, what?" Somebody get me a power wheelchair 'cuz I don't think I can walk... 24% off everything? I ALREADY shop here. I ALREADY love this store.

I noticed my new REDcard also said "VIP25"on it and I asked what that was for. People OMG.... listen to this!!!

She said anytime I shop there, they will give me 25% back in a gift card to buy almost anything in the whole store!!!

*"HOLY **$*%^^#$!!"*

"Usha, you're telling me that for every $100 I spend here, you will give me a $25 gift card????"

Usha nods her head yes. And I am picturing all the $25 gift cards racking up!!! Cha-ching!! 💰

Then Usha tells me in her excited accent that every time I spend $100, (is it possible to leave without dropping at least a hundo?) I would get a FREE gift!!!!

******Are you guys freaking out with me here???*****

I'm sitting in a Target power chair when she hit me with:

"AND..."

My eyes are wide like saucers 😃😃😃*.... "Every time you bring a friend into our store with you, you get $50..... AND that friend gets the same perks we are giving you!!!" Hello to all my friends that are signing up!!! I just scored us a HUGE win!!!*

Then this chick hits me with ANOTHER "And...."

The people are all gathering around me 'cuz I'm basically Target famous now and they are getting ticked 'cuz Usha keeps piling these deals on me and not them.....

She says, "and just for being a loyal customer, after you make just one purchase a month for 3 months, we are sending you another free gift. And at 6 months ANOTHER. And at 9 months, you guessed it- ANOTHER, and ANOTHER at 12 months!!!!!" 😊😊😊

You guys, I stink at math, but even I know this is SPECIAL. This is HUGE. This is a deal worth bragging about. This is news worth sharing. Which is why I am sharing this with ALL OF YOU!!

When I woke up from my amazing dream, I ran to my wallet for my REDcard, which is sadly just a regular REDcard. That 5% savings seems like a huge buzz kill now. A measly 5%??? I kinda wanna cry.

However... YOUNG LIVING actually IS a dream come true, people. All of that amazingness that happened in my Target dream happens every single day with YL!!!

- *As a member, you get 24% off retail for the rest of your life.*
- *With their rewards program, you get 25% back to spend on almost anything you want!*
- *When you place a 100pv Rewards order, you get a FREE gift every single month!*
- *You also get a FREE gift after 3, 6, 9 and 12 months of consecutive monthly orders!*

- *And you get $50 when you refer a new friend to YL and hook them up with their own starter kit.*

The BEST part is that I don't have to look up all the ingredients in YL's products. I KNOW they are safe for my family. So where would you choose to spend your hard-earned cash? My wallet, my precious children; and I will be getting ANYTHING and EVERYTHING I can from YL.

It. just. makes. sense.

Are you already using the Essential Rewards program? Drop a bag of cash below! 💰

Wondering if you're missing out on the best deal? Comment below with a question mark "?"

Before we walk away from Kelly's mic-drop moment, I had to ask her a question. I could not help it. I've been a news anchor for 23 years, and curiosity is part of my nature. If I meet you in person, I will likely ask you many questions, too. All I wanted to know is... DOES USHA REALLY EXIST?? That is an uncommon name!

Here's the story behind the story. Usha DOES exist. She IS Kelly's favorite cashier at Target. The above story DID happen in a dream. And Kelly is a very gifted writer. Here's Usha!

Instead of looking at the initial cost, look at the long-term cost to families when you stay silent on Essential Rewards. Stop sabotaging your business with fear!

We have completely derailed this chapter, but it gets the point across. Train your team to buy from their own business. If you owned a shoe store, you wouldn't go across the street and buy shoes from another store. Buy your own shoes. In the words of Kelly: It. Just. Makes. Sense.

Let's move to a different topic related to Essential Rewards: the process of signing someone on ER and the words you use. So far, this has been the most comprehensive write up I can pen to get you out of the gate with ER. Now we give you the words and the system and you're off and running. Ready? My goal with this chapter is CONFIDENCE. Because if you have confidence with ER, you have a business.

I want you to know the of how I get people on ER. I will walk you through exactly what my classes look like so you can see how I lay it out in front of newbies. I don't save it for the end of the class and drop it on them like a bomb. I pepper the lifestyle through the entire class. I pepper my "why" through the entire class. The bold close is the icing on the cake, because they've already been prepped for it.

Here is a laundry list of some of the things I do in my classes to set the tone for ER.

1. I open the class with my personal story and my oils journey and distrust for all things natural health.

2. I tell them I'm going to share some testimonial stories of what I've seen the oils do at the end of the class; and it's the most powerful part of the lecture. They should stick around till the end.

3. I jump into the 101 lecture and explain what oils are and start to pass around the oils, as I talk about them. For example, when I share my personal story, I pass the Peppermint around at the beginning of the class (it also wakes everyone up!)

4. I do a little tease of the ER promos right at the start of the lecture. I say, "this is the Premium Starter kit behind me on the table. It comes with 12 bottles of oil, NingXia, and a Thieves cleaning packet and hand sanitizer. This is where I started my journey, and where I recommend you start yours. When you order this, you are really close to getting all of this stuff for free *(point to the ER promos on the table and show them off. Pass them around.)* We'll talk more about the freebies later." This makes a really strong case for why you should get on ER at the 300pv or 400pv level monthly, because if you have the product to showcase in class, you're a lot more likely to have 300pv and 400pv orders. If they can see it, touch it, and smell it, it goes a lot farther than seeing an image on a computer screen. I'd recommend getting on YL Go+ so you can expedite the shipping. Put your order on the first of the month, and overnight ship it at a discount. Then, any class you have after the 4th or 5th, you'll have the promos to showcase.

5. When you pass the ER promos around, give a little tease on what each product can do. Tell them how you use them. Share any personal stories you have. It's not a bad idea to type up a little cheat sheet of that month's promos and their uses. I post promo uses written by the Diamonds every single month on the Oil Ability with Sarah Facebook page. Take from that if you need to and make it your own.

6. I'd also print off a quick picture of the freebies on ER with the uses, and hand it out to each person in the class as you pass around the kit. Drop little teases....

7. I like to promo the ER items at the beginning of class, because I usually go through the kit at the end of the class for the last part of the lecture. It lightens the amount of things being passed around the room in one sitting.

8. Once you're done with the 101 class, and you're on your close, it's time to bring up ER one last time. Let me give you a little script to help it roll off your tongue. In the Powerpoint presentation, there are slides I've made to showcase the benefits of Essential Rewards that pair perfectly with this little script.

ER Class Script:

Essential Rewards is the most affordable way to build your oils collection. When you get your reference guide in your hand with your kit today, you're going to want to start swapping things out in your home immediately. The *Fearless* book in your purple bag has a full list of every essential oil single and blend that Young Living has made. Cross off the ones you get each month as you build your collection.

How do I know what to add to my order? Make a list of the top three things you want to work on in your health journey. We have a reference guide in the back of the room where you can look those things up. Pick one or two and add it to your starter kit order. When you hit 190pv (and 100 of that is from your starter kit alone), these are the Essential Rewards freebies that come with that order. (*Showcase them*). When you hit 250pv, these are the freebies this month. Next month, they will be completely different. (*Showcase the free items*). When you hit 300pv (or 400pv), these are the free items. By stocking your home, you'll be getting ___ in free oils and oil infused products.

(Let me give you a sample of that sentence with the math included. "By stocking your home with products you want to try, when you hit 300pv this month, Young Living will give you 212-dollars-worth of free product. That's like spending 90 dollars for 300 dollars worth of items for your family. You can't get that at the grocery store!"

On top of the free products, you also get points to pick out things you want. It may be a supplement that you get for free, or a new oil you want to try, or something practical like swapping out your laundry soap or dish soap. That saves you cash out of your grocery budget, because you don't need to get it at the store. For any order over 50pv, you get 10 percent back immediately in points. If you spend 300pv today, and 100 of that is your starter kit, you will get another 30pv—the equivalent of 30 dollars— in free things you pick out. That's three bottles of oil (i.e. Lime, Lemon, and Cedarwood). It's an entire bottle of Thieves cleaner, which will last you six months, and can clean every surface of your home. It's Thieves foaming hand soap for your bathrooms. The points are IN ADDITION to the free products.

Essential rewards is the best program out there. You get 10 percent back immediately. After four months, Young Living doubles it and you get 20 percent back on your order. After 25 months consecutively, you get 25 percent back. One more math problem, and we'll wrap up. If you place a 300pv order today, you get 212 dollars back in free product (the number will be different each month as the promos change). Then you also get 30 dollars in ER points. You're effectively spending $300 and getting $242 back. That is the most affordable way to engage in the Simple Swap and start kicking all the chemicals in your home to the curb. This is how I protect my family from poisons in the home; and it's how I recommend you start your journey too.

You have heard it all. That's how I talk about Essential Rewards. I let them know they have to change their order every month or it will ship the same product. I tell them that it's like Christmas every single month. I know every box is getting garbage out of my cabinets that I don't want around my kids.

Let's recap.

- Have the promos at the front of the room, and pass them around.

- To do that, you'll have to place your ER order early in the month to have it on hand.

- Talk about what each product can do.

- Share your testimonies on the freebies.

- Type out a little cheat sheet with a photo and explanations of the ER promos, along with what they do.

- At the end of the class, give the 3 paragraph ER script and encourage them to sign up with Essential Rewards right when they get their kit (there are Powerpoint slides for this on the oilabilityteam. com website for free).

- You can offer a little gift for getting on ER right away, like a roll on of an oil that's not in a kit, or a $3 glass spray bottle for the Thieves cleaner that will come in their starter kit.

That's it for ER! It was one of the best Young Living decisions I've ever made. Our home looks vastly different now than it did the day I got my kit. It's about small steps. Each decision is another part of the process of tossing toxic chemicals, and drawing a circle around your home saying, "just because it's in the store, and deemed safe, doesn't mean it's for me."

Now that we hit on ER, let's talk about closing your class in a way that leads to kit sales.

You either sell to people or you invest in people. I choose investing.

Sarah is so wise and giving. Her books and trainings are life-changing. I would highly recommend her to anyone wanting to grow, not only in the Young Living business, but in life. She shares from the heart and helps others to reach their fullest potential.

Evelia Collins

CHAPTER 41

CLOSING A CLASS IN A WAY
THAT LEADS TO KIT SALES

This is the part of the class that everyone seems to dread the most. The education part is easy—but this is bringing down the hammer for the sale, and if you fail, then the last two hours of your life were for naught.

Well, not really, but that's the pressure you put on yourself when you walk away from a class without any kit sales. Don't do that to yourself. The close is actually my favorite part of the class, because it's where you get to get your passion on. End with a powerful testimony from your team. Share more stories. Read the bold close script and knock it out the ballpark with the powerful wording.

I don't need to give you the script again, because it's in the Appendix of this book; but I do want to say that having the room staged, set up, and ready to go is just as critical as the words coming out of your mouth.

Here are some tips that I do to help with kit sales just as I'm reading the bold close out of this book:

1. Have a table set up with a laptop or a tablet that's already connected to the internet and ready to go. If you have a leader or a family member manning that station, it will allow you to stay after and

answer questions without anyone waiting. I usually edify the person running the station. For example, I'll say, "my son Isaiah is back at our laptop with a whole table of gifts for you guys, (purple bags and *Fearless* books). Make sure you check in with him and get that before you leave. He can also help you get your kit tonight. He's taught many classes with me, and is excellent with the Young Living Virtual Office. If you want help navigating the website, take a seat next to him, and he'll make sure you get the freebies for Essential Rewards this month, and will help you pick out the best diffuser. Sign up takes less than 10 minutes; and for anyone that signs today, we have a really nice educational bundle desk reference you will get to take home right now."

2. Have desk references ready to go for those that sign.

3. Have the ER promos on display at the front of the room. Say, "if you didn't get a good chance to check out the freebies this month, I'm leaving them at the front of the room. Feel free to come smell or test any of the products."

4. Make sure you work the room. Go from person to person. Ask why they came. Ask what their biggest struggle is right now. Take them to the reference guide; and show them how to look their questions up.

5. Make sure everyone leaves with a purple bag.

6. Make sure you have the contact forms filled out for every person before they leave. I usually do those at the start of the class in case anyone has to leave early.

7. Keep the energy in the room high. A 1982 study by Milliman, Inc. found that when background music was played in a supermarket, customers spent 34 percent longer with a corresponding increase in sales. In you're at a place where you can play a song off your laptop or at someone's home, and can play music in the background after the class, it will keep the energy in the room high; and people may stick around long enough to snag their starter kit. Slower music causes people to move slower and stay longer, too.

8. Above everything, speak with passion. Share your story confidently. Be authentic. You're on this journey because you don't like toxic chemicals in your home. Tell them why. Convey it with feeling (not as though you're reading off a page). People will hear your enthusiasm. Remember, you're not really selling the kit. You're selling yourself. I like to say, "when you get your kit today, you're not just getting something worth over 400 dollars for $165. You're also getting this team. We are one of the top education teams in all of

Young Living. We love to come alongside you and empower you and train you for free. We can't wait to have you join this team." Sell you!

9. Have fun! Just the act of smiling, laughing, pulling the room into your lecture—it will make it fun for them too. Do a little giveaway. Keep the energy high. Honor the people in the room; enjoy the process. When you are at ease, they are at ease. If you feel tense with the close, practice it a few times. It will take the edge off so you fall into the rhythm of what you practiced at home, and somehow makes it all less scary.

Their feelings, their worries, their struggles take precedence over your fear.

If they have objections, like saying the kit is too expensive, I love that training Royal Crown Diamond, Teri Secrest, has in her book, "How to Be A Stunning Success in Network Marketing" (get it at <u>discoverlsp.com</u>). She uses four words to overcome any objection. They are: "that's the best part!" Let me demo it for you.

"I'd get the kit, but $165 dollars is a lot for some oil."

"Are you kidding me?? That's the best part! You are sitting in a room with the best essential oils in the world. The purest oils in the world. It's extremely rare! 97 percent of all oil is not therapeutic grade! You have the best of the best in front of you, from a company that's 25 years old. The price means you're not getting scammed with oils that won't work. I am so excited that you found this class and found us. I believe this is the answer you've been looking for."

What??!?! Ordering on Young Living is THE BEST PART! Oils ordered on Amazon could be tampered with! You can take the caps right off, dump the oil out and dilute with a carrier, or put synthetic oil in, and screw a new unopened cap on, so it looks like it's never been touched. When you order from Young Living, you know you're getting what you paid for, because it went right from the farm to your house. I would never trust an order that didn't come from the farm! There is no middle man! Ordering from Young Living is the best part; because you know exactly what you're getting: Seed to Seal!"

Why do I need to sign up for Essential Rewards right now, with my kit? I think I'll just wait until my order comes and decide later.

No way! Ordering now is THE BEST PART! Once we close out your order, that 100 PV you get for your kit is gone forever. I can't tack it onto anything else if you decide later on you want ER. If you snag a Thieves ER bundle, or (list xyz off their Contact Me card info), you only need 90VP to get the first tier of ER freebies, because your kit counts as the first 100! THAT'S AMAZING! I wouldn't check out without getting the free things for this month! Essential Rewards is the best part of Young Living!

I don't want to build the business. I'm not really sure why you're asking me to host a class.

Goodness THAT'S THE BEST PART. You want NingXia for your kids, right? You want Thieves to clean your home, right? You want oils for all the things, right? Don't you want FREE NingXia and FREE Thieves and FREE oils? My goal is not to build a business you don't want. It's to get you enough of a check that you never pay for your oils or supplements or cleaning supplies again. If we get ten people signed under you on ER that are also now going chemical-free (you're protecting their families, too), YOUR ORDER IS FREE. You can have unlimited NingXia in your home with no stress on the cost. I will do the teaching. You get humans in front of my face. That's how you get Young Living without any stress on your budget. Hosting a class is THE BEST PART.

Here is another example:

"I really just need one bottle of oil. I don't think I want the whole kit."

"What??!? No way! THAT'S THE BEST PART! The fact that we get 12 bottles of oil, 2 packets of NingXia, an entire packet of Thieves cleaner (that will last weeks), Thieves hand sanitizer, AND a diffuser. What company does that?? More than $400 dollars worth of products for $165? The one bottle of oil you want is a third of the price of the entire kit. I can't believe Young Living packs so much value into an intro kit. This is the best thing in the entire Virtual Office. If you get one oil, I can't teach you the playground of what these do. Let's REALLY study together. God showed off when He made the plants!"

And one more example:

"I'm not going to order right now. I need to go home and think about it first."

"What? Ordering here IS THE BEST PART! I get to put a pocket reference in your hands RIGHT NOW, so you can start your health journey tonight instead of waiting weeks. You are getting one of the top aromatherapy books of all time for free. I'm here tonight to help you navigate the website and set up your account, so you don't have that stress by yourself later on. Getting your kit in a room full of oilers is THE BEST PART!"

Do you see how you can turn the table with your enthusiasm and those four words? It works wonderfully for any objection. Teri is the Diamond I quoted that started her business by sharing a 101 class on cassette tape... and delivering it herself on horseback to her neighbors. What an incredible journey she has been on, and now, with all that fight, and never giving up, she stands before you today as a Royal Crown Diamond. Was it easy? No. I don't believe any Diamond in Young Living will tell you doing this was easy. Was it worth it? I believe you'd get a loud, unanimous, "yes" if you asked that in the halls of the Diamond lounge at convention.

One more thing as we close out the chapter on closing that I think is very important: expect the sale. If you go into your class in a cloud of negativity, you likely won't have anything to show for it in the end. Speak as though the sale of the kit has already happened. Use language like, "when you get your kit today" and "when you join our team" (not IF you join our team). Anticipate the outcome. The people in the room will anticipate it then, too. Don't sabotage your own work with doubt.

Remember, this business is about loving people. Always come from that place. Their feelings, their worries and their struggles take precedence over your fear. If you're focused on them, the close doesn't need to be tense. You have no time or space to be thinking of your emotions. You are giving your time tto show them a better way. Educate and train.

I think about that place where I was five years ago, days before my kit arrived. I had absolutely no idea what was in my house. I truly was living in the dark. I never would have made so many bad decisions had I understood that everything we bring into our home has a consequence. It was almost like living in a dark cave where I can't see my hand in front of my face. My whole world is different today. I view everything that enters our home with scrutiny. I feel a great weight and pressure to make sure people living just as I did have a chance to protect their homes. Arm them with the precious knowledge that you have.

They are worth fighting for. Don't be afraid of the moment they have to choose their kit. It may be one of the most important decisions they ever make. And you get to be in the room.

Expect the sale.

PART SIX

LIGHTEN YOUR LOAD: AVOID COMMON MLM MISTAKES

Sarah's work is everything I've wanted to say but couldn't find the words to say it. I've watched team members break thorough fears, step out of comfort zones, believe they can achieve success, and lead their teams like a boss. She's helping people break down brick walls!

Diamond Shelby Nowak

CHAPTER 42

THE GRASS IS GREENER ON THE OTHER SIDE SYNDROME

I'm definitely not a network marketing expert.

I am a mom.

However, I have been around long enough (a half decade now with Young Living; that's so hard to believe!) to watch a few trends. I always find it fascinating when many people post about what a bad business month they had, and then a few posts down on my wall, two or three other people make Diamond for the first time in the same month. Everyone says February is "a down month" for Young Living, but that was the month I hit Diamond. Some say the summer months are slow, or the month after Christmas; but there are always those that defy the naysayers.

Do you know what I think? I think it has nothing to do with trends, and everything to do with your personal goals. Other companies aren't blowing up while we are stagnant, and it's not time to jump ship or do other businesses as a backup. That's looking over your shoulder. If you have decided this is a rank up month for you, you're unstoppable. You will do the actions necessary to get there. You could also decide that your rank up is six months away—and guess what? It'll take at least six months to make it happen, because that's when you'll work for it. How do you get your runners to run with you? Show them how close they are. Then be there for them. Set the trend, showing that you won't quit. You are the pace of your team. If you clock out, so do they.

Is Young Living's heyday over? Shew. We are a 2-billion-dollar company. We are in the top ten in the WORLD for direct sales, according to Direct Selling News. There are no signs whatsoever of slowdown. Do you know what makes that so amazing? Our primary product is THOUSANDS of years old. I don't think we're going anywhere. Plants were made on the third day of creation, and they are still just as useful today. We have the best MLM in the world, because everyone needs the plants. Revelation 22:2 says, "the leaves of the trees are for the healing of the nations." God had a plan for the plants before He ever even made you and I. (That makes this better than pots and pans, books, supplements, and leggings.) You can't out-create God.

I believe we have a special anointing on this company (solely because of what it does). We propagate what the Lord has created, and train people to go back to the earth and pay attention to what we were given. That's a special burden to carry.

Many have asked me, "Is Young Living forever? Can I count on this income?" Here's the thing... it all goes back to classes. Even if you're a Diamond, it goes back to the work that you're doing behind the scenes: enrolling. It goes back to the action you did to get the rank you already have. You either have fire or you don't. You either build, or you don't. You either get people to catch the vision, or you don't. There is no ending of OGV... just distraction and stagnation, then discouragement.

The neat thing is that if you've landed in that pattern, you know exactly what to do to get out of it. Script. Kit. Human. Repeat. You control the growth of your organization.

But My Leaders Aren't Leading!

Do you have level 1's that are getting carried along? Do you have a family member or friend sitting atop a large OGV, and if they would just MOVE, their check would double with that second leg? Do you look at it every month, frustrated?

There are two things I do in that situation. The first thing I do is run a no-drama team. That includes you. You can't generate drama. Don't take part in it; and don't simmer in it. When you dwell on the speed or strategy of another leader, you are a drama creator. It's messing with your emotional health, and your ability to do what you need to do to rank up. Knock it off. Don't rubberneck other people's journeys, good or bad. Compare you to you. That's it. If your OGV isn't different from this time last year—go teach!

The second thing I do is drop all expectations of what I feel that leader needs to be doing. It's not their job to hold up a leg's OGV; and it's not their job to rank if God's got their head in other things. Do you know the fastest way to spike your paycheck? Collect Silvers. I mentioned it earlier. You get paid more for that action than any other action you can do. It's more than starter kit sales and overall OGV growth. Once you hit Silver, start collecting Silvers like people collect stamps and coins. You make about 128 dollars a month per Silver on your team, depending on how deep they are. Instead of being irritated, go build their second leg if they are in your top five levels. Whenever you are signing someone, build in sets of 2 under your leaders so they can hit Silver. Then collect the extra $128 a month forever. In a year, that one action of them holding rank equals $1536 in your check. If you do that with five other leaders, in a single month, you'd add more than $750 to your check monthly. Sometimes we forget that this is our business too. Grow it.

One of my friends came over this week, discouraged. She asked, "I have been working with a woman now for two years (sending her samples, training, planting seeds). She just signed with someone else. I'm trying not to get down, but this morning she was posting on her page, and she's now building the business. I am so discouraged."

Two years is a long time to pour into someone. I completely understand how that would hurt. Let yourself feel the sting of it, just long enough to never forget, then don't let it happen to you again. The reason the woman signed on another team is because they were persistent. They pulled a "7 to 15 times" on her. My friend planted the seed and did all the watering, and another leader collected the harvest. Whose fault is it? My friend's. Her follow up was not strong enough. It's not the woman's fault. She did not understand she was joining an oily family.

My friend is at a fork in the road. She can get discouraged and say network marketing doesn't work, and freeze in hibernation mode; or she can take an honest look at her follow up skills and get more aggressive, so she's not burned again. Here's what I'll tell you to help you process the loss: God makes no mistakes on where people land. It's why I don't respond when people shoot me a message stating they want to hop teams. The note is just deleted. Bloom where you are planted. If someone you pursued ended up elsewhere, even if it was a good friend. Take a deep breath and be looking to the next person. What do you do when the rank doesn't come at the pace you expect? I had a leader once who did five different network marketing companies in the span of six months.

She jumped from ship to ship, pulling her team in many directions. She became discouraged at the lack of growth.

When you feel demoralized in this business, a spirit of negativity flows over you (negativity, fear, and anxiety). Don't let a spirit of discouragement take over and paralyze you. Scripture is pretty clear about those feelings!

"Peace is what I leave with you; it is my own peace that I give you. I do not give it as the world does. Do not be worried and upset; do not be afraid." ~ **John 14:27**

"Have I not commanded you? Be strong and courageous. Do not be terrified; do not be discouraged, for the Lord your God will be with you wherever you go." ~ **Joshua 1:9**

Let's regroup! What do you do when you're having a "grass is greener on the other team" moment? First up, remember that the Lord orders your business. He draws people to it, raises leaders, fills classes, and grows you into the leader you need to be. There is no discouragement when you realize there are no mistakes on where people land. Hand out mini's in your class and say, "want to learn how to get your oils for free? Read this little book, and I'll call you tomorrow." End your 101 classes and say, "We're going to do a brief teacher training in 10 minutes if you want to stick around." Then get out there and make your grass the greener grass. Be so busy looking forward at the next thing that you don't notice the negativity.

Get out there and make your grass the greener grass.

When I think of Sarah, the word "Life" pops in my head. For all of the times I have heard her either live, via book or CD, life is what she's caused. Her words, her transparency, and her heart is such a blessing. Sarah, you have the gift of lighting a fire in all of us.

Jacquelyn E Lopez

CHAPTER 43

A Spirit of Contentment

I remember the thrill of seeing my first Silver check. It blew me away, because it was about what I was making at the radio station full time, after more than twenty years in my field. We hit Silver pretty fast because I taught for my friends who knew a lot of people. I drove to where I had friends, even if it was a couple of hours away; and I taught relentlessly, at least once a week.

It would have been so easy to rest at Silver. It was the check I was used to. It was easy to do a class a week and stay in radio. The lift was not too heavy for me. I loved radio and had no desire to leave. If my leaders plateau, I tend to see it at Silver, rank more than any other rank. I always itch my head on it, because by the time you hit Silver you know exactly what you need to do to rank. It's the same action for Gold that it is for Senior Star, just a different leg. You just have to keep repeating something you've already learned. Silvers are in the top 1 percent of all of Young Living.

There are two crowds of people I want to speak to in this chapter: those that get content with their rank, and those that are frustrated that their leaders are content with their rank. Both happen every single day in network marketing, but how you handle it is huge. It can determine if you stick with this or not. If you're frustrated with your leaders, remember that at some point, someone may have been frustrated with you. Your business has an ebb and flow to it. Sometimes you're riding high and the OGV growth is on overdrive and you're duplicating like no man's business, and other times you deliver a baby or move across the country and you're not sharing oils. And things begin to tank. Momentum is lost.

Having months where you don't teach isn't a deal breaker in Young Living. That's one benefit to this business: residual income. The check is still there even when you're clocked out. You're not going to slip from Gold to Star in two months. And there are times when other things absolutely must be the priority. You're going to be ok with this field unless that becomes the norm.

Let me tell you the tale of two leaders. To avoid throwing them under the bus, I'm not going to tell you which team they are on, and I'm going to make up completely fake names for them. They are real people. These are two stories of poor stewardship, but for different reasons. These are two stories of contentment. Since my 18-year-old son Isaiah is next to me as I'm writing this, I let him pick the random names for these two leaders. Isaiah says Person 1 is Steve from Minecraft. Person 2 is Rayquaza from Pokemon. Here's a photo of Isaiah and I, just for your pleasure. It has nothing to do with this chapter.

Let's continue.

Leaders That Are Content with Their Rank

Steve is not paying attention to strategy when he builds his team. He has over 40 legs on his front line, as level 1's. He has been sitting outside the rank of Gold for nearly three years. He has to have three legs at 6000 OGV to rank up. Leg 1 is well over 20,000. Leg 2 is at 5200. Leg 3 is at 4800. PGV is in place and his volume is well over the 35,000 needed to rank.

For three years, if he moved 2 people (one at 400pv and one at 300pv) under his second leg, he would have it in place. If he taught 2 classes and signed four people at each, he would have the 8000GV needed to get the third leg over. But instead of teaching two classes, or moving a couple of people, he sat outside the rank of Gold for 36 straight months. The difference in his paycheck monthly would be close to $1500 dollars if he ranked up. $1500 x 36 = $54,000 dollars lost.

I'm going to let that sit in your head for a moment.

Now we move to person 2, Rayquaza, from Pokemon. Rayquaza has a 55,000 monthly OGV. She has two solid legs for Silver, and both are well over the 4000 OGV each that are needed for the rank. She spends 100 PV each month. (Though I have had leaders who would easily have gotten a $300 or $400 dollar check say they can't afford their $100 order to get their paycheck. I sit down with them and say "I need you to hand me $100. I'm going to hand you back $400. Is that ok??" And they still don't get it...)

Back to Rayquaza.

Her OGV is five times what is required to hit the rank of Silver. She has two clear cut legs well over the volume needed for that check. She spends 100 PV a month. But for four and a half years, she has not had her PGV in place. That's the 1000 in volume you need outside your two legs to rank. She has about 300 of it, but not the other 700 needed. 700 OGV is seven kits. That's 2-3 classes. I told her to hold two to three classes and her check will triple. She said she doesn't know anyone. She works two minimum wage jobs. Her check is a few hundred dollars a month. But if she signed seven people, it would easily go to over $3000 a month. The hard work of volume (OGV) and legs is done. The easiest part is left. And yet she doesn't do the work to get the rank. For 4.5 years, she's lost her check. How much of a check? $3,000 dollars minus her $300 actual check times 4.5 years = $145,800. She has lost an entire house in paychecks, or 14 off lease cars. Yet she continues to work two part time minimum wage jobs because she does not think she knows anyone.

If you are one of those people who are sitting atop a goldmine but refuse to move out of fear, let me speak to you directly for one moment. I will say the things your upline wants to say, but out of courtesy, does not say.

ARE YOU CRAZY, MAN??!

This is FREE money. It's like taking a wad of $2700 one-dollar bills each month (Rayquaza) or $1500 one-dollar bills each month (Steve) and tossing it into a burning fireplace. That's poor stewardship. God has brought something amazing to you, and because of either fear, distraction, busyness, laziness, inattention or a lack of education, you are throwing the gift in the trash. You are burning through freedom without using a drop of it. I think of all the people that income would help, and the difference it would make in these builders that aren't building, if they only understood the concept of network marketing and cared enough to stomp out fear and the excuses that follow fear.

Now that I've horrified you, let's say you're in the second camp of people.

Business Builders That Are Frustrated with Their Content Leaders

I am going to sum this one up quickly: the only person you can control is you. You can't help people see a business they don't grasp. When I look out over the sea of people I signed the first year of my business, only a handful actually grasped it and kept ordering, and even fewer became builders. Let your frustrations go and be so busy teaching classes you don't notice who drops off, you don't notice who cuts their ER order, you don't have time to be disappointed at leaders you saw potential in. You just move your feet. You move your feet because you are responsible for your rank, and not any rockstar leader that you may be waiting for. Your business is your responsibility. I see so many people quit network marketing because they can't find leaders. I tell them "you haven't taught enough classes yet to find your leaders." Get out there and keep sharing. Leaders don't need to be hunted. They will find you on their own because they need hope.

A statistic that I think is strange is 92 and 8. 92 percent of all Young Living users are product users; and only 8 percent are business builders. I would love to believe if more people learned the one skill of relationship, that the number would be quite different.

Do you remember earlier in this book when I told you about my identity crisis? I was anchoring a newscast, when my intern dropped a bomb and said I was doing the wrong thing with my life. I ended up coming off morning drive and leaving my job full time.

It took me almost two years to mentally recover from the huge massive shift of what I believed was the only thing I knew how to do. It's because I thought my identity was in radio. I thought that was the only title I had. It took that long for the Lord to show that my identity is in Him. I didn't need to look for anyone's approval, because His was the only one that mattered. I still catch myself slipping, and not allowing my face to look up at God. Instead, I look all around me, rubbernecking, second guessing, and looking for approval.

In *Gameplan*, I shared a very sacred prayer for our family. I prayed it at my lowest point, when I was tired of being on public aid, and being the one always asking for help. I wanted to be the giver, not the taker. I prayed what our team has nicknamed the "Moses Blessing", which was just a prayer of favor, so that we were in a position to give.

For this book, I think it's important that we pray collectively once again; but this time... against that spirit of complacency. When the Lord has something amazing ahead of us, and we get distracted or content, we are missing out not just on a blessing for our family, but also the thousands of families that have yet to join our team. This is a prayer I've prayed many, many times as an adult; and I think it hits at the core of where we are when we're stuck.

We are stuck because we don't talk to people. We're stuck because we rely on leaders under us to build our volume. We're stuck because we lose our mind in an emotional game of what's going on around us. We let one "no" take our mind to the gutter. We allow lies into our heads of who we are and what we are capable of. We stall. We don't see forward movement. It's a snowball of feelings rooted in three words: lack of surrender.

Have you gotten to a place where you've completely let go? Where you've said, "This isn't mine. This business is yours Lord, and I release it?" Releasing it does NOT mean not working it. It means that you do what you need to do without drama, without excuses, and without distraction, but the outcome is 100 percent God's. He gets the glory for every good thing. We release all the emotions and refuse to carry them with us. I think something amazing happens when we don't have to be in control. Our guard is down and we aren't defensive. We release others when they don't live up to our expectations. We let petty things go and drama doesn't destroy our day. We draw people to us, because we are like Christ. It's a game changer for our business.

This is a little prayer of release. We'll do it live together during *Unstuck* bootcamp as well. It's so powerful to have tens of thousands of Young Living leaders praying together, especially for the same thing. When it's about God, and not about us, there is a fundamental shift in our business. It breathes oxygen into us and we re-center and re-focus.

Dear Lord—

I know I don't have this all figured out. I am weary. I feel like everything I do is running in a creek bed against the current. All my actions, in slow motion, despite my effort. And God, I'm tired. I'm tired of fighting to try to make this work. I see others do it well; but I can't seem to get to the same place. It must be possible if they have done it, so why not me??

I realize that the root of the issue is control. I get discouraged when I don't rank as fast as I see others ranking up. I feel like I can't find business builders who are all in, and don't need me to be there. No one seems to want to sit in an oils class. And building relationships is hard. Calling people is hard. Many times they don't even answer the phone. I feel like I'm standing in the middle of my business, in a great big desert, without any wind, alone. I need your wind, God.

I ask forgiveness, right here, right now. I ask forgiveness for my stubbornness, for my standards, for my expectations, for my fear, and for my anxiety and doubt. God, I lay that with you. I am sorry for the noise. I feel like I don't listen very well. I have a hard time being still to hear you. I know that you are bigger than any giant I face. Help me remember that I am a David, because I have you fighting by my side.

This is my year of surrender. I turn my hands up to the sky and release everything I've been gripping with tight fists. I release my downline, my leaders, my classes, my OGV, all my business statistics, my gifts and talents, my time, my family, my finances, my health, my past, present and future. I release it all to you. That means I hold none of it back for me. It's yours. I'm done taking glory that belongs to you. Everything good that I have came from you and you alone.

Lord give me the peace of the sun on my face. Clear the sky so I can be close to you. Be relentless with me Lord and never give up on me. Surrendering means this business is yours. It means my life is yours. It means I don't need to look over my shoulder or get discouraged, because you are in every detail. Thank you for never leaving and forsaking me! You are a good, good God. I can trust you. I am slowly learning to release. Thank you for fighting for me.

Amen

Remember that prayer forever. You just took all those emotions, fear, doubt, pain, and frustration; put them in a box and left them at the cross. It's over. Now we set realistic expectations.

―――――――――

We are stuck because we rely on leaders under us to build our income.

―――――――――

I loved receiving Unstuck at convention! Ignite lit the fire in me and Unstuck keeps me motivated to share from the heart. God bless you as you lovingly help us!

Stephanie Greene

CHAPTER 44

THE CURSE OF EXPECTATIONS

What if we lived in a world where there were no ranks? What if there was no hustle to achieve a goal, but we all slowly worked and one by one slid into an income that was more than we needed, without judgement?

What does hustle REALLY look like? Is it truly 120-hour work weeks? Is it a 40-hour work week atop our already full schedule? How hard do we need to push to win the rank up war?

Do people lose their rank? If they do, do they ever talk about it? How fast am I supposed to be sliding through each new title? Is it one rank a year? Does my upline notice when it takes me too long? How long do I need to work this hard until I can retire? What does freedom look like for us?

Can you have consistency and find time for your family? Is it possible to have both Young Living and a normal life? Have you ever thought, "I'm tired. I'm trying to decide if I want this and if I should put the work in. What does freedom look like for me? Why does everyone else seem to be moving, but I'm standing still? Can anyone help me?"

Let me lay it all out there right now: 10 truths about a Young Living Business that you need to know at every single rank. I'm going to shoot totally straight with you.

10 Truths About A Young Living Business

1. About three percent of your team will be lost monthly to attrition, where they naturally drop off. **Losing people that never grasp Young Living, even after they bought a starter kit, is NORMAL.** The good news is that if you're teaching a class a week, you won't even come close to feeling attrition. You're bringing in far more people than you lose. They got their kit, never reordered, and drop off your team a year later

2. On my team, I have 61 Silvers. Only about 30-40 hit rank every month. I'm not sure if those stats are across all of Young Living; but I know there are about 450 Diamonds, and our names are only printed in "The Essential Edge" newsletter if we hit rank that month; and there are only about 200 names are in that newsletter. **Losing rank, while preventable, is NORMAL.** You are not a failure if you lose your rank. Stop giving up lifelong freedom because you think you don't stack up against the rest of Young Living business builders. The image you have in your head of everyone holding rank every month is not accurate. Instead of giving up, fix the problem. The job you're at isn't going to get you the freedom you're looking for.

3. Yes, there are people who go Silver in 1; in one month from hitting Executive. On our team, there are 10-thousand people. Three in 10,000 have done it. **Silver in 1 is definitely not the norm.**

4. In our largest month, we had 9 people hit Silver for the first time. For almost half the months of the year though, not even one person a month will rank Silver. We see highs right after #ylunites rallies and retreats that I run with my leaders. For the most part, we have a slow steady growth. **Steady is normal.** Rocketship Diamond-in-a-year growth is really unusual if you look at how most of the Diamonds ranked. It's definitely not the majority. Building conversation by conversation, no matter the platform, is normal. If you're losing more people than you're adding, add classes. That's your Achilles heel. Then train your leaders to teach too. If you're OGV is the same time this year that it was last year, focus on the 3 Income Producing Activities: teach, train on ER, train leaders. Don't sit content with a stagnant OGV. Fight for your freedom. But also realize that Diamond a year after your starter kit is not the norm. It's possible, but not the norm. Don't stack yourself up against a standard that does not exist.

5. Paychecks dip and change. In network marketing though, if you are consistently sharing, the general trend is upward. I may have a

1,000 dollar change in my paycheck month to month (which, when I was at the radio station, that would have been crippling). Your check should go up year to year, **but it's very normal to have high checks and low checks in the same year.** This is not a regular 9 to 5 job with a nickel an hour raise once a year, or a white collar job with a 3-percent $100 monthly raise once a year. Your check can bounce by hundreds of dollars, up or down. One or two down months, or even four or five down months, doesn't mean you're not good at this. Every check is not necessarily going to be higher than the last. If you have a year of down months, or you don't like how much your check is dropping over a period of a few months, go back to your three key IPA's. **Do them and nothing else** until you turn the ship around. Don't base your success on a paycheck dip or two or five. Always evaluate yourself year to year, not month to month or quarter to quarter. And don't walk away because of a couple down checks. You have to fight through this if you want to make it all the way. If I look year to year, I am making more this year than I did last year simply because enough of my team holds classes.

6. There are 61 Silvers and 90 Executives on my Diamond team. More than half of them would be Silver if they bolstered their second leg, most by 10-20 kits. That's 7-9 classes. That's 2-3 months of work to get a rank back. **It's normal to have a leader clock out, even after they've seen the check.** It doesn't make you a bad leader. It also doesn't mean they'll never fight for their check again. No now does not mean no forever. (Remember, from *Gameplan*?)

7. I am a Diamond and I also have no-show classes. **No show classes are normal.** They happen to almost every builder. You are ENOUGH if you have no show classes. And after reading *Unstuck*, you know the solution; they didn't know they needed to be there. Build the relationship and they will come. Do the foundational work, and you'll still likely have occasional no-show classes, but you will have fewer of them. No show classes does not mean you can't do this.

8. The workload takes time. It took me 288 classes to get to Diamond. At four classes a month, that would take me 6 years if I did a class a week; but I hastened my pace significantly when I caught the vision at Gold and started to run. A lot of those classes were also online, or I did several in nearby locations in one day (which is how we did it in two and a half years). If it takes you six years to rank Diamond, that would be perfectly in line with a class a week schedule. Don't beat yourself up. **It's normal to build the business brick by brick, at a pace very different than the one you have in your head, the pace you think everyone around you works at.** Those time crunch-

es you place on yourself are not there because of anyone but you. Let them go and you'll likely keep doing the business all the way to freedom. Wake up and conquer this thing one day at a time. The brick-by-brick pace, without burnout, without expectations but with consistency, is what builds a Diamondship. Goals are good. Unrealistic goals are demoralizing. It's rarely the fairy tale story you envision looking at the page of Diamonds that have ranked. There is so much hard work under the surface. And guess what? You are still a brilliant network marketer if it takes you 14 years to get to Silver, because only one percent of people ever even try to get that far. They never see the release you are already fighting for. That puts you ahead of the game, not out of it.

9. Once you get to Silver, there is still work to be done. You have more momentum, but you don't just stop and rely on your downline to keep going without you. Don't underestimate how much of your check you'll use for your business. You have to pull taxes out. You need gas to get to classes. You have to place your ER order. You may do follow up mailings. Lay out realistic expectations of what a Silver income will look like. Just because you hit a rank does not mean you stop working. **It's normal to dedicate a chunk of your check to your business.** Retiring at Gold may not be possible, depending on how much of your check you use for business expenses. Don't kick yourself if your dreams take longer to achieve than you think. You are still good at this business if your dreams are a few more inches past your fingertips. Never stop reaching and never give up.

10. Despite the time I have to put in (alongside my regular job), it's still worth it. It's still more than I'd make with my degree, even if I only hit one new rank a year. No, I don't work 40 hours a week, yet as a Diamond, I am doing pretty well. **It's normal to spend more than two hours a week building your business. It's normal to have to juggle building your Young Living business while balancing all the other things on your plate. It's normal to feel spread thin.** Very few people start Young Living with nothing else going on. If your growth feels slow, remind yourself that you're still doing life alongside this thing. And in the words of Teri Secrest, THAT'S THE BEST PART. You don't have to leave your job to put 40 hours a week into Young Living to get your business off the ground, because it doesn't take 40 hours a week. It can be self-sustaining and thriving with a 2-hour weekly commitment, a 4-hour commitment, or occasional 10 or 20 hour a week commitment alongside your regular job. If you are disciplined with the time you put into Young Living and only do income producing activities if your plate is already overflowing,

you will make it. Here's the thing to remember: every hour you put into this business pays back far more than just a paycheck. It's a legacy. It's like owning a home instead of renting—you have equity. When people get on ER and you keep adding people and more ER to your team, and you talk to friends of friends, this gets a lot bigger than you ever thought it would. That 10,000 Silver OGV seems very attainable with friends of friends and ER. While you feel like you're the only one juggling a lot and dropping a lot, the actual truth is that most builders are juggling a lot and dropping a lot. Don't let that be the reason you lose freedom. Take it slower when you need to slow down. Speed up when you can speed up, but never stop. Stopping costs you everything. Freedom is freedom, not matter how long it takes and no matter how many plates you spin during the race. Your life won't stop for your business. And that's normal. Freedom is freedom, no matter how long it takes.

When I look out over my options, I still can't find anything that comes close to the benefits and blessings of doing Young Living. I'm not saying that to make vague promises to you. It's said after having worked more than 30 different jobs in my lifetime: from corn detassling to pizza delivery to book publishing to being a typist and a radio talk show host and a reporter and a public school teacher and a birthing doula. With all the things I have done, this has still been my best choice. It's worth the stress and the emotional rollercoaster. It's worth the people you desperately want to see succeed that don't try. It's worth the attrition and the dips in OGV. It's worth a rank loss, because I know how to get that rank back. It's worth it all.

Can I challenge you to set your expectations aside? Having a goal is smart. That gets your feet moving in the right direction. Putting a timeline on that goal and telling yourself you're not good at this if you don't hit the deadline, that could cost you this business. It's not the expectations Young Living places on us, it's the lines we draw in the sand for ourselves. No matter how you dice it:

- The income potential is ridiculous on the Income Disclosure Guide.
- The chance to work with family and friends is unusual.
- The ability to see the farms and Gary's work is generous.
- Being able to set your own hours and dictate your work clock is rare.
- Getting a paycheck after you're gone, and passing it down to your kids, that's UNPRECEDENTED in any other field.

Weigh it all. Then don't stop short of your rank. Keep moving. Fight against a spirit of contentment. If you go Silver, that changes a hundred lives for the better. If you go Diamond, about 4-thousand families are impacted. If you go Crown, it's more like 14,000 families changed forever. In the moments where you are weary and wondering if you'll ever make the rank you're running for, pause. Open the virtual office. Look at the size of your team. Those are all faces that forever changed from your yes. There's thousands more that aren't even there yet. That's why we fight to get oils in every home in the world.

Having a goal is smart. Putting a timeline on that goal and telling yourself you're not good at this if you don't hit the deadline; that could cost you your business.

PART SEVEN

KEEP THE MOMENTUM!

You are always amazing because you practice what you preach!

Shelley Greishaw Tomcho

CHAPTER 45

Rinse and Repeat to Diamond
The Story of Kathy: 12,000 to 19,000 OGV in 12 Weeks

Kathy, Feb. 2019	⊕ Ⓢ ████ ████	1	████	304.75	12,109.20
Kathy, March 2019	⊕ Ⓢ ████ ████	1	████	328.00	16,029.50
Kathy, April 2019	⊕ Ⓢ ████ ████	1	████	516.75	17,010.32
Kathy, May 2019	⊕ Ⓢ ████ ████	1	████	305.75	19,436.55
Kathy, June 2019	⊕ Ⓢ ████ ████	1	████	549.25	19,339.00
Kath, July2019	⊕ Ⓢ ████ ████	1	████	1,297.50	20,749.05
Kathy, August 2019	⊕ Ⓢ ████ ████	1	████	402.50	23,561.43

You read those images right. That's nearly a Silvership of growth from February to June alone, in just four months. I don't share the story with you to brag. I share it because it's a powerful tale about the testament of consistency and faithfulness in teaching classes.

In February, I lost my rank for the first time. We had a family emergency and my granddaughter was in the hospital for three weeks. I could not teach classes, because I was with her. That was the right decision. However, I watched my fifth leg leg dip from 17,000 to 15,000 and end the month at 12,000; three thousand shy of what I needed to stay Diamond. Though it is embarrassing, I'm publicly admitting I lost my rank. I lost it once, and I was determined never to lose it again. May that encourage those of you who think that once you hit Diamond, (or any rank), you are infallible. Even Diamonds fall.

I was one of them.

I fell because I stopped teaching. I was out writing books and speaking, and not following my own advice; which is why I'm not writing anything new until we hit Royal Crown Diamond. It sets a bad example for those watching. The freedom and protection of my children and grandchildren is more important than all the desires of my heart. Put those things in a box and focus while you build your freedom, or your priorities are out of order. I truly believe God won't bless the work of your hands when your family is at the bottom of your to-do list. Ask yourself if you are serving them with your actions, or serving you.

Losing my rank doesn't fall on my leaders. It falls on me. It's a statement of my work ethic. You might say that's being harsh, but I disagree. Being there for my granddaughter was absolutely the right choice. However, if I was teaching classes in December and January and was not clocked out, the rank would have been there during the emergency in February. The failure on my part was before the emergency, not during it. Use my mistake to avoid the same pit.

Let me tell you what happened after the shock of my fall from Diamond.

Once we were all out of the hospital, I met with the Silver on that leg and had a pow wow, and basically said this, "We had an emergency last month and it would have sent the wrong message to my family to leave the hospital and teach, but I am back on the horse. Our granddaughter is home and doing well, and it's time to hustle."

Then we did the only thing I know how to do well: classes. It's what I've had success with since I started in Young Living, in-person relationships. We tag teamed each other. Kathy set the classes up and marketed heavily. She built strong relationships and established needs. She edified me on the phone to the attendees and got them excited. She sent out text messages and called the people coming a couple days before and the day of to remind them.

When you are stuck after you've been successful, <u>the **best** thing you can do is do what you did before.</u> Anything less than that is an excuse. It makes no sense to talk yourself out of your gift set, because you clearly have talent if you've had kit sales. You have found your way of sharing. That means you're making an excuse when you've already had results. **Do what got you the rank all over again.** For me, it was sitting in front of humans with a script and a kit. If I can get them in front of me, I can get them signed. I put my arrogant "I'm too busy" ego away, rolled up my sleeves and fought to get my rank back. I had tasted freedom, and I was not going to lose it a second month.

The Silver leader I was working with, Kathy, worked twice as hard as I did. She tirelessly texted people and talked to people and built relationships. Every class I taught had at least 12 (and sometimes over 20) people in it. We were relentlessly signing people, sometimes doing three classes a week, many out of state. We went where we knew people. We signed naturopath doctors, chiropractors, respected Lyme's practitioners, successful businessmen, millionaire realtors, and so many others. I did Zoom calls with leaders across the country on her team, using the coaching sheets I designed in the Teacher Training section of the Appendix of this book.

Kathy did not rest. She lives alone and is retired, so her friend circles are dramatically limited. She never leaned on that as a crutch. If someone had power and influence and an audience, she got them in front of me. She even went to her own personal doctors and leaned on those relationships. We were looking for friends of friends for a fast rank up. You have heard me say this before: it's not about who you know, it's about who they know. Kathy did all the hard work after the classes, funneling them through aromatherapy training, training them on the lifestyle, and securing Essential Rewards.

Because Kathy set the tone for her team, they started duplicating what she was doing. Now she has more than a dozen amazing leaders: Nikki, Chele, Gary, Angie, Rhonda, Kathy, Cat and John, Jodie, Jenny, Andreanna, Melodee and Dave, Janelle, Thomas and Jan, Ben and Lisa, Valencia, and many others beneath them just getting started, that are teaching classes and doing the follow up necessary and the relationship work to get their people to classes and on Essential Rewards. The fire starts with one person and spreads across the field. Kathy has ignited generations with her integrity, persistence, leadership, and example. If you're not teaching, your leaders won't teach. If you're not relationship building, they will not relationship build, and will also have no-show classes and get discouraged. If you're not following up, they will not follow up, and they will not rank up. Be the example to your team. They will copy what they see you do. Kathy is a shining example that persistence works. When you think you have no leaders, but you keep leading anyway, they will show up, one person at a time. Kathy put three years into these relationships, and it's just starting to blossom. For three years she taught class after class alone. Kathy will never be alone again, because she knows how to rinse and repeat. If you're discouraged, don't make the mistake of quitting too soon. It could cost you everything.

Because of Kathy's endurance, we broke massive strongholds over powerful people in her community. She doubled the size of her team. One leader who had no interest in the business ended up on the Dream 1000 board as a winner. I'd love to say it was my work, but all I did was teach the class. Kathy did the hard work by relationship building to get them in the room and by following up afterward. The results don't lie: 12,000 to 23,000 in a little over half a year. Kathy is pacing at 30,000 this month and will have Gold before Christmas. We were both blessed by the hustle. I had my rank back that month, and I've not lost it since. In fact, John and I are 90 kits from Crown Diamond right now. And I have learned my lesson. I will never make the mistake of distraction again.

Let me tell you, step by step, what we did.

When I walked in to teach, Kathy took the floor first. She edified me and told her personal story with oils. Then I stood up and and edified her. I talked about the hard work she put in for her rank and honored her publically. That is huge. (Especially if there are Executive, Senior Star, and Star leaders in the room.) The people that were there just for the oils class got a real kick out of the positivity in the room, and it set the stage for a really great class. As soon as it ended, Kathy was in the back of the room with a tablet walking from person to person, asking their needs. Two other leaders were manning laptops. Every class we did resulted in 100 percent kit sales from her invites. Several people in those rooms she'd been working on for well over a year. Because of the tenacity, relationships, and asking their needs, she got them in the room.

We are now never looking back from Diamond again. It took steady, consistent fight. It took regular, once-a-week teaching.

Lord, all of our success is because of what you have done. Please give us peace. All the glory for our work, it goes to You!

Isaiah 26:12: "Open the gates that the righteous nation may enter, the nation that keeps faith. You will keep in perfect peace those who minds are steadfast, because they trust in you. Trust in the Lord forever, for the Lord, the Lord himself, is the Rock eternal."

If you're completely stuck, here's what I want you to consider:

- Does your OGV increase every month, or are you in a holding pattern, maintaining but not reaching new people?

- Do you check to see how many enrollers you have each month in the Oily Tools app? Doubling that number (the number of people that sign people up) is the fastest way to rank. Work with your runners.

- When was the last time you sold a kit? Are you expecting your leaders to do things you are not doing?

- Have you picked a method of sharing?

- Do you have an idea of what your gifts and talents are, and what you need to do to do this?

- If you've never sold a kit before, is there a certain type of class that resonates with you?

- If you are already a Star, Senior Star, or above, and you built your team, what did you do to build it? Since you became stagnant, have you done the same actions that initially led to your first rank up?

- Finally, the question of the entire book... *how bad do you want this*?

I cannot force you to freedom. You're reading this book because you need hope, so I have to believe that if I share my story, it may light your path just enough that you can see the way out. I have found my way out, and I will do just about anything to help you get there. If I have what it takes, I know you have what it takes. I lived in the projects for a quarter of my life. I lived with an alcoholic father a little less than half my life. I've been exhausted and watched my adrenal glands tank. I've gone to bed cold and hungry. I've slept in my car. I've suffered debilitating medical issues; bleeding that caused dead tissue on my brain and left me bedridden several days a month for 24 years, until I cured it with diet. I've pushed myself to the brink to escape the struggle. I've pushed hard in cycles over and over again. I was pushed to the edge the night I drove my son to Missouri and put him in a special school at the beginning of this book. I've been emotionally and physically at my end hundreds of times. If you are there, let me gently speak into that. <u>There is never an end to the cycle unless you choose it</u>. There is never a period where the stress is less, the crazy calms down, and life gives you enough of a break to pursue this business with the consistency required for multiple rank ups. You must make the decision to do this with all that craziness at the same time, or there is no way out for you. The life that you live will be your life until your last breath on the earth: no income change, no freedom, no rest, no emotional healing, limited ability to give time and resources to those that desperately need you, and no passing of the blessing to the people you care about the most.

May I be blunt?

If you know willable income and the protection of your family doesn't lie in what you're doing right now, *why is that where you put all your time?* Your actions show freedom is not a priority. Why do you complain about finances when you know the way out, but never walk toward the door? Why do you complain about stress and exhaustion, but never teach classes so you can lower your stress and exhaustion? You have the answer right in front of you!

I want you to try the theme sentence of this entire book directly on yourself: "I think this is the answer you've been looking for." Let me rephrase that: "*Young Living is the answer you've been looking for.*" If it's the answer, why do you sit immobilized, when you know how to fly? <u>Don't you know who you are??</u> You have the blood of a Diamond!! No one can hand this business to you. It's only the answer you've been looking for if you put the work in to *make* it the solution.

Do you want it bad enough to do a class a week, get every member of your team to the Core 4 classes in the back of this book and do *Fearless* challenges with them, and train your leaders with *Ignite, Unstuck,* and *Gameplan* once a year?

What do you think that would do for your OGV?

It's time to regroup. Recenter. We've already handed what we were holding onto back to the Lord. We've already let the outcome go. Now we move, and trust that our actions will have fruit, because we're doing things that lead to growth. This is what the building of a Diamondship looks like! One brick at a time, one class at a time, one investment in a life at a time.

When you do that, no one gets left behind. We all fight together.

It's time to group. Recenter.
No one gets left behind.

Every time I pick up Unstuck to read, I am both amazed and inspired by the content and can't put it down! It is such a power-packed book and resource and it is going to help and bless SO MANY people in countless ways!

Gary Westbrook

CHAPTER 46

CLOSING OUT WITH HOPE

It was a cloudy day. It was windy outside. It was blustery. It had been quite a while since I'd seen the sun. I was driving home, up the hill to our house. The winds had changed though, and things weren't quite the way they were before.

The last time I was there was a day exactly like this day. I was contemplating whether or not I wanted to be a mom. Everything was too hard. There was no way out. I was the kind of tired that you can't undo, not easily. I was wearing a lot of hats. Every mom wears a lot of hats and every mom is tired. This was the kind of tired that takes too much to repair. It takes a silent house (an impossibility when you have five kids), good food we could never afford, and sleep when my job called at 4am. This was unfixable. I was stuck.

Not long after that day, my oldest son, the one who had such a hard time articulating with his words, turned to his brother in our van in a moment of frustration, and put a mechanical pencil into his kneecap. He was charged with a felony for stabbing and two misdemeanors. Through a crisis, God brought a pause to our home. My son was sent to a school in Missouri where they could work with him on how to express anger and process consequences. Suddenly, the house was quiet. God gave me time to get on my feet.

The first thing that happened was an adrenal crash. I had been depleted for so very long that my adrenals needed to heal. I started sleeping 18 hours a day. I was awake for six hours, just long enough to go to work, anchor the morning drive, then come home and sleep until my next shift. Sometimes we only heard from our son once a month in an abbreviated call, based on his behavior. It was one of the hardest things I had ever done as a mom. I will never forget that week; driving 17 hours, leaving him in the school driveway, and pulling out with his face in my rear-view mirror as he said, "you're leaving me mom? You're really going?" Then I pulled away. He was safe. We were safe. We were both going to grow over the next year, just in different states.

I was in adrenal failure. I felt like my body was starting to shut down. The other four kids were amazing as we all acclimated to a strange new normal. It was an odd peace in the house we weren't sure we wanted. I wasn't processing emotions correctly. Most of the day felt like a big smear.

Then someone invited me to an oils class.

It was unassuming. I had no idea that the invite would lead to a massive team, and that I would re-learn the definition of friendship. These women and I would labor in the trenches together and our kids would learn entrepreneurship together. It's probably good that I didn't know what was coming, because in my exhaustion, I may never have chosen it. I still had bright blue dish soap on my counter. I still had the wrong smelly laundry soap that gave my son eczema in our cabinets; before I had any idea what was about to happen. This unassuming, weary homeschool mom was going to turn into a protective warrior; banning toxic chemicals from the homes of tens of thousands of people.

In the middle of that journey, my son came home. He grew into a man in a year. He wrapped his arms around me and was calm. He went to college. He got married. He had two baby girls, actually. God never left our family through it all.

Do you ever wonder how you'd respond if you could go back in time and tell your

old self what was coming? There is no way I would have processed a Diamondship then. We were in survival mode. We had 20 dollars a week to live on after food, our van, our mortgage, and student loans. There was nothing extra. Ever.

The photos in this chapter are shots of Gabe coming home. We had lost him for a year. When we saw him again, his younger brother (the one who was stabbed), ran to him and wrapped his arms around him and sobbed in joy. In those moments as a mom, all you can process is the homecoming. I was a Silver when this picture was taken. I'd gotten my kit while Gabe was gone. Even though I was in the top one percent of the company, the business was so far from my mind. I didn't see the possibility of Young Living for another year, when I hit Platinum. I wouldn't have wanted it when this picture was taken. It was more than I could emotionally process. Sometimes you have to walk without understanding why. Sometimes you have to go through the motions even when you feel like you're a shell of yourself, and it seems like no one would want a small piece of what you have to give. Here is the truth: there is always someone who needs you, whether you believe it or not. Your struggle is their answer.

What if, because the business was too much for me with the stress of our son, I'd never taught a class a week? What if I shut it down because my plate was overflowing? I would not have had the income to send Gabe to the special school. I would not have had the money to pay for his counseling and the counseling of all of our kids, after his homecoming. Young Living helped pull me through that crisis, because I taught classes and did the hard work alongside the chaos of a year-long emergency.

I have thought it out several times.

What if I had not said yes?

What if I never went to the class? I said "no" to it for several months before I finally went.

What if I never ordered the kit? What if I never reached for Peppermint to experiment?

What if my husband never saw it work?

What if I said I was too weary to build the business?

What if I gave up before I started?

What if I said the rank took too long to come?

What if I said I didn't know enough about oils?

What if I said I had no upline support?

What if I said I had too much on my plate with an autistic son and a full-time job?

What if I said I couldn't find people that would listen?

What if I never tapped into my friend's friend circles?

What if I never drove to classes with my kids?

What if I said it was too hard?

What if I didn't teach consistently?

What if I stopped at Silver?

What if just one of those things happened… and we never made Diamond? There would be no *Gameplan* or *Unstuck*. What if none of it ever happened? 1.5 million families were impacted just with some words on a page. The words were there because of a kit, a script, and some humans. That is how it all started.

What if you could see the impact you'll have on the people who aren't on your team yet? What if you could reach into their families and see what happens when you stand on top of fear, and say, "NO! You don't get the victory over me today!"

Just say yes.

Banish all the thoughts in your head that tell you you're not enough.

Banish all the lies.

Banish all the excuses.

Get out there and change the world. Turn your palms up and release it all. Surrender.

Because though there are so many no's on this road, weary one, it only takes one yes to change it all.

One yes to get Unstuck.

What if you could reach into their families-- look inside-- and see what happens when you stand on top of fear?

Appendices

Appendix A: Simple 101 Script (oils) • • • • • • • • • • • • • 357

Appendix B: 102 Script: Toxin Free Life (Thieves) • • • • • • • • 369

Appendix C: 103 Intro to NingXia Script • • • • • • • • • • • • 381

Appendix D: 104 Script: Savvy Minerals • • • • • • • • • • • 393

Appendix E: Closing Scripts • • • • • • • • • • • • • • • • • 403

Appendix F: Teacher Training • • • • • • • • • • • • • • • • • 409

Appendix G: Essential Rewards in Clear Language • • • • • • • 415

Appendix H: How to Use the Gameplan System • • • • • • • • 417

Appendix I: Gameplan Resources • • • • • • • • • • • • • • 421

Appendix J: Young Living Ease • • • • • • • • • • • • • • • 423

Appendix K: FAQ • 427

Appendix L: Who Gets Paid? • • • • • • • • • • • • • • • • 445

Appendix M: Poaching • • • • • • • • • • • • • • • • • • • 447

Appendix N: Advanced Strategy + Basic Compensation Plan Training • 449

Appendix O: Gameplan 3 Topics: Research Outlined • • • • • • • 453

SIMPLE 101 SCRIPT
BY YOUNG LIVING DIAMOND SARAH HARNISCH
TAKEN FROM THE 2ND EDITION OF GAMEPLAN

Note: Get your diffuser going with Peppermint for alertness before the start of class. Have Contact Me cards on hand from The Diamond Rising decks. They will collect the information you need for flawless follow up. Have them fill out the cards as they file into the class. Then start with your story! What got you into oils? What were your "wow" moments? Share that first. Then come up with your own personal stories for several of the oils at the end of the script.

WHAT ARE ESSENTIAL OILS?

They are the most powerful part of the plant.

They are distilled from shrubs, flowers, trees, roots, bushes, fruit, rinds, resins, and herbs.

Oils consist of hundreds of different natural, organic compounds.

In humans, many oils provide support for every system in the body: your skeletal system, muscular system, circulatory system, endocrine system, hormones, respiratory system, and immune system. They support brain health and a healthy weight. They are used extensively for spiritual support in your prayer life, as well as emotional support. They have been used for thousands of years as beauty aids. An oil in a diffuser can soothe a child's tough day at school, and provide a calming effect when you've had a stressful day at work. Oils can be used as an alternative to cleaning chemicals in the home. You can literally start swapping out every single chemical in your home to live a purer lifestyle; and you can do it without breaking the bank! The kit we're training on today is the Young Living Premium Starter kit, a $412 dollar bundle that's steeply discounted to $165 dollars. It comes with 12 full-sized bottles of oil and a Desert Mist diffuser with 11 different colored light settings (including a candle setting). This one kit contains respiratory oils, pain oils, immune support oils, stress oils, emotional oils, digestive oils, oils for alertness and oils for fear, as well as internal, aromatic and topical oils—and our powerhouse products of NingXia (a whole food liquid supplement loaded with antioxidants) and Thieves, the most affordable oil-infused plant based cleaning line on the planet. Thieves kills 99.9 percent of all germs and bacteria! I love this kit because it gives you a whirlwind sample of some of the best products we have. Let's jump right in.

You do not need to be an aromatherapist to use them. In most cases, just rub it topically onto the skin. There are three main ways to get oils into your system: the English apply it topically (rub it on the skin); the French ingest and cook with it; and the Germans diffuse and inhale, which is the most effective method because it doesn't have to pass through the digestive system.

How do they enter? How long do they last?

Tests have shown that oils reach the heart, liver, and thyroid within three seconds when inhaled. They were found in the bloodstream within 26 seconds when applied topically. Expulsion of essential oils takes three to six hours in a normal, healthy body.

ESSENTIAL OILS HISTORY

Oils were first mentioned by name in the Biblical book of Genesis, Chapter 37, when Joseph was sold to the slave traders. They carried spicery, balm, and Myrrh! Genesis ends with the burial of Joseph's father, anointed with Myrrh. There are over 1,100 direct and indirect mentions of essential oils in Scripture.

Some of the oldest cultures on earth used essential oils. The Babylonians used Cedarwood, Myrrh, and Cyprus. The Egyptians used essential oils for beauty and embalming. They have the oldest recorded deodorant recipe made with essential oils. Pakistan and Rome used essential oils in communal bath houses.

They were even used by Christ! Jesus was given gold, Frankincense, and Myrrh. Frankincense is sometimes referred to as "the coconut oil of essential oils," because it has over 10,000 uses.

Essential oils were used by the Medieval Europeans, many of whom brought oils back during the Crusades.

It was only after World War II when essential oils were "rediscovered." The science on their uses grows with every single year.

DO ESSENTIAL OILS WORK?

I used to buy my Lavender online, at farmer's markets, or at bulk foods stores. In the United States, there is no rating system for essential oils. It would be wonderful if there were; because then you'd know what you were buying! If you walk into a grocery store and look at a box of cereal, you'll see nutrition facts on the side. There are no "nutrition facts" on the side of oils. That means you must trust the source. You have to know the company you are purchasing from. What sets Young Living aside? Seed to Seal.

SEED TO SEAL EXPLAINED IN 2 MINUTES

The one thing that sets Young Living apart from all other oils companies is our Seed to Seal promise. Let me break down what Seed to Seal actually means.

At Young Living, we do not strip constituents to make our oils smell better. We do not mix species of the same oil. We do not spray weed killers or pesticides or herbicides or use genetically modified seeds. We spend $12,000 per acre to hand-weed Lavender, instead of the industry standard of $60 an acre for the same plant. The industry standard is $60 per acre because spraying pesticides is much cheaper than hand weeding. We do not distill with solvents like hexane.

Our soil is not tainted with mercury, arsenic, glyphosate or any poison because our fields are untouched by toxic chemicals. We harvest at the exact time of day that Young Living's research team has found to be the ideal time for that specific plant. We know when that peak is because of our extensive library on oils; the oldest and largest globally, compiled from nearly 30 years of research at farms on six continents.

Gary Young grew Helichrysum essential oil at St Marie's in Idaho, then Mona in Utah, then the Mediterranean country of Croatia to watch its scores on our Seed to Seal testing. We don't grow it where it grows natively. We grow it where it grows best and produces the most effective oil for the body. Our farms are all over the world, and you can visit them yourself, ANY of our farms, if you like, because we are transparent.

We test eight times at the farm, then again in Spanish Fork, Utah, then again after bottling. We do 24 tests per batch to make sure the oils meet our standards. Then they do third party testing with two accredited, respected, independent labs. Young Living's oils are tested by scientists with over 180 years of combined lab experience. Most of the scientists were hand-trained by founder Gary Young himself.

Young Living is a global leader in essential oils, with nearly two-billion-dollars in sales annually. That means those that use the oils keep returning, because they work. There are three-thousand global employees, 600 life-changing products, 16 corporate and partner farms, more than 20 international markets, 50 highly trained scientists, 12 independent partner labs, and six million global members.

To say we are the same as a generic off brand or a brand at the grocery store makes no sense. They are two completely different products.

Why use an oil to get away from chemicals, then use an oil laden with chemicals??

You cannot have quality without cost. The two go hand in hand. Irradiated mechanically separated rib meat is not the same as pastured grass-fed organic beef. You get what you pay for! We understand that in every other industry... except aromatherapy.

A third-party lab test doesn't make an oil pure. Saying your oils are better does not make them pure. Integrity, hard work, and high standards do. THAT is Seed to Seal. And that is why Young Living is different.

It's our promise of purity. You can learn more about Seed to Seal at seedtoseal.com. All of our oil is shipped from around the world to Spanish Fork, Utah, where it's run though vigorous 8-point testing to ensure purity. Those tests are run in triplicate at the farm, at Spanish Fork, and a third time before bottling. It's why Young Living has never had a recalled essential oil in over two decades of business. You can trust the integrity. Seed to Seal is based on three pillars: sourcing, science, and standards. Young Living's oils are tested by scientists with over 180 years of combined lab experience. They also do third party testing with two accredited, respected, independent labs.

Young Living is a global leader in essential oils, with nearly two billion dollars in sales annually. Those that use the oils keep coming back! There are three-thousand global employees, 600 life-changing products, 16 corporate and partner farms, more than 20 international markets, 50 highly trained scientists, 12 independent partner labs, and four million global members. What does that mean? The testing is thorough and precise. It's why I don't buy from a mom and pop oils shop. They don't have the team to do the testing that's needed to stay on top of hundreds of oils and blends. They don't have Seed to Seal. You can visit our farms.

Why can't you just buy oils at the grocery store? Purity. You get what you pay for. I have seen bottles of Frankincense for seven dollars at the grocery store; but it costs more than that just to distill! It's a red flag that the oil has been altered in some form.

All oils in the world fall into one of four categories: Authentic, Manipulated, Perfume, or Synthetic.

Authentic means the oils are 100 percent pure, with no added synthetics or other additives in the bottle. These are Young Living oils!

Manipulated means the final product has been made to smell more pleasing and less earthy. Some of the heavier molecules have been stripped out; or another additive has been introduced, to enhance the aroma.

Perfume oils are not pure. They are mixed with synthetics to enhance the aroma. These oils have no therapeutic action. Frequently, solvents are used to extract the plant.

Synthetic oils are not true oils at all. They smell nothing like the original plant and are typically labeled as "scented products."

Authentic is the only true pure oil. Synthetic oils would be like opening your fridge, taking a glass of orange juice, and diluting it 95% with chemicals before you drank it! It wouldn't have the same benefits of a full glass of pure orange juice. That's why you want authentic oils. Before you purchase, check to see if the company grows their own plants, has Seed to Seal, and controls the entire process from the farm to the sealed bottle. Pesticides, pollution, previously farmed land... all of it can affect the quality of an oil. Why would you go the extra step of using an oil to get away from a chemical, only to use an oil laden with chemicals. It makes no sense.

(Note: do not read the italicized lines if you're not using the 101 Powerpoint).

I want you to see the impact of what spraying a crop with pesticides can do to the human body. There was a study in Sweden that was catalogued in a video called "The Organic Effect." This is pertaining to food. However, when it takes tens of thousands of Rose blossoms to make an ounce of Rose oil, the oils are even more concentrated than food, so a pesticide sprayed on the crop with show in the oil even more concentrated than on food, like an apple skin. This is why we don't spray. Watch this video.

Young Living's Seed to Seal process is a promise of integrity. There are no pesticides used, no artificial fertilizers, and no weed killers. The plants are harvested at their peak. They're then put through a vigorous testing process. Then they go from the farm directly to your home. Seed to Seal is not a slogan, it's a promise.

WHY DO SOME OILS COMPANIES SELL OILS CHEAPER THAN OTHERS?

Most essential oils are sold cheaper than others because companies cut corners to save money. If you spray your crop with pesticides, you have more crop to distill. If you use a chemical solvent to extract the oil, you pull more out. If you dilute it with a cheaper oil, or a carrier oil, you stretch the oil you have distilled, and can easily sell it cheaper.

HOW OILS ARE MADE:

It takes a great deal of work to produce a tiny amount of essential oil!

60,000 rose blossoms provide only one ounce of Rose oil.

Lavender is abundant (220 pounds will provide seven pounds of oil).

Jasmine flowers must be picked by hand before the sun becomes hot on the very first day they open, making it one of the most expensive oils in the world! It takes eight million hand-picked blossoms to produce 2.2 pounds of oil.

A Sandalwood tree must be 30 years old and 30 feet high before it can be cut down for distillation. Gary Young's Sandalwood trees must be 90 percent dead before they are harvested.

A little goes a long way. Most oils are $10 to $30 a bottle. Depending on oil thickness (viscosity), a 5-ml bottle contains about 90-100 drops; and a 15-mL bottle contains about 200-240 drops. Each application is one to three drops, meaning even a small bottle will get you 45 to 90 applications. Thieves cleaner is made of plants only; and it costs about $1.50 a bottle to make. You can't even get that in the organic section at the grocery store! It replaces a multi-purpose cleaner, glass cleaner, and floor cleaner. The organic versions of those can run you four to six dollars a bottle. Thieves cleaner and Thieves hand sanitizer come in the starter kit. Two Thieves products come in the starter kit. There is an entire Thieves class I'd love to teach you on the power of this oil blend—it's our 2nd class is a Core 4 series of free aromatherapy training that our team offers. We love to come alongside you and train you in simple, easy steps. For today, I recommend you start with the starter kit and add the Thieves Essential Rewards bundle. In one swoop, you can affordably replace just about every chemical cleaner under your cabinet. Essential Rewards is a program that pays you 10 percent back immediately on everyday products you already use—like toothpaste, shampoo, and dish soap. When you order them from yourself instead of at the grocery store, you also earn points back and free oils for certain tiers. (Show ER freebies for that month). This is how I got most of my oils for free, by buying from myself to go toxin-free. AND your starter kit counts toward your ER points if you select Essential Rewards before you check out. The Thieves bundle will revolutionize how you clean your house. Check out these before and after photos of the power of Thieves in the home! That's where I began my oils journey, and where I recommend you start yours.

ARE THEY SAFE?

There are certain oils that are photosensitive, meaning you don't want to wear them and go outside. These are mostly citrus oils, like Citrus Fresh, Lemon, etc.

When using on your skin, always watch for redness and dilute with a carrier oil. Dilute oils on children, because their skin is more permeable and absorbs the oils more quickly. What is a carrier oil? It's a fatty oil (like olive oil or coconut oil), and its molecules are much larger than those of essential oils. Using a carrier oil with an essential oil slows down the rate the body can absorb the essential oil, because it must ping pong through the large molecules of the carrier oil to get into your skin

Be wary of putting the oils topically near your eyes. Some oils, like Peppermint, can cause a burning sensation. If you are placing an oil near your eye, apply the oil to a Q-tip instead of tipping the bottle toward your face.

You can become desensitized to an oil if you use the same one day after day. I rotate my oils every three to four days.

What about internal use of essential oils? NAHA, the National Association for Holistic Aromatherapy, one of the top aromatherapy organizations in the United States, doesn't advocate essential oils for internal use. Why? Most oils companies don't carry any GRAS (Generally Regarded as Safe) essential oils. Many argue that internal essential oil use is unsafe; and I would agree, in some circumstances. You need to make sure you're checking the labels first. Young Living Vitality oils are approved for internal use, just like a food additive. You have been consuming essential oils internally for most of your life, for instance, Wintergreen or Spearmint when you chew gum, or put Oregano in your pasta.

NAHA also bases a lot of their decisions on the British model, which advocates topical use only. Many of the British studies are flawed. For example: done at extremely high doses, or in ways the oils aren't used. Young Living utilizes all three methods, British, French, and German. The French have been safely using some essential oils internally for decades. Young Living's Vitality line has distinctive white labels so you can easily recognize which oils are safe to take internally.

ON THE FLIP SIDE...

Look at the ingredient list of what you have in your bathroom and kitchen. Every day we put products on our skin, in our body, and breathe them in; but many of these products contain damaging chemicals. The average woman applies over 300 chemicals every day to her body just through soaps, makeup, shampoos, and hair care products. Eighty of those products are applied before breakfast!

When you use Young Living's essential oils, you're using a product with one ingredient, like: Lemon, Oregano, or Tangerine. There are No synthetic additives and no yuck.

Is all this a bit overwhelming? Let me tell you how I started my oils journey: with a Young Living Starter Kit. It's the only item on the Young

Living website that is half off! If you're a frugal like me, this is the best bang for your buck! Let's run through the oils in the kit.

(Pass around the Premium Starter Kit with Diffuser, open the bottles, and smell them.)

Frankincense. One of the top skin oils. It helps smooth the appearance of skin. It's the key ingredient in Young Living's "Brain Power" essential oil blend. Diffuse during prayer time to help with grounding and purpose.

Lavender. Oil of relaxation. Diffuse for a calming, soothing aroma. Unwind by adding a few drops to a nighttime bath. This is one of the top oils to support healthy skin. It's referred to as the "Swiss army knife" of essential oils because of its many uses. I love this for bruises, blisters, rashes, bug bites, and burns.

Peppermint Vitality. It helps support gastrointestinal comfort. It promotes healthy bowel function and enhanced healthy gut function. It helps maintain efficiency of the digestive tract. It may support performance during exercise. I call this my "highway hypnosis" oil because 1 drop keeps me alert while driving.

Citrus Fresh Vitality. Diffuse to freshen the air. This blend is a mix of Orange, Tangerine, Grapefruit, Lemon and Mandarin oils. It's a replacement for chemical-based home fragrances. Spritz in rooms, closets, and over linens. Dilute with V-6 carrier oil, and use a perfume. It also helps to tone and smooth the appearance of skin. This is a powerful oil for immune support.

Thieves Vitality. This helps support a healthy respiratory system; and it helps maintain overall wellness when taken as a dietary supplement. Add a drop to hot drinks for a spicy zing! This is the first oil I use when I feel like I am "coming down" with something. Gargle with it in water.

Peace and Calming. This is one of my favorite kid oils! Though I have been known to sneak a few drops onto my hands and enjoy it as well! I use it to bring peace to the chaos in my head. It's different than Stress Away in that Stress Away is for prolonged use during the day, and specifically for the sort of "fight or flight" stress that comes on fast. Peace and Calming is more for the evening to slow your mind down. Peace and Calming contains Ylang Ylang, Orange, Tangerine, Patchouli, and Blue Tansy.

Stress Away. This promotes wellness and may be an important part of a daily health regimen. It's one of the top emotion oils blends! I use Stress Away before the onslaught of a heavier day. This oil contains Lime, Copaiba, Vanilla, and is like a massage for the senses.

Lemon Vitality. Its citrus flavor enhances the taste of food and water. The key ingredients are Thieves and NingXia Red. It may help support the immune system. Use it to get sticky goo off your hands or skin or to degrease pans.

PanAway. Apply after exercise to soothe muscles. It has a stimulating aroma. Apply to the back and neck for a soothing aromatic experience. It supports the appearance of healthy skin coloration. It's Also great for headaches.

DiGize Vitality. This is the top oil blend for supporting the digestive system. Add two drops, along with a drop of peppermint, to water for a stimulating beverage. Take it in a veggie capsule internally. Use with Essentialzyme at every meal to support a wellness regimen.

Raven. This is a cleansing blend of Ravinsara, Peppermint, Eucalyptus Radiata, and other essential oils. Raven creates a cooling sensation when applied topically to the chest and throat. Diffuse up to three times daily for a soothing aroma. This oil changes the game for anything involving breathing.

Valor. Valor contains Black Spruce, Blue Tansy, Camphor Wood, Geranium, and Frankincense. The Valor blend was used by the Ancient Romans in the bathhouses before they sent their soldiers into battle. Its smooth, relaxing scent is designed for courage and bravery.

I told you earlier that the kit comes with 12 bottles of oil, a diffuser (I recommend the Desert Mist), 2 packets of NingXia, two Thieves products, an aromaglide roll on cap that can turn any bottle into an instant roll-on, for $165. There is no yearly membership fee. If you don't order, you just go inactive after 12 months. When you hop on Essential Rewards, you can pick out products you want to try every single month as you start kicking toxic chemicals to the curb in your home. Going chemical free is a process that you do a step at a time.

Check out this quick video of Young Living Diamond Sarah Harnisch and her five kids showing what the inside of a Young Living home looks like.

(show Scavenger Hunt video)

I want to end the class with a challenge. It's called the 3-cabinet challenge. Go home and look at the products that are in your home right now in any three cabinets. Pick things you've used for years and take a look at the list of ingredients on the back of the bottle. If there's an ingredient you're not familiar with, type it in Google with the words 'dangers of'. You will be blown away at some of the poison lurking in your cabinets. Today I'm giving you a free copy of the Amazon best seller Fearless. In the back, it goes room by room, telling you how to have a chemical free kitchen, and a chemical free cleaning closet by swapping out the toxins for pure Young Living products. Start with the place where you're most convicted and take baby steps to kick the chemicals out of your home.

We want to come alongside you and train your friends and family in toxic-free living. My goal is for you to place your oils orders for free. If three of your friends sign up with Young Living, the cost of your kit is covered. If you have a five to ten friends fall in love with the lifestyle and get on Essential Rewards, you'll get a check each month that will cover your NingXia, Thieves, and oils so you don't need to take the cost out of your monthly budget. I'm willing to come and teach to your circle to educate them, for free, to give you the blessing of free oils for your family. Talk to me after class if you want to learn more. Young Living was one of the best decisions I've ever made for my family!

How do you order? Simply go to www.youngliving.com, click on "Become a Member," and use the number of the person who told you about oils as enroller and sponsor. It's that simple. Welcome to the world of oils!

The 30-Day Oiler Challenge

I want to look you in the eye and challenge you. We're going to kick this class up a notch. I believe in training you long after this class is over. We are an education-driven team, which means we work alongside you to train you on the Young Living Lifestyle. Let's train for 30 straight days, on oils alone.

This is a training you can do completely by yourself! I am going to give each of you a copy of the *Fearless* book. I've also printed a *Fearless* calendar (oilabilityteam.com/fearless). In the back of the book are 10 oils challenges, mapped out, like a scavenger hunt through your starter kit. Put this on your fridge. Fill it out by doing the challenges. And you'll learn how to get every drop of goodness out of your kit! Send me a screenshot of your completed calendar for some freebies. We want to come alongside you and train you in this new life. It's going to alter the way you look at every toxic chemical in your home. Young Living is a game-changer.

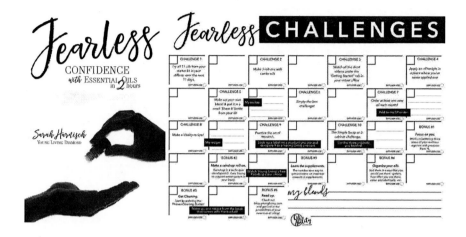

Note: End with the Bold Close script from the *Unstuck* Appendix

The entire *Oil Ability Powerpoint* presentation parallels this script perfectly and comes with embedded media and videos. There are Powerpoint presentations available for the Core 4 (101, 102, 103, and 104 classes,) and Textable classes for the Core 4 (101, 102, 103, 104); as well as (for the first time ever) the Gameplan mini (a prospecting textable class!) Free 30-day challenge calendars and graphics are free on the same site as well. Find it all at oilabilityteam.com/unstuck.

SIMPLE 102 SCRIPT:

TOXIN FREE LIFE (THIEVES)
BY YOUNG LIVING DIAMOND SARAH HARNISCH

Welcome to the Thieves class! I am excited to have you here! My name is _____, and I have been using Young Living since _____. I'll be handing out Contact Me cards as we kick this off so we can customize the aromatherapy training directly to your needs. You'll walk out of this class with a completely different perspective about how to clean your home and why it's critical to kick poison to the curb. This class centers around the Young Living Thieves line.

Let's take a peek at what a Thieves home looks like.

(Play video in 102 Powerpoint of the Murray Family.)

(Share Your Story)

Why Natural Health (And Natural Cleaning) is So Important

According to the cancer.org site, 609-thousand Americans will die from cancer this year, or 1,670 deaths per day. 1 in 3 men and 1 in 5 women will have cancer by the age of 60. Cancer is the second most common cause of death, exceeded only by heart disease. The American Cancer Society says only 5 percent of all cases are from gene defects. That means 90 to 95 percent are under our control, caused by excess weight, tobacco, or exposure to toxic chemicals. It's what we're allowing into our homes.

The National Institute of Occupational Safety and Health studied 2,983 ingredients in our products at home and found 884 toxic ingredients. 314 caused biological mutations, 218 caused reproductive problems, 146 (they knew) caused cancerous tumors; but were allowed in the United States, even though they were banned in other countries around the world.

To protect your family, begin making changes with your home, and the biggest offenders first. Start with laundry soap, dishwasher soap, cleaning supplies, candles, and plug ins, Toss the candles and plug ins. A candle is filled with dangerous petrochemicals. Dr. Andrew Sled, who specializes in Environmental Toxicology, says burning a candle in your home for two hours is the same as smoking a pack of cigarettes. 40 percent of candles are made with wics containing lead, which is not safe to breathe in. By make a swap from candles to a diffuser with Lemon oil in it, you're supporting your immune system instead of harming it.

Let's take a look at the labels of some of these products and their carcinogen ratings. No one else will be the gatekeeper of your home, save you.

(Click through 102 Powerpoint slides with EWG app photos on popular products at oilabilityteam.com).

Twenty-six seconds after exposure, chemicals are found in measurable amounts in the human body. The average woman applies 300 chemicals to her body a day (80 before breakfast). The top 10 most dangerous chemicals in our home: air fresheners, like plug ins or candles. Chemical cleaning supplies for your counters, floors, toilets, drain and oven cleaners, furniture polish, dishwasher soap, and dish soap are also culprits. What do you think the number one poison in the family home is? Laundry soap, fabric softener and dryer sheets. You're poisoned three ways: as you're cleaning your clothes it's filling your home with chemicals, then you wear them all day and have a topical exposure to your skin, and they outgas all night in your closet. Other dangers in the home are hairspray, gel, shampoo, and deodorant. Deodorant with aluminum is one of the leading causes of Alzheimer's and Parkinson's disease in the United States. The information about the most dangerous chemicals at home comes from a government study called the "U.S. Environmental Protection Agency's Top 10 Killer Household Chemicals".

What happens when your body is chemically overloaded? You may see it as something as catastrophic as cancer. Most of us feel it in other ways: lethargy, inability to focus, sleep trouble, chronic inflammation, unexplained pain, fibromyalgia, skin issues, adult acne, hormones, hot flashes, stress, anxiety, and fear. If you face any of these issues, it's time to kick chemicals to the curb. You can control what you allow within the walls of your home.

Seed To Seal Explained

The place to start is Seed to Seal. It is the standard of purity for Young Living. That means no chemical overload. You can trust the name. Young

Living is an essential oils company based out of Utah. The one thing that sets Young Living apart from all other oils companies is our Seed to Seal promise. Let me break down what Seed to Seal actually means.

At Young Living, we do not strip constituents to make our oils smell better. We do not mix species of the same oil. We do not spray weed killers or pesticides or herbicides or use genetically modified seeds. We spend $12,000 per acre to hand-weed Lavender, instead of the industry standard of $60 an acre for the same plant. The industry standard is $60 per acre because spraying pesticides is much cheaper than hand weeding. We do not distill with solvents like hexane.

Our soil is not tainted with mercury, arsenic, glyphosate or any poison because our fields are untouched by toxic chemicals. We harvest at the exact time of day that Young Living's research team has found to be the ideal time for that specific plant. We know when that peak is because of our extensive library on oils; the oldest and largest globally, compiled from nearly 30 years of research at farms on six continents.

Gary Young grew Helichrysum essential oil at St Marie's in Idaho, then Mona in Utah, then the Mediterranean country of Croatia to watch its scores on our Seed to Seal testing. We don't grow it where it grows natively. We grow it where it grows best and produces the most effective oil for the body. Our farms are all over the world, and you can visit them yourself, ANY of our farms, if you like, because we are transparent.

We test eight times at the farm, then again in Spanish Fork, Utah, then again after bottling. We do 24 tests per batch to make sure the oils meet our standards. Then they do third party testing with two accredited, respected, independent labs. Young Living's oils are tested by scientists with over 180 years of combined lab experience. Most of the scientists were hand-trained by founder Gary Young himself.

Young Living is a global leader in essential oils, with nearly two-bil-lion-dollars in sales annually. That means those that use the oils keep returning, because they work. There are three-thousand global employees, 600 life-changing products, 16 corporate and partner farms, more than 20 international markets, 50 highly trained scientists, 12 independent partner labs, and six million global members.

Integrity, hard work, and high standards do. THAT is Seed to Seal. And that is why Young Living is different.

What Are Essential Oils?

They are the most powerful part of the plant (the lifeblood of the plant). They repair and restore the plant when it is attacked or injured. In the human body, they have access to the limbic lobe of the brain. That part of the brain controls heart rate, breathing, memory, hormones, stress levels, and blood pressure. Oils are tiny (smaller than viruses). They hit your cells in 3 seconds when inhaled, and 26 seconds when applied topically.

Why would you want oils in your home? Oils have no yuck. They are just the distilled plant in steam form. There are millions of uses such as: to support systems in the human body like your cardiovascular system or your endocrine system (which effects hormones), supporting your joints, your brain, or liver. They are used to replace chemical cleaning supplies. Thieves cleaner is all I use to wipe down my bathrooms, my stove, and my kitchen. I even mop my floors with it. It's made of plants and five essential oils. You can use oils to replace your personal care products. Young Living has an entire line of shampoos, soaps, conditioners, eye creams, and face washes that are completely chemical free. If you use oil infused supplements, you get the benefit of the supplement along with the power of the oil.

It matters where the oils are sourced. There are four types of oils on the earth:

- ♟ Grade A: **Authentic**
- ♟ Grade B: **Manipulated**
- ♟ Grade C: **Perfume**
- ♟ Grade D: **Synthetic**

It's so important that you only use grade A oil because of the concentration in the bottle. It's like eating an entire apple tree sprayed with pesticide, instead of one apple. It makes no sense to go the extra mile to get away from chemicals, and then use an oil laden with chemicals.

Let's take a look at a powerful video that shows the effects of spraying crops. This study was done out of Sweden and is based on food. Essential oils are much more concentrated. When it takes 60-thousand rose blossoms to make an ounce of Rose oil, the concentration of the pesticides sprayed on those plants and in the ground is much higher. Look at what one month of clean eating, and getting rid of the chemicals, can do to the level of chemical exposure in the human body.

Play "Organic Effect" video in the 102 Powerpoint, available for free at oilabilityteam.com.

If you save 30 cents when you buy grapes at the grocery store by going for the sprayed grapes instead of the organic ones, I have just rocked your world! That is why Seed to Seal is SO powerful. It's not always about getting the cheaper version of a product that you possibly can. It's about the protection of your family. Now that you understand purity, let's switch gears and talk all things Thieves. We're going to do a little history class, a little math class, a little science class, and then send you home with some Thieves cleaner for you to make yourself. You'll wipe your kitchen down and fall in love!

What is Thieves?

Thieves essential oil is a blend of five powerful Young Living oils. It's spicy, hot, uplifting, and energizing. And it is one of the most famous oils in Young Living; one of the oils that put this company on the map in the early 90's.

Thieves oil is in Thieves Household Cleaner. To kick this section of the class off, let's take a look at a one-minute powerful video of what Thieves cleaner can do. The pan in this video had been through 11 dishwasher loads and a full scrubbing with a steel wool pad. Yet it could not stand up to Thieves!

Show Thieves Cleaner video in the 102 Powerpoint at <u>oilabilityteam.com</u>.

Let's take a look at the power of Thieves. I'll show you how it cleans and what it does to bacteria. Thieves kills 99.9 percent of all germs and bacteria. It's just as powerful to clean with plants over harmful chemicals. Look at these before and after photos of the power of Thieves.

(Click through photo montage in the 102 Thieves Powerpoint at <u>oilabilityteam.com</u>)

A Whole New Way To Clean

That video is pretty incredible! Thieves will revolutionize how you clean your home. It has been a game changer for me. I recommend you start with a $165 Young Living Thieves Premium Starter Kit. It's where I started my journey, and where I'd suggest you start, too. The starter kits are the only thing on Young Living's website that are HALF OFF. When you order, you get a 24 percent discount for life. Forever. Any oil you get from that point on, or any Thieves cleaning item, is 24 percent off. There's no yearly membership. There are no fees. Just snag your kit and enjoy a lifetime discount.

The Thieves Starter Kit comes with:

- 15-ml Thieves
- Thieves AromaBright™ Toothpaste
- Thieves Fresh Essence Plus Mouthwash
- 2 Thieves Cleaner

- 2 Thieves Foaming Hand Soap
- 2 Thieves Spray
- 2 Thieves Waterless Hand Purifier
- 5-ml Stress Away™
- AromaGlide™ Roller Fitment that turns any bottle of oil into a roll-on
- 10 Sample Packets of essential oils: Thieves, Lemon, Peppermint, Lavender, and Peace and Calming.

That means you get Thieves essential oil, toothpaste, mouthwash, cleaner (which replaces all the cleaner in my home), hand soap, spray that you can use for shopping carts or airplane seats (or to spray your kids hands down in a restaurant before you eat), and hand purifier.

What is Thieves cleaner used for? Here are 12 ideas:

- Put it undiluted into a roll-on and make a stain stick for your clothing with no chemicals.
- Pour it onto spots on your carpeting (undiluted) and get rid of stains.
- Let it sit on pots and pans with burnt food stuck to the bottom of them.
- Put a cap of it in a spray bottle of water and use it as surface cleaner for your kitchen, bathroom counters, sinks, your stove, or your bathtub.
- Add some to a bucket of hot water and mop your floors with it.
- Put a little Thieves cleaner in some baking soda and make your own soft scrub without any chemicals that you can use in your oven.
- Refresh a musty carpet by putting Thieves oil in some baking soda, let it absorb, and then sprinkle it over your carpets.
- After washing your clothes with Thieves laundry soap, add four to five drops to a dry washcloth and toss it in the dryer to make your clothes smell fresh.
- Put one drop of Thieves on anything sticky. Put one drop of Thieves on anything stuck to an object or a kid (or any sticky residue you don't want), and wipe it off.
- Clean your dishwasher by running an empty cycle with vinegar and two drops of Thieves oil.
- Add a drop to the cardboard insert of your toilet paper rolls to have Thieves freshness in your bathroom.

It's some of the best glass cleaner replacement I've ever seen. Spray it right on your windows to take gunk off. It's also great for detailing cars and cleaning the dashboard.

There is no yuck in Thieves; just plants and plant-based materials. You can literally replace everything under your counter with one bottle.

What about Thieves oil? That also comes in the Thieves Starter kit. Why would you want that? The oil is a lot more concentrated than the Thieves cleaner. Thieves oil doesn't contain the other plant ingredients that allow the oil to be evenly spread through the cleaning solution; so if you make it at home with straight up oil you'll end up with oil and water.

Five Uses for Thieves Essential Oil

- Put some on your feet and spine for immune support. Dilute it with coconut oil if you're putting it on kids.
- Take Thieves Vitality internally for the same reason. One of my favorite recipes is 10 drops of Thieves Vitality, 8 drops of Oregano Vitality, and 2 drops of Frankincense Vitality in a veggie capsule.
- Add a drop of Thieves Vitality to the toothpaste on your toothbrush to feel fresh.
- Put it in the diffuser as a favorite fall blend, it has cinnamon and clove in it.
- Clove has a numbing effect to it. I like to put Thieves on my teeth to sooth them when they hurt.

The History of Thieves

Let's talk for a moment about Thieves and what's in it. The Thieves blend contains Clove, Eucalyptus, Rosemary, Lemon, and Cinnamon. It's based on the legend of the four thieves in Marseilles, France dating from the time of the outbreak of the bubonic plague. Century after century, from the 1300's to the 1700's, outbreaks claimed up to half the population of Europe. There was a nasty outbreak between 1593 and 1608.

About that time, an aromatic legend developed around a brew called "Marseilles Vinegar" or "Four Thieves Vinegar." The group allegedly confessed they used it with complete protection against the plague while they robbed the bodies of the dead. There are a variety of recipes out there; but they included dried rosemary tops, dried sage flowers, fresh rue, camphor, garlic cloves, and vinegar, which were too steep for seven or eight days to fight (as history has it) the Black Plague. The vinegar was noted in a number of famous medical books published later on, including the Pharmacologia from 1825. As the legend goes, these Thieves covered themselves in this herbs and essential oils mixture before robbing the bodies of the dead. They were a mix of spicers, perfumers, and embalmers. The magistrate caught up with them and was going to behead them but offered them amnesty if they explained how they were touching the bodies of the dead without dying of the plague themselves. They gave him their oils secret. That is the story of Thieves.

D. Gary Young, founder of Young Living, is the most responsible for the story reaching the legendary status it has today. He created the Thieves blend in 1994 for immune support, as the result of his study at Warwick University in London. Gary said quote, "I must tell you I have read 17 different versions of the Thieves story. Some claim there were four thieves and some claim there were as many as 40. Most of the legends took place in the 15th century, but others put the date in the 18th century. The formulas varied from one story to the next, but through my research, I was led to four key botanicals that were mentioned again and again— clove, cinnamon, rosemary and lemon—four of the same ingredients that make up the Thieves oil blend today."

Young Living doesn't just have the Thieves Starter Kit; it has an entire line of Thieves products: bar soap, cough drops, dental floss, dish soap and dishwasher powder, mints, veggie soak, and even Thieves wipes. This is a better choice for your family. It's simple, requires no prep, and easy to swap. If affordability is an issue, consider this: when you get a Thieves starter kit, you get 24 percent off your oils for LIFE. It's a wholesale membership. When you sign up for Essential Rewards, (which ships Young Living products you pick out each month on a date you choose) you get 10 percent off right off the bat. That means they are paying you 10 percent back for buying your laundry soap and your dish soap; and there's no chemical yuck inside. After four months, you get 20 percent Back. After 25 months, you get 25 percent back, just for buying your cleaning supplies on Essential Rewards! No grocery store I know does that!

There is a laptop set up in the back of this room where you can snag your kit today. As a thank you, we have a whole educational bundle to put in your hands to train you how to use the kit. I'd also recommend we pick a date to do a 101 oils, 103 NingXia or 104 Savvy Minerals Makeup class together; because we believe in training you in the Core 4 Aromatherapy classes! When you know better, you do better.

Let's wrap up with the science of Thieves, I'll show you where to start, and we'll get you out the door.

Science of Thieves

Thieves is proven to kill 99.9 percent of all germs and bacteria. It's because of the constituents inside the oils. The science of Lemon, Rosemary, Eucalyptus, and Clove in the Thieves blend cannot be denied. One study out of Brazil showed Clove killed bacteria and yeast, with a concentration of only .2 percent essential oil. The study authors said Clove was so powerful that it could be used as a "preservation method". They recommended it for the food industry and dentistry. (https://www.ncbi.nlm.nih.gov/pmc/articles/PMC3769004/)

First, I'll show you some "mom studies" of the power of Thieves. Then we'll look at the science and what this oil looks like in a Petri dish.

Click through the Science of Thieves slides in the 102 Powerpoint at oilabilityteam.com.

Thieves + Math

It's time for a quick math lesson. We already covered history and science! You're getting a full school day in! I'm not terribly quick on my feet when it comes to calculating costs of products at the grocery store, but Thieves is a no-brainer. It's significantly cleaner than green cleaners, and even cheaper than chemical cleaners. Each spray bottle of Thieves cost 88 cents to make out of the concentrated cleaner. And it kills 99.9 percent of all germs and bacteria! With one bottle, (and you get two bottles in the Thieves Starter kit), I can get 27 spray bottles. Each bottle lasts me a week. Simply add 1 capful of the concentrated Thieves cleaner to a spray bottle of water and you're off and running. It's the cheapest green cleaner out there! And it works! This one simple swap will revolutionize how you clean and help you to toss most of the harsh chemicals under your kitchen sink.

If you're overloaded by the concept of oiling, Thieves is a brilliant place to start. Oils are the gateway to natural health. They are like fast-food natural health: apply and carry on. There is no tincturing, no fermenting, no weird things growing in jars on your counter. All the hard work is done at the distillery and out in the field. Then it goes from Young Living's farms to your home. In a single order you can knock most of the chemicals out of your home with Thieves alone. It's not going to break the bank. That's CHEAP. It's a simple easy gateway into the world of oiling. You're protecting your family from more than a dozen different toxic cleaning solutions with a single bottle of Thieves Cleaner.

If you don't have a starter kit yet, I'd recommend the $165 Young Living Thieves Premium Starter Kit. Add the Thieves Essential Rewards Bundle to clear out nearly all of your cabinets in one swoop. My favorite items to add to a Thieves-themed Essential Rewards order are Thieves laundry soap (item #5349), Thieves dish soap (item #5350), Thieves Whitening Toothpaste (item #26668), and the Thieves Home Cleaning Kit (item # 20421), with a full cleaning bucket and carrying case for your cleaning oils.

Where do you start?

Start small. Start slow. Start with what you're convicted on. Let me give you a simple tip. With your food, simply start by reading the ingredients. If you can't pronounce it, don't eat it. It doesn't mean you can't have ice cream; just go for the ice cream with milk, sugar, eggs, and vanilla, instead of an ingredients list of 35 items you can't even pronounce.

Learning to integrate oils into your home is about small, simple, baby steps. Take it one month at a time. Maybe the first month you focus solely on Thieves cleaner; and toss every chemical cleaning supply under your sink. Go home and wipe your kitchen down and fall in love, knowing you just boosted your immune system instead of taxing your liver.

The next month, swap out some laundry soap or dish soap. Month three, focus on your personal care products, like deodorant and shampoo. Month four, focus on beauty supplies, like face wash. Every day you leave your makeup on, your skin ages by seven days. Use a chemical free option to get it off.

I started this journey, myself, with a Young Living starter kit and have never looked back. We use the oils every single day in our home. Every oil you use is a chemical you're not using. This is where I began; and it's where I'd recommend you start.

There are photos of these bundles in the 102 Powerpoint at oilabilityteam.com.

The 30-Day Thieves Challenge

I believe in training you long after this class is over. We are an education-driven team, which means we work alongside you to train you on the Young Living Lifestyle. Let's train for 30 straight days, on Thieves alone.

This is a training you can do completely by yourself! I am going to give each of you a 30-day Thieves Challenge Calendar (oilabilityteam.com/unstuck). There are Thieves challenges every day for 30 days, mapped out, like a scavenger hunt through your Thieves starter kit. Put it on your fridge. Fill it out by doing the challenges. And you'll learn how to get every drop of goodness out of your kit! Send me a screenshot of your completed calendar for some freebies. We want to come alongside you and train you in this new life. It's going to alter the way you look at every toxic chemical in your home. Young Living is a game-changer. Accept the 3-cabinet challenge and look for poisons in your home. Look up the ingredients in the products you use the most, and start swapping them out.

Young Living is the best decision I've made in my chemical free journey! You matter. Your family matters. Your friends matter. You can take control of your own health. You don't have to feel the way you do. You don't have to feel tired, groggy, swollen, exhausted, or sore. Start kicking the chemicals out of your life and start living clean.

The entire Oil Ability Powerpoint presentation parallels this script perfectly and comes with embedded media and videos. There are Powerpoint presentations available for the Core 4 (101, 102, 103, and 104 classes,) and Textable classes for the Core 4 (101, 102, 103, 104); as well as (for the first time ever) the Gameplan mini (a prospecting textable class!) Free 30-day challenge calendars and graphics are free on the same site as well. Find it all at oilabilityteam.com/unstuck.

103 Intro To NingXia Script
By Young Living Diamond Sarah Harnisch

<u>Outline for the speaker:</u>

- What Is NingXia?
- Share your personal story
- How Gary found NingXia (sound file; play in free Powerpoint at <u>oilabilityteam.com</u>)
- What does NingXia do?
- Science: Why does it work? Here are 7 quick reasons!
- The Wolfberry Test
- Odd Ways to Use NingXia + NingXia shots from corporate
- Starter kit + ER
- The 30-day NingXia challenge

Prep: All media elements are inserted into the free Powerpoint. Place a bottle of NingXia on a table behind you to use later, where all can see it. Have NingXia shots prepped for those in the room. Have media ready to go (though the script can stand alone without the media; simply skip media elements). Have a NingXia Starter Kit on hand as well as the ER promos for the month. This script, just like the 101 and 102, covers simple topics with simple answers to share with a friend on a couch.

Video 1: Play this at the start of all your classes. *https://www.youtube. com/watch?v=hs82eTbo_cl*

Welcome to the powerful NingXia class! NingXia has changed my life; and I am glad to have you here to train on it! That video is a snapshot of Young Living, the company that produces NingXia. This is an intense, concentrated training on one of the most powerful whole foods on the planet. My hope is that when you leave, you start taking this as a regular daily supplement, and get as much of your family drinking it, too.

WHAT IS NINGXIA?

It's not always about what you're cutting out, it's also about what you're putting in. If I could only pick one Young Living supplement, I'd pick NingXia.

Can't you just get what you need from your food? No. Not anymore. The food the Lord created when He made this earth is not the food that's being grown here now.

Food is repeatedly grown on the same land, with pesticides and fertilizers. Scientists are creating new varieties of crops to grow faster and resist bugs. The plants don't have the time they need to absorb the same nutrients. The soil loses its vitamins, minerals, and microbes faster than they can be replaced.

A Kushi institute analysis of nutrient data from 1975 to 1997 (just in 22 years) found average calcium levels in 12 fresh vegetables dropped 27 percent, iron levels 30 percent, and vitamin C dropped 30 percent. You would have to eat eight oranges today to get the same amount of Vitamin A that your grandparents got. (Scientific American).

Maybe you can't get enough from plants, but you think you can make it up with meat. When plants contain fewer nutrients, the animals that eat them are also malnourished. A study from the "Journal of Nutrition and Health" found copper levels in the UK are down 90 percent in dairy, 55 percent in meat, and 76 percent in vegetables.

Water is also depleted of minerals because of the plants and modern production methods. Then there are town filtration systems. Many of them remove important minerals, like magnesium, which is essential for 300 biochemical reactions in the body. They top it off by adding chlorine and fluoride.

Beyond that, nutrient absorption declines with age. The older we get, the less we absorb.

Nutrient deficiencies hurt your performance, cause DNA damage, make you age faster, and cause chronic disease. That's why we need to supplement.

WHAT IS NINGXIA?

It's whole Ningxia wolfberry puree. If you leave your NingXia on the counter for a few minutes, you'll notice it divides into two colors. The color on the bottom is the pureed fruit. It's about a half to a third of the bottle. By using the entire plant and not just its juice, you now have a whole food supplement. That's much more powerful.

NingXia wolfberries grow in the NingXia river valley in China. On top of that, the juice is blended with blueberry, aronia, cherry, pomegranate, and plum juices, natural stevia extract, grape seed extract, pure vanilla extract, and Orange, Yuzu, Lemon, and Tangerine essential oils. It is the only nutrient drink on the market that combines whole Chinese wolfberries and pure therapeutic-grade essential oils into a single beverage.

There are at least 80 species of Lysium worldwide, but only Barbarum shows the highest nutrient levels in scientific testing. The NingXia region holds the Gold Certificate; China's equivalent of the USDA's organic certification. It is grown with no fertilizers, no pesticides, no sulfur, no irradiation, no dyes, and no heavy metals of lead, arson, mercury, or cadmium in the soil. The NingXia region's irrigation water comes from the Yellow River, which is upstream from all the pollutants of the major cities. The Yellow River floods the NingXia plants with a layer of minerals and silt every year. The farms in NingXia are in a semi-arid region with plenty of sunlight and a high temperature difference between night and day (think of the sap running in maple trees). Temperature differences are good for the liquids in plants, they keep them moving. The elevation is just right for the plant to be most productive. Any other place in the world would not have the same ecological condition of the pH of the water, or the nutrients in the soil, silt from the Yellow River. The conditions have earned NingXia the distinction of being China's recognized herbal medicine valley. NingXia has high nutritional content and natural organic sugar, (the sugar that allows your cells to talk). NingXia is China's only medicinal wolfberry production base. The Lycium Barbaram variety of the wolfberry is superior in vitamins, minerals, amino acids, and antioxidants, more than any other food. This is why the NingXia wolfberry is the best wolfberry in the world.

"If you want to be happy for an hour, go take a nap. If you want to be happy for a day, go fishing. If you want to be happy for a lifetime, help people." That is why I teach on NingXia. Because I believe in helping YOU."

(SHARE YOUR PERSONAL STORY)

If you do not have a NingXia story, share these: https://ningxiared. com/lifestyle/

Now let's talk about the journey that NingXia took to get to your doorstep. It's hard to bring something sacred from China all the way to the United States. I have a treat for you! The author of this manuscript, Sarah

Harnisch, has voiced the first few pages of the NingXia Wolfberry book by D. Gary Young, where he tells us what it took to bring NingXia to Young Living. Let's listen in.

(SOUND FILE: playable in the 103 Powerpoint at <u>oilabilityteam.com</u>)

Once Gary found NingXia, it took seven years to get it past customs in the U.S. and get it formulated. It started first as Berry Young juice, just the juice. Then it was reformulated to include the peel and the flesh of the wolfberry fruit.

THE SCIENCE BEHIND WHY NINGXIA WORKS: HERE ARE 7 QUICK REASONS:

Reason 1: Antioxidants

One ounce of Ningxia red = 2 pounds of wolfberries. There are 17 or 18 species of wolfberry, but only the NingXia wolfberry has the ability to deliver all the micro and macro nutrients that are bioavailable to the cells of your body. Antioxidants play a huge role in aging, memory, arthritis, inflammation, and so much more. Oxygen Radical Absorbance Capacity (ORAC) is a method of measuring antioxidant capacities. Presently, the highest antioxidant on the ORAC scale is vitamin E which comes in between 800 and 1200, followed by blueberries, raspberries, pomegranates, etc... A combination of fruits, together, reach around 3000 on the ORAC. The ORAC score of NingXia is 27,300.

Reason 2: Acid to Alkaline

In your body, you have alkaline acid. What creates disease? Acid. It breeds virus, bacteria, cancer, and fungus. When you can keep your pH neutral, you inhibit the growth of disease. Everything we eat converts in the stomach, which has a pH of 2.5. Wolfberry goes into the stomach and starts to break down as acid, but the minute it hits the small intestine, it immediately converts back to alkaline. It's acid binding and alkaline forming. Only one other food does that: the lemon. Wolfberry is chemically structured to convert because of the amino acid Tripsin, which is responsible for the conversion of amino acids in protein. Guess what NingXia is? It's alkaline protein. It's the most perfect food that exists.

Reason 3: Free Radicals

Where do free radicals come from? The air, electromagnetic fields, stuff we're eating, chocolate, and sugar. They are the army guys on the wrong side of the team. They wreak havoc. You outnumber the army with NingXia. Your body does a good job at taking care of oxidative stress, but one of the reasons we age, the reasons we get wrinkly, the reasons we feel tired, it's because of an excess of free radicals. Everything that is high in ORAC will flush your system really well.

Your body gets quadrillions of free radical attacks each day: 10,000 attacks **per cell** per day. The body needs a leg up. Most other "nutritional" drinks do little against superoxide (worst free radical) because the drinks are so heavily processed. Gary worked for years to protect the berry all the way to the bottle, so you get the full benefits. The NingXia wolfberry was saved during processing. That means it is a powerhouse designed to fight free radicals in the body.

Reason 4: Vitamin/Mineral Pairs

Minerals have to be properly balanced. Too much calcium will result in a zinc deficiency. Too much zinc can suppress immunity and lead to anemia. Both the mineral profile and the mineral balance of the NingXia wolfberry is without equal in the plant kingdom. With magnesium to calcium ratios 1:1, zinc to copper 2:1, and potassium to magnesium 8:1, it is exactly what the body needs in proportion.

Reason 5: It's A Macronutrient

You're getting whole food nutrition. It's coming from the plant, not a synthetic source. It's coming from a food-based source. That means it's easier for your body to process and you'll absorb more of what you're eating. It is also a liquid. If you did a digestive function test, 95-98 percent of us would come back with a weak or deficient digestive system, because of medications, stress, and processed food. To get NingXia in a liquid form means you absorb it faster, and your body doesn't have to break it down.

(This is a great spot to do a quick demo. Before the class started, I had you place a full bottle of NingXia on a counter. By now, the pulp from the berry should have settled in the bottom of the bottle. Show them how much of the bottle is fruit—and how much is juice. Not only do we not use "junk" juice like pear or apple—filler juice—but a quarter of the bottle is the pulp of the wolfberry.)

Reason 6: It's Infused with Essential Oils

Essential Oils in NingXia act as a delivery system to the body. Because it's infused with Young Living therapeutic-grade essential oils, it increases the absorption rate of the NingXia. The tiny oils act as a delivery system for the larger molecules.

Reason 7: It Has the Right Sugar and the Right Enzymes

Sugar is bad, right? Not all sugar. NingXia has the right sugar to open the door to your cell. When our cell membranes are 1) inflamed 2) oxidized 3) toxic 4) lacking in mitochondrial function to energize the receptors to open and close, we have no energy. NingXia's sugars open the door to our cells so good information can get passed to them. It crosses the lipid layer of the cell and passes inside. Only eight sugars on the earth can open the door. NingXia has 4 of the 8, naturally.

Enzymes. By age 40, you start losing digestive enzymes in the gut. NingXia is loaded with the right enzymes to help you break food down and get the nutrients out of what you eat.

Feed your body exactly what it needs.

Other important things about NingXia:

It contains every essential amino acid. It contains 13 percent protein, the highest protein content of any fruit. It has trace minerals. It has naturally occurring vitamins B1, B6, and B2, the energy vitamin. It has more vitamin c than all the fruits and veggies on the earth: 148 milligrams. Parsley and Spinach have 133 milligrams. Oranges have 50. It has more calcium than cherries (16mg) and cruciferous veggies (50mg) at 110 milligrams, and more beta carotene (12,600mg) than carrots (11,000mg). It is loaded with fiber because the skin of the berry was preserved.

Perhaps the best thing the Wolfberry does for your body is what it does to cells. The cell membrane is made up of oils, fats, and phospholipids. There are proteins floating on a liquid and very flexible sea of fat. The proteins are like antennas that pick up messages from other cells. You know the messengers that come into a cell. They have fancy names like insulin, thyroid enzymes, digestive enzymes, neurotransmitters like dopamine and serotonin. They are messengers that do not work well until you attach the right sugars to them. You can see the power of nutrition! Fats, proteins, and sugars are needed. If you are eating the wrong sugar, you are rendering the whole structure of the cell membrane dysfunctional. If cell communication breaks down, your health breaks down.

If you mess up the cell membrane, you need more insulin to get the job done. 40 percent of you are insulin resistant. If a man has a waist of more than 40 inches, and a woman more than 35 inches, they are insulin resistant. To wrap all this science up in two sentences; the NingXia wolfberry and good nutrition can impact your cell membrane. It corrects the pH of your blood so cellular communication can take place. It gives the mitochondria the energy it needs to open the gates of communication. It corrects inflammation in the cells by providing micronutrients. It has the right sugar to open the door.

When you eat poorly, your cells get mucked up. That lipid layer gets sticky. Then the cells stack on top of one another like coins. NingXia wipes that doorway clean and increases the surface area so that good information can get passed to the cell. Let's look at it play out on a microscope.

Video 3: https://www.youtube.com/watch?v=b5pbjSmleD4

These are available in the free 103 NingXia Powerpoint at oilabilityteam. com/unstuck)

LET'S TRY IT OUT!

How long does it take to notice the benefits of the juice? Some notice immediately, some in the first couple of weeks, and some a few months. It takes four months for every cell in your body to be replaced. I'd say drink 2-4 ounces a day for four months, then take a week off and see how you feel. That's how you can feel the benefits of NingXia on your body. Let's do a little in-class experiment right now.

THE NINGXIA WOLFBERRY TEST

Hand each person a shot of NingXia. (You can do the dollar store shot glasses and it is less than an ounce.)

- **Step 1:** Take note of a few reference points that are easy to self-evaluate; like lung capacity, vision, and the sense of energy you feel. Look around the room and assess the quality of your eyesight. Are you feeling tired, energized, or somewhere in between?

- **Step 2:** Take a large sip of NingXia Red and hold it in your mouth for 10 to 20 seconds. Under the tongue is best. Close your eyes and swallow.

- **Step 3:** Take another good evaluation of how you feel. Usually almost immediately, you'll feel a warmth through your body. You may feel tingling down to your toes. Take another deep breath. Are your lungs able to take in more air? Do you feel more awake? Are your sinuses more open? NingXia has anti-inflammatory properties. Look around the room. Do things appear more vivid? NingXia contains Zaexanthin and Lutein (zee-uh-zan-thin and loo-teen), which basically act as a natural sunscreen for the eyes. Do you feel more calm and centered? Many say the Wolfberry helps them relax. Do you feel more energized? Wolfberry juice helps improve circulation.

ODD WAYS TO USE NINGXIA

NingXia Shot recipes from Young Living corporate (all are Vitality oils):

- **Atomic fireball:** 1 oz NingXia Red, 2 drops Cinnamon, 1 drop Ocotea; **Mind Blaster:** 1 oz NingXia Red, 1 drop Lime, 1 drop Peppermint, 1 drop Citrus Fresh, 1 drop Frankincense, 1 drop Cinnamon Bark;
- **Hot Flash:** 1 oz. NingXia Red, 2 drops Cinnamon Bark, 2 drops Peppermint;
- **Dreamsicle:** 1 oz. NingXia Red, 1 drop Sacred Frankincense, 1 drop Orange, 1 drop Lime, 1 drop Tangerine, 1 drop Copaiba, 1 drop Citrus Fresh, 1 drop Lemon;
- **Cimply Smooth:** 1 oz. NingXia Red, 2 drops Tangerine, 2 drops Lime, 1 drop Sacred Frankincense.

As a mouthwash: Use for mild sores on the tongue, gum or cheeks, just swish.

NingXia Gargle: This is good for an occasional sore throat.

Make NingXia Tea: Heat one cup of water, add 1 ounce of NingXia Red. Sip as you would a tea.

NingXia poultice: Select a gauze pad. Add a tablespoon of NingXia to the cloth. Put a heat or cold pack behind it. Apply to the spot directly for a few hours.

NingXia Wolfberry paste: Pour an ounce of juice onto a plate. Let it sit for a few hours. As the water evaporates, it will get sticky and gooey. Apply that to a wounded area.

NingXia abdominal conditioner: I like to use this to get things moving. Add to Genesis Hand and Body Lotion and massage over your abdomen, just under your ribs to your hips. Move in large clockwise circles over your large intestine.

NingXia lotion: Add 1 tsp of Wolfberry juice to a small amount of Rose Ointment or Genesis Hand and Body Lotion.

NingXia for your ears: Add a few drops of the juice on a cotton swab, and swab on the inside of your ear (not deep). Your ears will feel clean. Wolfberry juice has a naturally occurring compound that can dissolve or loosen waxy substances.

NingXia enema: Add warm water to an enema bottle. Add one tablespoon to two ounces of NingXia. Lay on your right side, insert the applicator and squeeze liquid into your colon. Hold for at least seven minutes, longer is better. It takes seven minutes for the blood to circulate through your body.

Finger or toe soak: Soap the finger or toe in undiluted NingXia Red for a few minutes. Massage the juice into your skin.

NingXia foot baths: (This is great for calluses, cold feet, dry skin, poor circulation or stiff feet!) Get two one-gallon ziplock bags. Add 2 ounces of NingXia per bag. Fill your bathtub or a foot tub with warm water. Put your foot in the bath and the bag in the water and soak for 20 minutes.

NingXia massage: When you get your next massage, take a half ounce of V-6 with you, and add 1-2 ounces of NingXia to it. Have them do the massage with this mixture.

NingXia nail and cuticle treatment: (This is good for broken or brittle nails, hangnails, or breaks in the skin). Dip half a cotton ball in a small bowl of NingXia until it's dripping wet. Press onto injured area and let sit for 30 minutes or overnight.

NingXia scalp application: Place one tablespoon of NingXia in a small dish. Wrap a towel around your head and shoulders to protect your clothing. Massage the juice into your scalp. (I like to use a small plastic squirt bottle for this to get it into my roots). Let it sit on your skin for at least 15 minutes before showering.

NingXia frozen snacks: NingXia doesn't freeze entirely. If you put the packets in the freezer, they'll come out like slushies. It's pretty amazing. Likewise, if you want frozen NingXia, you can add some water to it and put it in trays. The little cubes feel amazing on bumps, bruises, cuts and blisters.

NingXia gummies:

- 1 cup fresh-squeezed orange juice
- 1/2 cup NingXia Red
- 5 tbsp grass-fed gelatin (my favorite is Great Lakes brand)
- 2 tbsp organic maple syrup or raw honey
- 4 drops Orange essential oil
- 2 drops Lemon essential oil

In a saucepan, heat the NingXia and maple syrup or honey. Add gelatin until it's fully dissolved, with no clumps. Add oils and pour into a silicone mold. Let harden (3-4 hours on the counter, or 10 minutes in the freezer.)

THAT WRAPS UP OUR CLASS!

How do you get this goodness in your life??

There are two ways: the **NingXia Premium Starter Kit**, and the **NingXia Essential Rewards Bundle**. One gets you started, and one keeps you going. The starter kit comes with a 2-pack of NingXia Red, 30 NingXia Red Singles, NingXia Nitro (a concentrated form of NingXia infused with B vitamins) which is AMAZING for energy and focus. It is Young Living's top-selling cognitive fitness booster. The kit also comes with an Aroma-glide Roller Fitment, a full bottle of Stress Away oil, Thieves mints, and lots of literature to read.

To continue on NingXia after month one, get on NingXia Essential Rewards. This gives you 10 percent off your NingXia, and is the cheapest way to get it in Young Living. After four months you get 20 percent off, and after 25 months you get 25 percent off your NingXia. NingXia ER is 1.16 an ounce, instead of 1.60 an ounce! The ER bundle comes every month and includes a 4-pack of NingXia Red and a 30-pack of Singles.

Recommended daily amount: two ounces, (one ounce for those under the age of six.)

If it bothers you, drink one-quarter teaspoon two to three times a day until you can up your dose. After a week, move up to ½ tsp a day. After two weeks, move to one teaspoon daily. Continue until you get it up to two tsp daily. Take Sulfyrzyme to detox while you up your dose slowly for 30 days, then start on a 2-ounce daily regimen.

We end with a story, from Young Living's Convention in 2015, a story about Ghandi.

Ghandi used to give advice to people 2 or 3 hours a day. He'd sit under a tree and people would line up. After waiting all day long in the heat, finally a mom with her child gets up to Ghandi and says, "please, tell my kid to stop eating candy." Ghandi says, "come back tomorrow." The woman is puzzled, but hey, if Ghandi says, you do it. She lines up in the heat of the sun the next day and gets to the top of the line again, and says, "please Ghandi, tell my son to stop eating candy." Ghandi says, "quit eating candy." She says, "why didn't you tell him that before?" He says, "well before, I was eating candy myself."

I want to look at you in the eye, and I want to challenge you. Do you want to share NingXia with those you know? You will have more power of conviction, you will sell more, if you speak truthfully and say, "I quit refined sugar today." Refined sugar does the opposite of what NingXia is doing for your body. Let's kick this entire class up a notch. I believe in training you long after this class is over. We are an education-driven team, which means we work alongside you to train you on Young Living products. Let's train for 30 straight days, on NingXia alone.

THE 30-DAY NINGXIA CHALLENGE

How do you incorporate all this NingXia training as a lifestyle change?

You have 2 options, depending on where you are on your wellness journey.

Option 1—Just start drinking it. Get it in your system. You're going to feel changes just from that one simple move.

Option 2—Take the full-on 30-day NingXia challenge. I will add you to a challenge group (Speaker: this is something you create on Facebook; samples are at oilabilityteam.com) where we will hold each other account-able. It's 30 days with 2 ounces of NingXia, no sugar, and a 30-minute walk. Let's do this side by side, and feel good together!

To study more:

The NingXia Wolfberry: The Ultimate Superfood, Gary Young.

53 Ways To Use the NingXia Wolfberry: A Handbook of Oral and Topical Applications (by Sound Concepts).

The Superior NingXia Wolfberry: A Powerful and Natural Ally Against Disease and Aging, Dr. Hugo Rodier.

The entire Oil Ability Powerpoint presentation parallels this script perfectly and comes with embedded media and videos. There are Powerpoint presentations available for the Core 4 (101, 102, 103, and 104 classes,) and Textable classes for the Core 4 (101, 102, 103, 104); as well as (for the first time ever) the Gameplan mini (a prospecting textable class!) Free 30-day challenge calendars and graphics are free on the same site as well. Find it all at oilabilityteam.com/unstuck.

SAVVY MINERALS CLASS SCRIPT
BY YOUNG LIVING DIAMOND TINA DAILEY CIESLA AND SARAH HARNISCH

You have made it to your very first Young Living Savvy Minerals Makeup Class! I am so stoked to get some time with you! This is a great class because you get a little of everything: a little science, a little play time with some foundation, a little color matching, a little laughter with our blooper real, and a lot of learning about how chemicals in your makeup hit your body. You will leave with full training, conviction, and action steps on how to give your makeup bag its own makeover.

Let's start with a few hard facts.

Europe bans 1,328 toxic ingredients from their cosmetics. Those ingredients are connected to cancer, hormone disruption, infertility, skin issues, and respiratory issues. Did you know your MAKEUP can trigger food allergies??

The United States bans **11** toxic ingredients from the makeup sold to consumers. Then we apply it to our faces all the time.

Do you know how many ingredients Young Living has banned from Savvy Minerals makeup? Not 11. Not 1,328. **2500 HUNDRED ingredients are banned**. It's made all the difference for me with breakouts. Getting sick (my immune system isn't taken down fighting toxic ingredients; it's doing what it was made to do; fight germs and bacteria!) My skin feels healthier and my body feels better. Let's open the class with a few before and after pictures of what Savvy has done for the skin of people in Young Living. When you're not putting talc, bismuths, phthalates and parabens on your skin, there is always a consequence. Savvy sets the standard for what clean makeup really looks like. Let's see what confidence looks like!

Show before and after pictures in the 104 Savvy Minerals Powerpoint, available at <u>oilabilityteam.com/unstuck</u> for free.

SHARE YOUR PERSONAL STORY

Why Savvy?

26 seconds after exposure, chemicals are found in the bloodstream in measurable amounts in the human body. The average woman applies

300 chemicals to her body every day. 80 of them are applied before breakfast. Most chemicals come from four items: soap, makeup, shampoo, and hair care. Your skin ages seven days every time you don't take your makeup off at night.

Even if you're not wearing makeup daily, Savvy will wow you. It covers sunspots and age spots, fills in fine lines, and makes your lips and eyes pop. It covers acne and redness. 70 percent of aging isn't wrinkles, it's skin discoloration. Savvy covers that up without using toxic chemicals that will cause more damage. You're not hurting your liver when you apply your makeup every single day.

Savvy History Lesson

As with all of our Core 4 classes, we're going to take you school today. You'll get a little history, a little science, and a lot of recess as we play with the makeup and do some color matching with swatches. After this class, I'd love to plug you into a 101 oils class and show you what Young Living is all about. Our mission is education. Our mission is to protect you from toxic chemicals. Our mission is oils. All our makeup today is oil infused. That means you get the benefit of the oil, without the toxins on your skin.

This is the story of how Savvy Minerals was birthed! Crown Diamond Melissa Poepping came up with her own makeup line. Young Living was so in love with it that Melissa sold the whole thing to them. Now we have the benefits of oil infused makeup.

(Play the Intro Video of Melissa Poepping in the 104 Savvy Mineral Powerpoint for free at <u>oilabilityteam.com</u>)

Savvy is naturally derived and held to Young Living's Seed to Seal standard. That means the makeup has no fertilizers, no pesticides, no sulfur, no irradiation, no dyes, and no heavy metals of lead, arson, mercury, or cadmium. A lot of mineral based makeup will have those things because they source their minerals from tainted soil. Young Living protects your face before we ever pull the minerals from the ground, because we only use clean, unsprayed soil.

There's also no gluten in our makeup, no mineral oil (**Mineral Oil** can damage the skin barrier and increase water loss, making your skin look more wrinkled. It also clogs pores and suffocates the skin. Mineral oil causes premature aging and messes with your hormones.) There are no petrochemicals in Savvy, no talc, no parabens, no nanoparticles that tear the pores of your skin, no phthalates, no bismuth (which is the number one ingredient that causes acne when you use makeup), no synthetic dyes, no synthetic ingredients at all, and no fragrances. There are no fillers.

Dangers of Talc: It's a skin irritant, carcinogen, causes organ system toxicity to your lungs and ovaries, and may contain asbestos. It's found in eye shadow, blush, foundation, face powder, and baby powder.

Dangers of Bismuth: It's a skin irritant and synthetic filler found in eye shadow, blush, bronzers, and nail polish.

Dangers of Phthalates: It's an endocrine disruptor. That means your makeup could lead to your hot flashes, inability to lose weight, and thyroid issues. Your makeup may be why you are tired. It causes reproductive and development issues for teens using the makeup. They use this as a plasticizer and fixative in color cosmetics, skin care, lip balm, and nail polish. It's listed as DEP, DBP, DEHP, and fragrance on the bottle.

Dangers of Parabens: It's linked to skin cancer, reproductive issues and endocrine disruption. It's a preservative in cleansers, lotions, sunscreens, and moisturizers.

Let's kick this up a notch with some action. I'm going to issue a challenge. I call it the **Makeup Bag Challenge.** I printed these few ingredients we just talked about on a small card. I want you to take it with you and go home to your makeup bag, and make sure none of these ingredients are in what you are using. Look up several of the ingredients in your makeup and type in Google "dangers of" with the name of the ingredient. You will be shocked at some of the things your own makeup is doing to your skin right now.

(Pass out the Makeup Bag Challenge handout. That printable is free at oilabilityteam.com/unstuck).

Why Savvy?

It's what's inside. Savvy is made from Kaolin clay, jojoba (hoe-hoe-buh) oil, mica, aloe, pure essential oils, aspen bark extract, arrow root powder, sweet almond oil, beeswax, sunflower oil, and Vitamin E. None of those ingredients will hurt your skin. Jojoba softens your lips!

Kaolin clay reduces oily skin and detoxifies. Arrowroot powder absorbs excess oil and provides a natural glow. Aloe is nourishing and helps you maintain a youthful appearance. It's hydrating. Aspen Bark has skin softening properties but is also a natural preservative. It allows us to use it instead of those nasty parabens!

Savvy Introductions

It's time to introduce Savvy! We'll talk through it the same way you introduce your makeup, starting with the foundation first. There's a bit of a learning curve to putting on natural makeup. But once you have it, you'll never look back again. You'll go to bed every night knowing you're preserving your skin by not poisoning your skin. I'm going to walk you through foundation, blush, bronzer, the mineral veil, eye shadow, eye liner, mascara and lips. We'll watch quick demo videos on some of them.

Then I'll let you test the foundation on your skin just to see how it feels. We'll color match you using swatches with the makeup next to your skin. And I'll have you fill out your own color palette sheets to take home with you today, so you know what to order here and in the future. You'll be fully decked out in Savvy!

Foundation

Savvy Foundation can get confusing because there are cool tones, warm tones, and dark tones. If your skin is dark, the dark tones are simple to pick. But if it's lighter, you may not know whether you are cool or warm. Let's take a little test together to help you sort it out.

The Foundation Skin Test

1. Check your veins. Are they blue or green? If they are blue, you're cool. If they are green, you likely would look good in warm colors.

2. Jewelry. Do you prefer gold or silver against your skin? Cool foundation looks good with those who are stunning in silver and platinum metals. Warm foundations look better with those who shine in gold.

3. What clothing do you wear? Does your face and eyes look better in bright white and black, or in ivory, off-white, grey and tan? White and black look better in cool tones. Ivory and off-white are usually warm foundations.

4. The color of your eyes and hair. Usually, cool shades pair well with blue, grey or green eyes and blond or brown hair. Warm shades look good with brown, amber, or hazel eyes and strawberry blonde, red, brown or black hair with gold, red, yellow or orange undertones.

5. What does the sun do to you? If you turn golden brown, you're likely warm toned. If you turn pick first, cool tones like to burn.

If those questions put you in different categories, I like to sample the foundation and see what works best, then write it down on a Young Living Swatch card. I have one for you today. (If you need to order the swatch cards, they are item #21840 in the Virtual Office.)

Why use this foundation over other foundations? It minimizes the size of your pores, absorbs excess oil, you can apply it once and wear it all day, and it's great for sensitive skin. The Foundation comes in many colors, including: three Cool, three Warm, and four Dark shades.

Let's take a look at this quick video where Melissa is showing us some tips applying Savvy Minerals foundation. Snag this video in the 104 Savvy Powerpoint at oilabilityteam.com.

OPTIONAL DEMO: We're going to do a little demo with the foundation, because I want you to color match the foundation directly to your skin. Clean never felt so good! I'm going to pass around some color-matching swatches made by a 19-year-old in Texas, named Havalah Puccio. You can see which shade looks best on you. Then take that shade and put a little on the skin of your hand and rub it in, to experience the gentleness of Savvy yourself.

(Note: Order one of each of the foundation colors to have as a tester. Use a q-tip or brush for application. [No double dipping for sanitation purposes]. To save on cost, I don't do full makeovers on each person in the class. I do like to have them sample the foundation so they can feel Savvy on their skin, and to color match the foundation, because it's the trickiest to match through an online order. This demo is optional. You can order the color-matching cards directly from Havalah at Savvyswatches. com).

Blush

Next, we'll take on Blush. These compliment any skin tone giving you a radiant glow! **(Show off the blush colors.)** The neat thing about blush is that it can double as a shimmer for your eyes, too.

Bronzer

When I'm doing my makeup in three minutes, I usually just do foundation, mascara and sometimes some lip color. I have always skipped bronzer. But bronzer is actually great because it contours your face— which means you can make your face appear **thinner** just by using a little shading. It also makes you look like you have a tan, especially if you're really white. Savvy minerals bronzer is one of their best products. **(Show bronzer).** Let me show you makeup gone wrong. This is what bronzer can do!

Show in 104 Savvy Powerpoint before and after photos of the human Barbie as a joke.

Don't worry—we won't do that to you! Crowned All Over and Summer Loved are our bronzer colors. Either is versatile and blends nicely on any skin tone.

Mineral Veil

Mineral Veil is the finishing powder from Savvy Minerals. I used to think I could cut this product to save a little, then I got it and tried it, and it's like using pressed powder for me. It makes your face glow after all your foundation and blush are on. It's truly amazing. Diamond Dust is the name of the mineral veil. Dust it over your neck, chest, and shoulders for a beautiful effect.

Eye Shadow

Eye shadows are one of the most incredible tools in your makeup bag. We offer a couple of matte as well as shimmery choices for your eyes; including all the new shadows just released, that you can add to your Essential Rewards order. Unlike other brands, the shimmery colors are very forgiving on mature skin. You must give them a try! The great thing about mineral makeup is that you can layer it to get a more dramatic effect if you're going to a wedding or just need heavier coverage. You can go big or go light. These are the colors of the Savvy Mineral Eye Shadows. I haven't met a single one I didn't LOVE! **(Show the colors)** There's now even an entire eyeshadow palette that is stunning!

Eye Liner

The eye liner used to scare me a bit, because I'm used to a pencil—not liquid liner. I had a hard time drawing a straight line on my eyelid! But after I read the ingredients in the pencil, I never wanted to touch it again. It's not worth the cost to my body. I wear eyeliner almost every day. That choice, repeatedly, with a chemical-laden liner is costly. So after decades of using a pencil, I learned a new skill and started to apply liquid liner in a straight line with some practice. Young Living has an amazing eyeliner brush that makes it really easy. Our Savvy Mineral Eye Liner is a jet-black mineral eye shadow. Use it dry for a soft liner or spritz your brush with Misting Spray to achieve a liquid eye liner. If you go into the Virtual Office, it's not called Eyeliner—it's called Multi-Tasker, because that's what it does!

First, let's see video of how NOT to apply eyeliner. (Video is in the 104 Savvy Powerpoint at oilabilityteam.com.)

Now, let's watch it done right. Let's take the fear out of using a brush to apply eyeliner.

Melissa's video is in the 104 Savvy Powerpoint at oilabilityteam.com.

Multi-tasker is the perfect name for this mineral powder in several colors: including black, brown, medium, and tan. You can use it as a shadow, an eyeliner, to fill in your brows, or even cover up some of those grey hairs around your face. You can mix a bit of it to get a darker or lighter foundation or eye shadow color. Use it dry or use it wet (with the Misting Spray) for a more dramatic effect.

Mascara

I don't know anyone that makes Lavender-infused mascara. What's the benefit of having Lavender? It's good for your lashes. Some studies-show it even helps them to grow; which makes sense, because Lavender is also really good for your skin and hair. Mascara is one of the most dangerous things in your makeup bag. Swap it out with something smart.

Young Living's mascara:

- Conditions and nourishes lashes
- Is made with naturally derived ingredients
- Is formulated without parabens, phthalates, petrochemicals, bis-muth, talc, dyes, synthetic colorants, or synthetic fragrances
- Is not tested on animals
- And was clinically tested for ocular irritation
- Also contains jojoba and coconut fruit extract

Lips

For soft lips, you'll love Savvy Minerals Lipstick! It is smooth, vegan, and velvety. Young Living's lipstick line provides weightless, buildable coverage and nourishing ingredients for your skin. It glides on smoothly and has a creamy texture. It moistens and hydrates your lips. What's in it? Jojoba. Coconut oil. Shea butter. Citrus orange peel. Peppermint and Spearmint and Cinnamon. Or go with the Tangerine infused lipsticks!

Lip Gloss is all the rage right now. But did you know that the brighter the color and the longer the wear, the more toxins may be in the formula? Lip glosses that are slick and oily feeling contain petrochemicals. You don't want anything but the cleanest, most pure ingredients by your MOUTH!

You lick your lips, eat food and sip drinks all day! Savvy has colors you can feel good about. **(Show off lip glosses.)**

Durability

One of the things I love so much about Savvy is that it lasts so long. But did you know you can make it last even longer? The Savvy Minerals Misting Spray is one of my favorite products. You'll get better coverage and longer wear from your Savvy Makeup by just doing a quick spritz over your face. Made with pure essential oils, trace minerals, and entire-ly plant-based ingredients, our Misting Spray gives you more thorough foundation coverage, all while nourishing and freshening your skin. It provides more control with mineral powder makeup application.

Have No Time?

Some women tell me they do not have time to put on makeup. What if I told you that you could do your face in five minutes? Let's review the steps and keep it crazy simple.

1. Wash your face with ART gentle cleanser. Use ART Light Moistur-izer and Renewal Serum. Now your skin is clean, hydrated, pH balanced and ready for makeup.

2. Makeup step one in the five-minute face: foundation.

3. Step 2: bronzer.

4. Step 3: blush.

5. Step 4: eyeliner and shadow.

6. Step 5: mascara.

7. Step 6: lip gloss or lipstick. And you are off and running.

If you want a 60-second look, do foundation, eyeliner, mascara and a smidge of lip gloss. You'll look polished, but simple.

Let's watch a time lapse video of a five-minute application! (Show video from 104 Savvy Powerpoint at <u>oilabilityteam.com</u>).

Young Living is known all over the world for being the leading producer of pure essential oils. We do oils. That's who we are. No Young Living makeup system would be complete without using essential oils. Here is a glance at some of the top essential oils for the skin. I use Frankincense on my skin every day. Lavender is also wonderful to add to your skin care products. And the top five anti-aging essential oils are: Sandalwood, Geranium, Myrrh, Lemon, Tea Tree, and Frankincense. Pick any of them and add 20 to 30 drops to your Cleanser, Moisturizer or Renewal Serum right after you open the bottle.

Starting With Savvy

How do you order Savvy? It's so simple. We have a computer at the back of the room and someone willing to help. Simply go to youngliving. com, click "Become a Member", select wholesale—because I want you to get 24 percent of all your makeup for life. You'll want to put in the sponsor and enroller number of the person who invited you, because you're blessing their family with your order.

Pick your kit, based on the color of your foundation. Each Savvy kit comes with one foundation, one blush, three eyeshadows, one lip gloss, the misting spray, foundation brush, a 5-mL bottle of Lavender oil, a Savvy Minerals book to train you how to use it, and an Introduction to Young Living booklet.

I would encourage you to set up Essential Rewards today, because it's the most cost-effective way to order. It's how our members are getting close to 50 percent off retail prices. (These are the freebies this month at 190, 250, and 300pv. Show the products). Your kit counts toward 100 of these points! You get 10 percent back immediately, 20 percent back in 4 months and 25 percent back in 25 months. Right now, I earn 25 dollars for every 100 I spend. I don't know anywhere that pays me for ordering clean makeup! Some of my favorite products to get on my first makeup Essential Rewards order are:

• The Savvy Minerals Essential Brush set (item #21257) $85

- Silicone cleansing pad and brush cleaner (items #25005 and #24504, $12 and $20
- Mascara (item #21072) $29.75
- Primer (item #23684) $35
- Multi-tasker (item #20794) $20.75
- Lipstick (item #21751) $29.75
- Bronzer (item # 20787) $27.75
- Diamond Dust Veil (item #20793) $45
- The eyeshadow palet (item #23954) $55
- Makeup removal wipes (item #24503) $18

Do you want to continue learning? For a quick look at a product before you use it, try scanning it with an app like Think Dirty. Sometimes products are not in the database, so it helps to visit websites like SafeCosmetics. org to look up an ingredient. For the serious label reader, the book "The Consumer's Guide to Cosmetic Ingredients" is an excellent resource. It is just like a dictionary. Simply find the ingredient and read what it is, why it is used in a product, and if you should stay clear of it. I'll also give all of you in the room a purple bag with a copy of *Fearless* in it—my go-to for understanding and reading the dangers of labels, and how to incorporate essential oils into my life. Also printed in those bags: a 30-day Savvy challenge to help you kick chemicals to the curb! If you place your Essential Rewards order today, our team will gift you $25 dollars back just for filling out the 30-day challenge calendar as well. We want to come alongside you as you grow in the knowledge of protecting your family. That means a $300 ER order would yield $55 dollars off—$25 from the 30-day Savvy challenge and $30 for getting 10 percent off today.

Thank you for giving up your time to learn about Savvy! By now, you're ready to make some changes in your routine. We are an education-driven team and want to help you learn! Fill out the "Contact Me" card and tell me some other areas where we can train. I want to help you get every drop out of your starter kit, and beyond. Let's get that makeup bag cleaned out and filled with the good stuff!

The entire Oil Ability Powerpoint presentation parallels this script perfectly and comes with embedded media and videos. There are Powerpoint presentations available for the Core 4 (101, 102, 103, and 104 classes,) and Textable classes for the Core 4 (101, 102, 103, 104); as well as (for the first time ever) the Gameplan mini (a prospecting textable class!) Free 30-day challenge calendars and graphics are free on the same site as well. Find it all at oilabilityteam.com/unstuck.

OIL ABILITY CLOSING SCRIPTS

Here are two strong closes to use at the end of your classes. Start your close after you have gone through the start kit.

Why oils?

Because you need them in your home as part of a simple, chemical-free lifestyle. When you see what the oils do for your own body and how they help create a chemical-free home, it's impossible to walk into the homes of your friends and family members and see their bright blue dish soap or their chemical-laden shampoo that is in their bloodstream in 26 seconds and not speak about what you know! You share it because you love and care for your friends, and you want to see them living a healthy life. When you take care of yourself, you can fully do what God created you to do, what you were called to do.

How do you begin?

With a Young Living Premium Starter Kit. I'm a frugal momma, and it's the only thing on the Young Living site that's half off. If you take the diffuser off, you're literally getting 12 bottles of therapeutic grade oil for $70. You can't even get it that cheap at the grocery store. Each bottle has 90 drops of oil in it—that's 90 applications.

The kit also comes with bottles to share the oils with your family and friends, an AromaGlide roll-on fitment to apply the oils on the go, and samples of NingXia Red® for full system support. I want to see every single person in this room on NingXia! It's your first line of defense in immune support!

You also get a diffuser with the kit AND a lifetime wholesale membership. That means 24% off your oils FOR LIFE. Every single order you place is 24% off. To maintain a wholesale membership, you have to spend $50 in a calendar year of products YOU select. That's like two bottles of Thieves cleaner, which is the only stuff I use to clean my counters, my stove, my floors, and my windows. Without any chemicals, in one swoop, it eradicated my multipurpose counter spray, my glass cleaner, and my floor cleaner. If you need a small step to start using oils in your home, use them to clean!

Where do you start?

That's as hard as going to www.youngliving.com, click on "Become a Member," and filling out the form. You'll need a sponsor and enroller number because Young Living is a multi-level marketing company. Many people tell me they can't buy from an MLM, but when you shop at Walmart, you're supporting a CEO's third home. When you shop at a MLM, you're buying local. You're supporting my family business. You're paying for gas in our car or food on our table. It's the best form of business out there, and one of the most important reasons is that you get to see your friends and family financially blessed. The Oil Ability team now has, in five years, more than 10-thousand members in all 50 states and several countries. It's because the oils work. A company which sells 100,000 starter kits a month is selling them for a reason! People are tired of the chemical yuck around them, and they are taking control of their homes.

If you look around you—Chipotle is cutting all their GMO's. Panera has placed signs in their restaurants that they're cutting all the chemicals from their salad dressings. Kraft Mac and Cheese has cut their dyes. Heinz has cut all corn syrup from their ketchup. People are starting to flip over and read the backs of the bottles of products they put on their skin, eat, clean their homes with, and say, "no more." That's where oils come in. Can you live a completely toxic free life? No, but you can minimize your exposure. You can take control of your laundry soap, your dish soap, your cleaning supplies, your supplements, and say, "I want a less toxic life." That's where oils come in. The starter kit has 10,000 uses, from cleaning your home, to emotional balance, to fitness, and to personal care products like toothpaste and deodorant.

I'd like to issue the three-cabinet challenge. When you get home, I'd like to encourage you to start flipping over the bottles that you use in any three cabinets in your home, and then read the ingredients. If there's anything on there that you can't pronounce, it's time to start swapping it out. I wouldn't slather that stuff on my skin, or plug it into my walls and smell it; giving it access to the limbic lobe of my brain! I wouldn't cook with it and ingest it. I wouldn't wash my hair with it and have it in my bloodstream over my brain in 26 seconds. I wouldn't clean my counters and butcher block with it and then eat my food off that same block; or wash my clothes with it. We're at a place where people aren't just taking everything at face value anymore; that is, thinking that a product is safe.

You are the gatekeeper of your home. Only you control what crosses the threshold of your doorway. You alone are responsible for the health and safety of your family within the four walls of your house. You can say NO. It's time to start kicking chemicals out of your home. To get a starter kit, we've set up a station where you can enroll right now, and we are here to help navigate the website with you. We will walk you through every step. If you'd like to do it at home, we have bags filled with a picture of the kit so you can see what comes in it, as well as a FREE copy of this 101 lecture on CD. Take it home, share it with someone who should have been in this class with you. It's my gift to you. Also in the bag is my contact information, so you have a way to get back to me. Feel free to contact me absolutely any time! It is my job to walk you through this and to be there as a resource for you. There are no dumb questions. Also in the bag is a paper which walks you through how to order online.

Thank you for generously giving your time to learn about essential oils! I believe with all my heart that you're about to have the best year you've ever had. You will not recognize your home a year from now, and I am SO excited for you!

You have survived essential oils 101!

THE BOLD CLOSE

(Tweak it and include your story!)

Let me get real with you for a moment as I wrap up—and tell you the true reason I teach so emphatically about this. Why does chemical free living matter so much to me? Because I have seen the other end of a chemical filled lifestyle, and I want everyone to know what they are putting in and on their bodies.

There are 100,000 chemicals on the market today. The Toxic Substance Control Act (TCSA) of 1976 grandfathered them in. What does that mean to you? Simply put: these chemicals have not had any safety testing, and we know very little information about their side effects. Dr. Samuel Epstein, chairman of the Cancer Prevention Coalition, says, "it is unthinkable that women would knowingly inflict such exposures on their infants, children, and themselves if products were routinely labeled with explicit warnings of cancer risks. But they are not labeled."

Since the 1940's, prostate cancer is up 200%. Thyroid cancer, 155%. Brain cancer, 70%. And the American Cancer Society estimates a 50% rise in cancer rates by 2020.

What happens when your body is chemically overloaded? You may see it in something as catastrophic as cancer. But most of us feel it on other ways: lethargy, inability to focus, sleep trouble, chronic inflammation, unexplained pain, skin issues, adult acne, hot flashes, stress, anxiety, and fear. If you face any of these issues, it's time to kick chemicals to the curb. You can control what you allow within the walls of your home.

I was invited to my first oils class, got my starter kit, and began right where you are now, taking this chemical-free living thing one day at a time; kicking one chemical out of my home at a time. You can do this. It's about taking small steps, and saying- no more. I will not allow these things in my home. You can't control all the places you are exposed—but you are the gatekeeper of your house.

Learn alongside our team. Let us guide you through the process in simple, easy steps. Step one is to start with the starter kit—a diffuser and 12 bottles of oil, some of the most common oils on the earth for supporting systems of the body. They each have just one ingredient; Lemon is just cold pressed lemon rinds. Frankincense is resin, properly steam distilled at the right temperature to make essential oil. Lavender is freshly distilled at the peak of the harvest—with thousands of uses in the home. Let us come alongside you and train you how to kick chemicals to the curb. You can DO this.

Start by heading to www.youngliving.com, click on "Become A Member" and enter the sponsor and enroller number of the person who introduced you to the oils.

Once you have put in the sponsor and enroller number, it will take you to a second page and ask for personal information where you'll set up your account. Write it all down so you're able to log in later. The third page asks which starter kit you want. My personal favorite is the Rainstone diffuser with the Premium Starter Kit. If your budget is tight, the Desert Mist diffuser works wonderfully too. I'd also encourage you to sign up for Essential Rewards. You get to pick the oils that come to your door every single month, you switch them out—and you get paid 10% back for everything you order in reward points. That's 10% back on your laundry soap, dish soap, and Thieves® cleaner—which is all I use to clean my house. It's one of the best choices I ever made. If you'd like to add those to your order, I recommend the Thieves® Essential Rewards Kit—because in one swoop, it contains just about all you need to get rid of nearly every chemical cleaner in your home. It's simple and easy. And if you're taking chemical-free living head on, it's the best place to start.

The final window asks for payment, and you're off and running. We're honored to have you as a part of this team. Look for a welcome package in the mail! Connect with us online at Oil Ability with Sarah on Facebook. Find more resources at oilabilityteam.com. Welcome to the Oil Ability family!

This is something you NEED to take seriously. No one is watching your home but you. You are the gatekeeper. I'd be willing to bet my life that there are things in your home right now—that you're exposed to every single day—that could be killing you. And the thing is, it's totally preventable.

What do you do until the box arrives?

Start small. Start slow. Start with what you're convicted on. Let me give you a simple tip. With your food, flip the container over and start reading the ingredients. If you can't pronounce it, don't eat it. It doesn't mean you can't have ice cream—just go for the ice cream with milk, sugar, eggs, and vanilla instead of an ingredients list of 35 items you don't recognize.

With your home, start with the biggest offenders first—laundry soap, dishwasher soap, cleaning supplies, candles, and plug-ins. Toss the candles and plug-ins. Swap them out with a diffuser and pure essential oil. Young Living has oil-infused Thieves® cleaner, laundry soap, and dish soap that's affordable and simple to use. Add them to your Essential Rewards order once you have that starter kit.

This is about small, simple, baby steps. Take it one month at a time as you swap things out in your home. Maybe the first month you focus solely on Thieves® cleaner and toss your cleaning supplies. You can start that today by grabbing a $22 bottle of Thieves® cleaner. Go home and wipe your kitchen down and fall in love—knowing you just boosted your immune system instead of taxing your liver.

The next month, swap out some laundry soap or dish soap. Month three, focus on your personal care products—deodorant and/or shampoo. Month four, beauty supplies—like face wash. Every day you leave your makeup on, your skin ages by seven days. Use a chemical-free option to wash it off. The Young Living ART line is my favorite.

I started this journey myself two years ago, with a Young Living starter kit, and have never looked back. We use oils every single day in our home. Every oil you use is a chemical you're not using.

You matter. Your family matters. Your friends matter. You can take control of your own health. Kick the chemicals out of your life and start living clean.

UNSTUCK TWO-PAGE

Teacher Training

Intro to Teacher Training

Ninety-five percent of what I do is action. That is how you get to Diamond; not by thinking about what you're going to do, but by doing it. The tighter you keep your classes, the tighter you keep your teacher trainings, the tighter your advanced coaching, the easier you can be copied. I have consolidated the Teacher Training into two pages (or one page printed back to back), because it's how I train a new leader without giving them information overload. Most of the training is done in photos so you're capturing your visual learners, too. Run through the Income Disclosure Guide, give the why, explain the comp plan in five minutes or less, show them the four things they must do to get a higher paycheck with the Rank Qualification graphic, show them how to log in and place their Essential Rewards order (and find the Rank Qualification and My Organization buttons), and give them their first homework assignment. Then set a date to meet again.

These final sheets in this section are coaching sheets. The Teacher Training pages are your very first business training. The coaching sheets are for following up with advanced leaders. I usually only use two sheets when I coach: rank mapping, to plot out how far they are from their next rank, and the Coaching Sheet, where I map out action steps to help them achieve the goals laid out on the Rank Mapping Sheets. If you have them track their stats as well (they take that sheet with them), when you meet again you can identify weaknesses. A dropping ER percentage rate means their leaders aren't training the lifestyle. A dip in the number of Stars or Senior Stars means there's not enough Teacher Training and Coaching going on. A dip in the number of new members means the leaders aren't teaching classes. For the coaching sheets, I print two sets. As we work through it, we both write down the numbers. One set goes home with me in my leader binder, the second set goes home with them to work on. We meet again in 3 months and see how close they've gotten to their goals.

The great thing is that these are FREE RESOURCES. You don't need to copy them out of this book. You can print them directly off my website, over and over again, at no cost. Go to oilabilityteam.com/unstuck and look for the coaching resources section. May this bless you as you train your leaders!

❶ **Let's talk compensation!**

This is what
#diamondrising
looks like

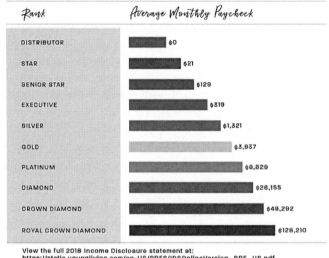

YOUNG LIVING *Ranks* AVERAGE MONTHLY INCOME

Rank	*Average Monthly Paycheck*
DISTRIBUTOR	$0
STAR	$21
SENIOR STAR	$129
EXECUTIVE	$319
SILVER	$1,321
GOLD	$3,937
PLATINUM	$9,829
DIAMOND	$26,155
CROWN DIAMOND	$49,292
ROYAL CROWN DIAMOND	$128,210

View the full 2018 Income Disclosure statement at:
https://static.youngliving.com/en-US/PDFS/IDSOnlineVersion_PDF_US.pdf

❷ **Why Do A Young Living Business?**
- no income ceiling
- you're your own boss and set your own hours
- take time off and still get paid (residual income)
- oils are easier to share than a pan, clothing, or makeup because they are consumable
- see the people around you experience financial freedom as they teach
- build time economy
- build relationships with those that love natural health
- it doesn't matter how many people you know
- you don't have to be good at speaking (or know a lot of people) because there are many ways to build
- willable income

❸ **Young Living Compensation Plan (Let's break the check down!)**
You're paid four ways:

1. Starter Kit bonuses ($50 per kit; $25 for the Starter Kit bonus and $25 for Fast Start)

2. Fast Start (25 percent on everything they order after the starter kit; only for 3 months)

3. Unilevel (8% on your level 1's, 5% on your level 2's, 4% on your level 3's, 4's, 5's)

4. Rising Star or Generation Leadership Bonuses (bonuses for strategizing your rank a certain way or for raising leaders once you hit the rank of Silver). For the purposes of just starting the business, keep your strategy simple. Everyone goes under you as a Level 1 until you have ten people on Essential Rewards.

❹ Rank Qualification chart from the Virtual Office (Simple Strategy Coaching)

This is how you rank up! The nine ranks in Young Living are across the top. The four rows represent four things you need to do to hit the next rank: spend 100 PV, hit a certain volume (OGV), build your legs, and sustain 1000 PGV outside your legs. There are 9 ranks in Young Living: Star, Senior Star, Executive, Silver, Gold, Platinum, Diamond, Crown Diamond and Royal Crown Diamond. There are four things you must do to rank: 1) Spend 100PV. 2) Hit a certain OGV (volume) for each rank. That resets the 1st of every month (unless you get your people on Essential Rewards!) 3) Build legs. A leg is a person and a team under them. 4) Have PGV, or volume outside your legs. The four requirements are broken down below.

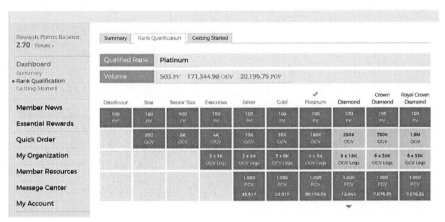

❺ Log in and do a quick tour of the Virtual Office so you understand how to place an ER order. Your order as a business builder must be 100pv to get your full paycheck. As a builder, being on Essential Rewards is good financial stewardship. To spend the $100 to get your full check, you're actually spending $90 because of Rewards Points. To pick out what you'd like, go over the reference guide and the YL catalogue side by side and build an ER wish list!

❻ Homework 1: Teach your first class + read two books: "Your Gameplan: Build A Life Beyond Survival Mode" and "The Essential Gameplan: Ignite Your Business In 2 Hours" before our next coaching session. Next time, we will cover Fearless, the Fearless 30-day calendar, and the Diamond Rising Deck for follow up training. You can do this!

This is my cell phone number if you have questions: _____

Print this sheet for free at oilabilityteam.com/unstuck to track your leader coaching!

UNSTUCK #DIAMONDRISING LEADER
Coaching Sheets

Gameplanner Rank-Mapping Sheet

Name _____ Distributor # _____ Date _____

Last six month's OGV

1_____ 2 _____ 3 _____ 4 _____ 5 _____ 6 _____

Set OGV goals.

Current OGV _____ OGV Goal _____ OGV Needed _____

	current	goal	need	break it down
• Leg 1				
• Leg 2				
• Leg 3				
• Leg 4				
• Leg 5				
• Leg 6	*ex: 1500*	*2000*	*500*	*5 kits / 2*
3 Month OGV targets				

Schedule 4-6 classes this month.

Dates of classes:

_____   _____

_____   _____

_____   _____

Raise leaders.

Based on your rank mapping sheet, make a list of all the leaders in the last 6-12 months that have sold a kit on your weakest leg. Put down their names. Those are the people you work with, coach, and teach classes with and for this month. Work in your weakest places when you are fighting for a rank up.

_____

_____

_____

When you fill these sheets out, print two copies and work on them side by side. Both of you keep a copy until you check in again three months later.

Print these for free at oilabilityteam.com/unstuck.

Unstuck #diamondrising Leader
Coaching Sheets

Coaching + Action Steps

Name_____ Distributor #_____ Date_____

Every 3-6 months, sit down for a 30-minute coaching session and revisit their goals, do rank mapping and stat tracking from the Gameplanner and work on their weak areas.

Do they need coaching on: ☐connecting with cold market   ☐closing their classes   ☐ meeting needs of people   ☐doing strong follow up ☐teaching 1-2 classes a week (consistency)   ☐ training their leaders   ☐excuses ☐doing non income-producing activities (distraction) ☐ making sure each person on their team has the Core 4 classes ☐ tapping into friends of friends to build their team

Dates I coached this leader: _____

Action steps with 10 lines for notes and suggestions.

_____

_____

_____

_____

_____

_____

_____

_____

_____

_____

• Leg 1 _____

• Leg 2 _____

• Leg 3 _____

• Leg 4 _____

• Leg 5 _____

• Leg 6 _____

Print these for free at oilabilityteam.com/unstuck.

UNSTUCK #DIAMONDRISING LEADER
Coaching Sheets

Stat Tracking Homework

Track your statistics from the data on the Young Living Oil Tools app!

January
Rank:_____
Paycheck:_____
OGV:_____
Team size:_____
New members:_____
Going inactive:_____
Pace OGV on Day 1:_____
Projected OGV on Day 1:_____
Super recruiters:_____
Total ER:_____
Member % ER:_____
Enrollers:_____
Stars:_____
Senior Stars:_____
Executives:_____
Silvers:_____
Golds:_____
Platinums:_____

Februrary
Rank:_____
Paycheck:_____
OGV:_____
Team size:_____
New members:_____
Going inactive:_____
Pace OGV on Day 1:_____
Projected OGV on Day 1:_____
Super recruiters:_____
Total ER:_____
Member % ER:_____
Enrollers:_____
Stars:_____
Senior Stars:_____
Executives:_____
Silvers:_____
Golds:_____
Platinums:_____

March
Rank:_____
Paycheck:_____
OGV:_____
Team size:_____
New members:_____
Going inactive:_____
Pace OGV on Day 1:_____
Projected OGV on Day 1:_____
Super recruiters:_____
Total ER:_____
Member % ER:_____
Enrollers:_____
Stars:_____
Senior Stars:_____
Executives:_____
Silvers:_____
Golds:_____
Platinums:_____

April
Rank:_____
Paycheck:_____
OGV:_____
Team size:_____
New members:_____
Going inactive:_____
Pace OGV on Day 1:_____
Projected OGV on Day 1:_____
Super recruiters:_____
Total ER:_____
Member % ER:_____
Enrollers:_____
Stars:_____
Senior Stars:_____
Executives:_____
Silvers:_____
Golds:_____
Platinums:_____

May
Rank:_____
Paycheck:_____
OGV:_____
Team size:_____
New members:_____
Going inactive:_____
Pace OGV on Day 1:_____
Projected OGV on Day 1:_____
Super recruiters:_____
Total ER:_____
Member % ER:_____
Enrollers:_____
Stars:_____
Senior Stars:_____
Executives:_____
Silvers:_____
Golds:_____
Platinums:_____

June
Rank:_____
Paycheck:_____
OGV:_____
Team size:_____
New members:_____
Going inactive:_____
Pace OGV on Day 1:_____
Projected OGV on Day 1:_____
Super recruiters:_____
Total ER:_____
Member % ER:_____
Enrollers:_____
Stars:_____
Senior Stars:_____
Executives:_____
Silvers:_____
Golds:_____
Platinums:_____

July
Rank:_____
Paycheck:_____
OGV:_____
Team size:_____
New members:_____
Going inactive:_____
Pace OGV on Day 1:_____
Projected OGV on Day 1:_____
Super recruiters:_____
Total ER:_____
Member % ER:_____
Enrollers:_____
Stars:_____
Senior Stars:_____
Executives:_____
Silvers:_____
Golds:_____
Platinums:_____

August
Rank:_____
Paycheck:_____
OGV:_____
Team size:_____
New members:_____
Going inactive:_____
Pace OGV on Day 1:_____
Projected OGV on Day 1:_____
Super recruiters:_____
Total ER:_____
Member % ER:_____
Enrollers:_____
Stars:_____
Senior Stars:_____
Executives:_____
Silvers:_____
Golds:_____
Platinums:_____

Weakness:_____   Action Steps:_____

Print these for free at oilabilityteam.com/unstuck.

ESSENTIAL REWARDS IN CLEAR LANGUAGE

I get asked at least once a day how the Essential Rewards program works, even by leaders, and when I see leaders with 288 PV or 187 PV, I want to kick a wall. So here's a simple explanation (for my own sanity).

1. Essential Rewards Freebies

If you spend 100 PV, 190 PV, 250 PV, or 300 PV, you get oodles of freebies! Example: The one this month—a free Everyday Oils Kit—for 300 PV is actually worth $270 (retail). With this amount of money, you can literally restock most of your starter kit, or your cleaning supplies, supplements and oils. The freebies change every single month. Look for January's to be released around December 31st. You cannot add to an order from earlier in the month to hit 300PV. It's got to be in one single order.

Earn gifts available only to members of the Essential Rewards program when you place consecutive Essential Rewards orders over 50 PV. Get rewarded when you consecutively order for 3, 6, and 9 months—and beyond. Plus, you'll get an exclusive blend after your 12th consecutive month!

2. Discounted shipping

Essential Rewards orders qualify for discounted shipping rates.

3. Cash back

For the first three months you're on Essential Rewards, you get 10% back. Beginning month four, you get 20% back, and after 25 months, you get 25% back. Most of my oils were free this way.

4. Kits only available on Essential Rewards

The NingXia Red® Essential Rewards kit, for example, costs $1.16/ounce instead of $1.60/ounce buying it in a One Time Order bundle. It's the cheapest way to buy NingXia, and if your whole family drinks it, like mine does, that's a big savings! The same is true of the Thieves® and Everyday Oils Essential Rewards kits.

5. The Requirements

You must spend 50 PV a month to place an Essential Rewards order, and you can always change the date to a better date for you. You must check your cart before your ship date and update it.The items in your cart from last month are left in the cart to order again. Why? Because most people use this to order the same supplements every month and don't want to keep adding them in month after month. Make sure you have what you want in your cart before it ships out.

Why should business builders be on Essential Rewards? Because you have to spend 100 PV to get your paycheck anyway, which is a good idea since it gets you familiar with the product. If you are on Essential Rewards, you get 10% back. That would mean you're actually only spending $90. And that's better financial stewardship. It's a wiser way to get paid.

Three other Essential Rewards questions I get every week:

1) Where do I order it?
   Under the Essential Rewards button only in your Virtual Office. I try to put my entire monthly order on it every month because it's free money back.

2) How do I claim my Essential Rewards points?
   Under the One Time Order button. All Essential Rewards points need to be claimed under One Time Order tab, not under the Essential Rewards tab.

3) Can I get the freebies under One Time Order?
   Yes. Hit the same benchmarks: 190, 250, or 300PV. You can get many of the freebies twice: once under One Time Order, and once under Essential Rewards. I frequently place an order under both the One Time Order and the ER buttons. You will only earn points under ER, and some of the freebies may be ER exclusive, just check that month's promotion.

Based on points earned plus estimated value of monthly promotions

	3 MONTHS	6 MONTHS	12 MONTHS	2 YEARS	5 YEARS
50PV	$15	$45	$105	$225	$765
100PV	$75	$165	$345	$705	$2,325
190PV	$312	$681	$1,419	$2,825	$7,665
250PV	$495	$1,065	$2,205	$4,485	$14,995
300PV	$690	$1,470	$3,030	$6,150	$16,050

How to Use the Gameplan System

When I first wrote *Gameplan*, it was just a book. It was a simple high-light-it-and-shelf-it two-day read. It has become so much more than that, because of you. I am honored to say because of your suggestions and your probing me to make this even better, it's now a complete duplicatable training system, the first put on paper in all of Young Living. It's affordable. And it keeps you and your leaders on the same page.

It started with the book. After running my team through bootcamp, they requested a workbook to mold the principles in the book to their teams specifically. Once we released it, there was a request on the Platinum page of Young Living to create a prospecting book for those that weren't ready for *Gameplan* yet. That's how the mini was developed: *Your Gameplan*.

I recorded the bootcamp videos to flesh out what was in the book and make it personable. And we ended up with a 25-day system: one chapter of the book, one set of workbook worksheets, and one video a day. 25 chapters, 25 worksheets, 25 videos. Rinse and repeat. Simple and easy, yet fully equipping your leaders with everything they need to succeed. In 2019, we tightened up the training and made it shorter and better. *Gameplan* can now be done in 12 days, for free, here: https://oilabili-tyteam.com/gameplan-bootcamp/

I knew after bootcamp we needed one more step to the system for long-term commitment and focus — and that's why I just wrapped up the *Gameplanner*, which is unlike anything you've ever seen in a planner before. It marks a year of research and work. There's rank mapping, stat tracking for eight months in a sitting so you can watch trends on your team, places to chart classes, track OGV, focus on certain leaders and certain legs, watch those ranking up who are doing the work, keep in touch with your top leaders, track your oils collection, *Fearless* challenges to boost Essential Rewards, follow up and warm and cold market pages, and more. This is all the actions I've focused on and sketched into my planners for the past three years. It's based off market research on hundreds of different planners, over 1,000 of your planner requests, and includes every element of the *Gameplan* book, putting it into planner form. It's the definition of accountability.

How do I use the *Gameplan* system now that it's complete?

1) Hand out the mini (*Your Gameplan*) like candy (this will help you find leaders!).

2) Do the Teacher Training in *Unstuck*.

3) Coach them through their first 101 class using the script

4) Hand them the *Gameplan* book and the *Gameplan* workbook and direct them to the FREE *Gameplan* bootcamp at oilability.team.com.

5) Have them pick two leaders and do the first four steps

6) Once they have trained their first two leaders, reward them with a *Gameplanner* to keep them on task. It is a full year of business accountability.

7) Rinse and repeat.

For a year of accountability after they have completed bootcamp, there are two amazing resources for keeping them focused. The first, mentioned briefly above, is the *Gameplanner*. It allows them to track *Gameplan* bootcam with their leaders, focus on teaching classes, doing follow up, tracking their stats, rank mapping to see how far they are from their next rank, and so much more. It is a powerhouse. I also recorded *Gameplan* as an audio book. When you listen to something, you use a totally different part of your brain. They can download it on Apple iTunes or Audible on Amazon and listen through their cell phone, and get *Gameplan* training as they drive. Solidify the concepts through audio learning!

What would happen to your family business if you committed to doing only income-producing activities for one year? If you held a class a week, did follow up once a month on your classes, and held twelve *Gameplan* bootcamp, training two to train two, and getting your leaders to duplicate? You'd have a totally new business in a year. You'd be building a legacy income. A Young Living business is built one brick at a time, with a little Essential Rewards mortar in between. Is it easy? No. Is it worth it? Yes.

GAMEPLAN

The Complete Strategy Guide to go From **Starter Kit to Silver**

STEP 1
Read "Your Gameplan" (the mini)

STEP 2
Do the Teacher Training from the "Gameplan" Appendix

STEP 3
Market and Host the 101 Class from the "Gameplan" Appendix

STEP 4
Get "Gameplan" and "Gameplan Workbook" in your hands

STEP 5
Go to oilabilityteam.com and do the bootcamp *(25 FREE videos, 25 chapters in Gameplan, 25 workbook chapters)*

STEP 6
Train two people with the first five steps

STEP 7
Rinse and repeat.

To listen to a full 101 oils class for FREE - go to:
oilabilityteam.com

GAMEPLAN RESOURCES
THAT WILL EXPLODE YOUR BUSINESS

To rank, stay focused on the only three things that directly grow your business:

- **Hold classes** • **Follow up** *and get people on Essential Rewards*
- **Train your leaders using Gameplan**

Hold Classes

Essential Oils 101 Audio CD

This is a 45 minute class on audio cd, recorded in a professional studio. The who, where, when, what, why of oils. Sarah uses these in her purple bags as a "class in a bag" to hand to complete strangers… and friends.

Toxin Free Life Audio CD

This is a 30 minute class on the Thieves line on audio cd, recorded in a professional studio. This targets cleaning supplies and toxins in the home. It's designed for those who aren't ready to jump in with oils yet, but really like the concept of a toxin free life.

FREE RESOURCES

The textable 101 audio class and Toxin Free life classes, the online Beauty School, and the 101 powerpoint at oilabilityteam.com! Look under "Share".

Follow Up

Fearless

This little book is a powerhouse, and the first of its kind in all of Young Living. For the majority of the people you share oils with, this is their first exposure to natural health. They are overwhelmed. This book is a systematic step-by-step oils explosion to get your new oiler emptying their bottles with courage. It trains the toxin-free lifestyle. It's the first book that should go out to every new kit holder.

Diamond Rising Decks

Are a full-on follow up system. You've had tools for your new oiler—this tool is for YOU. It takes the FEAR out of follow up for the very first time. The average person needs to be approached 7 to 15 times before they will commit to the

lifestyle. This gives you specific steps, tools, and concise training so you know exactly what comes next in each of those conversations, and it's never awkward for you. You simply stick to the system. Contact Me cards are for prospects. You'll learn their biggest health struggles, what areas of aromatherapy they want to learn more about, if they're already in Young Living, and how to best contact them. The Distributor cards are for people who have joined your team—and they're run through a powerful aromatherapy funnel that will drive them to research, label read, and take control of their own health. The Diamond Rising Leader cards take your budding leaders through an entire business funnel, step by step, from the starter kit all the way to Royal Crown Diamond. You track their entire Young Living journey on a series of three 4x6 cards, with simple checkmarks and minutes a day. It's a powerful and duplicatable system that works.

oilabilityteam.com

Train Your Leaders

Gameplan Book

The first duplicatable affordable training system in all of Young Living in the form of a book. This series went to number 1 on Amazon's entrepreneur catagory and sold over 700-thousand copies. How do you train your leaders? Use the book, workbook, and the free bootcamp at oilability-team.com. 25 chapters in the book, 25 worksheets, 12 free videos averaging 30 minutes each. Take it at your pace, pull two leaders through it, and rinse and repeat your way to Diamond. The system has worked for thousands upon thousands of Young Living distributors.

Gameplan Workbook

This is a critical part of the training system. It customizes the Gameplan book for you. This puts action to the things you read in the book and gets you to move.

Your Gameplan (the mini)

This is the first digestible prospecting book in all of Young Living. This book does the talking on the business for you. It covers the eight perks to a Young Living business, the Income Disclosure guide, and gets your prospect stacking up their job against a Young Living home based business.

Unstuck

Is the 2ND BOOK IN THE GAMEPLAN TRILOGY! Sarah collected thousands of responses and categorized them into 15 types of classes that have results. She lists four tried-and-true mojo methods to pull you out of a rut. There's 100 pages of Young Living specific mindset training, coaching to craft your personal story, how to lead with Essential Rewards in a compelling way that trains the lifestyle, training to set up an aromatherapy and business funnel that makes it comfortable to have multiple conversations to get your new oiler on ER. There are four scripts for the four starter kits—including a powerful NingXia script and a new Savvy Makeup script. She's collected dozens of leading sentences, tips for opening conversations with cold and warm market leads, and suggestions for following up. If your struggle is finding and connecting with humans, this will be the catapult your business has been waiting for.

Unstuck Workbook

Pairs perfectly with the Unstuck book. Unstuck gives you the knowledge and tools. The workbook tailors that knowledge directly to your needs and custom fits your experiences to the book to make it come alive for you. You'll find practical, tangible homework assignments inside that drive your business forward and pull you from a place of fear. It's not to be skipped! This is your personal Unstuck accountability system!

Ignite

Is a cliff-notes version of the full Gameplan book. This concise book is designed for your leaders that are not "all in" yet—those that are whetting their appetites with Young Living or are overwhelmed by a large book. Beta tested on dozens of blue personalities, the average read time for this book is 42 minutes. Yet it hits all the important topics that a new builder needs to know from the get-go: ER, the Virtual Office, the compensation plan, simple strategy, how you are paid, and the power and importance of consistently teaching. It ends with two scripts and a challenge to teach their first class to a family member or friend that night. If your leaders have clocked out or have stopped doing the things that got them to their rank in the first place—or if they're new and you have a blank slate, Ignite is the perfect tool.

YOUNG LIVINGEASE: LEARN THE LANGUAGE

YOUNG LIVING BUSINESS TERMS

Personal Volume (PV): Many products sold by Young Living have a PV amount. Not all products are dollar for dollar, so if you're trying to hit a certain rank, make sure you check the PV of an item and not its retail price. (Tax and shipping are not added into PV either). PV is one of the requirements for ranking within the compensation plan, and it accumulates throughout each commission period.

Organization Group Volume (OGV): OGV is the entire sales volume of a sales organization. This can be determined by calculating the sum of the PV of all the distributors and customers within a particular organization. OGV accumulates throughout each monthly commission period, and resets to zero with the start of a new month.

Personal Group Volume (PGV): For Silver or higher ranks in the compensation plan, PGV comes into play. It is determined by the sales volume of the organization directly supported by the distributor. Basically, it's all the volume outside of people who have ranked Silver or above. It is the sum of PV from the distributor down to, but not including, the next Silver or higher rank for each leg of the sales organization. If you are out there selling, you'll not have any problem hitting the 1,000 PGV requirement once you hit Silver (1,000 of your volume must be outside your legs). Let me explain to you how this works. If you have three people outside your legs that are spending 300 PV each, and you spend 100 PV to get your check, you will have 1,000 PGV. If you have nine people outside your two Silver legs spending 100 PV each, and you spend 100 PV to get your paycheck, you will have 1,000 PGV.

Sales Organization: Also known as a downline, this encompasses all members located beneath a particular distributor. This includes the distributor and all levels within his or her organization.

Level: The position of a distributor within a sales organization. Those distributors who are immediately sponsored by another distributor would be considered the sponsoring distributor's first level. Those distributors who are sponsored by a distributor's first level would be considered that distributor's second level, and so on.

Enroller: The person responsible for personally introducing a new distributor to Young Living. Enrollers are eligible to qualify for financial bonuses, including the Fast Start and starter kit bonuses.

Sponsor: A new distributor's direct upline and main support. The sponsor may also be the enroller.

Upline: Any distributor above another distributor in a sales organization.

Customer: A member who chooses not to participate in the Young Living compensation plan, but desires to purchase the product at retail price for personal use. Customers need to be sponsored and enrolled by a current Young Living distributor.

Unilevel: Unilevel is a form of commission that is earned through the compensation plan. Qualifying distributors earn 8% on the sales volume, or PV, of each distributor on the first level within their organization, 5% on the second level, and 4% on the third through fifth levels.

Compression: In circumstances where a distributor does not meet the 100 PV qualification to earn commissions, his or her volume, if any, is combined, or "compressed," with all the volume of distributors down to and including the next qualifying distributor in the sales organization with at least 100 PV. For instance, if in the third level a distributor places an order of only 30 PV, then the fourth-level distributor's PV in the organization who has ordered 100 PV compresses up with the third level for payout purposes. This creates a single unilevel to be paid out with a total of 130 PV for that commission period. Compression maximizes compensation in cases where there are inactive distributors in an organization who may not be purchasing regularly but may have others below them who are doing so.

PV Minimum: In order to qualify for retail earnings and enroller-based bonuses, and to be considered "active," a distributor must maintain a monthly order of at least 50 PV. In order to qualify for a paycheck, a distributor must maintain a monthly order of at least 100 PV. If an account becomes inactive by dropping below 50 PV for a period of 12 consecutive months, the account will be dropped.

YOUNG LIVING RANKS

Star: In order to qualify as a Star in the compensation plan, a distributor must achieve 100 PV and 500 OGV within a commission period. As a Star, the distributor qualifies to receive compensation on the volume of three unilevels in his or her organization (paid at 8%, 5%, and 4%, respectively) in addition to any retail earnings. Stars may also qualify to receive the Fast Start, Starter Kit, and Rising Star Team bonuses.

Senior Star: In order to qualify as a Senior Star in the compensation plan, a distributor must achieve 100 PV and 2,000 OGV within a commission period. As a Senior Star, the distributor qualifies to receive compensation on the volume of four unilevels in his or her organization (paid at 8%, 5%, 4%, and 4%, respectively) in addition to any retail earnings. Senior Stars may also qualify to receive the Fast Start, Starter Kit, and Rising Star Team bonuses.

Executive: In order to qualify as an Executive, a distributor must achieve 100 PV, 4,000 OGV, and two separate legs with 1,000 OGV each within a commission period. As an Executive, the distributor qualifies to receive compensation on the volume of five unilevels within his or her organization (paid at 8%, 5%, 4%, 4%, and 4%, respectively) in addition to any retail earnings. Executives may also qualify for the Fast Start, Starter Kit, and Rising Star Team bonuses.

Silver: In order to qualify as Silver, a distributor must achieve 100 PV, 10,000 OGV, 1,000 PGV, and two separate legs with 4,000 OGV each within a commission period. As a Silver, the distributor qualifies to receive compensation on the volume of five unilevels within his or her organization (paid at 8%, 5%, 4%, 4%, and 4%, respectively), personal generation commissions (paid at 2.5%), generation commissions on 2 levels (paid at 3%), in addition to any retail earnings. Silvers may also qualify for the Fast Start, Starter Kit, and Generation Leadership bonuses.

Gold: In order to qualify as Gold, a distributor must achieve 100 PV, 35,000 OGV, 1,000 PGV, and three separate legs with 6,000 OGV each within a commission period. As a Gold, the distributor qualifies to receive compensation on the volume of five unilevels within his or her organization (paid at 8%, 5%, 4%, 4%, and 4%, respectively), personal generation commissions (paid at 2.5%), generation commissions on 3 levels (paid at 3%), in addition to any retail earnings. Golds may also qualify for the Fast Start, Starter Kit, and Generation Leadership bonuses.

Platinum: In order to qualify as Platinum, a distributor must achieve 100 PV, 100,000 OGV, 1,000 PGV, and four separate legs with 8,000 OGV each within a commission period. As Platinum, the distributor qualifies to receive compensation on the volume of five unilevels within his or her organization (paid at 8%, 5%, 4%, 4%, and 4%, respectively), personal generation commissions (paid at 2.5%), generation commissions on four levels (paid at 3%), in addition to any retail earnings. Platinums may also qualify for the Fast Start, Starter Kit, and Generation Leadership bonuses.

Diamond: In order to qualify as Diamond, a distributor must achieve 100 PV, 250,000 OGV, 1,000 PGV, and five separate legs with 15,000 OGV each within a commission period. As Diamond, the distributor qualifies to receive compensation on the volume of five unilevels within his or her organization (paid at 8%, 5%, 4%, 4%, and 4%, respectively), personal generation commissions (paid at 2.5%), generation commissions on five levels (paid at 3%), in addition to any retail earnings. Diamonds may also qualify for the Fast Start, Starter Kit, Generation Leadership, and Diamond Express Profit Sharing Pool bonuses.

Crown Diamond: In order to qualify as Crown Diamond, a distributor must achieve 100 PV, 750,000 OGV, 1,000 PGV, and six separate legs with 20,000 OGV each within a commission period. As Crown Diamond, the distributor qualifies to receive compensation on the volume of five unilevels within his or her organization (paid at 8%, 5%, 4%, 4%, and 4%, respectively), personal generation commissions (paid at 2.5%), generation commissions on six levels (paid at 3%), in addition to any retail earnings. Crown Diamonds may also qualify for the Fast Start, Starter Kit, Generation Leadership, and Diamond Express Profit Sharing Pool bonuses.

Royal Crown Diamond: In order to qualify as Royal Crown Diamond, a distributor must achieve 100 PV, 1,500,000 OGV, 1,000 PGV, and six separate legs with 35,000 OGV each within a commission period. As Royal Crown Diamond, the distributor qualifies to receive compensation on the volume of five unilevels within his or her organization (paid at 8%, 5%, 4%, 4%, and 4%, respectively), personal generation commissions (paid at 2.5%), generation commissions on six levels (six levels paid at 3% and 1% paid on the seventh level), in addition to any retail earnings. Royal Crown Diamonds may also qualify for the Fast Start, Starter Kit, Generation Leadership, and Diamond Express Profit Sharing Pool bonuses.

FAQ SECTION

Every Tuesday at 8:30 PM Eastern, I do a Facebook Gameplan round-table for 30 minutes on our Facebook page, at Oil Ability with Sarah. I get on with tens of thousands of you and answer your questions about the business and about the book. Some fantastic questions have come in the past year since we released the book. We compiled the most common ones and put them in this brand new second edition section of Gameplan. These are based on leaders who have led teams through bootcamp or are doing one right now. I have picked the most common business questions that I see.

Do you have ideas on who to share with when you've exhausted your friend circles and you have no one who wants to have a class?

Yes. This issue is not your friend circles, it's your way of approaching your friends. One on-fire oiler is enough to ignite a Silvership. One on-fire oiler will be a megaphone for your business. So start with the simple act of igniting one person. Build the relationship. Make it about them, not about the sale of your kit. Ask them what their needs are. Drop seeds. Loan out product. And then stand down and watch it work. Make sure your follow up is good.

I will tell you too—that when we first start in network marketing, we're so excited we can scare many of our closest friends and family members away, just with our passion. It's ok to return to them, tell them you are sorry for your initial approach, and ask for forgiveness. Then work to rebuild that relationship, and eventually, a need will arise that will require oils. Be there in that moment, without being pushy. It's ok to re-engage with people you have scared off.

If you truly have not one person left in your warm market that wants the oils, I'd recommend vendor events to meet new people.

People have asked how much I have made, and honestly it's very little. How do I collect business builders when I have no story?

Tell them you are just seriously starting your business. Then share stories of people that have done it. They don't always need to hear of your success to get interested. Get good at using third party tools. *Your Gameplan* is great because it shares a truly rags to riches story, eight reasons why Young Living is the best job on the earth, then gets them stacking up what they are doing now against a Young Living business. See if you can get them to read that first.

I also love to point people to the website at oilabilityteam.com, the "Start Here" button and "Sarah's Why". That is a good way to ignite just about anyone.

But if they need more 'proof' that they can do this, just go into your virtual office and show them the 450 Diamonds that have already done it. (You can find that under "benefits" and "global recognition.")

Your story is coming. But for now, lean on others that have done it. This falls under the same category as having to know it all to do the business. Just get good at using third party tools. "I don't have the answer to that, but here's where you can look." Point them to reference guides for medical questions, Gameplan for business questions, the D. Gary Young book for purity questions as well as the Seed to Seal website. You don't need to be the expert or the success story. You just need enough passion to ignite a leader and show them it can be done. And you need enough passion to believe in them, even if you're still building your own belief.

Can you give me specific steps on how to grow my business?

Absolutely. This book.

How do you actually 'build' a leader?

Besides giving vision and training them, which is what this book is for, it really comes down to one word—serve. With my team, my leaders before me. Their kit sales matter more to me than mine, their few moments to vent matters more to me than what I am doing in that moment—the simple pause, the listening ear, the encouraging text. It goes so very far. If you launch your business with an ear for your leaders, it's amazing how far it will go. Use the same training so you're all on the same page, create a team culture and do rallies and events together, but above all, wash their feet—just like Jesus did. Serve. I picked up over 800 business builders in the first two years after getting my kit. I didn't have a system to follow. I just met needs and listened. Then grow together, right beside your leaders.

What do you gift your leaders when they rank up?

One of my goals when I was a teenager was to live on 10% and tithe 90%—the reverse tithe. I have had that focus for more than 20 years, and this is the first year that John and I have been able to make leaps and bound toward it. So my giving is probably a bit higher than the average leader. But I will tell you what I do, and you choose to take it and run with it, or take bits and pieces and make it your own.

I believe that until Silver, every uprank should get business tools. I think it's wonderful to hand out diffuser necklaces and pretty bracelets and spa days, but my number one goal as their Diamond upline is tools to make the next rank easier than the rank they just achieved. Once they hit Silver, my leaders have a pretty good idea where this goes. Many have left second jobs (or even their primary job), relieved the burden on their spouse and have more free time. They are not stopping until Royal Crown Diamond. They have caught Diamond fever. But it takes tenacity and tools to keep them focused.

This is what I do on my own team. Cherry pick what works for you!

Star:
> One Toxin Free Life cd
> One Essential Oils 101 cd
> One *Your Gameplan* mini book
> One copy of *Fearless* and a *Fearless* calendar
> One free month of Oily Tools subscription
> One Nitro

Senior Star:
> Supplies for making ten purple bags (flyers, cd's, mini's and *Fearless*)
> Two *Gameplan* books
> Two *Gameplan* workbooks (to train 2 to train 2)
> Intro To Young Living DVD (to play if they have timid leaders)
> A sample of Pure Protein complete and my Mango Smoothie recipe

Executive:
> Supplies for making 20 purple bags
> Two *Gameplan* books
> Two *Gameplan* workbooks (to train 2 to train 2)
> *Gameplanner* to keep them organized for 12 months. (Of the 43 Silvers on our team right now, 36 made Silver in Six because of focus and organization!)
> NingXia and Nitro packets

Silver:

> Six *Gameplan* books
> Six *Gameplan* workbooks
> Desert Mist diffuser
> *Gameplan* training 7-DVD set
> Private coaching session to strategize to Gold
> Fifty *Fearless* and *Fearless* calendars
> Aromacomplete case (if it's in the budget!)
> NingXia and Nitro packets and wolfberry crisp bars

What am I doing with these gifts? Giving them tools to grow. There are three things that lead to direct OGV growth: sharing (purple bags), getting people on Essential Rewards (Fearless and the calendar), and training your leaders (Gameplan and the workbook). The tools make it easier to rank up.

Did I do all of this when I was a Star? Absolutely not. I gave roll ons and coaching sessions and hand-written notes. Live within your budget. But as your check grows, set a portion aside to say thank you to your leaders. They will duplicate that generosity to their leaders. Are gifts necessary to grow? No. Will they make you rank faster? In some cases, perhaps, and in others, no. Are they an act of love and generosity to your leaders, and appreciation? Yes. That is why I give.

Do you have a list of resources to give people who are still convinced that buying their oils from a super market is a good idea!??

I will shoot straight with you here—you can only save so many people. If you have taught the 101 and explained purity, if you have told them that they get what they pay for—that they are using oils to get rid of chemicals, so why would they use an oil laden with chemicals—and they still think $7 Frankincense is a good idea, kick the dust off your feet and move on. Don't waste time and energy and live in a land of drama with people that are insistent that all oils are equal. You are in the oils business, and you know better. Plant gentle seeds with them and move on.

If it's the first time you're approached by a person, and they genuinely seem interested but there isn't enough "science" on Seed to Seal to make them comfortable, there is a tool generated by Jen O'Sullivan that I love. It's a chart of all the major oils companies in the world pitted against one another for purity, sourcing, number of farms, distillation methods, etc. You can find that chart at 31oils.com.

I find it a struggle handling questions of how to show those interested which oils to use for different issues. I feel like our tongues are so

tied up by the FDA. I need help trying to help those that want it and still staying compliant.

Here is my trick: just use what's on the Young Living website. What they've written has been through a team of lawyers and it's safe to say. Young Living has knocked it out of the ballpark with YL Central. It has scripts, videos, PowerPoints, and all sorts of things you can share now if you don't have the words to say. Just log into your Virtual Office and click on "Member Resources", and you'll find it.

Let me put in one more word of encouragement here, too. Don't live in the land of fear. The Lord has brought this business to you, and He will make a way for you to share. It says in Scripture to be anxious for nothing. When we live in a land of fear, we aren't trusting that God made no mistakes when He put you on the team you're on, brought your leaders to you, filled your classes and gave you a passion for the things He created. You can do this! Just learn the lingo. Instead of diagnosing, say, "I don't know about that. I've never dealt with that before. Why don't you take home this oil and my diffuser and see how you feel?" That one line gets you off the hook. If you want to up your game, add in, "here's a place where you can begin your research" (and point to a reference guide). Now they are standing on their own two feet, as well, and looking things up.

I could use some tips on how to invite, teach, and lead men. Obviously, this is a very female driven company which is amazing! But I would love some guidance on how to help men be interested in the oils and the business!

Can I be totally frank with you? I do nothing different. Absolutely nothing. Men are faced with the same needs for respiratory support, immune support, personal care products and supplements. I teach my 101 class to men and women and get the same response. I'd say, after the class ask them why they came, and build relationships with them. Meet their needs with oils from the starter kit. That will get you farther than any "man" script!

About purple bags... when one is first starting out with the business do we include sample product? You have mentioned not spending more than you make. Is this something we add once our bonus checks start coming in?

Yes. I firmly believe in not spending more than you make. When I first started, I could not afford a $20 Vistaprint order for business cards, so I typed out my information, printed it on regular white paper and cut it out with scissors and handed it out. I took the first six months of my check and put it in my gas tank to get to classes. Your number one responsibility as you climb to Silver is to teach classes. You can't find leaders without classes. You can't get people on Essential Rewards without classes. You need to get that script in front of faces.

So how can you do purple bags on the cheap? Print the textable classes on your business cards and direct them to listen to it. Print off the free-bies on the oilabilityteam.com website under purple bags and use those: the how to order sheet, the cover page. I'd hold off on samples until you have more income. If you feel convicted, put one drop of Peppermint in the palm of their hand while they are at class. That's my "wow" oil. That's a lot cheaper than giving away all your Share It bottles, ordering more, and buying carrier oils—and going through a bottle or two of oil each night of teaching. Be faithful with the small things, and the Lord will make you ruler over more.

Where do I sign people up to begin to build legs when I have no established leaders? How do I get people on ER so I can build under them and no one loses commission?

That's a great question! I got it so often that I added a whole section on Rising Star bonuses on the new edition of this book. Go check out "A Young Living Strategy Guide on Where to Sign New Oilers" on page 89 for structuring.

To get people on ER utilize Fearless. See "Follow Up For Those Who Got a Kit" on page 48

What should a day look like when you are doing your business full time from home?

Eighty percent of your time should be spent prospecting. So if you're home full time, put that time to good use by teaching classes. The other 20% should be spent on behind the scenes stuff: training your leaders, teaching classes other than the 101 for your new members, doing follow up mailings, marketing your upcoming classes, possibly running a busi-ness or product Facebook page, etc. Always ask yourself if what you are doing is the best use of your time, and if it will lead to income producing activities. If they answer is no—why are you doing it? Cut back on those things and focus on the three things that build your OGV and make it last.

What does my day look like? I work about ten hours a week right now as a Diamond (but I do delegate a lot of my mailings to people that I pay). Eighty percent of my time is spent in training and teaching. I believe even as a Diamond that you can lose your rank when you stop teaching! The other 20% is what I just mentioned above, but mostly leader training and follow up mailings.

Follow up and social media: How do I follow up after doing a FB Live class?

The real work begins when the class ends, because follow up can be time consuming. But many, many Diamonds have been successful building online—it works. Start by going through your class and finding every "like" and every "comment". Message each person based on what they said or liked and start building the relationship. It may be something like "you liked the post about my dog in the class tonight. Do you have any dogs?" (Don't say 'want me to send you a sample for your dog?' Or 'want a Young Living starter kit for your dog?' You aren't there yet. You always start by asking questions to build relationship, not selling the kit.) Go for a back and forth exchange, asking questions about them, and lead into a sample, a tool, more knowledge, or the kit if they are ready for it.

How do I give a 1 on 1? A lot of my classes are 1 on 1 and it feels awkward since I'm talking to them like I would a class. It needs to be more intimate—but I'm not sure how to do that.

It may feel awkward to use a script when you are face to face with just one person, often a close friend or family member. But the great thing about scripts is that they are duplicatable—anyone can read a script. So if use one during a one-on-one, your new member will see that all they have to do to share is read a script!

There are two things that I've done to make it feel more natural and personal. First—practice. Seriously! Get that bad boy out and read it in front of a mirror 20 times. You'll have that sucker down pat. I'm not telling you to memorize it—that's not duplicatable. But if you have a good idea where you're going, you don't have to look down so much. Then what I do is highlight the first sentence of each paragraph and just glance down and then up again to give details.

The second thing is to start with your story. Don't use the script for that. Just share your passion. Why did you get a kit? Why have you fallen in love with it? Where did your journey begin? What prompts you to share them with everyone? Facts tell, stories sell. You start with your reasons, and they will fall in love.

What about people that really just want to be retail customers? There really are those people out there.

May we agree to disagree on this? I don't ever believe in selling one oil. Let me tell you why. Oils have been a course correction for my family. If anything, I don't live in fear anymore. I know I have what it takes on my oils shelf to calm my kiddos down and support multiple systems of their body when the need arises. But beyond that, I have kicked chemicals out of my home.

You see, oils aren't one bottle. They are a lifestyle. If you communicate that, you have nailed the entire reason why this network marketing company is the best in the world: consumable product. I don't need a bunch of pots and pans every month, or lots of books—but I use oils every single day, many times a day. I wash my hair with oil infused products and make smoothies for breakfast with Pure Protein complete. I have the diffuser running all day and all night, and include Vitality oils and supplements for wellness. It's part of the deal. You don't kick some poisons out of your home, but keep others. Don't train one bottle of oil. Don't train the starter kit. Train the lifestyle. That's the missing link in getting people on Essential Rewards and training them in the playground of oiling.

What do I say to them? "I can't train you how to clean out your cabinets with one bottle of oil. The Premium Starter Kit is a playground. It's got a diffuser—which is the fastest way to get oils into your system—and 11 full bottles of oil. Think you won't use it? Do you need respiratory support? Immune support? Joint and muscle support? That's what's in this kit. Snag it, and I am committed to training you every step of the way. We'll start with lifestyle training and Fearless. I know there's a part of you that doesn't want the garbage in your house. We'll do this together, one room at a time, one bottle at a time."

Why don't you do more themed classes (health, beauty, kids, pets, etc)?

Because they don't sell Starter Kits. There are four Premium Starter kits on Young Living's website: the oils kit, Savvy, NingXia, and Thieves. If you're not driving to one of those four kits, you're not setting up wholesale accounts. I have included a 101 and there is a Toxin Free Life Class on my website. As much as I adore Oils of Ancient Scripture (it's still my favorite class to teach!) I don't teach it often. If someone sits in that class, the likelihood of them getting a $185 starter kit, a $200 Ancient Scripture kit, and getting on Essential Rewards is pretty remote. Always funnel to the PSK's. That's where your longevity is.

How do I reengage business-minded members when they say they want to do this but then won't take any action?

Two tools I use are the mini—*Your Gameplan*—and the "Sarah's Why" video on the oilabilityteam.com website. That's under the "Start Here" button. Have them watch the video and read the mini, then meet with them for lunch and talk about their why. Talk about their need for freedom. Talk about where they are. Listen to their needs. Then offer gentle coaching to start teaching classes. If they won't commit, kick the dust off your feet and move on. Be so busy teaching 101 classes—and gathering leaders through them—that you don't have time to notice the naysayers.

If you call someone to invite them to a class you are hosting what do you say on that initial call? Then when you call back to remind them about the class and you get voicemail what message do you leave?

I never leave voicemail messages. It gives them a chance to opt out. I wait until I get an actual person, then I focus on the relationship. My first question isn't "My name is Sarah Harnisch, would you like to buy my starter kit???" (bats eyes). It's usually "talk to me about how you have been. What's going on in your life?" Then I tailor my oils response based on their need.

How do I get my spouse on board the Oil Train?!?

Oh this is a simple one! Show him the paycheck! Most spouses don't want you working harder and making less. Commit to one class a week and see where it leads. Then show him the fruit. Don't tell him how great oils are or how wonderful the business is—just show him results.

My struggle is getting three to invite 50. I know you are from a small town as well, but when those three people all know the same 50 people, how do you make that work???

You are overthinking it. It's not about the size of the town. It's about the art of the relationship. One person has a reach far beyond your little town. They know people all over the United States, and sometimes in different countries. What happens when that one person gets excited about oils—and their home starts to look just like yours, with Thieves dish soap on the counter and shampoo in every shower? They get passion. And all it takes is the passion of one to build a team. That's where all the magic starts.

If you have 50 people in your town, that's a chance to build a pretty large organization with their contacts list. It's because they don't only know people in the town. They have been to school elsewhere, maybe had jobs far away, they have family members that don't live there, etc. All those faces could be part of your team. Don't see your town as a single town. See it as the city that could be your organization, if only you start a relationship with one.

If you walk out your door and see humans on the other side, those humans should be on your team. I think the bigger thing is fear. We fear what people will think of us, we fear rejection. We fear that we can't make this work. We feel the pressure of the need and desire to rank up, but get paralyzed by the art of building relationships and talking to people we do not know.

Here's the thing: you have a wide world of wisdom under your belt. You have been gifted something precious in the knowledge that you have of oils. It's knowledge that can help every person out there. When you do not share with them, you are robbing them of something precious that they need to care for their families. Your love for them must be greater than your fear of rejection. That's how you share oils.

I just don't know anyone. I live in a small town, and there's one church. There are eight distributors in that one church. What do I do? Everyone I know is oiling.

The real issue is that you must get better at asking questions. You do know people, but you are not connecting with them. How do I know that you know people? Is every family member and every friend and every social media contact on your team? If not, you have untapped resources.

The secret to connecting with people is asking better questions. Answer questions with questions. For example: "why is the kit so expensive?" I'd respond with "I spend money every week to take care of my family. This is just moving the money from a store into a place where there are healthier choices. Tell me one thing you struggle with—one thing you'd love to work on for your family's wellness, and let's start from that place." Ask a question. Then offer an oil from that place. The reason they say it's expensive is simply because they do not know they need it.

I have yet to see a family using Thieves that is craving the chemicals back in their home. It's simple knowledge to walk from yuck to purity. Meet them where they are and respond to their objections with questions. Find common ground and start there, then offer an oil. Here is another good question to ask, "what questions do you have of me?" Always put the ball in their court. Meet them in the place where they are, without judgement.

How do you handle it, or what do you say when a level 1 leg that's huge decides to stop her association with YL and go to another MLM? How do you recover that leg?

Your heart always needs to be for the distributor. When I first was building to Silver, I lost my level one leg twice as that leader decided to jump to another MLM. I believe with my whole heart that Young Living is the best company in the world, because we have a product that is consumable that people need every single day. It's easier to share than pans or books, because you need oils and oil infused products every day, all day long. But not everyone catches that vision and that's ok! If you try to force them into the business when their heart is elsewhere, you will lose more than a business builder—you may lose a friendship, too, and that is a far bigger cost. Dig farther down into your organization and find another leader—under that leader—that is willing to work. And work with them to keep that leg afloat.

I do explain how I feel, gently, one time, to that distributor that wants to leave. If they still have no interest in continuing, kick the dust out from under your feet, and move on. Then when you speak to them in the future, have no animosity. Love them in the place where they are.

How do I follow up with prospects from a vendor event, kiosk, or a casual meeting in the grocery line? How do I get them to respond to my voice mail, email, or hand-written notes (this also applies to current team members)?

Part of the issue with connecting is not giving an expectation during the initial contact. If it's a completely cold market person, it's usually awkward to ask for a cell phone number, address, or email. The average person gets 115 emails a day anyway, that's not an effective way to build a network marketing business. Your message will go in a pile. Instead, Facebook friend them. Give them something—like a purple bag, a sample, a mini or a Fearless. Then expect something back in the exchange. Tell them the date you'll call and check in with them. Then check in on that date. As soon as I walk away, I text their name to myself and set a reminder on my phone to touch base—then I don't lose them in my sea of friends on Facebook.

A Facebook 'friending' is very effective, because it's informal. If they truly didn't want to connect with you, then can unfriend you when you walk away and nothing is lost. There's a distancing with it that makes them feel safe—much more than giving out a cell phone number to a total stranger (though we get in the car with random strangers who work for Uber—so who knows, maybe it will eventually be acceptable!).

If you set the expectation that you've given a gift and will be checking in, they are usually expecting your call. I don't ever leave voicemail messages, because I don't want to appear to be a pest. I simply try again later if I can't get through. I will try for a couple of weeks at different times of day, and if I'm still not getting through, I let it go and move on to the next person. Be so busy making contacts that you don't have time to hunt down all the rogue leads.

When people say, "send me the link!," and then they still don't sign up... how do I keep following up then, without being pushy?

I just answered that above. I'll give it a few weeks, and if I'm still not getting anywhere, I let it go. But if they are not a totally cold lead (maybe they are a mom you see at soccer practice), I'll do what I call seed dropping. That means you'll have a few conversations that don't have the word essential oils in them. You're not actively pursuing them. After that, watch for a need. Offer an oil. And check in.

I have a really good example of it from one of my executives, Colleen. This is a text she sent me this morning:

"I signed a friend up over a year ago. I taught him about the oils, gave him pamphlets, DVD's, digital recordings, and talked to him occasionally about life and oils. He still decided to go inactive about four months ago. I finally got to see him a few weeks ago, and as soon as I walked into his home, I grabbed his oils and started using them. He has an 18-month-old who was not feeling the best. I also brought my Thieves cleaner and started using it. He immediately fell in love and started asking about it. As a parting gift, I left a few packets of NingXia, which his wife used last night. She felt depleted. I oiled her like I oiled his daughter. His wife woke up this morning and said "order that stuff. I don't care about the cost." He is calling Monday to go active with a Thieves Premium Starter Kit and is starting Essential Rewards with NingXia"

I can summarize her work with two simple hashtags: #carrythieves-cleaner #livewiththemtosellit

No, for real—this falls under the category of why I wrote *Fearless*. You need to train the lifestyle, not the Starter Kit. That's what makes that book so awesome. He didn't know how to use the products he had. If you train lifestyle, label reading, researching, Simple Swap, etc., you will grow on-fire oilers. Or go live with them for a night. That works too.

What's the best way to approach an existing business? Is there a script for sharing our products with chiropractors, dentists, massage therapists, etc.?

Yes. The 101 script.

Seriously.

I use it for EVERYTHING. Just because you are a chiropractor doesn't mean you don't need to know the 'who-where-what-when-why-how' of oils. Start with the basics. Start with your story. Lead with your heart. Lead with your passion. It's not the script they are after—it's you. If you can tell a story with conviction, purpose, passion, and confidence—it doesn't matter who is listening. Start from that place.

In places of business, I never offer professional accounts, because they lose their chance at a downline, and that's the greatest blessing. I simply get their family to fall in love with oils first. I work on that relationship with the owner. Get them reading *Fearless* and doing the challenges. Get the diffuser going in their home. Oil up their kiddos. In the interim, I encourage them to keep a diffuser going in their office constantly—that's the best sales tool you have in a business environment. And I keep a basket with purple bags right by it that says "want to learn more about this diffuser?" It will draw a LOT of attention. Put the sponsor and enroller numbers of the team members you want to build under in the bags, and build relationships with each person that shows up on your team.

How do I ask someone to host a class for me?

It depends who you are asking. If you're asking an on-fire oiler that you have already built a relationship with, it's simple. Tell them you want to train them how to use their kit. Ask them to invite a few friends and promise a hostess basket. I put some Thieves cleaner in mine, a roll-on of an oil not in the starter kit, a couple cd's with classes like *Essential Oils 101* or *Toxin Free Life*, *Fearless*, and a couple samples like Thieves cough drops or Cool Azul pain cream.

If it's someone who is not signed yet, then you have to take a step back and build the relationship first. If they are a friend, it's simple—ask them to do something to help your family business. Get an oil on their body based on a need that they have and ask if they will host. If they are not a friend, then you need to spend more time on the relationship aspect. A totally raw conversation might look something like this:

"Have you had any exposure to essential oils?"

"Yes, I think my mom's friend sells them."

"Tell me what's going on in your life right now. If you could list your top three wellness struggles, what would they be?"

"Stress is definitely one. I have a high stress job."

"Boy do I understand that! I am a mom of three! (Meet them where they are). I have something that you may like. Smell this. (offer Stress Away). Try it at work tomorrow and see if it takes the edge off your day."

Then check in—and see how they are doing the next day. That opens a door for them to get a kit. If they are not ready yet, offer to teach a class—either in their home or in yours, so you can give them some basic aromatherapy training. It's all in the art of the relationship and meeting needs. If you are meeting their needs, it does not matter whether you are getting them started with a starter kit or asking to set up a class—the language is the same. You want to educate, to train, and to meet them where they are.

Help! All the local farmer's markets require that you sell things that you have grown or made. Where do I find events that will welcome an oils booth?

Yes, there are a lot of vendor events that are crafts only. But they are not your only option. You will have to get creative and do some more homework to find events that will work for you. Look into concert settings, conferences, trade shows, state and county fairs, and definitely call the Chamber of Commerce for your town and the ten towns around your town. They will have ideas of festivals and upcoming events. I just did an event this weekend that was set up at a christian concert with 2,000 women. They wanted a vendor hall—and there I was.

There was also a vendor event that told one of my leaders 'no'—that it was "crafts only", so I asked if I could make my case before their jurist panel. After appearing before them, they allowed to let my leader in—and she built from 8,000 OGV to 42,000 OGV in 18 months with that once a week Saturday fair. Get creative in how you ask, make a strong case, always have your eye out for festivals and fairs, and make some phone calls to make sure you're not missing local events.

How do I get my team to come to monthly classes/meetings? They always have excuses, do I just let them go?

Develop the skill of listening and vision casting. When I first get to know a leader, I ask their why. What do they want in their life? Where are they going? What is their bucket list? What do they want out of this business? Then gently, from time to time, remind them of their why. Remind them of the reason they began in the first place.

It's also really good to encourage attendance at events. Events always pump up my team. It may be a Gameplan Live event near you, or Go Pro, or an event from a Young Living Diamond like Elevate or Ignite. Set them on fire. And do it with all the other leaders around them. That's social proof, when they get to see everyone else fired up too, and hear their stories of how they have ranked. They begin to believe it's possible.

I believe the greatest weapon that Satan has in his arsenal against us is busyness and distraction. That's what leads to a lack of focus and puts your team on the road to giving up. Plan or attend #ylunites rallies, do events, do team classes, do retreats with your leaders. Let them grow in community with one another so they are constantly poured into by people that believe in this business. Encourage them to get some daily mindset training (see "Train your brain" on page 63) They need to get their head in the realm of possibility. When you get them dreaming, they will fight. A leader without vision goes nowhere.

What do you say to people who are content with other oils? It breaks my heart to know they're using inferior oils.

Your heart is big and your motive is good. But not everyone is ready to hear. I know you've heard me say it so many times—but it goes back to the art of building the relationship first. Eric Worre is one of my favorite network marketing trainers, and he once said that when you first start your business, you're so excited about it that you are like a puppy that is potty training. You piddle in every corner of the room. You spew information out to every person in your friend circle without concern of where they are. Sometimes you have to go back and fix those relationships. Apologize, stand down, have a few conversations without bringing up oils, wait for their need and make an offer—but only if they are ready.

I did this with my brother. For two years I sent him samples and big baskets at Christmas. He wasn't having it! When I came to visit, his hand went up in my face and said "don't mention Young Living." I had piddled in his corner! I did not meet him where he was. I only offered my need, not his need. But a later conversation led to getting the smoke smell out of his basement, which then became a starter kit, and he is now an Executive halfway to Silver.

They may not be ready for what you have to offer right now. And that's totally ok! Keep moving, and wait until the right opportunity to meet their needs.

What's your favorite oil for getting people's attention fast in line at the grocery store or at vendor events?

Peppermint is my wow oil. A sniff of peppermint is a memorable experience that it gets attention fast. I put one drop in the center of their hand and let them experience it for themselves.

What do you say to when you follow up with contacts you got at a vendor event?

"Thank you for coming to ___ event! I am so glad that our paths crossed. Young Living has changed my life. Tell me why you checked that you'd like more information on the card I gave you. What's going on right now with your health and wellness?"

Listen, respond, offer a sample, send a purple bag, make contact for the kit. Let your passion, belief, warmth, vision, and desire for them to be blessed with oils come out in your tone of voice. Relationship all stems from authenticity.

Do you struggle with authenticity? Try inviting *you*. Re-recruit yourself. Look in the mirror and use your own script on yourself. What would get your attention? Use those words. People need to hear the passion in your voice. They need to see that you are certain. That you have composure. That you can guide them where they want to go. You portray that through your voice, eye contact, tone, passion, belief, and most importantly—your story. Use it as a tool to connect.

What do you say to follow up after handing out the *Your Gameplan* mini?

I thank them for coming to the class. And then I stand down and ask for their story. "What would you do if you made an extra $1,000/month? What is your bucket list? Why would you do this? What is your biggest dream?" Ask leading business questions, then ask if they have 30 minutes to do a Teacher Training where you can show them how simple this is—without large friend circles, lots of time, or a big bank account.

I have stalled out. I am not sure I am able to do this business. How do I get momentum and motivation again?

You lose motivation when you get comfortable with a rank. You lose momentum when you slip into leadership mode. If you let your team do the work and forget that 80% of your time in this business NEEDS to be spent prospecting. Sharing with new people is how you built to the rank that you have already—you must never stop doing that one activity!

If you go months without selling a kit, that's how you lose your mojo. It's said that 7-figure earners invite as many as seven to ten people a day to take a look at their opportunity. That's seven people a day that you're building relationships with, dropping seeds, leaving purple bags, and oiling up. Keep the initial conversation short and lead them to a tool, like the mini, the textable classes, *Fearless*, or the CD's that they can listen to in their car.

You should always be inviting. The day you stop doing that, your business slips. You are either growing or you are shrinking. If you're not prospecting, you're shrinking. The key is consistency. You can't invite people one day a month. It's got to be something you get into the practice of doing regularly, because it's more important than any other thing you do for your business. It leads to kit sales and keeps you moving forward.

Help! I believe this works, but what would you say to those of us so mentally and emotionally exhausted from life—divorce, etc. that do not have anything left to give past their day job, children and surviving?

Oh weary warrior, I was you. I was the momma up at 3 a.m. to work, 52 weeks a year. I was the beaten down traveler. I was the mom of an autistic high-needs son. I was at the brink of collapse. I know that place like it was so real and so raw that it was yesterday. There are moments when I still pause and ask myself if I'm truly free of those burdens!

As I write this, I'm on the Diamond Retreat in Banff, Canada—looking out at the Rockies. I pinch myself and wonder if this life truly is the life the Lord has laid out for me. Can it be real? Will I stay humble—and give the glory to the Lord, or soak it up for myself? Can I stay momma and still be a millionaire? I have so many thoughts running through my head. Our life has been completely changed and altered forever because of the hands of Gary Young and the incredible corporate staff at Young Living.

May I offer some gentle wisdom? There is no release where you are. There is only decades more of pain, frustration, insecurity, exhaustion, and loss of hope. If your feet stay in those waters, you stay in a place of stagnation and weariness. You are looking at decades more of emotional turmoil, mental exhaustion and physical collapse. I know deep in my heart that is not the life you want for yourself.

Start by putting good things in your mind. Separate yourself from the things that tear you down. Look over your life at the things that drag you into the deep, dark places—and stand back. It may be a difficult marriage, friends with no vision, or wayward adult kids. Step back. Allow yourself personal distance. Spend more time with those that inspire you. It was once said that you are the combination of your five closest friends. Who do you let in?

Once you have cut toxic relationships out, start pouring into YOU. Start filling your head with mindset training that will give you hope. I gave you a list of my favorite mindset training in Chapter 13, "Keys to Confidence" on page 79, and there is a list of Diamond resources in "Appendix O: Follow the Diamonds" on page 295 too. Start on YouTube—do something free, and get lost in hope. I'd also encourage you to get your nose in the Bible. That's where I find my greatest source of hope! Just start reading, even if you don't know what you are doing. The lines of that book have ancient wisdom and truth that have pulled me from some of my darkest places. Read it cover to cover, then do it again.

You can slowly put one foot in front of the other. But it takes one thing: courage. You have to see this life for yourself. You have to imagine your check, the freedom from emotional baggage, you have to WANT it for yourself. It's not hard to fight once the vision is in place. So head to your Gameplan workbook and work on your vision board. Allow yourself to dream. You may have been hurt ten thousand times. But you don't need to stay there. You are the one that controls where your feet and your mind go. Start walking.

You know what is on the other side. If I could, sweet one, I would pick you up and carry you there myself! This momma from the projects knows pain and rejection and hurt. If I had a magic Diamond veggie cap that would release all that pain and toss ranks at your feet, I'd hand it to you right away. But the truth is, the first step is knowing you were made for more. The first step is allowing yourself to picture freedom for your family. The first step starting to dream. Writing it out. Letting your mind go to the places of where this goes. Vision leads to belief. And belief leads to action. And then action makes your vision truth. But the first step is to move from where you are. And only you can make that choice.

You see, everyone has fight. You don't need a loud personality or a large friend circle for fight. It was born into you. But that fight won't come out without a plan. The plan is inside you, if only you will move from the places where you stand right now. You CAN do this, no matter how much you hurt. Do not be content with pain.

Pick up your mat and walk. There is peace on the other side of the climb.

WHO GETS PAID?

This is a good place to explain something that needs a bit more clarity from the *Gameplan* book, because I have been asked about it a lot. Who gets paid if you teach a class for someone else?

THEY DO.

Huh? So if I give my time, and I teach, I give up my paycheck to my new leader?

Yes.

Why do I advocate for that? YOU already know where this goes! You have the vision! You will keep walking and won't stop till you get there. The best way to pick up leaders is by showing them the paycheck. If you teach, and you put yourself as the enroller, cash in on the Starter Kit and Fast Start bonuses, you just potentially cost yourself a leader (and leaders are the most valuable thing you have in Young Living). They are far more valuable than the fifty dollars you get for the starter kit. They are more valuable than the classes you can teach, because you can only teach one at a time. If you have ten leaders teaching on a Saturday, it's as if you just taught ten classes yourself. That's the power of duplication. like getting the Boardwalk piece when you're playing Monopoly. Leaders are your most valuable real estate.

One leader that duplicates and teaches, as they rank to Silver, Gold, Platinum and beyond, will add hundreds and in some cases thousands of dollars to your paycheck every month IF they see the vision. They see it when you invest in them. Give up the fifty dollars and make the investment.

Go teach for them and show them how to do it. Some will catch the vision and take off, and some may never see it. The chance of getting their attention is worth the fifty dollars you will lose. It's worth the blessing of the possibility of a spark. Their friend circle is enough for 20 Silverships. Make the investment! I give my new leaders both sponsor and enroller. I only put my name down if I'm the only leader in the room, doing my own classes.

POACHING

There are a few things in the network marketing world that are very taboo because they are unethical or illegal. Poaching falls in that category. Poaching is when you actively seek out people on other teams, and try to recruit them to your own team. Poaching is NOT signing a member who *has never been signed* to your team. That falls under poor follow up. If a person is approached by two people at the same time, ethically decide with the other leader how you will handle it. If it generates drama, let it go. There are many fish in the sea! I believe the Lord will honor your business when you run it with integrity. What you do when no one is watching is key. It determines what type of a leader you are. It would be incredibly painful to have someone stolen from your team. Don't do it to someone else.

I hear about poaching a LOT when people have small warm market circles. "I can't do Young Living, EVERYONE in my church does it." "Because EVERYONE I know already does Young Living, I'm going to try a different company." We already debunked the whole "everyone" statement. There are 6 million active distributors, and 300 million living in the United States. I assure you, "everyone" is not doing Young Living. It does matter what network company you're in. You're going to have a hard time if you can't build relationships with people you don't know. Within my first class, someone was signed that I did not know who lived in Mexico! They were a friend of a friend. You have to think bigger than the circle in which you live.

Back to poaching...

In the regular world, talking to a close friend about oils really isn't that big of a deal. In the network marketing world, if they are already signed on another team, and you're trying to get them to jump ship, it's a VERY big deal. It's a big deal because you are dismantling another person's business, and undoing the hard work they have already poured out to train and lead that person. Think about the cost of the purple bags you assemble, the gas you use to drive to classes, and anything else you may have poured into an incoming distributor. Poaching is the equivalent of walking into a storefront and walking out with items you didn't pay for. It's stealing.

What do you do when someone approaches you, and says they are already on another team, but "don't have upline support", and want to join your team? Two things: First, ask them to log into their virtual office and go to "my account", and look at the name of their upline Diamond. Then contact your Diamond and ask them to pass the name along; or shoot that Diamond a Facebook message yourself, and connect them with their downline leader. That's the ethical way of handling the situation. Second, run. Seriously. Run away. That person is a drama generator. You don't need drama on your team.

How do I know that? Because it does not take an upline to build a Diamondship. It just takes reading a three-page script. If you can read, you can build. You can build without anyone living near you that does the business, and without an upline constantly coaching you. If you feel terribly bad about it, point them in the direction of this book and the Gameplan series. There is enough information in these books to explode their team. They can invest in themselves; and you can invest in the leaders that are already on your team. I firmly believe in blooming where you are planted. God makes no mistakes in where people end up.

If they pursue you, honestly, I just delete the email messages. Run your business with honor. Let the Lord handle the rest. Just don't poach! Go back to your training on listening to people and building relationships earlier in this book; and tap into new friend circles. If everyone in your church is already doing Young Living, it's time to look at the workplace, homeschool co-ops, PTA's, and your husband's co-workers. You have other opportunities. The Lord will open even more doors to you than you thought imaginable, if you do the right thing.

ADVANCED STRATEGY + BASIC COMPENSATION PLAN TRAINING

Let's pause here for a little English lesson, because I keep using all this crazy terminology: PV, OGV, ranks... and your head may be spinning. That's ok! Mine was too when I first started! Just share the script. Get the script in front of faces while you learn the rest of it. If you have no leaders yet, use your number for sponsor and enroller until you find some. Don't know your distributor number? Call Young Living member services at 1-800-371-3515, or contact the person that signed you to get the number.

We went over this earlier on. I've included a chart that lays out all the ranks in Young Living: Distributor, Star, Senior Star, Executive, Silver, Gold, Platinum, Diamond, Crown Diamond, and Royal Crown Diamond.

Distributor	Star	Senior Star	Executive	Silver	Gold	Platinum	Diamond	Crown Diamond	Royal Crown Diamond
100 PV	100 PV	100 PV	100 PV	100 PV	100 PV	100 PV	100 PV	100 PV	100 PV
	500 OGV	2K OGV	4K OGV	10K OGV	35K OGV	100K OGV	250K OGV	750K OGV	1.5M OGV
			2 x 1K OGV Legs	2 x 4K OGV Legs	3 x 6K OGV Legs	4 x 8K OGV Legs	5 x 15K OGV Legs	6 x 20K OGV Legs	6 x 35K OGV Legs
				1,000 PGV	1,000 PGV	1,000 PGV	1,000 PGV	1,000 PGV	1,000 PGV
				12,197	5,762.25	3,431.5	2,066.25	1,369.25	1,369.25

The chart is not too tough to read; and you can access it by logging into your Virtual Office at youngliving.com and hitting "sign in." It will dump you right on to your dashboard. If you click on "rank qualification" in the middle of that page, you'll be able to see the exact chart you're looking at above. As you fulfill certain requirements, they light up in green in your Virtual Office.

Down the left side of the page are the four qualifications to rank up. You must spend 100pv to get your full paycheck. That never changes, no matter how high you go in the company. There are certain OGV benchmarks (OGV is organization group volume, which means your purchase and the purchase of those under you) for each rank. For example, a Star's monthly OGV is 500. When you cross 500 OGV, or about five kits, (each kit is 100PV), you'll hit the first rank in Young Living. A Royal Crown Diamond does 1.5 million OGV every single month. It sounds crazy, but it's coming for you! It's all in the power of duplication. Dream big!

The third requirement is legs. Arguably, this is the toughest because it requires strategy. Everything else can happen with minimal effort if you are regularly training on oils. A leg is a person and a team. You don't need legs until you hit Executive. Then you need two separate legs doing 1000 OGV in sales monthly. A Silver has two legs doing 4000 OGV monthly. A Gold has three legs doing 6000 OGV monthly, etc...

The fourth requirement is the PGV I was telling you about earlier. That's volume outside of your legs. You don't need it until Silver; but it's a lot easier to build it when you don't have leaders on your mind, at the beginning of your business.

Recap:
1. Spend 100 PV to get a check
2. OGV attained determines your rank (500 = Star, etc....)
3. You need legs once you hit Executive and beyond
4. PGV is volume outside your legs

That's your strategy training to get to Silver. Sign everyone under you and build 1000 PGV. Wait to see who "pops"; pick two people; and build equally under both. Stay laser focused on areas you need to grow. Teach a class each week, and you will rank up.

A second way to strategize sets you up for all the bonuses Young Living gives to early builders (those under Silver rank). It's called the Rising Star bonus system. If you build seven legs to 3000GV (the person on the top has to spend 100PV on ER for the leg to count), then take two legs to 5000GV, and then those same two legs to 10000GV and two new legs to 5000GV, you can cash in on all the bonuses. It sets you up strongly for the structure you need for Royal Crown Diamond. This is what that structure looks like:

Getting Paid: In Simple Terms

Now that you have strategy under your belt, let's talk about your pay-check for a moment. This is especially for those that are using this as their first introduction to a Young Living business. This little book also serves as your Quick Start Training guide. In a simple paragraph, you earn $50 for each kit sold. That means Young Living immediately gives you nearly a third of the kit sale, even though the kit is discounted 50 percent from the retail price. Under the Fast Start program, you also get 25 percent back on everything they order (after the kit) for the first three months. After three months, they slip into the Unilevel system. Then, if they are on your first level, you are paid eight percent on all they purchase. Second level is paid at 5 percent; and the third, fourth and fifth levels are paid at four percent. Don't sign anyone under your fifth level, or you won't be paid Unilevel pay for them.

Recap:

1. You earn 50 dollars for each Premium Starter Kit

2. Fast Start: you get 25 percent of all they order for the first 3 months (except their kit)

3. Unilevel: you are paid 8 percent on level 1's, 5 percent on level 2's, and 4 percent on level 3's, 4's, and 5's

Based on pay, you don't want to build too deep, not more than five levels, or you forfeit some of your check. Based on strategy, you don't want to build too wide. There is no need for ten legs, because you only need six legs to get to Royal Crown Diamond.

One of the tools I use when I am coaching my own leaders in a strategy session is a rank up sheet, a goal page, and a stats page. I have included them in the Gameplanner each year, but now, I'm going to offer those to you as printables on my website at oilabilityteam.com so you can sit with your leaders (and work on the sheets yourself) to map out your next move. The next Appendix covers these in depth. These are completely FREE. May they bless you as you map out your way to Royal!

GAMEPLAN 3 TOPICS: RESEARCH OUTLINED

Look for these upcoming topics from Sarah!

You can't get to gold alone. It is lonely doing the business with no builders. You are in the top 1 percent of the company! That's HUGE! How to stretch yourself and build a team. You find leaders by teaching.

☐ Getting back to the basics

☐ Big OGV jumps: how to double your OGV with examples, training, and 10 targeted areas for growth

☐ Reactivations 101: How to get people focused on oils again

☐ How To Spike Your ER percentages

☐ How to Double the Number of Enrollers on your team

☐ Focusing on new blood over reactivations; why 80 percent of your time must be spent prospecting

☐ A study of the actions that many of the Diamonds used to rank up

☐ Comparison

☐ How to handle spouses that won't buy into the business

☐ What really makes Young Living different from every other company out there

☐ What is Seed to seal, in non-scientific terms?

☐ A checklist of Income Producing Activities for beginning of the month and end of the month hustles

☐ How to run challenges on your team page to get your leaders engaged

☐ How to train EVERY member of your team on the Core 4

☐ Sarah's master packing list for convention (and how to do it in a carry on)

☐ Training on the story of Gary Young; and how to train your team to be like Gary

☐ Finding crossline friendships; and what they do for your business

☐ How to get people to sign up for ER right at their first class

☐ The new land of compliance: what it looks like now

☐ Running successful #ylunites rallies

☐ How to read a reference guide and train your team to do the same, with action steps

☐ How to read a Zyto Balance scan and use it to boost OGV

☐ My Favorite aromatherapy reading lists

☐ Signing transfer forms for your team for them to switch teams; a discussion on Young Living ethics

☐ Getting back on the horse after a season of being distracted or dismayed

☐ Retiring your spouse: why it's a myth, and what you should shoot for instead

☐ How to do professional accounts successfully

☐ Rank up blends at each level: Star, Senior Star, Executive, etc...

☐ A Simple Retreat Script

☐ Write ups for recognition at the end of the month

☐ Traveling 101

☐ Posts that look professional without hiring a graphic artist

☐ In-depth Project Broadcast training

☐ Training your kids how to go Diamond; tricks you can use right now while they are still young to instill the business

☐ What "be a product of the product" looks like, with action steps on how to use that to ignite your product users

☐ How to speak your personal goals over your team; how to track your stats in front of your team

☐ How to lead a successful Teacher Training that results in fire; Rank Mapping/Coaching/Strategy 101

☐ Getting your level 1's to rank with you, building in sets of 2, and why that's critical to get the highest paycheck possible

- ☐ Breaking down the check: what it all means; advanced training on Generations Pay
- ☐ What if means if you're on the low end of the pay scale
- ☐ Never give up on your leaders: the story of the leader with 12 legs
- ☐ How To Lead with Confidence
- ☐ Edification: How to show off your leaders
- ☐ Gratitude for Young Living; why we don't bash the company we work for
- ☐ How to handle dissident leaders
- ☐ An oil to lead each chapter, with targeted brief aromatherapy training on oils for business
- ☐ Business testimonies of the Diamonds
- ☐ Humility, and why it's so important in upper leadership
- ☐ GETTING TO EVENTS = rank ups
- ☐ Letting your team see you in the trenches
- ☐ When leading takes the place of prospecting
- ☐ What to do when you plateau, with action steps
- ☐ Taking care of you; resting 101 while still running a business (marriage
- ☐ first, staying off your phone, time management and sacred circles)
- ☐ Training your family to respect the business. Training you to respect your family.
- ☐ Listening to your leaders
- ☐ The Art of delegation and letting your leaders lead
- ☐ Upper level strategy session for faster ranking
- ☐ How to get the highest paycheck possible
- ☐ How to inspire your leaders
- ☐ Husband's roles
- ☐ What your class count should look like after Silver
- ☐ Hustle months vs growth months + how to identify what you did wrong if you backslide
- ☐ Taxes 101: How to keep the most out of your check; how to do taxes for network marketing
- ☐ What are the specific perks for each rank?
- ☐ Utilizing online tools to connect with leaders: Facebook Live, Marco Polo, Sway

☐ Hidden software gems to track your business online

☐ Running with your runners

☐ Contest ideas for your team

☐ Engaging Facebook posts to get product users to interact with you

☐ Talking to different color personalities on your team and how to connect with opposite personalities

YOUNG  LIVING
ESSENTIAL OILS

D. Gary Young

FATHER OF THE MODERN-DAY
ESSENTIAL OIL MOVEMENT.

—— 1949 - 2018 ——